An Introduction to the Study of Spectrum Analysis

W. Marshall Watts

Alpha Editions

This edition published in 2020

ISBN : 9789354012655

Design and Setting By
Alpha Editions
email - alphaedis@gmail.com

As per information held with us this book is in Public Domain.
This book is a reproduction of an important historical work. Alpha Editions uses the best technology to reproduce historical work in the same manner it was first published to preserve its original nature. Any marks or number seen are left intentionally to preserve its true form.

AN INTRODUCTION

TO THE

STUDY OF SPECTRUM ANALYSIS

BY

W. MARSHALL WATTS

D.Sc. (LOND.), B.Sc. (VICT.), F.I.C.

WITH COLOURED PLATE AND 135 ILLUSTRATIONS IN THE TEXT

LONGMANS, GREEN, AND CO.
39 PATERNOSTER ROW, LONDON
NEW YORK AND BOMBAY

1904

All rights reserved

PREFACE

WHATEVER discoveries the century now opening may bring us, there can be no doubt of the enormous advance in scientific knowledge witnessed by the nineteenth century. That one hundred years ago there was no travelling by rail, no electric telegraph, no telephone, no electric or gas lighting, no photography, no chloroform—not to mention such trifles as matches—this shows that no mean advance has been made. But, amongst all the discoveries of the past century, there is none more important—from some points of view, at least—than the discovery of spectrum analysis, by means of which the composition of the sun and stars has been revealed and new elements have been discovered, and which is now the most powerful means we possess of investigating the constitution of matter. Before the discoveries of Bunsen and Kirchhoff no philosopher had ever ventured to think it possible that we should be able to analyze the sun and stars. The idea of its possibility is said to have occurred to these philosophers of Heidelberg on the occasion of a fire at Mannheim, when, looking at the distant conflagration through the newly constructed instrument, they recognized the presence of strontium amongst the burning material, and the thought occurred to them, "If it be possible to recognize a substance by the nature of the light emitted a few miles off, why not also at any distance?"

"By the methods which have become possible since 1860 by the introduction into the observatory of the spectroscope and the modern photographic plate, a great harvest has been gathered by many reapers. Spectroscopic astronomy has become a distinct and acknowledged branch of the science, possessing a large literature of its own, and observatories specially devoted to it. The more recent discovery of the gelatine dry plate has given a further great impetus to this modern side of astronomy, and has opened a pathway into the unknown, of which even an enthusiast forty years ago would scarcely have dared to dream.

"In no science, perhaps, does the sober statement of the results which have been achieved appeal so strongly to the imagination and make so evident the almost boundless powers of the mind of man. By means of its light alone to analyze the chemical nature of a far distant body; to be able to reason about its present state in relation to the past and future; to measure within an English mile or less per second the otherwise invisible motion which it may have towards or from us; to do more—to make even that which is darkness to our eyes light, and from vibrations which our organs of sight are powerless to perceive, to evolve a revelation in which we see mirrored some of the stages through which the stars may pass in their slow evolutional progress—surely the record of such achievements, however poor the form of words in which they may be described, is worthy to be regarded as the scientific epic of the century." *

As the handmaid of astronomy, spectrum analysis has thus opened up to us a field of research of the greatest interest and importance. But in the opposite direction, also, it has been, and will be, of the utmost service as a means of investigating the minutest structure of matter. In a drop of water, we are told, the number of molecules is so great that, if we could see them when the drop was magnified till it had, apparently, the dimensions of our earth, they would appear like a heap of tennis balls in number something like 9,556,000,000,000,000,000,000,000. Yet in each molecule we have two atoms of hydrogen and one atom of oxygen, and, according to the latest views, within each atom of hydrogen there are some thousand electrified "corpuscles;" and it is the rhythmical vibrations of these infinitely minute particles, executed perhaps five hundred million million times every second, which we are able to investigate by means of the spectroscope.

The reality thus exceeds the imagination of the poet—

> "A globe of dew,
> Filling in the morning new
>   Some eyed flower whose young leaves waken
> On an unimagined world:
>   Constellated suns unshaken,
> Orbits, measureless, are furl'd
>   In that frail and fading sphere,
>   With ten millions gather'd there,
> To tremble, gleam, and disappear."

These investigations into the infinitely great, and infinitely small, will have for some minds the greatest attraction; others will,

* Sir William Huggins.

Preface. vii

perhaps, attach more importance to the utilitarian applications of spectrum analysis and the services it has rendered in the discovery of new elements, the certain detection of traces of rare substances in ordinary chemical analysis, and so on. In the present work, the Author has sought to explain principles and procedure from the very beginning, as well as to give an account of the refinements and achievements of this method of analysis, which have marked its latest developments. There is a very large amount of work waiting to be done, both by those who have the command of fine instruments and elaborate apparatus, and also by those who have only the simplest means, and it is hoped that to these last, especially, this book may prove a useful guide.

The Author desires to express his thanks to many friends for permission to reproduce photographs, etc., in illustration of this work, which show, better than pages of description, the results which have been obtained in spectrum analysis; to the Editors of the *Astrophysical Journal;* to Sir W. Huggins; to Mr. Higgs, for the use of his admirable photographs of the solar spectrum, obtained with Rowland's grating; to Professors Kayser, Runge, Paschen, Eder, and Valenta, and others.

W. M. W.

June 21, 1904.

CONTENTS

CHAPTER		PAGE
I.	How to produce a Spectrum	1
II.	Flame-spectra	11
III.	Spectra produced by Means of Electricity . . .	18
IV.	Absorption Spectra.—The Electric Arc	34
V.	The Diffraction Spectrum.—Measurement of Wave-lengths.	40
VI.	On the Production of Dark Lines by Absorption.—The Fraunhofer Lines of the Solar Spectrum	58
VII.	Spectra of the Stars and Nebulæ	75
VIII.	The Sun, its Photosphere, Chromosphere, Corona, Sun-spots, and Prominences	95
IX.	New Stars.—Double Stars.—Comets	107
X.	The Concave Grating. — Photography of the Spectrum	120
XI.	Relationships between the Different Lines of a Spectrum, and between Lines of the Spectra of Allied Elements	138
XII.	Band-spectra.—Spectra of Compounds	160
XIII.	The Spectroheliograph. — Electro-magnetic Theory of Light.—The "Zeeman Effect" . .	165
XIV.	The Michelson Echelon Diffraction Grating. .	174
	Catalogue of Spectra	185
	Appendix	311
	Index	321

AN INTRODUCTION
TO
THE STUDY OF SPECTRUM ANALYSIS

CHAPTER I.

HOW TO PRODUCE A SPECTRUM.

BEFORE we enter upon a description of the methods of spectroscopy, and of the various instruments as they are supplied by the optician, it will be well to consider what a spectrum is, and the simplest and most inexpensive method by which it can be produced. We shall thus gain some general idea of the subject at the outset, and it is hoped that the reader to whom the subject is entirely new may be induced to construct an instrument and to make observations for himself.

We must have, in the first place, a prism—a wedge-shaped piece of glass or other transparent material, with plane polished surfaces. In default of anything better, the lustre of a chandelier will answer our present purpose, such as shown in Fig. 1. If we place this upright, and look through it in the proper direction at a flame some distance off, we shall see a spectrum—the spectrum of the flame. The best sort of flame for our purpose is a long narrow flame and non-luminous, such as the flame of a Bunsen gas-burner, or of a spirit-lamp, but if these are not at hand a candle-flame will do. What we shall see depends upon the nature of the light emitted by the

FIG. 1.

flame. If the flame is non-luminous, and is then coloured yellow by putting common salt into it, or by bringing a bead of melted sodium carbonate on the end of a thin platinum wire into it, we shall see a yellow flame, but not where the flame actually is. The rays of light from the flame are bent in passing through the prism, as shown in Fig. 2, where A represents the position of the flame, and B that of the observer's eye ; a yellow image of the flame is seen at Y.

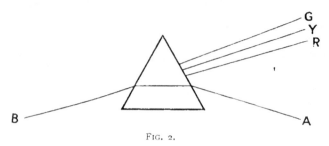

FIG. 2.

Now, let a little lithium chloride be brought into the flame ; this colours it a brilliant red, and we see a *red* image of the flame at R, less refracted than the yellow image. In like manner, some thallium chloride colours the flame a beautiful green, and we see a *green* image of the flame at G, more refracted than the yellow image. These differently coloured and differently situated images of the flame constitute what we call the spectrum of the flame. We shall improve our arrangements somewhat by putting in front of the flame a narrow vertical slit in a piece of cardboard or thin metal, so as to allow only a thin slice of light from the flame to fall upon the prism. The substances we have used to colour the flame were chosen because each of them gives only one colour, or, in other words, gives *monochromatic* light ; but white light is a mixture of light of many different colours, so that an ordinary gas-flame placed behind the slit at A gives us a succession of images of the slit of many colours without break, forming what is called a *continuous* spectrum ; red at one end, passing through orange, yellow, green of many tints into blue and violet.

If we burn a short piece of magnesium ribbon behind the slit, we shall see a very brilliant continuous spectrum, with some bright green lines superposed upon it : these are due to the vapour of the metal and to the oxide which is produced when the magnesium burns.

If we place coloured glasses, or pieces of coloured gelatine, or coloured liquids between the slit—illuminated by white light—and the prism, we get *absorption* spectra : certain colours being cut out of the white light. Thus, if we put a test-tube containing a very dilute solution of potassium permanganate (Condy's fluid) in front of the slit, we shall see five dark bands in the green, due to the absorption of light of this particular colour by the solution, which must be only faintly pink.

The Refraction and Dispersion of Light.

From any luminous source—a red-hot poker, a candle-flame, burning magnesium, the sun, or any other source—waves of light are emitted, which are conveyed to the eye through the luminiferous ether with inconceivable rapidity, and which are spoken of as forming rays of light in straight lines from one point to another.

The velocity with which light travels is (in vacuo) the same for all colours of light, and amounts to 300,000,000 metres per second, or 186,000 miles per second. In glass or water or other transparent medium the velocity is less, and different for different colours, being greater for red and less for violet light. The ratio of the velocity in vacuo to the velocity in a transparent medium is termed the refractive index of that medium, and this is different for different colours. Thus for water the refractive index is 1·331 for red light, 1·336 for green, and 1·344 for violet light. For crown-glass the corresponding numbers are 1·526, 1·533, and 1·547; for flint-glass, 1·628, 1 642, and 1·671; and for carbon disulphide, 1·621, 1·646, and 1·709. We may note, in passing, that while for green light the numbers for flint-glass and carbon disulphide are about the same, the differences between the numbers for red light and violet light are 0·043 for flint-glass, and 0·088 for carbon disulphide: this is what is meant when it is said that carbon disulphide has a greater dispersive power than flint-glass has, and consequently, when using prisms of flint-glass and carbon disulphide of the same angle, the colours are more widely separated by the carbon disulphide than by the glass.

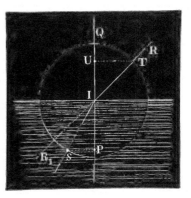

FIG. 3.

Let us now consider a little more closely the change in direction which takes place when a ray of light passes obliquely from one medium to another. In Fig. 3, suppose RI to represent the path of a ray of monochromatic light incident at I from air upon the surface of water. If it suffered no change in direction it would have passed into the water along IR₁, but it will be found that it actually takes the path IS. The angle R₁IS, the change in direction, is called the deviation, and is greater the less the angle between the incident ray and the surface of the water. Let us describe a circle QTS with I as centre, cutting the incident and refracted rays in T and S respectively; also draw IQ (the normal) at right angles to the refracting surface. From T and S let fall perpendiculars TU and SP upon the normal.

The law of refraction is that $\frac{TU}{SP}$ is equal to the index of refraction, whatever the angle of incidence may be. The angle QIR is called the angle of incidence, and SIP is called the angle of refraction. The ratio $\frac{TU}{TI}$ is called in trigonometry the sine of the angle QIR; and the ratio $\frac{SP}{SI}$ is called the sine of the angle SIP. The refractive index, usually denoted by the symbol μ, is then the ratio of the sine of the angle of incidence to the sine of the angle of refraction; for, since TI = SI,

$$\frac{\left(\frac{TU}{TI}\right)}{\left(\frac{SP}{SI}\right)} = \frac{TU}{SP}$$

The formula $\frac{\sin i}{\sin r} = \mu$; or $\sin i = \mu \sin r$, we shall, no doubt, want later on.

If we look through a prism at a distant flame, as explained by Fig. 2, and gently turn the prism round a little while watching the image, we shall observe that the image of the flame moves up to a limiting position Y (for the yellow light), and then moves away from this position again, although the prism is turned in the same direction all the time. This limiting position is the position of minimum deviation, and is the position in which the prism of a spectroscope is used.

Fig. 4 shows the path of a ray of light through a prism, at the angle of minimum deviation, when the course of the ray within the prism is equally inclined to the two polished surfaces. The angle of incidence at the first surface Def is equal to the angle of emergence at the second surface ghE, and the deviation is twice the angle heD$_1$, and this angle is $i - r$ where $\sin i = \mu \sin r$. If the angle of the prism BAC is denoted by a, we have $a = 2r$, and the deviation $\delta = 2(i - r) = 2i - a$. Hence

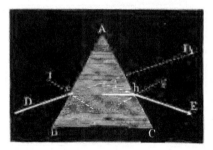

FIG. 4.

$$i = \frac{\delta + a}{2} \text{ and } r = \frac{a}{2}, \text{ so that } \mu = \frac{\sin i}{\sin r} = \frac{\sin \frac{\delta + a}{2}}{\sin \frac{a}{2}}$$

This is the formula generally used in determining the refractive index of a substance, which is found by observing the minimum deviation and the angle of the prism.

We may use a simplified form of the above formula when the angle of the prism is only small. Since the sines of small angles are to one another nearly as the angles themselves, we may put $i = \mu r$ instead of $\sin i = \mu \sin r$, or $\dfrac{\delta + a}{2} = \mu \dfrac{a}{2}$, or $\delta = (\mu - 1)a$.

When a beam of parallel rays of light falls upon a converging lens, the rays are differently bent according to the distance from the central point of the lens upon which they fall, so that after refraction they are all collected approximately in one point, known as the focus.

This is represented in Fig. 5, where F is the focus of the equiconvex lens DBE.

FIG. 5.

Let us suppose that in Fig. 6, ABC represents a converging lens (in this case a plano-convex lens), that O is the centre of curvature

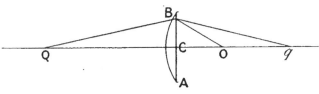

FIG. 6.

of the spherical surface, and that a luminous point at Q sends out rays of light which are refracted by the lens. Let QCO be one of these rays, which, travelling along the axis QO, passes through the lens without any change of direction, and QB another ray which is refracted at B to meet the axis in q. This ray is refracted as if it passed through a prism whose angle is that between the plane surface ABC and the tangent plane at B, which angle is equal to BOC. The deviation of this ray is equal to the sum of the angles BQC, BqC. If we call BQ u, Bq v, BO r, and BC a, since for small angles the sines are nearly proportional to the angles themselves, we may put $\dfrac{a}{u} + \dfrac{a}{v} = (\mu - 1)\dfrac{a}{r}$; or $\dfrac{1}{u} + \dfrac{1}{v} = \dfrac{(\mu - 1)}{r}$.

The fact that a disappears from the equation shows that the distance of q from C does not depend upon the distance of B from C; in other words, that all rays emanating from Q and falling upon the lens are collected at q, which point is called the focus of Q, or the focus conjugate to Q. If we suppose Q to be very far off from the lens, then the incident rays become parallel, and since u is now infinite, $\frac{1}{u} = Q$, and we have $\frac{1}{v} = \frac{(\mu - 1)}{r}$. In this case q is nearer the lens than is shown in the figure, and becomes the principal focus of the lens: putting F for the distance of the principal focus from the lens, we have $\frac{1}{F} = \frac{(\mu - 1)}{r}$, and $\frac{1}{u} + \frac{1}{v} = \frac{1}{F}$, the formula which connects the distances of the conjugate foci with the distance of the principal focus from the lens. This formula is applicable to all converging lenses, provided that the pencil of rays is a small one, so that no ray falls upon the lens very far from the axis.

If the pencil of rays is not a small one, then, after refraction, all the rays will not go accurately to one point, and those furthest from the axis will show the most deviation from the true focus. This error is called spherical aberration, and is illustrated by Fig. 7. This

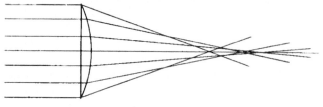

Fig. 7.

defect may be remedied by the use of a stop, but, of course, at the cost of loss of light.

There is in each lens a point called the centre of the lens which has this property, that any ray of light passing through the centre suffers no angular deviation. The direction of any such ray is called an axis of the lens. That axis in which the centres of curvature of the surfaces lie is called the principal axis, the others are termed secondary axes. In an equi-convex lens, such as shown in Fig. 8, the centre of the lens is the geometric centre; in a plano-convex lens the centre lies upon the curved surface. All the rays of light starting from any one point of a luminous object, therefore, after passing through the lens, are collected into one point on that secondary axis which passes through the luminous point, at the distance given by the formula $\frac{1}{u} + \frac{1}{v} = \frac{1}{f}$. We see, therefore, that a convex lens gives an inverted image of the object, larger or smaller than the object, according as the distance of the image from the lens is greater or less than the distance of the object from the lens. This is illustrated in Fig. 8.

What has been said about lenses is true for light of any one colour or monochromatic light, but when using white light the image will be found to be coloured, and this defect of a single lens is termed "chromatic aberration." Since violet light is more refrangible than red, there will be formed a violet image somewhat nearer to the lens than the red image. This defect can be partially remedied by the use of an achromatic lens, made of two lenses cemented together; a convex lens of crown-glass, and a concave lens of smaller curvature made of flint-glass. The possibility of constructing an achromatic lens depends upon the fact that the dispersive power of flint glass is greater than that of crown-glass in proportion to the deviation pro-

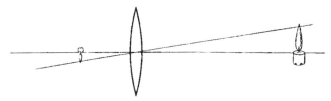

FIG. 8.

duced, so that if we have two prisms, one of crown-glass and the other of flint-glass, of such angles that they produce the same deviation of a green ray, the red and blue rays will be more widely separated by the flint-glass prism than by the crown-glass prism. This will be seen from the following table of the refractive indices of flint- and crown-glass for light of different colours:—

	Red light.	Yellow light.	Green light.	Blue light.
Flint-glass	1·62775	1·63504	1·64202	1·66028
Crown-glass	1·52431	1·52798	1·53137	1·53991
Water	1·33093	1·33358	1·33585	1·34129
Carbon disulphide	1·6182	1·6308	1·6439	1·6799

The differences between the numbers for red light and blue light are then, for flint-glass, 0·03253; for crown-glass, 0·01560; for water, 0·01436; and for carbon disulphide, 0·0617. A prism of flint-glass must have a smaller angle than a prism of crown-glass if it is to produce an equal deflection of the green rays, and if it then is placed in contact with the crown-glass prism, with its refracting angle in the opposite direction, the green ray will pass through without deviation, but the blue and red rays will be separated. Such a prism is a direct-vision prism, such as used in certain forms of spectroscope, viz. direct-vision spectroscopes; but if the angles of the prisms be so chosen that the separation of the blue and red rays produced by the one prism is exactly neutralized by the other, then the blue, red, and green rays will pass through without separation (or nearly so), but will be deviated through a certain angle.

8   *An Introduction to the Study of Spectrum Analysis.*

Fig. 9 represents an achromatic lens, and Fig. 10 a direct-vision prism composed of three prisms of crown-glass and two prisms of flint-glass.

The spectroscope with one prism, as employed for chemical analysis, is represented in Fig. 11. The light from the flame c passes through a fine slit in the plate at the end of the tube A, which is called the collimator-tube, through the prism P, and into the observing telescope B. An

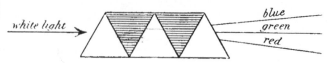

FIG. 9.   FIG. 10.

FIG. 11.

enlarged view of the slit-plate is given in Fig. 12. The adjustment required is that parallel rays should pass through the prism

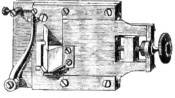

FIG. 12.

at the angle of minimum deviation. The collimator is furnished with a convex lens at the end nearest the prism, and the slit is adjusted at the principal focus of this lens, so that the rays fall upon the prism as if they came from a slit at an infinite distance. To put the instrument into adjustment, the observing telescope should first be removed and focussed exactly on a distant object; it is then screwed into its place, and the arm which carries it turned round until the telescope is in a line with the collimator; the slit-tube is then drawn out until it is seen in sharp focus on looking through the telescope, and the adjusting screws α and β are moved until the middle of the slit is seen in the middle of the field of view. The prism is then placed on the table, and fixed in the position marked for it by means of the clamp γ. This position is that of minimum deviation for the green rays, but it is not necessary to alter the prism for the red or blue portions of the spectrum.

The third tube, C, carries a photographed scale and a lens at the end near the prism, similar to the collimator. The next adjustment is to get this scale (which is seen by reflection in the face of the prism) in the right place and in sharp focus. The arm carrying this tube turns round the central pillar, and can be fixed in the right position by the set-screw k; the scale can be raised or lowered by means of the screw δ; the tube can be pushed in or out to focus it exactly. It is usual to make the image of the fixed edge of the slit coincident with the number 50 of the scale, the scale being illuminated by a small luminous gas-flame placed behind it. The use of the small movable prism shown in Fig. 12, which covers up half of the slit, is to enable the observer to directly compare two spectra. The little prism sends the light of the flame D through the slit by total reflection, whilst the light from the flame E passes through the upper portion of the slit directly.

It is not possible to construct scales for different instruments which shall give *exactly* the same readings, and of course the scale is an arbitrary one. Bunsen's maps are given on the scale of his own spectroscope, in which the sodium line is placed at 50, and the lithium, strontium, and thallium lines read as follows:

$$\text{Li } 31\cdot5, \text{ Sr } 105\cdot5, \text{ and Tl } 67\cdot8.$$

The image of that edge of the slit which does not move when the width of the slit is altered is made to coincide with the division 50. If this be on the left of the observer, then always the position of the left-hand edge of each line and band is to be recorded, and in the case of a faint line the slit may be opened to admit more light, and yet an accurate reading may be obtained. This refers, of course, only to lines which are sharply defined, and not to bands of considerable breadth.

The most convenient plan in making a map of a spectrum is first to put down, as exactly as possible, the positions of the well-defined lines on a millimetre scale on paper, opening and closing the slit as convenient, and then to go over the work again, keeping the slit at one uniform width, and noting the relative intensity of the lines, and

10　*An Introduction to the Study of Spectrum Analysis.*

the width and character of the bands, whether sharply defined at the edges, or sharp at one edge and fading away at the other, or bright in the middle and fading away at both edges. There is no better plan of recording the peculiarities of a spectrum than that employed

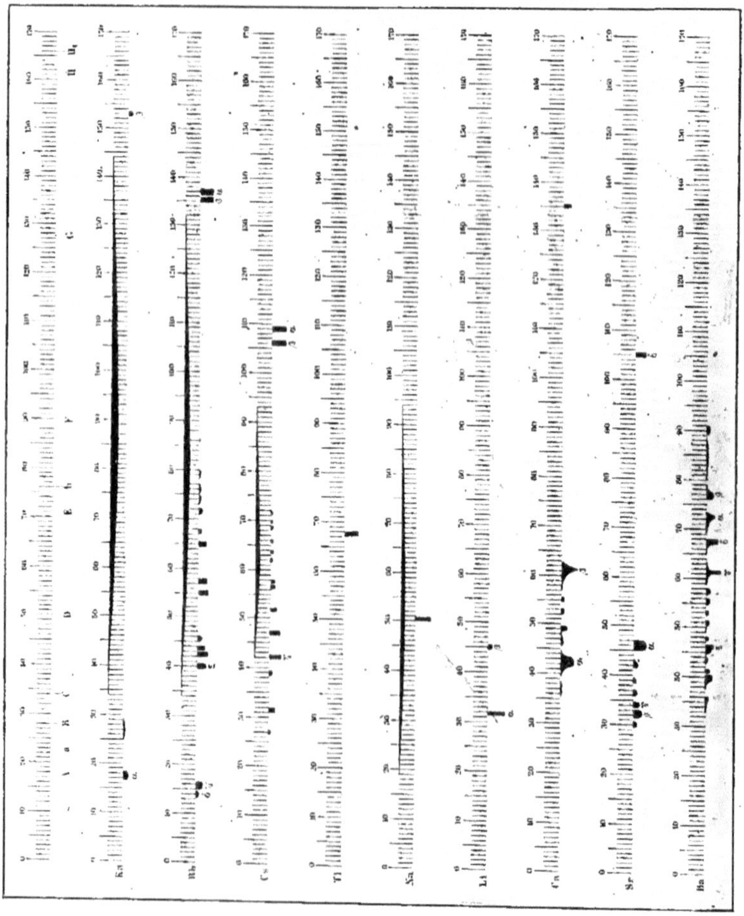

FIG. 13.

by Bunsen, in which each bright line is represented by a black mark on the paper, the height of which represents the intensity of the line. In Fig. 13 we have a copy of Bunsen's map of the spectra of the metals of the alkalies and alkaline earths, constructed upon this plan.

CHAPTER II.

FLAME-SPECTRA.

THE spectrum of an incandescent solid is continuous ; a discontinuous spectrum of bright lines is produced only by an incandescent gas. The yellow line seen when a salt of sodium is introduced on a fine platinum wire into the non-luminous flame of the Bunsen burner is due to the vapour of sodium set free by the high temperature of the flame, or by the chemical changes taking place in the flame between the hot gases of the flame and the salt introduced. Bunsen remarks that all sodium salts give the same reaction ; although it is obtained more vividly from the more volatile compounds, such as the oxide, chloride, bromide, iodide, carbonate and sulphate, yet the non-volatile phosphate, silicate, and borate show the line plainly. This reaction is of extraordinary delicacy : Bunsen showed that 0·0000003 milligram of sodium could be detected with certainty by the spectral reaction. Indeed, the reaction is *too* delicate for the comfort of the spectroscopist, who finds the sodium line almost always present, even when no sodium compound has been intentionally brought into the flame. Spectrum analysis thus reveals the wide diffusion of substances previously accounted rare ; as of lithium in sea-water, river and mineral waters, in tea, coffee and tobacco, and in human blood. The invention of spectrum analysis was quickly followed by the discovery of new elements ; of rubidium and cæsium by Bunsen, in the mineral water of Durkheim ; of thallium by Crookes, in 1861 ; of indium by Reich and Richter, in 1864 ; of gallium by Lecoq de Boisbaudran, in 1875 ; and now of the new gases, argon, helium, krypton, neon and xenon.

In Fig. 14 we have shown a large spectroscope of nine prisms, constructed by Browning for Mr. Gassiot, known as the Kew Spectroscope. Fig. 15 shows the path of the rays of light through the prisms ; A represents the collimator, seen on the left in Fig. 14, and B represents the observing telescope.

The carbonates, chlorides, or nitrates of the alkalies and alkaline earths are convenient salts to use ; but the chlorates—if they can be obtained—are perhaps to be preferred, as in consequence of the liberation of oxygen the flame is hotter, and the reaction more brilliant. In a flame of low temperature the reaction is much less distinct ; thus in the flame of hydrogen burning in chlorine the

12   *An Introduction to the Study of Spectrum Analysis.*

sodium reaction is not obtained, and the yellow line is hardly seen in the flame of sulphuretted hydrogen burning in air. The use of a hotter flame may bring out new lines; thus in the oxy-hydrogen

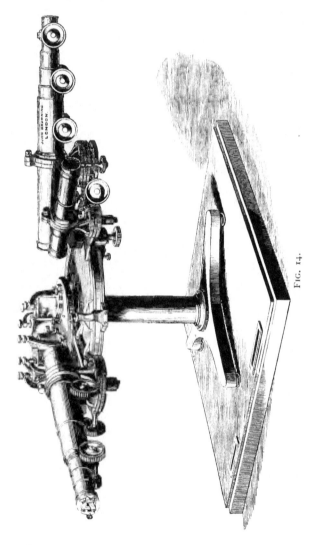

FIG. 14.

flame sodium salts show, besides the usual yellow line, a series of lines at 43·2, 56·0, 76·0, and 83·6.

Lithium salts colour the flame a splendid crimson, the spectrum

Flame-spectra. 13

of which consists of two lines, a very brilliant one at 31·7, and a much feebler line at 45·0. If the oxy-hydrogen flame be employed, there is seen in addition a blue line at 105·2 close to, but a little more refrangible than, the strontium blue line. All lithium compounds show the red line distinctly, even minerals containing lithium such as lepidolite only need to be held in the flame to give the reaction distinctly.

The spectrum of potassium is remarkable, consisting of a line in the extreme red and one in the extreme violet, at 17·5 and 153·0 respectively, besides a certain amount of continuous light. Other lines come out in the oxy-hydrogen flame at 51·8, 52·4, 53·2, 67·1, and 152·7. Some of the silicates containing potassium do not show the potassium lines until they are heated with sodium carbonate; the potassium felspar "orthoclase" is in this way easily distinguished from the sodium felspar "albite."

The spectra of cæsium and rubidium show a remarkable analogy to the spectrum of potassium, the characteristic lines in all three being at the ends of the spectrum, and all three showing a continuous spectrum in the centre. Rubidium (from ῥύβιδος, dark-red)

FIG. 15.

is named in allusion to the red lines at 15 5 and 13·5, even less refrangible than the potassium red line; it has also characteristic lines in the violet at 135·5 and 137·0, and several less characteristic lines in the yellow and green. Cæsium gets its name from the bright blue lines at 106 and 109 (from *cæsius*, sky-blue); the spectrum has several other lines in the red, yellow, and green, the brightest of which is at 42.

Like potassium, rubidium and cæsium are precipitated by platinum chloride; if the quantity of these rare substances in the substance under examination is small, the spectrum test is best made with the precipitate obtained with platinum chloride, by heating this precipitate in a current of hydrogen and boiling the residue with a few drops of water.

The *spectra of the alkaline earths*, barium, strontium, and calcium, are not quite so simple as those of the alkalies. When first introduced into the flame there are seen certain bands which are different according to the particular salt of the metal used, and which are supposed to be due to the compound employed; but the final spectrum obtained is the same with all the different salts of any one metal, and is partly due to the oxide of the metal produced by the reactions taking place in the flame, besides which there appear the brightest lines due to the metal itself; for example, the strontium blue line at 105, and the calcium violet line at 135, are due to the metal. The lines attributed to the special compounds, *e.g.* chloride, bromide, and iodides of these metals, are maintained and strengthened by introducing into the flame a current of hydrochloric acid or bromine vapour, or iodine vapour, as the case may be. These differences are clearly shown in Fig. 16, copied (by permission) from the drawings by M. Lecoq de Boisbaudran, given in his valuable work "Spectres Lumineux," on a scale a little different from Bunsen's scale. The spectrum of calcium is at once recognized by the characteristic orange band, 40 to 43, and the green band, 61 to 63. The chloride, chlorate, bromide, and iodide give the reaction best; the non-volatile salts must be treated with hydrochloric acid (if it decomposes them) or heated with ammonium fluoride.

The strontium spectrum is characterized by the absence of green lines; the brightest lines are the orange band at 44 to 47, and the red lines at 30 and 35, but the most characteristic line is the blue one at 107·6. The reaction is given best by the chlorate or chloride or other haloid salt; but it is not given by the sulphate, phosphate, silicate, etc. These salts require a preliminary treatment. The sulphate may be reduced to sulphide by heating in the reducing flame of the Bunsen, and then moistening the bead with hydrochloric acid; the silicate or phosphate should be fused with sodium carbonate in a little spiral of platinum wire; the residue, after being washed with hot water, is moistened with hydrochloric acid, and brought into the flame.

The barium spectrum is given brilliantly by barium chlorate, chloride, etc. It presents a splendid series of green bands, the brightest of which are at 73 and 78. The non-volatile salts of barium require the same treatment as those of strontium.

In Fig. 16 the lines due to the metal are marked M, and those due to the oxide are marked O. In the Bunsen-flame spectrum of barium chloride there are three metal lines, 44·0, 61·6, and 69·9; the strontium spectrum shows two metal lines, 47·7 and 107·6; whilst the calcium spectrum shows only one line, at 138·2, due to the metal. The lines due to the compound of the metal with chlorine are 69·8, 72·9, 74·5, 76·0, 77·6, and 81·0; the rest of the lines are no doubt due to the oxide.

In the strontium spectrum the lines due to the chloride are 30·3, 33·0, and 38·25. In the calcium spectrum the lines due to the chloride are 41·75, 42·25, 45·0, 45·7, 48·8, 52·2; whilst 61·2 and 62·1 seem to be due to the oxide. We may therefore conclude, from spectroscopic evidence, that calcium has a greater affinity for chlorine than strontium and barium have, and that barium has a greater affinity for oxygen than strontium and calcium have.

Other metals (besides those of the alkalies and alkaline earths)

Flame-spectra.

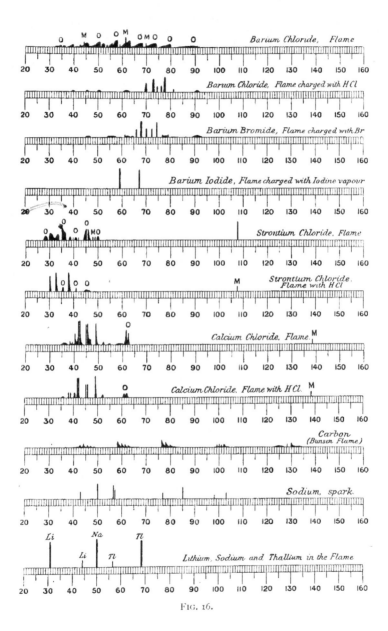

Fig. 16.

16 *An Introduction to the Study of Spectrum Analysis.*

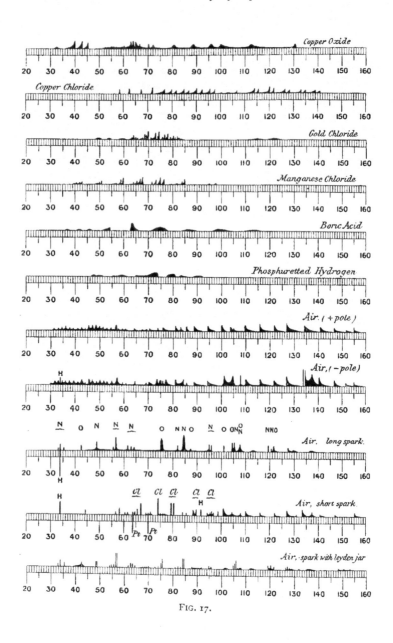

FIG. 17.

do not, as a rule, give spectra when their salts are brought into the Bunsen flame, either because they are not volatile enough, or because they are not decomposed at the temperature of the flame ; and for these it is necessary to employ a higher temperature by the use of electricity. There are, however, a few substances which give flame-spectra, and these may conveniently be described here before we proceed to describe the various ways of using the electric discharge.

Copper chloride colours the flame green or blue, according to circumstances ; a bead of the substance brought into the flame melts and gives a yellow patch of light bordered with a reddish tint, outside this central colour is seen a blue colour, and beyond this, on the outside of the flame, a green colour. On continued heating, the chloride of copper becomes converted into oxide, the blue colour disappears, but the green persists; on bringing hydrochloric acid into the flame the blue colour is restored. Professor Smithells has shown that the green colour is due to an oxide of copper, the blue colour to cuprous chloride, and the yellowish-red coloured portion of the flame is due to metallic copper.

The spectra of oxide of copper and chloride of copper are shown in Fig. 17 ; the two spectra are generally seen together.

Gold chloride gives a greenish colour to the flame, the spectrum of which is drawn in Fig. 17. Hydrochloric acid is essential to its production, and the spectrum is therefore regarded as due to the compound of gold and chlorine.

Lead chloride colours the flame blue, and behaves very much as copper chloride does, giving a spectrum due to oxide of lead, besides lines due to the chloride.

Bismuth chloride gives a spectrum of bands due to the oxide, and on continued heating a line at 100 (wave-length, 4722·7) due to the metal.

Manganese chloride and manganese oxide give a fine spectrum of bands due to the oxide, especially in the oxy-hydrogen flame. This spectrum is drawn in Fig. 17.

Other substances giving flame-spectra are boracic acid and phosphuretted hydrogen ; their spectra are also given in Fig. 17.

A trace of a phosphorus compound brought into a hydrogen-flask suffices to colour the flame of the hydrogen green, and to give the three green lines at 73, 79, and 59.

CHAPTER III.

SPECTRA PRODUCED BY MEANS OF ELECTRICITY.

IN order to produce the spectra of the less volatile metals, electricity must be employed; either the electric arc produced by a battery or by a dynamo, or the spark of an induction coil, or, in the case of gases, the discharge of the coil through an exhausted tube containing the gas. The most convenient method of obtaining these spectra in the laboratory is by the use of an induction coil and battery, unless the laboratory is fitted with the electric light, in which case there is no need of a battery. An induction coil, or "Ruhmkorff coil," is shown in Fig. 18; it should be large enough to give at

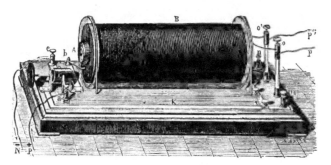

FIG. 18.

least a two-inch spark in air when worked by four or five Grove cells, or the same number of bichromate cells, if these are found more convenient. The spark may be made to pass between a piece of the metal under examination in the form of wire, or pieces held in the forceps of a spark-discharger as shown in Fig. 19. Sometimes a Leyden jar is used, which is connected as shown in Fig. 20. The spark between metal electrodes gives both the spectrum of the metal and also that of the air or other gas surrounding the spark. To distinguish the lines due to the metal from those due to the air, the spark may be surrounded by hydrogen; it is for this purpose that the little glass tube shown on the right in Fig. 19 is used. The lines due to hydrogen are few in number and easily recognized, whereas those produced by air are exceedingly numerous, and may all but obscure the lines due to the metal. The relative extent to which

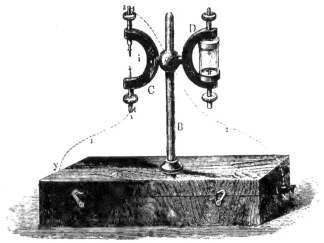

FIG. 19.

the lines due to these two sources appear depends very much upon the volatility of the metal, and the length of the spark. If the spark is only weak, the metal lines may be seen only in the close neighbourhood of the poles, and are thus discontinuous, whilst the air lines

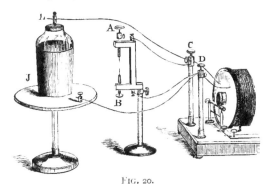

FIG. 20.
(*From Glazebrook's " Physical Optics."*)

go right across from one pole to the other. The appearance of the spark may be altered by regulating the adjustment of the contact-breaker of the coil. When this is made to work more slowly by slackening the tension, the metal lines become brighter, and those of the air less marked. With electrodes of platinum the metal lines are very few; iridium is, perhaps, still better.

It is, therefore, very important to make oneself familiar with this spectrum of air, and it is therefore given, under different conditions, in Fig. 17, where No. 7 shows the spectrum of the positive pole with a spark of moderate length (the band spectrum of nitrogen); No. 8, the spectrum of the negative pole under the same conditions; No. 9, the spectrum of a long spark (lines of oxygen, nitrogen, and hydrogen); and No. 10, the spectrum of a very short spark between platinum wires moistened with hydrochloric acid. In this last drawing there are shown lines of hydrogen at 33·7, 91·75; lines due to chlorine at 64·25, 64·72, 65·58, 66·80, 74·00, 79·18, 80·30, 88·47, 89·67, 94·30, 95·47, 96·05, and 96·80; and lines due to platinum at 63·55 and 70·38.

There is sometimes an advantage in using a lens between the

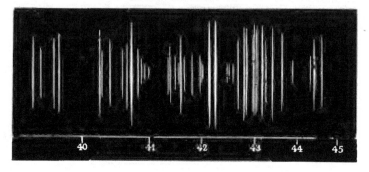

FIG. 21.

source of light and the slit; this is adjusted so as to throw a sharp image of the source of light—flame or spark—upon the slit. By this means we can distinguish the different spectra proceeding from different portions of the spark or flame.

If the experiment be tried with an ordinary candle-flame, using a small hand-spectroscope with the slit horizontal, we get, when the middle of the image falls across the slit, the continuous spectrum of white light; but if the very tip of the flame falls on the slit, we have the one bright yellow line of sodium, and if we make the image of the blue base of the flame fall upon the slit, then we get the spectrum of bright lines (to be afterwards described) known as the "Swan" spectrum.

If the spark is placed horizontally, and the image of it thrown on to a vertical slit, the spectrum of the vapour surrounding each pole can be more clearly distinguished from that of the surrounding gas. With this arrangement all the lines of any one substance are seen not to be of the same length. This is shown in Fig. 21, which is copied from a photograph of a portion of the spectrum obtained from the arc between poles of carbon impregnated with a strontium salt which contained calcium as an impurity. The longest lines at 4078 and 4215 are due to strontium; there is a long line of calcium at 4227, and the four short lines on the left are due to impurities of calcium and aluminium contained in the carbon poles. These four lines (of which the two outer ones are due to calcium, and the two inner ones to aluminium) are always seen in the photographs of arc spectra, whatever the substance used.

We get a hotter spark and brighter spectra by using a Leyden jar, of which the inner coating is connected to one terminal of the coil, and the outer coating to the other terminal. This arrangement is shown in Fig. 20; in Fig. 19 the Leyden jar is contained in the box which forms the base of the instrument.

Instead of using metallic electrodes of the substance to be in-

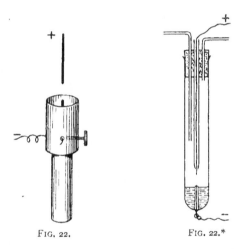

FIG. 22.   FIG. 22.*

vestigated, we may employ its salts in the solid form or solutions of the salts. Convenient arrangements for this purpose are shown in Figs. 22 and 22*. The apparatus shown in Fig. 22 is for the use of dry salts. It consists of a little conical cup made out of an aluminium rod about $\frac{1}{4}$ inch in diameter; a fine hole is drilled in the bottom of this cup, into which a platinum wire is inserted (like the wick of a candle); this cup is employed in the spark-holder as the bottom electrode, the upper electrode being a piece of wire of copper or some other metal; the salt to be examined is pressed into the cup, the use of the platinum wire being to confine the spark to the centre of the salt, and thus to render it steady.

The apparatus shown in Fig. 22* is for use with solutions; it is made out of a piece of glass tubing, about $\frac{3}{4}$ inch in diameter, closed at the bottom like a test-tube. A platinum wire is melted through the bottom to serve as the lower electrode, and a bit of thin glass tubing is dropped over this; the solution to be examined is put into the tube and adjusted to such a height that it rises by capillary attraction to just cover the electrode. The upper electrode is a platinum wire, melted into a glass tube which passes through a cork fitting the top of the test-tube, and which is easily adjusted within the required distance from the bottom electrode. The two other glass tubes shown, passing through the cork, enable a current of hydrogen or other gas to be passed through the tube to displace the air, if required.

The work of M. Lecoq de Boisbaudran, entitled "Spectres Lumineux," contains a very careful series of measurements of the spark spectra of the metals, as seen in a short simple spark in air, between platinum poles moistened with the solutions of the metallic salts. These are accompanied by an atlas of drawings, from which many of our figures are copied by permission. M. Lecoq de Boisbaudran employed a coil giving a spark of from 2 to 5 cm. length; he recommends the use of a rather short spark with solutions of the chlorides of the metals; he finds that, under these conditions, the lines due to the air and to the electrodes do not interfere with the results to any great extent.

On comparing the drawings of the spark spectra of sodium, lithium, and potassium with those of the flame spectra of the same elements, we see that the higher temperature of the spark gives rise to many more lines; so that, for example, instead of the one line of sodium and the two lines of lithium in the flame, we have in the spark eight lines due to sodium and four lines due to lithium, and thirty-one lines in the case of potassium. Some of these additional lines are obtained in the flame spectrum by feeding it with oxygen instead of air. It seems, therefore, as if these additional lines were due simply to the higher temperature of the source of light. With barium, strontium, and calcium the case is somewhat different, since in the flame spectra we have bands due to the oxide of the metal and to the chloride or other salt used, and some of these bands disappear at the higher temperature and are replaced by additional lines due to the metal itself.

In the spectrum of manganese chloride produced in the gas, we have a series of bands due to the oxide of manganese. In the spark, not too short, we have these bands again, as well as certain conspicuous lines due to the metal itself; and if we make the spark short enough, the bands of the oxide disappear, and the lines of metal become more numerous and decided. These spectra of manganese are shown in Fig 17, No. 4. We get also a spectrum of bands due to the oxide with aluminium, if we employ electrodes of the metal, or if we use aluminium chloride at the negative pole.

The bands of copper chloride, shown in Fig. 17, are obtained, together with the lines due to copper itself, in the spark with copper chloride. The spectrum obtained with magnesium chloride is shown in Fig. 23. It shows a very strong double line at 76, and a shaded band beginning at 83·8,* and fading away towards the blue end of the

* In the figure this band is shown at 88·8 by mistake.

Spectra produced by Means of Electricity.   23

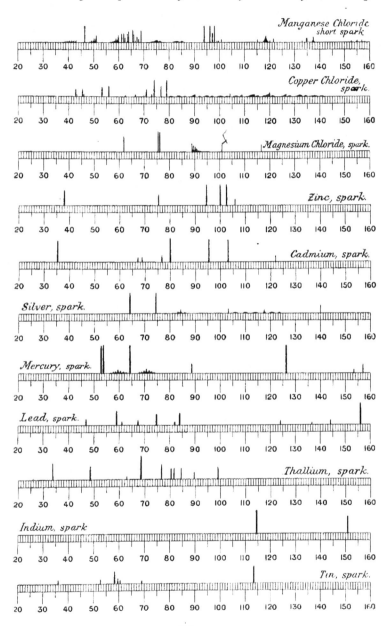

FIG. 23.

spectrum. This band is due to the oxide of magnesium, and is obtained very brightly in the spectrum of burning magnesium together with the double line at 76, which is due to the metal itself. This line is really triple, and can be seen as such if the slit be made very narrow. It coincides with the dark line known as "little b" in the sun's spectrum. Three other less conspicuous lines of the metal are seen at 61·7, 101, and 116·6. These are the chief examples of oxide spectra produced in the spark; in all other cases the lines seen in spark spectra are those of the metal. In the spectrum of zinc we have three bright lines at 94·6, 100·05, and 102·6, forming a wide triplet, and in the spectrum of the allied metal, cadmium, we have three similarly spaced lines at 80, 95·4, and 102·8. In the spectrum of silver the chief lines are two green ones at 64 and 74·4.

Mercury and mercury salts give a spectrum in which the chief lines are a yellow double line at 53·0 and 53·7, a green line at 64·1, almost in the same place as one of the silver lines, and a blue line at 126·4. This spectrum may also be obtained from a vacuum-tube containing mercury highly exhausted, and is given very brilliantly by the Cooper-Hewitt mercury-light, where the arc-light is produced between mercury electrodes.

In the spark spectrum of lead the chief line is a blue one at 155·9. If a solution of lead chloride is employed, this is the only line seen, but with a solution of the nitrate we have also the lines at 84, 74·7, 59, and 46·8. The spectrum as drawn was obtained by the use of electrodes of metallic lead.

Salts of thallium in the flame give one brilliant green line at 68·4, and a second faint line at 56·5. When the spark spectrum is examined, besides the flame-line in the green there are seen two lines in the red and orange, several lines in the green, and a well-defined line in the blue. Thallium was discovered in 1861 by Sir W. Crookes by means of its spectrum.

In 1864, Drs. Reich and Richter observed two deep-blue lines in the spectrum of a variety of zinc ore, and were thus led to the discovery of a new metal, which received the name "indium." Indium chloride colours the flame deep blue, and the spectrum shows two lines in the blue at 114·5 and 150·8.

The spark spectrum of tin is characterized by two lines, a blue line at 113·4, and a yellow line at 58·2; two lines a little more refrangible than this yellow line, at 59·6 and 60·6, are feeble, but if a Leyden jar is used these two lines become the strongest in the whole spectrum.

The most characteristic lines of bismuth in the spark, are 99·9, 60·9, 74·3, and 149.

Antimony only gives a bright spectrum with strong solutions; the chief lines are in the red and greenish yellow at 46·8, 60·3, 43·5, and 44·8.

A solution of chloride of gold subjected to the spark gives a brilliant spectrum, containing some of the bands of the flame spectrum, and in addition, sharp lines due to the metal. The most characteristic

Spectra produced by Means of Electricity. 25

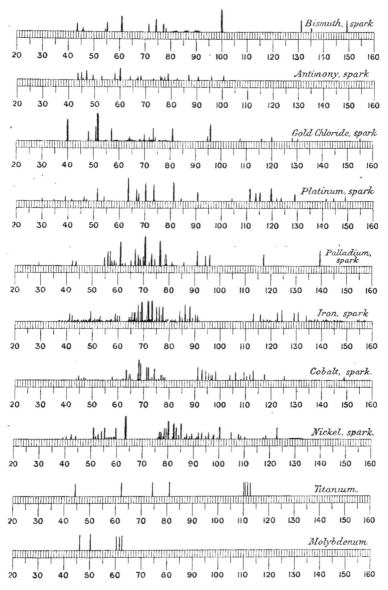

Fig. 24.

of these are a yellow line at 51·6 and a red line at 39·9, then green and blue lines at 95·7, 73·4, 81, and 57·3.

The spark between electrodes of platinum does not give lines due to the metal unless the spark be very powerful or a Leyden jar be employed; with the ordinary spark only air lines are seen; but if the electrodes are moistened with a solution of chloride of platinum a brilliant spectrum of fine lines is obtained. It is advisable to employ a short spark and moderately concentrated solution. The chief lines are 63·6 and 70·3, then 81·25, 73·5, and 66·8.

With a solution of chloride of palladium the chief lines are green lines at 70·7, 76·3, and 61·1.

Iron, cobalt, and nickel give very complicated spectra. They are best obtained from solutions of the chlorides of the metals.

The most characteristic lines of iron are three green lines at 71·8, 69·3, and 73·4, then two blue lines at 86·3 and 88·25, and a violet line at 124·3.

The most characteristic lines of cobalt are a fine double line at 68·25 and 68·75 in the green, a somewhat wider double line at 71·3 and 71·9, a single line at 74·2, and blue lines at 91·3 and 92·9.

The most characteristic lines of nickel are a bright green line at 63·6, another at 80·2, and a blue line at 100·4.

The most characteristic lines of titanium are 40·4 in the red, 62·2, 74·3, 80·9 in the green, and a group of blue lines, 110·1, 110·7, 111·6, and 112·7.

Molybdenum is recognized by a group of three lines in the green at 60·3, 61·6, and 62·5; and lines in the yellow and orange at 50·1 and 46·1.

The simple spark between fragments of arsenic gives only a continuous spectrum, but if a Leyden jar be employed, a very large number of lines are obtained. Arsenic may, then, be recognized in minerals containing it by red lines at 42·5 and 44, green lines at 57·5, 60·7, 62·8, 69·2, and others. Only the strongest lines are shown in the figure.

Beryllium is recognized by the blue line at 110; minerals containing it must be fused with an alkaline carbonate. Count de Gramont, in his treatise on the application of the spectroscope to the analysis of minerals, recommends carbonate of lithium; the mineral in fine powder is fused with the lithium carbonate in a loop of platinum wire placed in a Bunsen burner, and the spark is made to play upon it while in the flame, so that the bead is kept liquid or pasty.

The silicon in silicates can be easily recognized by the same method. The most characteristic lines of silicon are two lines in the red at 47·8 and 48·4, and a double green line at 81·2 and 81·9; the double blue band at 147 to 148 is also very characteristic, especially if the method of photographing the spectrum be employed.

Germanium is recognized by two broad and bright lines in the orange at 46·3 and 50; this last line is apparently coincident with the sodium line, but it is really a little more refrangible.

Spectra produced by Means of Electricity. 27

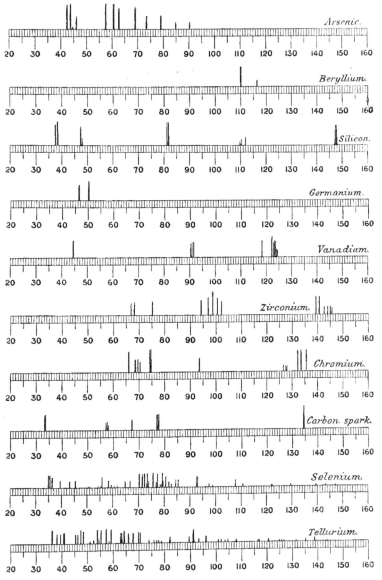

Fig. 25.

Vanadium can be recognized in a mineral by a group of lines in the indigo at 122·3 to 124·5.

Zirconium gives a brilliant spectrum of lines in the green, blue, and violet. A silicate containing zirconium fused with lithium carbonate shows the group of blue lines at 94·4 to 102, and the pair of violet lines at 139·4 and 140·7.

Chromium is recognized by a group of three lines in the violet at 132·3, 133·7, and 135·6, and by the close triplet of lines in the green at 74·3 to 74·5; with a single prism this will appear as a strong single line.

Carbon can be recognized in the spectrum of fused alkaline carbonates by the line at 134·5, which with increase of spark strength becomes a nebulous band. Without the Leyden jar this and the red line are the only lines seen; the spectrum is best obtained by the use of a Leyden jar and air-break. The same spectrum is obtained from the spark between electrodes of graphite.

The spectrum of selenium is shown in Fig. 25. It is obtained by taking the spark with Leyden jar between platinum wires covered with melted selenium, or between fragments of any of the selenides. The most characteristic lines are those in the green: 70·2, 71·7, 72·4, 73·6, 75·8, 77·4, 79·5; and the three lines in the red: 35·1, 35·4, 36·4.

The most characteristic lines of tellurium are 36·3 in the red, 47·6 and 48·7 in the orange, 54 and 55·5 in the yellowish green, 57·5 and 59·5 in the green; it is necessary to employ the jar.

Sulphur gives both a line spectrum and a spectrum of bands, which are shown in Fig. 26. If the spark, with jar, is made to pass between wires of platinum covered with sulphur, or between fragments of sulphides, the most characteristic lines are the red group of five lines at 36 and 39, the green lines at 64·5 and 65·1, 68·5 and 69·6.

The band spectrum of sulphur is obtained by passing the current from the induction coil through an exhausted tube containing sulphur which is heated by means of a Bunsen burner.

In Fig. 26 are shown the spectra of the minerals berzelianite and argyrodite, a comparison of these spectra with the spectra of the various elements given, shows that berzelianite contains selenium, copper, silver, and thallium; and argyrodite contains sulphur, silver, and germanium. It was in this mineral, one of the silver ores found at Freiberg, that germanium was found by Winckler in 1886.

In the case of the elements which are gaseous at the ordinary temperature, or which are easily vaporized, the spectra are often very conveniently obtained by the use of exhausted tubes, known as Geissler or Plücker tubes. Such a tube is shown in Fig. 28. The electrodes consist of platinum wires melted into the glass, one at each end of the tube, and the central portion of the tube ab is made narrow. This portion of the tube—the "capillary"—is placed in front of the slit, while the discharge from an induction coil passes through the tube. The colour of the discharge varies with the nature of the gas enclosed, *e.g.* with hydrogen the colour is red, with nitrogen violet,

Spectra produced by Means of Electricity. 29

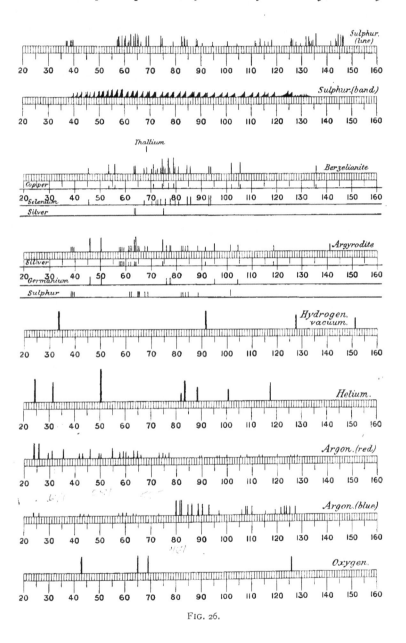

FIG. 26.

30   An Introduction to the Study of Spectrum Analysis.

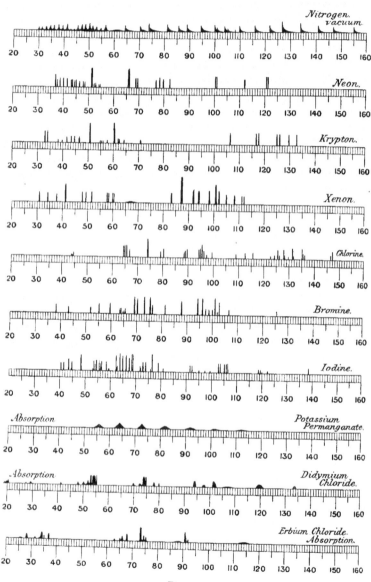

Fig. 27.

Spectra produced by Means of Electricity. 31

and with helium it is yellow. The pressure of the gas left in the tube is usually only a few millimetres of mercury; if the pressure is too great the discharge refuses to pass, or takes place only as a thin thread-like spark, but as the pressure is reduced the light given out by the tube becomes brighter, and the discharge fills the whole tube. The colour is often different in the wider portions of the tube from that of the capillary, and the colour (and spectrum) of the negative pole, B, is often different from that of the positive pole, A, and different again from that of the capillary, ab. It is, however, the capillary portion always which is adjusted in front of the slit.

FIG. 28.

The spectrum given by a Geissler tube is not always that of the gas present in the tube in the largest proportion. It is extremely difficult, in filling the tube, to avoid the presence of impurities, and it may happen that the electric discharge picks out one of these impurities, and renders it luminous, so that the tube may give the spectrum of something quite different from the gas supposed to be contained in the tube. Thus it has happened more than once that the spectrum of some unsuspected impurity has been described as that of a new element, or as a new spectrum of an element. Tubes which have been exhausted by means of a mercury pump commonly show the spectrum of mercury, often to the exclusion of all else, and at high exhaustions the commonest spectrum is that of an oxide of carbon, due to dust in the tube, or to the grease used in lubricating the taps, so that the evidence obtained by the use of tubes only is to be received with very great caution.

If the gas in the tube is hydrogen, the spectrum consists mainly of three bright lines, shown in Fig. 26. Hydrogen vacuum tubes generally show, besides these three lines, a large number of feeble lines filling up the whole spectrum; these constitute the so-called secondary spectrum of hydrogen, but it is not certain that they are due to hydrogen itself. It is very difficult to obtain absolutely pure hydrogen, and especially to free it from all traces of water. A tube filled with water vapour gives practically the same spectrum as has been described.

Helium is one of the gases discovered by means of spectrum analysis. The most characteristic line in its spectrum is an extremely brilliant yellow line, a little more refrangible than the sodium line. This line was first seen in 1868, at the time of a solar eclipse, in the light from the prominences and chromosphere of the Sun, but no substance of terrestrial origin giving the same line was known. Nevertheless, it was concluded by Lockyer that there must be an element characterized by this particular line, and he gave to it the name "helium," from the Greek word for "Sun," and for twenty-seven years helium was known only as an element existing on the sun. But in 1895, Sir W. Ramsay obtained from the mineral clévite a new gas, which turned out to be the long-sought helium. Since then this new gas has been obtained from other minerals, and has been found to exist in small proportion (one in a million) in air. At a pressure of 7 or 8 millimetres the helium tube glows with a brilliant yellow light, and gives the spectrum shown in Fig. 26. If the tube is more highly exhausted, the green line at 83·3 becomes much the brightest, and the tube emits a brilliant green light, but only if the gas is pure. When mixed with other gases, helium is best detected by the green line in tubes highly exhausted.

Argon is another gas existing in the air, discovered in 1894 by Lord Rayleigh and Sir W. Ramsay; it appears to constitute about 1 per cent. of the atmosphere. A vacuum tube containing argon glows with a red light; the spectrum is complex; showing chiefly red lines and only feebler lines in the blue; but if the tube is connected with a Leyden jar, the colour of the light becomes blue and the spectrum changes, the red lines having become fainter, and many new green and blue lines having appeared.

The behaviour of oxygen in a vacuum tube is peculiar; it is not to be detected when mixed with other gases, and as already remarked, air in a vacuum tube shows the same spectrum as nitrogen. A tube filled with pure oxygen, when not much exhausted, shows a continuous spectrum with a thin thread-like spark. As the exhaustion is increased, four lines make their appearance from the capillary, and these get brighter as the tube is further exhausted, while the glow from the negative pole spreads into the capillary, so that we now have the four lines superposed upon the special spectrum of the negative pole. If a Leyden jar and air-break be used, the four lines disappear and give place to the "elementary line spectrum," which is mapped in Fig. 16, No. 9. The four lines constitute the "compound line spectrum" of oxygen; it is mapped in Fig. 26.

It appears that oxygen is capable of giving no less than seven different spectra.

Nitrogen in a vacuum tube gives a spectrum of bands, shown in Fig. 27, No. 1. It shows a number of bands of one character in the orange and yellow, and an extensive series of bands of a different character in the blue and violet. This spectrum is entirely different from that given by the gas at atmospheric pressure when the spark with Leyden jar is sent through it. The line spectrum then obtained forms part of the air spectrum shown in Fig. 16. There is also a different band spectrum seen at the negative pole, so that it appears that nitrogen, like oxygen, is capable of giving several different spectra.

Besides argon and helium, Ramsay and Travers have found in air three other new gases, neon, krypton, and xenon, the spectra of which are shown in Fig. 27. Of neon there appear to be one or two parts in 100,000 parts of air; the spectrum has a yellow line a little more refrangible than the characteristic helium line, and a mass of orange lines to the left of this, besides a characteristic triplet in the green.

There is about as much krypton as helium in the air—one in 1,000,000 parts. The most characteristic lines in the spectrum are a bright green line at 60·2, and pairs of lines in the red, orange, blue, and violet.

Xenon occurs in still smaller quantity; its brightest lines are in the blue.

Chlorine seems to give only one spectrum—a line spectrum. This is obtained either by the discharge through a vacuum tube containing chlorine, or by sparks in the gas at ordinary pressure, or from fused chlorides, or minerals containing chlorine. The vacuum tube gives the best result with chlorine at a pressure of 50 to 100 mm. The lines by which the presence of chlorine is best detected are four lines in the yellowish-green at 64 to 67, a bright green line at 74, which is seen to be double on employing a higher dispersion, and a group of blue lines at about 95, in which three lines are very strong.

A vacuum tube containing bromine shows a spectrum of lines; the same lines are seen with fused bromides or minerals containing bromine when the spark is made to play upon them. The brightest lines are a group of blue lines at 94·4, 96·1, 101·1, and 102·8; green lines at 69·1, 70·2, 73·1, 75·5, and 76·4.

The spectrum of iodine is still richer in lines than the spectra of chlorine and bromine. The principal lines are at 48·3 in the red, a group in the yellow from 53 to 58, lines in the green at 62·8, 62·9, 63·9, 65, 6·2, 68·6, 68·9, 76·5, besides many blue lines.

CHAPTER IV.

ABSORPTION SPECTRA.—THE ELECTRIC ARC.

SOME few substances are best recognized by means of their absorption spectra. The substance to be examined will generally be in the form of a solution, placed between a bright white light and the slit of the spectroscope. Fig. 29 shows a two-prism spectroscope arranged for the observation of a solution contained in the test-tube

FIG. 29.

fixed before the slit of the instrument; and Fig. 30 represents a glass trough to contain the solution to be used instead of the test-tube of Fig. 29. It is better, however, to use a wedge-shaped trough, since in this way the effect of different thicknesses of the absorbing medium on the spectrum is seen. Fig. 31 shows the absorption spectrum of a solution of chromium chloride, of which a dilute solution appears green to the eye, while a strong solution or a greater thickness of solution appears purple or red. The red end of the spectrum is shown to the right in the figure, and the position of the dark lines of the solar spectrum are marked below, B in the red, D in the yellow, E and *b* in the green, and so on. The bottom of the figure corresponds to a small thickness, and the top to a much greater thickness. The small thickness cuts out some light in the yellowish-green and in the blue, and the light transmitted is therefore of a green colour, but as

FIG. 30.

FIG. 31.

the thickness or strength of the solution increases, the absorption increases until at last nothing but red light makes its way through.

In Fig. 32 we have the absorption spectrum of a solution of potassium permanganate; a very weak solution shows five dark bands between D and F, but as the thickness or strength of the solution increases, all the light in this region is absorbed and the bands disappear, a solution of moderate strength being purple, and a very strong solution allowing nothing but red light to pass. This same spectrum, as shown by a weak solution, is drawn again in Fig. 27, No. 8; it must be understood that in such a drawing of an *absorption* spectrum the black marks represent *dark* bands. Some colourless or all but colourless solutions show well-marked absorption bands, often useful in detecting the substance. Thus didymium and erbium salts are easily detected by means of their absorption spectra. Fig. 27 shows the absorption spectrum of a solution of didymium chloride in dilute solution; the strongest bands are at 53 to 55, and at 73·9 to 74·6.

The position of these dark bands in didymium salts is not quite the same in the sulphate as in the chloride, each band being slightly shifted towards the red, and in a solution of the acetate the bands are still further shifted towards the red. Bunsen remarks that "these differences in the absorption spectra of different didymium compounds cannot, in our present complete state of ignorance of any general theory for the absorption of light in absorptive media, be connected with other phenomena. They remind one of the slight gradual alterations in

36   *An Introduction to the Study of Spectrum Analysis.*

pitch which the notes from a vibrating elastic rod undergo when the rod is weighted, or of the change of tone which an organ pipe exhibits when the tube is lengthened." Bunsen further calls attention to the fact that the molecular weight of the acetate is greater than that of the

FIG. 33.

sulphate, and that the molecule of the sulphate again is heavier than that of the chloride.

Fig. 27 shows the absorption spectrum of erbium chloride; the most conspicuous bands are at 73·4 and 91·0.

Coloured gases also give absorption spectra, often of great complexity. Bromine, iodine vapour, nitrogen peroxide, iodine monochloride give innumerable dark lines. The relationship of

Absorption Spectra.—The Electric Arc.

these absorption spectra to the emission spectra of the same substances will be discussed later on.

Another mode of ignition of the substances to be examined is by the use of the electric arc. Unless we have at command the supply of electricity from a dynamo, we must employ batteries, and as at least forty cells of Grove or Bunsen are necessary, the method is somewhat inconvenient. The carbon, whether volatilized or not, is carried across from the positive pole to the negative, thus producing a "crater" in the positive pole. Fig. 33 shows the incandescent poles of the arc; they may be projected upon a screen by the arrangement shown in Fig. 34. To obtain a steady arc some

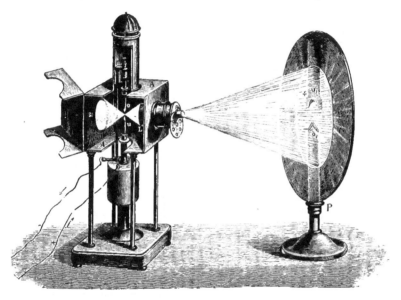

Fig. 34.

form of regulating lamp must be used. Fig. 35 represents Foucault's electric lamp; in this the carbons are moved by two trains of clockwork, the one of which causes the carbons to approach each other, and the other causes them to separate. When the arc is in exact adjustment, both trains of clockwork are held by a catch governed by the armature of an electro-magnet working against a spring. If the carbons come too close together, the electro-magnet draws the armature forward and releases the set of wheels which make the carbons separate from each other; if, on the other hand, the carbons get too far apart, the current is enfeebled and the spring draws the armature back and releases the other train of wheels, but so long as the distance between the two carbons is exactly right, both trains of wheels are locked. As the positive carbon wastes away about twice as fast as the negative carbon, the clockwork is so made as to move the former twice as fast as the latter. An alternating current may also be used to produce the arc; in this case both carbons wear away at the same rate. There are many other forms of automatic regulators for the arc, but some form or other is necessary.

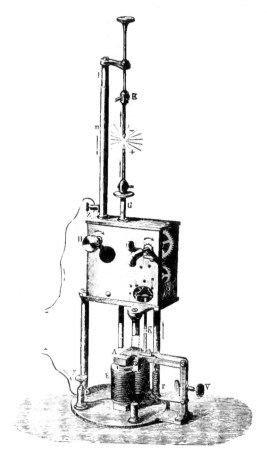

FIG. 35.

The spectrum of the electric arc is, in the first place, a continuous spectrum due to the incandescent solid carbon. Then, in the next place, it gives certain bands, the same as seen in the spectrum of the Bunsen flame (see Fig. 16, No. 9), which are believed to be due to the vapour of carbon, the temperature of the arc being that due to

Absorption Spectra.—The Electric Arc.

the volatilization of carbon, or perhaps 3500° C. It must be observed that the temperature of the arc is much *less* than that produced by the spark from the induction coil, either with or without Leyden jar; and as a result the arc-spectra of the metals are usually much simpler than their spark-spectra. Thus in the arc-spectrum there are no lines due to arsenic in the portion visible to the eye, whereas in the spark-spectrum there are some 50 lines. In the complete arc-spectrum of zinc there are about 73 lines, but in the spark-spectrum something like 400 lines have been measured.*

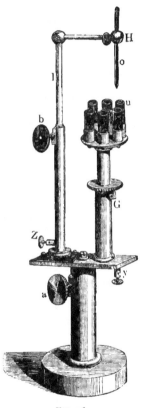

FIG. 36.

In order to produce the arc-spectrum of a metal, the lower carbon is hollowed out to form a cup, in which fragments of the metal or of one of its salts are placed, we then obtain bright lines of the metallic vapour superposed upon the continuous spectrum of the carbon poles. The upper pole is a rod of carbon, or sometimes a rod of the metal under examination is used. A convenient arrangement for producing the arc-spectra of the metals is shown in Fig. 36, in which there are six hollow carbons, any one of which may be brought under the top carbon rod, and thus into the right position for obtaining the spectrum.

The continuous spectrum due to the carbon is fortunately much weakened by the introduction of metallic substances into the arc, more particularly if volatile metals such as cadmium are being employed.

Then the presence of lines due to metals other than those intentionally introduced and resulting from impurities in the carbon rods employed must always be expected; in particular lines due to iron, calcium, aluminium, magnesium, and silicon, as well as the

---

* The arc- and spark-spectra of the elements (according to wave-lengths) are given together in the tables at the end of this work. A comparison will show that in some cases the spectra are very different (*e.g.* barium, arsenic, antimony, chromium, etc.), and that while generally the spark-lines are more numerous than the arc-lines, there occur cases in which the arc-spectrum contains lines not seen in the spark. When extremely exact measurements are made there is observed a very slight shift of the lines in the spark as compared with the same lines in the arc, a slight increase of wave-length. This is attributed to greater pressure in the spark than in the arc.

carbon bands already spoken of. Even if the carbons have been heated for hours in a current of chlorine, the lines of iron and calcium are still to be seen. In Fig. 21, which shows a portion of the arc-spectrum of strontium, the first line on the left is due to calcium, the next two are due to aluminium, and the next to calcium. These four " impurity " lines can be recognized in all arc-spectra.

CHAPTER V.

THE DIFFRACTION SPECTRUM.—MEASUREMENT OF WAVE-LENGTHS.

So far we have only spoken of one method of producing a spectrum, viz. by the use of prisms. But there is another method—and a very important method—of producing a spectrum, by the use of what are called "diffraction gratings." In order to understand this it will be necessary to consider at some length the nature of light, and the mechanism by which it is propagated from a luminous source to the eye.

The velocity of light has been measured by several different methods, which give concordant results. Römer, in 1676, by observing the eclipses of Jupiter's moons, found that light required 16 minutes and 26 seconds to traverse the diameter of the earth's orbit, or 185,600,000 miles.

Bradley determined the velocity of light from the aberration of light. The velocity of the earth in its orbit combined with the velocity of light has the result of causing a star (apparently) to describe a small circle or ellipse once in a year round its true position, the diameter of this circle is foundtos ubtend an angle of 20·445 seconds of arc, and the velocity of light is found by dividing the velocity of the earth in its orbit by the tangent of this angle.

Fizeau, by an arrangement of a rapidly revolving toothed wheel, found how long it took light to travel a distance of about ten miles, and his method was employed with improved apparatus by Cornu.

Foucault, employing a rapidly revolving mirror, found it possible to measure the velocity of light in a room through a distance of only a few metres. Foucault's apparatus is shown in Fig. 37. $m\ o\ n$ represents a rapidly revolving plane mirror; the source of light is at S, and an achromatic lens, K, is so placed as to throw an image of S somewhere on the circle R' S' M M', of which the centre is at o, the axis of the revolving mirror. If this image, after reflection at the revolving mirror, is formed at s', and if a concave spherical mirror is placed at M, whose radius of curvature is $o\ s'$, the light is sent back again to the revolving mirror and reflected back again to S, if the mirror has not had time to move sensibly while the light was passing from o to s' and back again. $a\ b$ is a plane, unsilvered plate of glass, and O the lens of a micrometer. Observation shows that there is a measurable displacement of the image when the mirror is in rapid motion, the ray of light which started towards R' entering the eye at O as if it came from S'.

By placing a tube filled with water, T, between the revolving

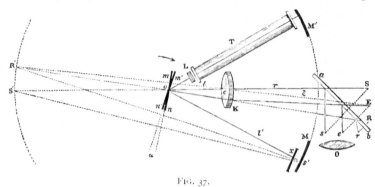

Fig. 37.

mirror and a concave mirror at M', it is possible to measure the velocity in water, and it is thus shown that in water the velocity of light is just three-quarters of the velocity in air. Foucault's method has been employed with improved apparatus by Michelson. His result is 186,330 miles per second, or 299,890,000 metres per second, or $2\cdot9989 \times 10^5$ kilometres per second. The result obtained by Cornu was $3\cdot004$; by Fizeau, $3\cdot15$; by Römer, $3\cdot10$; and from the aberration of light, $3\cdot083$.*

Light consists in a very rapid vibration of a highly elastic medium, called the luminiferous ether, which fills all space, and pervades all transparent substances. Light travels from a star (or the sun) to the earth by means of waves, in which the particles vibrate at right angles to the line joining the star and the eye of the observer, that is, the ray of light. This is represented in Fig. 38, the motion of the particles in the row a a' is communicated to the next row, which move down, and come back to their positions of rest at c c', then move up and come back to their original positions at b b'. The length ab is called a wave-length, and the time of oscillation of any one particle is the time required for light to travel from a to b.

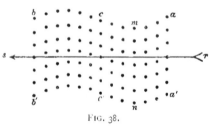

Fig. 38.

---

* Listing, from a discussion of all Cornu's measurements, thinks the most probable value to be $2\cdot999$; and Newcomb has obtained $2\cdot998$. The value may therefore be taken as 300,000 kilometres per second.

The Diffraction Spectrum.—Measurement of Wave-lengths. 43

We have seen that when light falls upon a plate of glass, or other transparent substance, it undergoes a change in direction, part being reflected according to the law of reflection, and part passing into the glass, being refracted according to the law of refraction.

The explanation of these phenomena given by the undulatory theory of light is as follows:—when the wave of light reaches the surface of the reflecting and refracting surface, each point of that surface becomes the centre of a disturbance, which spreads out in each medium, but with less velocity in the glass than in the air. Let MN in Fig. 39 represent the plane surface of the glass, and sa, $s'b$ the

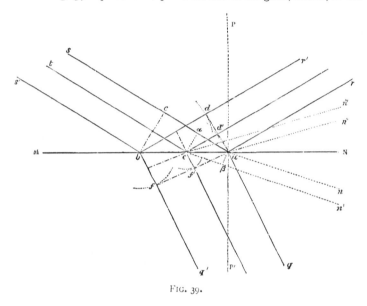

FIG. 39.

direction of an incident beam of light, of which the wave-front is at right angles to sa. When the wave-front reaches the surface at b, a spherical wave starts from b as centre, and by the time the wave-front has got to a, the new wave has a radius bd equal to ca in the original medium, and in the glass the new wave has a radius of only two-thirds of ca, since the velocity of light in glass is only two-thirds of that in air. If now from a in the plane of incidence we draw tangents to the two spherical surfaces at d and f, these will be the wave-fronts of the reflected and refracted beams respectively; the direction of the reflected beam will be bd, and that of the refracted beam bf.

It will easily be seen that, in the first medium, the triangles abc and abd being similar, the angle abd is equal to the angle bac, that is, the incident and reflected rays make equal angles with the reflecting surface MN, and, therefore, also with the normal, aP; and the angle which the refracted ray makes with the normal is equal to baf, the sine of which is $\frac{bf}{ab'}$ and the angle of incidence is equal to abc, the sine of which is $\frac{ac}{ab'}$.

The sine of the angle of incidence, therefore, bears to the sine of the angle of refraction the constant ratio $ac : bf$, which is the law of refraction. The ratio $ac : bf$ is called the index of refraction, usually denoted by μ, it is simply the ratio of the velocity of light in the first medium to the velocity in the second medium.*

We have now to consider the phenomenon known as the interference of light. When any portion of the luminiferous ether is affected by two waves of equal intensity, they may combine so as to produce increased motion and, therefore, greater intensity of light, or they may neutralize each other. If in Fig. 40 two waves come

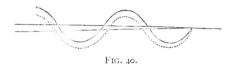

FIG. 40.

together so that they are in the same phase, that is, so that the crests and troughs of the one wave coincide with those of the other, we shall have an increased effect; but if the one wave is behind the other by half a wave-length, or by an odd number of half wave-lengths as shown in Fig. 41, the two disturbances will neutralize each other

FIG. 41.

and darkness will be the result. This result may be realized experimentally by the arrangement of Fresnel, shown in Fig. 42. A beam of sunlight enters a dark room by a narrow slit in the shutter, and, after passing through a plate of red glass, falls upon a cylindrical lens, L, of short focus, and is thereby reduced to a narrow line of red light at S.

The light from S falls upon two plane mirrors Im Im', which meet at a very obtuse angle, and after reflection proceed as if it had come from the two points s s' behind the mirrors. The line in which the mirrors meet is parallel to the line of light at S. The spherical waves which proceed from s and s' as centres are in a condition to interfere.

---

* There is no light in directions oblique to the reflected and refracted rays, because disturbances in these directions destroy each other by mutual interference.

The circular arcs represent successive positions of these wave-fronts, each arc being further from the origin by half a wave-length than the preceding arc. Upon a screen placed at right angles to the line A*a* we obtain a series of fringes alternately dark and light. There will be increased light wherever a dotted arc crosses another dotted arc, or where one drawn full crosses another; but there will be darkness where a dotted arc crosses one drawn full. It will be

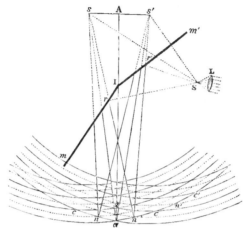

FIG. 42.

seen that where the screen meets the line A*a* we shall have the central bright fringe, and on each side of this we shall have a dark fringe at the points determined by the condition that the distances from *s* and *s'* differ by half a wave-length for red light, *i.e.* at the points *n n*; we have also dark fringes at the points *n'*, whose distances from *s* and *s* differ by three-halves of a wave-length, but at the points *c c*, whose distances from *s s'* differ by one or two wave-lengths, *i.e.* by an even number of half wave-lengths, we have bright fringes. If, therefore, we can measure the distances *ns ns'* we can determine the length of a wave of red light. This is found to be less than the thousandth part of a millimetre, or denoting the one-thousandth part of one millimetre by the symbol μ, the length of a wave of red light is found to be 0·656 μ, and of violet light about 0·4 μ.

A different method of producing these diffraction fringes is by the use of a "grating." Such diffraction gratings were first employed by Fraunhofer, who made them by winding very fine wire round two parallel screws of very fine thread and equal thickness, or by ruling parallel lines on glass with a diamond point by means of a dividing engine.

The finest gratings now are those known as Rowland gratings, ruled by a fine dividing engine on polished metal, having in one inch 14438 lines (or 568·44 to a millimetre).

In Fig. 43 let s represent a luminous point, and p a screen; and let the circular arc nAm represent any position of the spherical wave-front (whose origin is s) between s and p. The effect at p is the same as if each point of this arc were itself the origin of a wave. From p as centre let a series of circles be drawn with radii increasing by half a wave-length, the first having the radius pA, the next pa, then pb, pc, and so on. We thus divide the wave-front nAm into "elements of interference." The element Aa is larger than ab, ab larger than bc, and so on, but the elements approach more nearly to equality as they get further away from A. Now, considering the

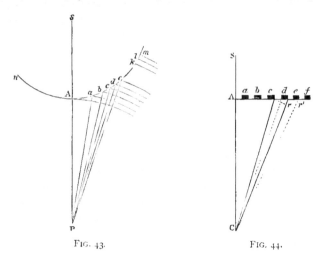

FIG. 43.   FIG. 44.

effect at p, for each point in ab, there is a point in Aa half a wave-length nearer p; interference will take place, and the effect produced by ab will be completely neutralized by Aa, but the effect produced by Aa will be only partially neutralized by ab. In the same way bc is partly neutralized by cd, and so on, and the elements of interference, taken in pairs, will neutralize each other more completely the further away from A they are.

The light which reaches P from s, therefore, comes altogether in the direction sP; none comes in the direction mp, i.e. light travels in a straight line, and not round a corner. But the case is different if at km a grating is interposed so as to stop off the alternate elements of interference, then light will reach P in the direction mp.

This result is, perhaps, seen more clearly from Fig. 44, in which S A C represents the direction in which light falls upon a grating at Aabc. The distance dC being greater than cC by half a wave-length, cC greater than dC by the same amount, and so on, light

The Diffraction Spectrum.—Measurement of Wave-lengths. 47

reaches C in the direction dC, making an angle dCA with the direct line SAC. If cr be drawn at right angles to dC, the angle dcr is equal to the angle dCA; dr is the length of a wave, and cd is the width of a bar and a space of the grating. Hence $\frac{dr}{dc}$ is equal to the sine of the angle dCA, so that if there are N bars and spaces in one millimetre, $cd = \frac{1}{N}$ and sine dCA $= $ Nλ, where λ denotes the wave-length in millimetres. To an eye placed at C, then, the appearance represented in Fig. 45 will be presented; the line of light at S is seen

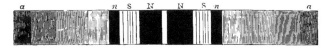

Fig. 45.

just as it would be if the grating were not there, but on each side of it will be seen a dark space, followed by a spectrum having the violet nearest the centre and the red furthest off. This is called the spectrum of the first order, and beyond it may be seen a spectrum of the second order, with the colours just twice as widely spaced as in the first spectrum. The spectrum of the third order overlaps that of the second, and the fourth, fifth, etc., overlap the others more and more, so that their colours become more and more indistinct.

The measurement of the exact wave-length of the lines of a spectrum is a problem of the highest importance, and one to which a vast amount of care has been devoted by many observers. To give some idea of the accuracy with which these measurements can now be made, the following measurements of the wave-lengths of the sodium yellow lines may be quoted:—Fraunhofer, using two wire gratings, found 5888 and 5896, while with a glass grating he obtained 5888 ten-millionths of a millimetre, for the mean of the two lines. Ångström, of Upsala, in 1868 published his "Recherches sur le Spectre Solaire," in which he arrives at the values 5895·0 and 5889·0 for the two sodium lines.

Ditscheiner obtained 5905·3 and 5898·9; Van der Willigen 5898·6 and 5892·6. Ångström published a map of the solar spectrum on the scale of wave-lengths, in which the chemical origin of a large number of the Fraunhofer lines was marked, and this map and the measurements based upon it were accepted for many years as the standards. This "spectre normal" of Ångström marked a very great advance in accuracy; but the construction of more accurate gratings by Rowland, and the publication of a photographic map made by Rowland with his new gratings, showed that Ångström's work needed revision. Rowland's values for the two sodium lines were 5896·08 and 5890·12.

Other measurements of the less refrangible sodium line are 5896·25 by Müller and Kempf, 5895·90 by Kurlbaum, 5896·20 by Pierce, and 5896·20 by Bell. The most probable value is 5896·161 in air at 20° C. and 760 mm.; or in vacuo 5897·8.

The distribution of the colours in the diffraction spectrum is different from that in the spectrum produced by any prism; the blue end is more compressed in the diffraction spectrum, and the red end is proportionally lengthened out. This is clearly shown in the coloured frontispiece. No two prisms can be relied upon to give exactly the same distribution of colours, and it is therefore necessary to reduce the readings obtained with a prism-spectroscope to the standard scale of wave-lengths; we must therefore explain how this may be done. The following table shows the relative positions occupied by the Fraunhofer lines B, D, E, F, and G, in dispersion spectra produced by prisms of 60° of crown-glass, flint-glass, and carbon disulphide, with which are compared the positions of the same lines in a spectrum obtained by diffraction. The interval between B and G is in each case divided into 1000 equal parts.

	Crown-glass.	Dispersion. flint-glass.	Carbon disulphide.	Diffraction.
B	0	0	0	0
D	236	220	194	381
E	451	434	400	624
F	644	626	590	784
G	1000	1000	1000	1000

To reduce the readings of a prism-spectroscope to wave-lengths, we have first of all to obtain accurate measurements of a number of standard lines whose wave-lengths are known exactly, and from these data to draw an interpolation-curve on accurately ruled squared paper. A scale of wave-lengths is marked off along one edge of the paper, and the edge at right angles to that has a scale marked on it corresponding to the scale of the instrument. The positions of as many lines as possible are then mapped on the paper, and through these points a curve is drawn as uniformly as possible. Then the position of any line to be measured being found on the curve will have opposite to it the wave-length required on the scale of wave-lengths.

The following list of lines will be found useful in constructing the curve of wave-lengths for a one-prism-spectroscope. The wave-lengths are given in tenth-metres* (or ten-millionths of a millimetre); there is also given the approximate position of the line on Bunsen's scale, and the reciprocal of the wave-length, or "oscillation frequency" —*i.e.* the number of waves in one centimetre. There are many advantages in using these "frequencies" instead of the wave-lengths themselves, as will be afterwards explained.

* A "tenth-metre" is $(\frac{1}{10})^{10}$ metre.

The Diffraction Spectrum.—Measurement of Wave-lengths.

(a) Flame-Spectra.

	Scale number.	Wave-length in air.	Oscillation frequency in vacuo.
Lithium	31·8	6708·2	14902·7
Sodium	50·0	$\left\{\begin{array}{l}5896·154\\5890·182\end{array}\right\}$ Mean 5893·168	$\left\{\begin{array}{l}16955·6\\16972·8\end{array}\right\}$ Mean 16964·2
Thallium	67·8	5350·65	18683·7
Magnesium *	74·5	5183·791	19285·6
Strontium	105·5	4607·506	21697·7

(b) Fraunhofer Lines.

	Scale number.	Wave-length in air.	Oscillation frequency in vacuo.
A	17·5	7594·059	13164·6
B	28·9	6867·461	14557·5
C	35·0	6563·054	15232·7
D	50·0	$\left\{\begin{array}{l}5896·154\\5890·182\end{array}\right\}$ Mean 5893·168	$\left\{\begin{array}{l}16955·6\\16972·8\end{array}\right\}$ Mean 16964·2
E	70·9	5270·085	18969·8
b_1	74·5	5183·792	19285·6
b_2	74·8	5172·871	19326·3
b_3 and b_4	75·0	5168·366	19343·1
F	90·0	4861·496	20564·1
G	127·3	4308·034	23205·9
H_1	161·2	3968·620	25190·6
H_2	165·7	3933·809	25413·4

(c) Spark-Spectra.

	Scale number.	Wave-length in air.	Oscillation frequency in vacuo.
Cadmium	36·9	6439·30	15525·4
Lithium	44·6	6103·77	16378·5
Copper	53·2	5782·30	17289·5
Lead	58·4	5607·30	17829·0
Cadmium	66·5	5379·30	18585·0
,,	68·2	5338·60	18726·0
Copper	69·9	5292·75	18888·6
,,	73·1	5218·45	19157·6
,,	75·6	5153·40	19399·4
,,	77·8	5105·75	19580·4
Cadmium	78·7	5086·06	19656·3
Air	82·4	5005·70	19978·0
,,	82·7	5002·70	19983·0
Barium	86·2	4934·24	20260·9
Cadmium	100·8	4678·37	21369·3
Barium	108·8	4554·21	21951·6
,,	110·8	4525·19	22092·3
Calcium	135·5	4226·91	23650·4
Barium	147·1	4130·88	24201·1
Calcium	161·2	3968·620	25190·6
,,	165·7	3933·809	25413·4

If the observer is not familiar with the Fraunhofer lines, or has difficulty in recognizing the particular bright lines of the metals given in the preceding list, the following plan is recommended: First observe accurately the positions of the lines of the "flame-spectra" given, and from these construct an interpolation-curve; then mark

* Least refrangible line of the (b) group, seen in the flame of burning magnesium.

on the curve the wave-lengths of the Fraunhofer lines, and so determine their positions approximately on the scale of the spectroscope. On directing the instrument to the sun or to a bright cloud, the Fraunhofer lines will certainly be found at or near these positions. Now let these Fraunhofer lines be read off as exactly as possible, and from their positions, and those of the lines of the flame-spectra, let a more accurate interpolation-curve be drawn, and let this curve be used to find the positions of the lines of the spark-spectra. The final curve should be drawn when the positions of these spark-lines have been carefully observed. If it is not convenient to make use of the spark-spectra, a very fair curve may be constructed from the lines of the flame-spectra and from the Fraunhofer lines, but a little trouble in obtaining as accurate a curve as possible will be well repaid. As a sample of what may be done with a one-prism spectroscope and reflected scale, the following numbers, taken from Lecoq de Boisbaudran, for the wave-lengths of bismuth lines, are compared with Thalén's numbers:—

Lecoq de Boisbaudran.	Thalén.	Lecoq de Boisbaudran.	Thalén.
6130	6129·0	5144	5143·5
6048	6050·0	5123	5123·5
5719	5716·5	4724	4722·0
5552	5553·0	4303	4302·0
5268	5270·0	4259	4259·5
5209	5208·0	4118	4119·0

The lines from which Lecoq de Boisbaudran's interpolation-curve was drawn are the following:—

	Scale reading.	Wave-length.		Scale reading.	Wave-length.
Potassium	65·55	7680	Silver	114·00	5464
Solar a	72·50	7185	Thallium	118·40	5349
Solar B	77·81	6867	Silver	124·40	5208
Lithium	80·78	6706	Cadmium	130·03	5085
Hydrogen	83·71	6562	Hydrogen	141·75	4861
Cadmium	86·25	6438	Cadmium	152·83	4677
Zinc	88·00	6361	Strontium	157·60	4607
Lithium	94·15	6102	Iron	174·28	4383
Sodium	100·00	5892	,,	180·80	4307
Copper	103·25	5781	Calcium	188·25	4226
,,	105·90	5700	Indium	200·83	4101
Lead	109·00	5607	Calcium	216·33	3968
			,,	220·75	3933

Fig. 46 is a reduction of the interpolation-curve, drawn from these data.

The different methods of measuring the positions of the lines of a spectrum may conveniently be put into two groups, which may be called methods of consecutive coincidences and methods of simultaneous coincidences. The chief plans employed are the following:—

Consecutive coincidences.

(1) The graduated arc and vernier.
(2) The tangent-screw micrometer.
(3) The bright-line micrometer.

The Diffraction Spectrum.—Measurement of Wave-lengths. 51

Simultaneous coincidences.
(4) The reflected scale.
(5) The double-wire micrometer eyepiece.
(6) The divided lens micrometer.
(7) The photographic method.

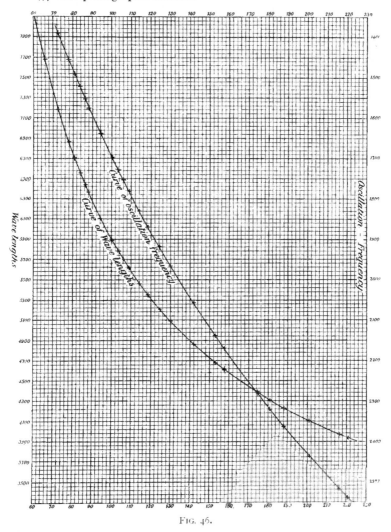

FIG. 46.

Some of these methods are more suitable for a small spectroscope, and others for a large one; or, again, particular methods may be employed in one case and not in another. For example, cross-wires can be employed with the solar spectrum, or with any spectrum of sufficient brightness, while they are useless with very faint spectra.

A favourite plan with the opticians is that of the divided arc and vernier; in which the telescope carries cross-wires, the intersection of which is brought first to coincidence with one line, then with a second, and so on. This, of course, is a method of consecutive coincidences, and it is a necessary condition of obtaining correct results that the collimator and slit shall remain rigidly in the same position, and that the cross-wires of the telescope and the vernier shall retain the same relative position during the motion from one line to another. These conditions are attended to in the massive construction adopted by Steinheil and some other continental makers, but are fatally disregarded when the instrument is constructed of slender metal, and when the collimator and observing telescope, instead of being firmly grasped at the centre of gravity, are merely screwed by one end into a slender upright of brass, further weakened at the most important point by being attenuated into some (so-called) ornamental shape.

Certain precautions must be observed in the use of a spectroscope with cross-wires to obtain good results. The eyepiece should first be removed and so adjusted that, on looking through it at a sheet of white paper, the cross-wires are seen in sharp focus; then, replacing the eyepiece in the observing telescope removed from the spectroscope, the telescope should be exactly focussed on some distant object. Having replaced the telescope in the instrument, the *collimator* should then be adjusted till some lines in the green—say b in the solar spectrum—are in accurate focus. The instrument is then in adjustment.* When used on the red or blue portion of the spectrum, the focus may be adjusted with the observing telescope, but the collimator should not be altered.

It is necessary that the ray to be measured should be in exact focus together with the cross-wires. If this is not the case, the ray will alter its position slightly with reference to the cross-wires, if the eyes be slightly moved. The adjustment may therefore be tested by moving the eye slightly and observing whether the ray and the cross-wires move together. There is also a slight movement of the rays consequent on lateral shifting of the source of light; this is less the narrower the slit is, and the more distant the source of light is.

Some instruments are provided with a tangent-screw micrometer —that is, a long screw, the head of which is divided into a hundred equal parts, by means of which a slow motion can be given to the observing telescope, and the number of turns of the screw, and parts of a turn necessary to carry the cross-wires from one line to another, is noted.

---

* For a different method of adjusting the collimator of a spectroscope, see a paper by Dr. Schuster, *Phil. Mag.* [5] vii. 95.

In the bright-line micrometer * the image of a fine slit in a brass plate is seen by reflexion at the first surface of the prism, and so is superposed upon the spectrum; the plate and slit have a slow motion given by a micrometer screw. This form of micrometer is specially useful with very faint spectra, when cross-wires would be useless. In observing with cross-wires a luminous spectrum, the lines of which are faint, it is necessary to admit a certain amount of light into the observing telescope, sufficient to illuminate the wires (conveniently by raising an edge of the cloth used to cover up the prisms). This general light renders very faint lines invisible. In all these methods of consecutive coincidences it is necessary that no shifting of the parts of the instrument by bending or shaking, nor any disturbance of the position of the source of light, nor of the exact position of the eye, should take place during the passage of the cross-wires from one line to the next. In the methods of "simultaneous coincidences" all these sources of error are avoided by observing at the same instant two lines—one a known line, used as a reference line, and the other the line to be measured.

The method of the reflected photographed scale, already described at some length, may be employed as a method of simultaneous coincidences, and so made more exact if, when the reading of any line is noted, care be taken to observe that the sodium line is still exactly at 50; or if the sodium line is not in the field, then that some other line used as reference line is exactly in its right position at the moment of observation.

The most accurate measuring instrument for use with large spectroscopes is the bifilar micrometer eyepiece. This is an eyepiece similar to those employed for astronomical purposes, provided with two crosses of fine spider lines in the focus of the eyepiece, which must therefore be of the Ramsden construction. One of these cross-wires remains fixed; the other is moved by means of a micrometer screw. The interval between the line to be measured and a line of known wave-length can thus be determined with great precision. In taking an observation, a slight motion is given to the fixed cross-wires by means of the slow motion or tangent-screw of the observing telescope, the micrometer screw of the eyepiece being at the same time adjusted by the other hand, till the observer is satisfied that each line is truly coincident with the inter-section of the corresponding spider lines.

Another device for measuring the interval between two lines, quite equal in accuracy to the bifilar micrometer, is that of the divided-lens micrometer.† In this instrument the micrometer screw moves one-half of a lens placed just in front of the prisms, and divided along a horizontal diameter. The effect is to cause one-half of the spectrum to move along under the other half, and the sodium line or any other convenient line is used as a substitute for the cross-wires, and is brought into coincidence with each of the lines to be

* *Microscopical Journal*, January, 1870.
† *Phil. Mag.*, August, 1875. *Proc. Physical Society*, vol. i. p. 160.

measured. It will be seen that the necessity of admitting extraneous light to illuminate cross-wires is avoided, and this instrument can therefore be used with faint spectra with precision.

The photographic method is, of course, a method of simultaneous coincidences, inasmuch as the positions of the known lines employed as references are recorded at the same instant as those of the unknown lines.

The bifilar or the divided-lens micrometer may have fitted to it a device for mapping the spectrum at the same time as the positions of the lines are measured. For this purpose the steel rod on which the micrometer screw is cut is made about three times as long as usual, and the extra length has cut on it a much coarser thread. On this there travels a little brass piece carrying a steel point, with which a trace can be made on a slip of blackened glass. We thus obtain a mark on the blackened glass corresponding to each line of the spectrum.

Another instrument, very useful in measuring photographed spectra or in drawing maps of spectra from measurements, is Beckley's spectrograph. This consists of a brass cylinder, on which the photograph is stretched, and the edge of the cylinder is graduated and provided with a vernier. There is also a straight edge which can be brought down upon the photograph parallel to the lines of the spectrum. Each line in succession is brought up to the straight edge, and the position of the cylinder is read off by means of the vernier. The accuracy of reading is increased by substituting for the straight edge a small microscope with a three-inch objective, and with cross-wires in the eyepiece.

Whatever the method of measurement, the numbers obtained must be reduced to the uniform scale of wave-lengths, so as to be independent of the peculiar construction of the instrument, the number, position, and refracting angle of the prisms, the dispersive power of the material of which they are made, of variations in the temperature, and of all other disturbing causes. It is clear that in such a method each line can be mapped only by means of its colour, that is to say, by the length of the wave of light by which it is produced; and a spectrum so represented must be such a one as is produced by *diffraction*, and not by dispersion. Dispersion spectra obtained by the use of prisms of different materials vary greatly in the relative breadth of the colours, so that in mapping a spectrum it is by no means sufficient to give the positions of only two or three lines as points of reference. Many otherwise valuable observations of spectra are entirely useless from the insufficient number of reference lines observed.

Three spectroscopes (each with a single prism and reflected scale), constructed by Duboscq and intended to be exactly alike, differed as shown in the following table. The numbers show the difficulty of constructing two instruments with exactly similar scales :—

| | Spectroscopes. | | |
Lines observed.	No. 1.	No. 2.	No. 3.
Potassium	65·6	64·0	68·0
Lithium	80·8	80·0	81·5
Sodium	100·0	100·0	100·0
Thallium	118·4	119·0	117·5
Strontium	157·6	160·0	152·5
Rubidium	189·9	195·0	183·0
Potassium	207·4	214·0	198·0

In a *diffraction* spectrum the position of the lines is dependent solely on their colour, and is precisely the same by whatever method the spectrum is obtained.

If it is desired to determine wave-lengths accurately to five figures (or more), the reference lines should be chosen from those found in the "Table of Rowland's Standard Wave-lengths" (given at the end of this book). The wave-length may be determined from the wave-lengths of two standard lines, between which it lies, by the method of graphical interpolation, or it may be calculated by the use of a formula.

The formula employed may be Cauchy's formula—

$$\lambda_2^2 = \frac{n_3 - n_1}{\dfrac{n_2 - n_1}{\lambda_3^2} + \dfrac{n_3 - n_2}{\lambda_1^2}}$$

where n_1 and n_3 are the readings on the scale of the spectroscope of the two known lines, λ_1 and λ_3 their wave-lengths, n_2 the reading of the line to be measured, and λ_2 its wave-length. It is desirable that the two known lines should be as close as possible to the one to be measured; when sufficiently close the formula gives the same result as a simple proportion.

A more accurate formula, and one applicable over a greater range of the spectrum, is that due to Hartmann [*]—

$$n = n_0 + \frac{c}{(\lambda - \lambda_0)^a}$$

where λ is the wave-length of a line, and n its refractive index, and n_0, λ_0, c, and a are constants depending upon the substance of which the prism is made. For the kinds of glass in ordinary use $a = 1·2$, so that there are three constants to be determined.

This formula may be much simplified. If we put $a = 1$ (instead of 1·2), the formula may be written $\lambda = \lambda_0 + \dfrac{c}{n - n_0}$; and, instead of refractive indices, we may use scale readings for n and n_0. To determine the constants λ_0, n_0, and c, we must choose three suitable reference lines, and measure their readings on the scale. Let the lines have the wave-lengths λ_1, λ_2, and λ_3, and the scale readings n_1, n_2, and n_3. We must now find the differences $\lambda_1 - \lambda_2$, $\lambda_1 - \lambda_3$, $n_3 - n_1$, and $n_2 - n_1$, and also the products $\lambda_1 n_1$, $\lambda_2 n_2$, $\lambda_3 n_3$.

[*] *Astrophysical Journal*, November, 1898.

Then λ_0 is found from the formula—

$$\lambda_0 = \frac{(\lambda_1 n_1 - \lambda_2 n_2)(\lambda_1 - \lambda_3) - (\lambda_1 n_1 - \lambda_3 n_3)(\lambda_1 - \lambda_2)}{(n_3 - n_1)(\lambda_1 - \lambda_2) - (n_2 - n_1)(\lambda_1 - \lambda_3)}$$

We can then find n_0 from the formula—

$$n_0 = \frac{\lambda_0(n_2 - n_1) + \lambda_1 n_1 - \lambda_2 n_2}{\lambda_1 - \lambda_2}$$

and c from the formula—

$$c = (\lambda_1 - \lambda_0)(n_0 - n_1)$$

The following example of measurements of a portion of the solar spectrum by Professor Hartmann will show the degree of accuracy which may be obtained. The constants were found to be—

$$\lambda_0 = 2232 \cdot 8 \qquad n_0 = 464 \cdot 251 \qquad c = 658860$$

The first column of the table gives the scale reading of the line, the second column its true wave-length, and the third column the wave-length calculated from the formula—

$$\lambda = 2232 \cdot 8 + \frac{658860}{464 \cdot 251 - n}$$

I.	II.	III.	I.	II.	III.
17·794	3709·6	3709·3	75·414	3928·2	3928·1
23·130	3727·1	3727·2	81·060	3953·0	3953·1
M 23·323	3727·7	3727·8	82·961	3961·7	3961·7
27·928	3743·6	3743·6	92·349	4005·2	4005·3
29·298	3748·5	3748·4	100·677	4046·0	4045·9
32·492	3759·5	3759·6	104·324	4063·9	4063·8
33·035	3761·5	3761·5	h 111·542	4101·9	4101·8
34·219	3765·8	3765·7	119·307	4143·9	4143·8
40·406	3788·0	3788·1	129·516	4202·1	4202·1
42·351	3795·0	3795·3	g 133·685	4227·0	4226·9
43·574	3799·7	3799·8	140·938	4271·7	4271·7
47·137	3813·1	3813·2	G 146·598	4308·0	4308·0
53·699	3838·5	3838·4	Hγ 151·535	4340·7	4340·8
54·341	3841·0	3841·0	157·787	4383·7	4383·8
60·555	3865·8	3865·7	160·793	4405·0	4405·1
63·696	3878·6	3878·5	193·578	4668·0	4668·2
67·834	3895·7	3895·7	F 213·523	4861·7	4861·9
69·590	3903·2	3903·1	b_1 239·565	5167·7	5166·6
70·195	3905·8	3905·7	b_2 239·991	5172·8	5172·2
74·254	3923·0	3923·1	b_4 240·820	5183·9	5183·2

The calculated values agree remarkably well with the true values except for the last three lines on the list (the b lines); the differences in these arise from want of sharpness in the photograph measured.

On the whole, probably the graphical method will be preferred, since, with care, it may be made to give accurate results, and has, further, the great advantage of enabling us to detect at once any reading inconsistent with the rest. If the positions of as many reference lines as possible are mapped on the paper, and a smooth curve is drawn through these points, or through as many as possible, and having the rest as near the curve as possible, and as many above the curve as below it, then one observation is corrected by another. The curve so drawn is more likely to give correct results than an irregular line made up off many straight portions so as to pass through all the points. In drawing the curve it will be found convenient to use a steel rule, which may be bent by the hands into the curve required; this, however, requires the co-operation of two persons—one to hold the rule down on the paper (stretched on a drawing-board), and the other to rule the curve with a finely pointed hard pencil.

If oscillation frequencies be employed instead of wave-lengths, the line obtained is less curved, as may be seen from Fig. 46. This is an advantage, since the less curved the line is, the more easily is it drawn, and the more exactly can it be employed.

A map of oscillation frequencies is intermediate between a diffraction spectrum and a dispersion spectrum, the red end being less extended when compared with the blue end than in a diffraction spectrum, and more extended than in the dispersion spectrum. A map drawn to wave-lengths is too much distorted to be advantageously employed with a dispersion spectroscope; and, on the other hand, a spectrum mapped with a dispersion spectroscope does not sufficiently resemble the same spectrum seen with a diffraction spectroscope; but a map of oscillation frequencies, being intermediate between the two, is not so different from either but that it is suitable for use with a spectroscope of either kind. Further, a map of oscillation frequencies exhibits most clearly relationships between the lines of a specturum; as, for example, in the spectra of silver or copper, where pairs of lines are repeated always with the same difference of oscillation frequency, or in the spectra of zinc and cadmium, where the same triplets are repeated again and again.

CHAPTER VI.

ON THE PRODUCTION OF DARK LINES BY ABSORPTION.— THE FRAUNHOFER LINES OF THE SOLAR SPECTRUM.

THE rule has been laid down that a discontinuous spectrum of bright lines is in general due to an incandescent gas, but that an incandescent solid gives a continuous spectrum. Thus from the light of glowing lime in the oxyhydrogen flame we get a bright continuous spectrum, in which the colours follow without break in succession from red through every shade of orange, yellow, green, and blue, into deep violet. If, now, the flame of a spirit-lamp coloured with common salt—which itself gives the bright sodium line—be brought between the glowing lime and the slit of the spectroscope, we see a dark line in the place of the bright sodium line. The cause of

FIG. 47.

this phenomenon is explained to be that sodium vapour possesses the power of absorbing exactly that particular light which it is itself able to give out. The experiment may be made in various ways. If a glass tube containing a few pieces of metallic sodium be exhausted and sealed up, then, on heating the sodium so as to fill the tube with sodium vapour, and holding it in front of a sodium flame, the tube appears dark; and if a spectroscope be used, and the tube be held between the flame and the slit of the instrument, a dark line is seen exactly in the same place where the bright sodium line appears the moment the tube is removed. Or, by the use of the electric light, the dark line may be projected on a screen.

On the Production of Dark Lines by Absorption. 59

The observation of the exact coincidence of the dark line in the Sun's spectrum with the bright line of sodium seems to have been first made by Fraunhofer. So long ago as 1814, Fraunhofer concluded that the dark lines of the Sun's spectrum were somehow produced in the Sun itself. He also observed that the light of the moon and the brighter planets (being only reflected sunlight) contained the same dark lines as seen in the direct light of the Sun. Foucault, in 1849, seems to have been the first to observe the dark sodium line in the spectrum of the electric arc, but he did not explain how it was produced; and it is to Kirchhoff that we owe the clear explanation of the phenomenon, and its application to the discovery, by spectrum analysis, of the composition of the solar atmosphere.

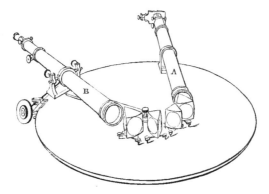

FIG. 48.

Kirchhoff mapped the spectrum of the Sun with very great care, using four prisms (Fig. 48), and giving the positions of the lines on an arbitrary scale of equal parts. A comparison of these lines with the bright lines of the elements showed that the following elements must be present in the sun: sodium, calcium, barium, magnesium, iron, chromium, nickel, copper, zinc, and hydrogen. This list has been increased by subsequent researches by the addition of the following elements: titanium, manganese, cobalt, carbon, vanadium, zirconium, cerium, scandium, neodidymium, lanthanum, yttrium, niobium, molybdenum, palladium, silicon, strontium, aluminium, cadmium, rhodium, erbium, silver, beryllium, germanium, tin, lead, gallium, and potassium, and possibly also iridium, osmium, platinum, tantalum, thorium, tungsten, uranium, and oxygen.[*]

---

[*] Fig. 50 is a copy of part of Kirchhoff's map, showing the b lines. It may be compared with the photograph of the same portion of the spectrum shown in Fig. 51. Fig. 47 shows a convenient arrangement in observing the absorption spectra of gases.

The chief lines of the visible portion of the solar spectrum, as seen under small dispersion, from the red hydrogen line marked C to the H lines in the violet, are shown in Fig. 49; D is the double sodium line, E is a double line due to calcium and iron, *b* is a group

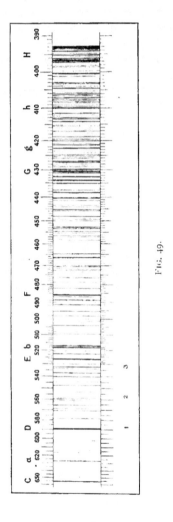

Fig. 49.

of four lines due to magnesium and iron, F is due to hydrogen, G is due to iron and calcium, *g* is due to calcium, *h* is due to hydrogen, the H lines are due to calcium.

An immense amount of labour has been expended on the careful

The Fraunhofer Lines of the Solar Spectrum.

mapping of the lines of the solar spectrum by Ångström, Fievez, Cornu, and others, but all this has been superseded by the photographs obtained by the use of Rowland's concave gratings. The complete map of the solar spectrum made by Rowland is something like forty feet long, and contains something like 20,000 lines.

One of the best drawings of the ultra-violet portion of the spectrum is that of Cornu, a small portion of which is reproduced in Fig. 52; with this may be compared the photograph of the same

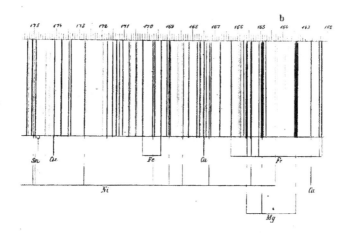

FIG. 50.

portion of the spectrum made by Mr. Higgs with a Rowland grating, and reproduced by permission (Fig. 53).

In Fig. 51 we have a reproduction of Mr. Higgs's photograph of the b group, in the upper portion of the plate, and below it a portion of the spectrum from the violet. The upper portion was photographed in the spectrum of the third order, and the lower portion in the fourth order. The scale of wave-lengths shown applies to the upper spectrum; the wave-length of a line in the lower spectrum is exactly three-quarters of that shown by the scale. It is a valuable property of the concave grating that it allows the photographing of two portions of the spectrum at the same time, and on the same plate, the wave-lengths of which have an exact numerical ratio. Of the lines which can be distinguished in the upper spectrum, thirty-seven are due to iron, eleven to titanium, seven to nickel, and seven to chromium, four to magnesium, two to cobalt, and one each to calcium, vanadium, and yttrium. The b line most to the right (known as b_1) is due to magnesium, b_2 is also due to magnesium, b_3 is a double

62 *An Introduction to the Study of Spectrum Analysis.*

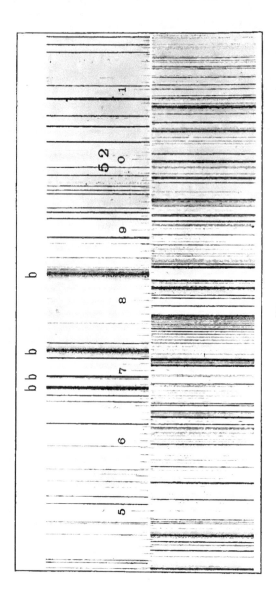

FIG. 51.

The Fraunhofer Lines of the Solar Spectrum. 63

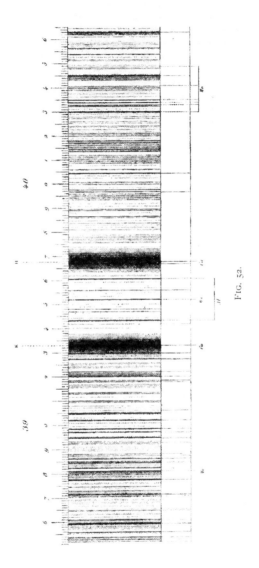

FIG. 52.

64 *An Introduction to the Study of Spectrum Analysis.*

line due to iron, and b_4, also a double, is due to magnesium and iron.

In the lower spectrum there is a remarkable shaded band between

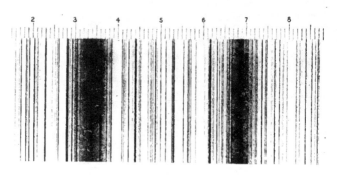

FIG. 53.

5172 and 5178, due to cyanogen; its least refracted and strongest edge is on the right, and has the wave-length 3883·48.

The apparatus employed by Mr. Higgs in photographing the solar spectrum is shown in Fig. 54.

FIG. 54.

In the portion of the solar spectrum shown in the upper half of Fig. 51 Rowland has measured about 282 lines. Their wave-lengths are given in the following table, a copy of a very small portion of Rowland's "Table of Solar Spectrum Wave-lengths":—

The Fraunhofer Lines of the Solar Spectrum.

Wave-length.	Substance.	Intensity and character.	Wave-length.	Substance.	Intensity and character.
5141·918s	Fe	3	5153·687		oo
5142·074		oooo	5153·848		ooo
5142·279		oooo	5153·985		ooooNd?
5142·458		oooo	5154·244s	Ti, Co	2
5142·693	Fe	4d?	5154·505	C	oooo
5142·958s	Ni	2	5154·579		ooo
5143·111s	Fe	3	5154·913		oooo
5143·288		oooo	5155·028		oooo
5143·511		ooo	5155·303	Ni	1
5143·764		ooo	5155·694	C	ooo
5143·901		oo	5155·935s	Ni	2
5144·031		oooo	5156·239		ooo
5144·203		oooo	5156·530		ooo
5144·543		oooN	5156·728	C	oooo
5144·758	C	ooo	5156·823	C	ooN
5144·847	Cr, C	oo	5157·163		oooo
5145·098		oooo	5157·376		ooo
5145·271	Fe	1	5157·783	C	ooo
5145·403		oooo	5157·915	C	ooo
5145·636	Ti	o	5158 152		oo
5145·907		ooooN	5158·701	C	ooo
5146·291	C	oo	5158·832	C	oooo
5146·486		ooo	5159·026		ooooN
5146·659s	Ni	3	5159·231s	Fe	2
5146·945	Co	oood?	5159·452		oooo
5147·273		ooo	5159·634	C	ooo
5147·458		ooooN	5159·776	C	oooo
5147·652	Ti	o	5159·946		oooo
5147·871	C	ooo	5160·138		ooo
5147·992	C	coo	5160·419	C	ooN
5148·222	Fe	2	5160·554		oooo
5148·410	Fe	3	5161·006		ooooN
5148·627		oooo	5161·194	C	ooo
5148·851		ooo	5161·353	C	ooo
5149·013		ooo	5161·849	C	oooo
5149·267	C	ooo	5161·910	C	ooo
5149·392		ooo	5162·153	C?	oooo
5149·512		oooo	5162·449s	Fe, C	5
5149·685		ooooN	5162·690	C	oooo
5149·964		ooo	5162·902		oooo
5150·363		oo	5163·074	C	ooo
5150·525		oooo	5163·200	C	ooo
5150·736	C	ooo	5163·327		oooo
5150·842	C?	oooo	5163·585	C	ooo
5151·020s	Fe	4	5163·756	C	oooo
5151·112	Mn	coo	5164·007		oooo
5151·344		ooooN	5164·172	C	oooo
5151·628		ooooN	5164·404	C	ooo
5152·087	Fe	3	5164·562		oooo
5152·361	Ti	o	5164·724	Fe?	1
5152·700		oooo	5164·855	C	oooo
5153·129	C?	ooo	5164·950	C	oooo
5153·337	C	oooo	5165·080	C	ooo
5153·414	Fe	1	5165·209	C	oooo
5153·584		oo	5165·297	C	oooo

F

66　*An Introduction to the Study of Spectrum Analysis.*

Wave-length.	Substance.	Intensity and character.	Wave-length.	Substance.	Intensity and character.
5165·416 *	C	0000	5181·498		00
5165·588s	Fe	2	5181·719		0000N
5165·746		0000	5181·010		000
5166·133		0000	5182·123		0000
5166·454	Cr, Fe	3	5182·518		0000
b_4 { 5167·497s	Mg	15	5182·761		0000
5167·678s	Fe	5	5182·907		000
5167·885		00	b_1 5183·791s	Mg	30
5168·123		0000	5184·364		000
5168·360		000Nd?	5184·445	Fe	2
5168·832	Ni	1	5184·738	Fe, Ni, Cr	1
b_3 { 5169·069s	Fe	3	5184·998		0000
5169·220s	Fe	4	5185·201		0000
5169·469		00	5186·073	Ti	2
5169·664		0000	5186·274		0000
5169·871		0000	5186·497	Fe	000N
5170·271		0000	5186·718		000
5170·655		0000	5187·432		0000
5170·767		000	5187·620		000
5170·937	Fe	0	5188·004		0000
5171·192		0000	5188·079	Fe	1
5171·778s	Fe	6	5188·227		0000
5172·386		00	5188·409		0000
b_2 5172·856s	Mg	20	5188·571		0000
5173·499		0000	5188·863s	Ti	2
5173·652		000	5189·018s	Ca	3
5173·917s	Ti	2	5189·300		000
5174·077		0000	5189·503		0000
5174·203		000	5189·744		000
5174·595		000N	5186·948		000
5175·099		000	5191·244		000
5175·423		000	5191·629	Fe	4
5175·575		000	5191·768		000
5175·923		000Nd?	5191·911		0000
5176·191	Co	000	5192·033		0000
5176·305		000	5192·155	Cr	00
5176·735	Ni	1	5192·523	Fe	5
5176·954	V	000	5192·659		000
5177·179		0000N	5192·785		000
5177·410	Fe	0	5192·924		0000
5177·577	Co	00	5193·139s	Ti	2
5177·784		0000	5193·339		0000
5177·979		0000	5193·500		0000
5178·156		0000	5193·669	Cr	000
5178·644		000	5194·027		0000
5178·970		00	5194·216	Ti	000
5179·293		000	5195·113	Fe	4
5179·695		0000	5195·647	Fe	2
5179·958		000	5196·227	Fe	1
5180·233	Fe	1	5196·434		000N
5180·572		000	5196·613	Cr	0
5180·747		000	5196·741	Mn	00
5181·041		0000	5197·332	Ni, Mn	00
5181·334		000	5197·540		0000N

* The first line in the "head" of the carbon group "δ" (at 76 in Fig. 16).

The Fraunhofer Lines of the Solar Spectrum.

Wave-length.	Substance.	Intensity and character.	Wave-length.	Substance.	Intensity and character.
5197·743		2	5207·791		oooN
5197·954		oooo	5208·038		oooo
5198·108		o	5208·111	Ti	oo
5198·512		oooo	5208·276		ooo
5198·888s	Fe	3	5208·596	Cr	5
5199·033		oooo	5208·776	Fe	2
5199·766		ooo	5208·779		oooo
5199·879		ooo	5209·949		oooo
5200·355	Cr	oo	5210·059		ooo
5200·590	V	o	5210·204		oooo
5200·989		ooooN	5210·421		oooo
5201·260	Ti	ooo	5210·555s	Ti	3
5201·458		ooooN	5211·015		ooo
5201·771		ooooN	5211·106		oooo
5202·125		ooo	5211·367		ooo
5202·249		ooo	5211·700	Fe	oo
5202·439 }s	Fe?	2	5211·976		oooo
5202·516	Fe	4	5212·398		oooN
5202·945		oooo	5212·503		oooo
5203·118		oooo	5212·859		oooNd?
5203·658		ooo	5213·155		oooo
5204·414		oooo	5213·515		ooo
5204·680 }s	Cr	5	5213·977		ooo
5204·768	Fe	3	5214·286	Cr	oo
5205·113		oooo	5214·781		oo
5205·467		oooo	5215·353s	Fe	3
5205·897	V	o	5215·737		oooN
5206·215	Cr, Ti	5	5216·437	Fe	3
5206·372		oo	5216·648		oo
5206·712		ooo	5217·552s	Fe	3
5206·986		oooo	5217·836		ooooN
5207·259		oooo	5218·030		oooo

In this table the intensities of the lines are denoted by the numbers 30, 20, 15, 5, 4, 3, etc., and after o, oo, ooo, oooo, so that oooo denotes the very faintest line. N signifies "nebulous," and d "double." Lines chosen as "standards" are marked "s."

Fig. 55 is a reproduction of Mr. Higgs's photograph of a portion of the solar spectrum, very crowded with lines, from 4252 to 4326.

Besides the dark lines due to substances vaporized in the sun's atmosphere, there are in the solar spectrum a number of groups of dark lines which have their origin in the earth's atmosphere. Of these "telluric" lines, the most remarkable are A, B, and a, due to oxygen, and a, due to water-vapour. These groups of lines are more intense when the spectrum is observed near the setting of the sun, when the sun's rays have to pass through a greater thickness of air. In Fig. 56 we have a reproduction of two photographs by Mr. Higgs, showing the group B: the upper one taken when the sun was high, and the lower one taken when the sun was low down. The remarkable

68 *An Introduction to the Study of Spectrum Analysis.*

symmetry in the structure of the band is very interesting; it must indicate some connection between the vibrations of the molecules of oxygen which give rise to the absorption lines, and it is most

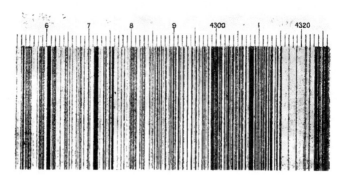

FIG. 55.

interesting to find the same structure reproduced almost exactly in the other group A, which lies further in the red.

Fig. 57 is a reproduction (by permission) from a photograph of this group by Mr. McClean.*

A group of lines due to water-vapour in the neighbourhood of the D lines, has been called the "rain-band"; it is darker when there is much water-vapour in the air, and may be used to foretell rain with some success. It begins at 5860 and extends to 6030.

Fig. 58 shows Ångström's map of the telluric lines of the solar spectrum; and Fig. 59 shows the rain-band.

It is possible to distinguish the telluric lines from the real solar lines in the spectrum of the light which reaches us from the sun by an application of Doppler's principle carried out by Cornu. In consequence of the sun's rotation, the position of a true solar line is slightly different, according as the light which reaches the spectroscope comes from the advancing or receding limb of the sun. If a small image of the sun, produced by a lens, is thrown upon the slit of the spectroscope, and if the lens is made to oscillate through a distance about equal to the diameter of the image, so that the slit is illuminated, first by the light from one edge of the sun, and then by that from

---

* Olszewski found that a layer of liquid oxygen, 30 millimetres thick, gave rise to an absorption band agreeing in position and character with the Fraunhofer band A, shown in Fig. 57. Professor Janssen, in 1888, observing at Meudon the electric light at the top of the Eiffel Tower in Paris, observed the A and B groups just as they appear in the "High Sun" spectrum. In travelling from Paris to Meudon the light would have to pass through about as much oxygen as the sun's rays would in traversing the atmosphere.

In the invisible infra-red region of the solar spectrum, bands due to the carbonic acid and aqueous vapour of our atmosphere have been observed.

The Telluric Lines of the Solar Spectrum.

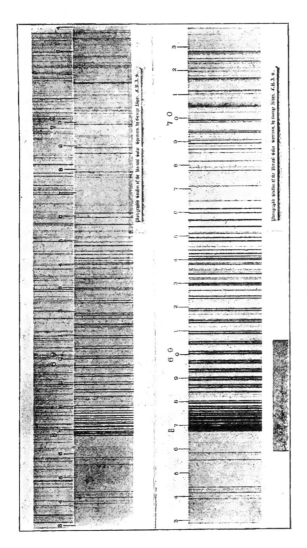

FIG. 56.

70   *An Introduction to the Study of Spectrum Analysis.*

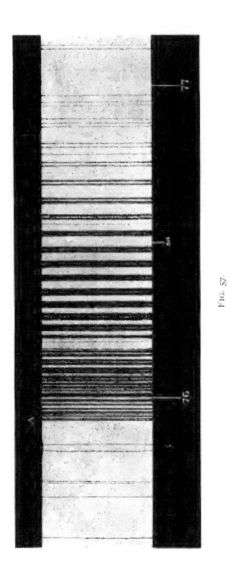

Fig. 57.   Fig. 58.

the opposite edge, the solar lines will appear to tremble in consequence of the slight alternately opposite displacements; but if the lines are produced by absorption within our own atmosphere, it will matter nothing from what part of the sun the light comes originally, and the position of the line will not be affected by the vibration of the lens.

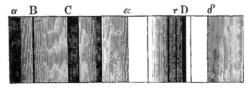

FIG. 59.

Fraunhofer, in 1814, examined the spectra given by the brightest of the fixed stars, and recognized that they differed from the spectrum of the sun. Fig. 60 is a copy of a drawing of the spectra of two bright stars made by Huggins and Miller in 1864, giving the result of a direct comparison of the bright lines of some metals with the spectrum of the star. It thus appears that Aldebaran contains hydrogen, sodium, magnesium, calcium, iron, bismuth, tellurium, antimony, and mercury; and that Betelgeux (α Orionis) contains sodium, magnesium, calcium, iron, and bismuth.

Infra=red and Ultra=violet Extensions of the Solar Spectrum.

The portion of the spectrum visible to the eye is only a very small portion of that which can be observed by the use of photography at the blue end, and by the use of the thermopile, or Bolometer, for the red end.

The portion of the solar spectrum which can be seen by the eye is little more than that shown in Fig. 49, extending from wave-length 6500 to 3900. By the use of photography lines of wave-length only 1000 have been observed, and by the use of the bolometer radiations of wave-length of 100,000 have been detected. These radiations beyond the red form the *infra-red* spectrum; those beyond the visible violet form the *ultra-violet* spectrum. Photographing with glass prisms and glass lenses, a limit is put to the spectrum because the glass itself absorbs the radiations which would affect the photographic plate.

With flint-glass the spectrum is cut short at about 3176, with crown-glass at about 2980, but if quartz be employed, the spectrum can be photographed as far as 2099. If a Rowland concave grating is employed, the image is formed by the concave mirror of speculum metal on which the lines are ruled, and all lenses are avoided; but

72 *An Introduction to the Study of Spectrum Analysis.*

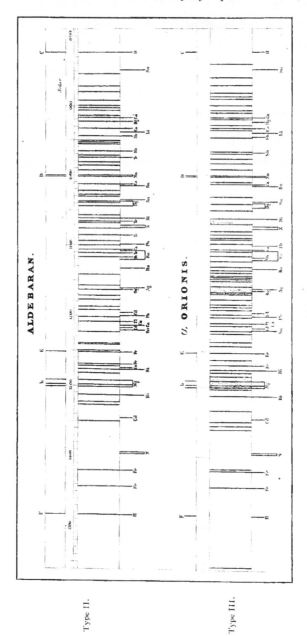

FIG. 60.

The Fraunhofer Lines of the Solar Spectrum. 73

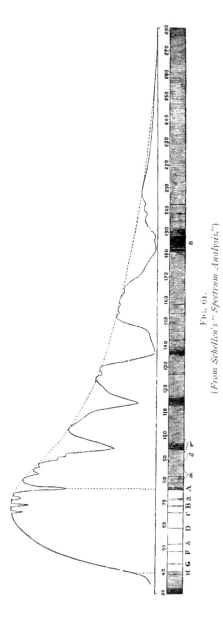

FIG. 61.
(From Schellen's "Spectrum Analysis.")

even then a limit is put by the absorption of the air, and of the gelatine used in making the photographic plates, as a support for the sensitive silver salts.

The extreme limit of wave-length 1000 mentioned above was attained by Schumann by working in a vacuum, and with sensitive plates of emulsion on glass without gelatine.

Beyond the red end of the visible spectrum the lines have been photographed, by the use of proper plates, as far as wave-length 12,000, with the diffraction grating, but beyond this point the heating effect of the spectrum must be utilized. Here prisms and lenses must consist of rock-salt or other material transparent to dark heat.

Professor Langley, in 1884, employing a large Rowland concave grating of short focus with a rock-salt prism and a bolometer, measured the heating effect in the spectrum down to wave-length 53,000.

The Bolometer consists of a narrow strip of metal, on which the lines of the spectrum fall; this strip forms one arm of a Wheatstone bridge, and consists of some metal whose resistance varies rapidly with change of temperature. Such an instrument will detect a change of temperature of one-ten-thousandth of a degree Centigrade.

Fig. 61 shows Langley's infra-red solar spectrum. The dark line ω at 14,000 is due to water-vapour, as are also Ω at 18,300, X at 26,400, and a strong band from 50,000 to 110,000 with maxima at 71,000 and 81,000. A band Y at 46,000 is due to carbon dioxide.

Langley, working on Mount Whitney at an elevation of 12,000 feet, has measured 700 dark lines in the infra-red invisible spectrum.

CHAPTER VII.

SPECTRA OF THE STARS AND NEBULÆ.

In 1862, only three years after the publication of the discovery of Bunsen and Kirchhoff, Huggins had observed the spectra of about forty stars with a small spectroscope attached to an eight-inch telescope. Shortly after, Secchi, from the observation of some 4000 stars, attempted a classification of stellar spectra, which, with small alteration, is still adhered to. Secchi distinguishes—

Type I. White stars (such as α Lyræ, Sirius, Altair, Regulus, Rigel, etc.), spectra with few dark lines chiefly due to hydrogen; the hydrogen lines are broad and strong.

Type II. Yellow stars (such as Arcturus,* Aldebaran, Capella, Procyon, Pollux, and the Sun), spectra with numerous strong lines; the hydrogen lines less marked.

Type III. Red stars (such as Antares, α Orionis, α Herculis, Mira, β Pegasi, etc.), spectra with numerous dark lines, but also shaded bands, darkest on the violet side and fading away towards the red.

Type IV. Red stars, fainter than the fifth magnitude, such as 152 Schjellerup. The spectra are characterized by shaded bands, apparently due to carbon, darkest on the side of the red and fading away towards the blue. To these four types must now be added that of the Helium stars, such as γ Orionis. The spectra show the helium line near D and the hydrogen lines. Some stars of this type (Type O) show the lines of hydrogen bright instead of dark.

The spectra of the stars are almost infinitely diversified, yet they can be arranged, with some exceptions, in a series in which the adjacent spectra, especially in the photographic region, are scarcely distinguishable, passing from the bluish-white stars like Sirius, through stars more or less solar in character, to stars with banded spectra, which divide themselves into two apparently independent groups, according as the stronger edge of the bands is toward the red or the blue. In such an arrangement the Sun's place is toward the middle of the series.

A difference of opinion exists as to the direction in which evolution is proceeding, whether by further condensation white stars pass into the orange and red stages, or whether these more coloured stars are younger and will become white by increasing age.

* See Fig. 64.

These different types of spectra are believed to indicate different stages in the evolution of stars from nebulæ. According to the nebular hypothesis of Laplace, the stars have been formed by the

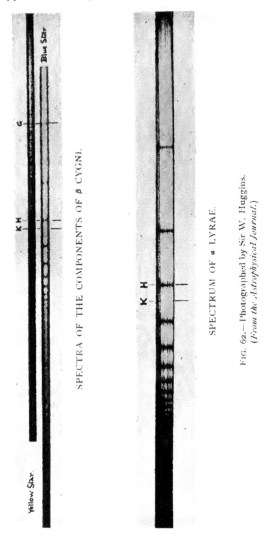

FIG. 62.—Photographed by Sir W. Huggins. (*From the Astrophysical Journal.*)

condensation of the original widely diffused nebular matter. The spectra of well-defined nebulæ exhibit bright lines, as if the radiating bodies were altogether gaseous, the hydrogen lines being prominent.

Spectra of the Stars and Nebulæ. 77

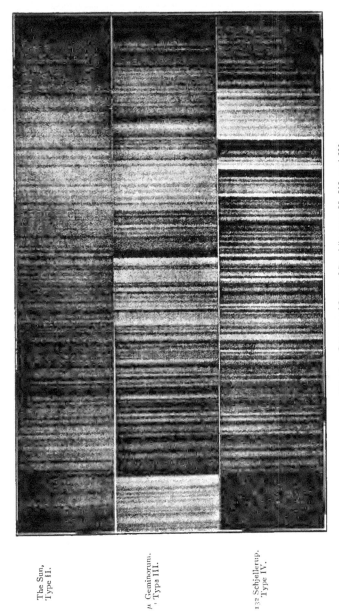

FIG. 63.—Spectra of Stars of Secchi's types II, III, and IV.
(*From the Astrophysical Journal*, April, 1899.)

The Sun, Type II.

μ Geminorum, Type III.

152 Schjellerup, Type IV.

78 *An Introduction to the Study of Spectrum Analysis.*

Certain stars (often called the "Wolf-Rayet" stars) have spectra consisting chiefly of bright lines, those of hydrogen and helium being conspicuous.

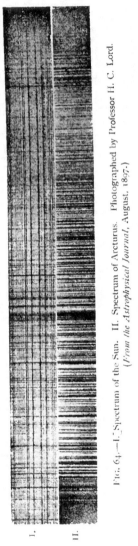

FIG. 64.—I. Spectrum of the Sun. II. Spectrum of Arcturus. Photographed by Professor H. C. Lord. (*From the Astrophysical Journal,* August, 1897.)

These, then, are the newest stars, after which follow in order of age the stars of types O, I, II, III, IV, in order. The stars or nebulæ which have the highest temperature have the simplest spectra.

Spectra of the Stars and Nebulæ.

As a star cools its spectrum becomes more complicated; thus the temperature of Sirius is supposed to be higher than that of Arcturus or of our sun.

In Fig. 62 (see also Fig. 66, No. 3) we have the spectrum of α Lyræ showing the complete series of the hydrogen lines, and in Fig.

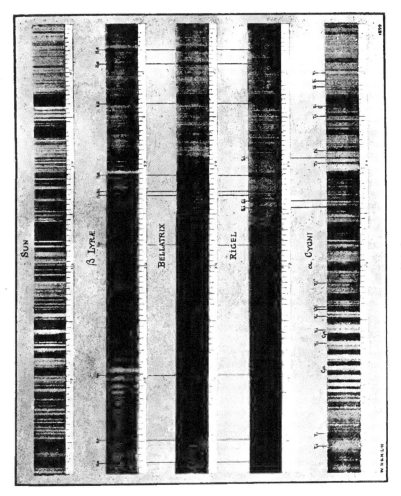

FIG. 65.

63 we have photographs of stars of Secchi's types II, III, and IV, taken by Professor Hale, with the 40-inch Yerkes telescope, and reproduced by kind permission of the Editors of the *Astrophysical Journal*.

Sir William and Lady Huggins have published a magnificent

80 *An Introduction to the Study of Spectrum Analysis.*

"Atlas of Representative Stellar Spectra" (London, 1899), from which Figs. 65 and 66 are reproduced by permission. They show some of the principal changes which are supposed to have taken place in the gradual evolution of stars. We quote the following description from the "Atlas":—

FIG. 66.

"We begin the series with the Bellatrix subdivision of the white stars, which we regard as in the least condensed condition (omitting Wolf-Rayet stars). These stars exhibit strong absorption lines of helium.

"In the early white stars the series of hydrogen lines continues thin, defined, and distinct, to the end of the series, while, on the contrary, as the solar stage begins to set in, the ultra-violet members of the hydrogen series become less distinct, and when the full stage is reached have practically disappeared.

"In Bellatrix and in β Lyræ a very strong sub-characteristic presents itself in the strong lines of helium, so that these stars may be distinguished as Helium stars. In Rigel this sub-characteristic includes a strong pair of lines at about 3860 which belong to silicon, so that this star and any similar ones might be known as Helium-Silicium stars.

"One glance at the ultra-violet region of α Cygni shows as its chief characteristic, next to hydrogen, a pair of strong lines and a thin line on the more refrangible side, forming a triplet at about 3760 (due to Titanium), and the pair as in Rigel at 3860. This star may appropriately be known as a Titanium-Silicium star.

"The gradual incoming and the advance of the characteristics of the solar stage can be well followed in the photographs, becoming successively stronger as we pass from Sirius to the fainter star of Castor, and then to α Aquilæ. A great advance is made when we reach Procyon, and the progress is still more rapid through γ Cygni to the complete solar stage as it presents itself in Capella, of which the spectrum is not distinguishable from that of the Sun."

Spectra of the Nebulæ.

The nebulæ are masses of more or less vague luminosity. Some of them, when seen in a large telescope, appear to consist of clusters of very minute stars, others cannot be resolved by the telescope, and present the appearance of a luminous cloud, often surrounding a star of considerable brilliancy. One of the most famous nebulæ is that situated in the constellation Orion (see Fig. 71). This was discovered in 1656 by Huyghens, and has been often drawn and described, and in recent times photographed. Sir J. Herschel, in 1824, gave a careful drawing of this object as it was seen in his large reflecting telescope of twenty feet focal length and eighteen inches diameter.

Splendid work in the photography of the nebulæ has been done by Sir Isaac Roberts and Dr. Common, and at the Lick Observatory by means of the Crossley reflector. Professor Keeler concludes that there must be something like 100,000 nebulæ in the heavens.

Huggins found that while the stellar and resolvable nebulæ gave spectra resembling the spectra of the fixed stars, the planetary and irresolvable nebulæ gave spectra consisting of bright lines, thus showing that in these bodies we have masses of incandescent gas. He observed generally three bright lines—one due to hydrogen and coincident with Fraunhofer's line F, one supposed to be due to nitrogen, and the third was not identified.

In Fig. 67 is shown a nebula, resembling a sickle in shape; Fig. 68 shows the spiral nebula in Canes Venatici; Fig. 69, the spiral nebula H 604, and Fig. 70 the annular nebula in Lyra; Fig. 71, the great nebula of Orion, photographed by Sir Isaac Roberts with an exposure of three and a half hours.

Sir William Huggins thus describes his discovery of the true nature of the nebulæ—

"I was fortunate in the early autumn of 1864 to begin some observations in a region hitherto unexplored, and which, to this day,

FIG. 67.

remains associated in my memory with the profound awe which I felt on looking for the first time at that which no eye of man had seen, and which even the scientific imagination could not foreshow.

"The attempt seemed almost hopeless; for not only are the nebulæ very faintly luminous—as Marius puts it, 'like a rush-light shining through a horn'—but their feeble shining cannot be increased in brightness, as can be that of the stars, neither to the eye, nor in the spectroscope, by any optic tube, however great.

"The view of the nebulæ as parts of a fiery mist out of which the heavens had been slowly fashioned, began, a little before the middle of the century, at least in many minds, to give way before the revelations of the giant telescopes which had come into use, and especially

Spectra of the Stars and Nebulæ.

of the telescope, six feet in diameter, constructed by the late Earl of Rosse.

"Nebula after nebula yielded, being resolved apparently into

FIG. 68.—Spiral nebula in Canes Venatici.
(*From Morgan's "Advanced Physiography."*)

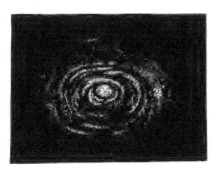

FIG. 69.

innumerable stars, as the optical power was increased; and so the opinion began to gain ground that all nebulæ may be capable of resolution into stars. According to this view, nebulæ would have to be regarded, not as the early stages of an evolutional progress, but rather as stellar galaxies already formed, external to our system—cosmical 'sand-heaps' too remote to be separated into their component stars. Lord Rosse himself was careful to point out that it would be unsafe from his observations to conclude that all nebulosity is but the glare of stars too remote to be resolved by our instruments.

"On the evening of August 29, 1864, I directed the telescope for the first time to a planetary nebula in Draco. I looked into the spectroscope. No spectrum such as I expected! A single bright line only! At first I suspected some displacement of the prism, and that I was looking at a reflection of the illuminated slit from one of

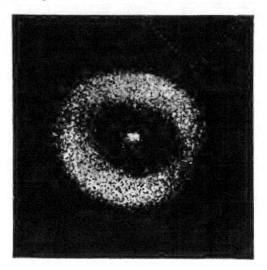

FIG. 70.—Ring nebula in Lyra.
(*From Morgan's " Advanced Physiography."*)

its faces. This thought was scarcely more than momentary; then the true interpretation flashed upon me. The light of the nebula was monochromatic; and so, unlike any other light I had as yet subjected to prismatic examination, could not be extended out to form a complete spectrum. After passing through the two prisms, it remained concentrated into a single bright line, having a width corresponding to the width of the slit, and occupying in the instrument a position at that part of the spectrum to which its light belongs in refrangibility. A little closer looking showed two other bright lines on the side towards the blue, all the three lines being separated by intervals relatively dark.

"The riddle of the nebulæ was solved. The answer, which had come to us in the light itself, read: Not an aggregation of stars, but a luminous gas. Stars after the order of our own sun, and of the

brighter stars, would give a different spectrum; the light of this
nebula had clearly been emitted by a luminous gas. With an excess
of caution, at the moment I did not venture to go further than to
point out that we had here to do with bodies of an order quite
different from that of the stars. Further observation soon convinced

FIG. 71.—The great nebula of Orion. Photographed by Sir Isaac Roberts.
(*From Morgan's " Advanced Physiography."*)

me that, though the short span of human life is far too minute
relatively to cosmical events for us to expect to see in succession any
distinct steps of so august a process, the probability is indeed over-
whelming in favour of an evolution in the past, and still going on, of
the heavenly hosts. A time surely existed when the matter now

condensed into the sun and planets filled the whole space occupied by the solar system, in the condition of gas, which then appeared as a glowing nebula, after the order, it may be, of some now existing in the heavens. There remained no room for doubt that the nebulæ, which our telescopes reveal to us, are the early stages of long processions of cosmical events, which correspond broadly to those required by the nebular hypothesis in one or other of its forms.

"It is necessary to bear distinctly in mind that the old view which made the matter of the nebulæ to consist of an original fiery mist, in the words of the poet—

> '. . . A tumultuous cloud
> Instinct with fire and nitre'

could no longer hold its place after Helmholtz had shown, in 1854, that such an original fiery condition of the nebulous stuff was quite unnecessary, since in the mutual gravitation of widely separated matter we have a store of potential energy sufficient to generate the high temperature of the sun and stars.

"The solution of the primary riddle of the nebulæ left pending

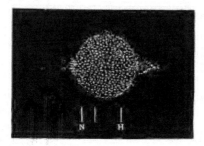

FIG. 72.—Planetary nebula in Aquarius.

some secondary questions. What chemical substances are represented by the newly found bright lines? Is solar matter common to the nebulæ as well as to the stars? What are the physical conditions of the nebulous matter?

"Further observation showed two lines of hydrogen; and recent observations have shown associated with it the new element recently discovered by Professor Ramsay, occluded in certain minerals, and of which a brilliant yellow line in the sun had long been looked upon as the badge of an element as yet unknown. The principal line of these nebulæ suggests probably another substance which has not yet been unearthed from its hiding-place in terrestrial rocks by the cunning of the chemist."

The different kinds of nebulæ, no doubt, represent different stages in condensation of the original nebular matter. The planetary nebulæ show edges sharply defined in the form of a circle or slight ellipse, but a higher type still is that of the stellar nebulæ, in which a tolerably well-defined bright star is surrounded by a disc or halo of light.

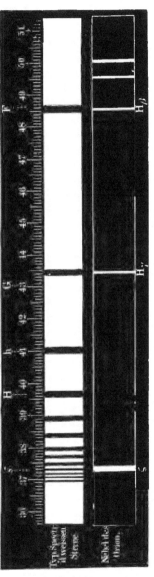

FIG. 73.—Spectrum of a white star. Spectrum of the nebula in Orion.

In Fig. 72 is shown the planetary nebula in Aquarius, with its spectrum of three lines, and in Fig. 73 is shown the spectrum of the

88   *An Introduction to the Study of Spectrum Analysis.*

great nebula in Orion, with which is compared the spectrum of the white stars.

In Fig. 74 we have a fine photograph of the great nebula in

FIG. 74.—Central parts of the great nebula in Andromeda. Photographed with the two-foot reflector of the Yerkes Observatory, by G. W. Ritchey.
(*From the Astrophysical Journal.*)

Andromeda, taken with the two-foot reflector of the Yerkes Observatory, with an exposure of four hours; and in Fig. 75, a photograph taken with the Crossley reflector of the Lick Observatory, on July 6, 1899, with an exposure of three hours, of the remarkable trifid nebula in Sagittarius.

The latest determinations of wave-lengths of nebular lines are given in Lick Observatory Bulletin, No. 19. They are—

5006·89	
4959·05	
4861·5	Hβ, due to hydrogen.
4740·1	
4685·8	
4471·7	due to helium.
4363·4	
4340·6	Hγ, due to hydrogen.
4101·9	Hδ, ,, ,,
4068·8	
4026·7	due to helium.
3970·2	Hϵ, due to hydrogen.
3967·7	
3965·1	due to helium.
3889·2	Hζ, due to hydrogen.
3868·9	
3835·8	Hη, ,, ,,
3729·0	
3726·4	

No one nebula shows all of these lines.

Spectroscopic evidence leads to the conclusion that the different chemical elements as we know them on the earth are widely diffused throughout the universe, and also no doubt others with which we have not yet made acquaintance upon the earth. The example of the gas helium whose existence as a new element was first inferred from the observation of the bright yellow line in the spectrum of the sun's chromosphere, but which has now been found upon the earth, teaches us caution in supposing that we have as yet made acquaintance with all the chemical elements. Only a very small proportion of the lines photographed in the spectrum of the sun have been identified.* No doubt some of the others are due to some of these—as yet—undiscovered elements.

Chemists and physicists have been gradually coming to the conclusion that the elements are in some way connected together, as would be the case, for example, if they were all modifications of the same primary material. The name "protyle" has indeed been given to this hypothetical primary "stuff." The relationships between the properties of the elements exhibited in the statement of the "periodic law" make it almost certain that there is some such connection between the different elements. The relationships which have been shown to exist between the different lines of one and the same element, and between the similar lines of chemically related elements, lead to a similar conclusion. There is some evidence that certain lines observed in the spectrum of the star ζ Puppis form a series due to hydrogen, but these lines have not yet been obtained from hydrogen in the laboratory. The Fraunhofer lines H and K, due to calcium, are frequently seen at the highest levels in solar

* In Fig. 51 there are one hundred and sixty-seven lines whose origin has not yet been determined.

prominences, accompanied only by the lines of the very light gases hydrogen and helium, and without the strong calcium line at 4226·9, while in the Bunsen flame this line is strong, but H and K do not appear. Schuster and Hemsalech have observed that in the electric discharge the elements of small atomic weight, such as magnesium and aluminium, are projected from the pole with greater velocity than heavier ones, such as zinc, cadmium, and mercury, and that in

FIG. 75.—Trifid Nebula Sagittarius.
(*From the Astrophysical Journal.*)

some cases certain lines of an element are projected with greater velocities than other lines of the same element. These facts seem to show that the particles whose vibrations give rise to certain lines in the spectrum of an element may exist independently of the particles which give rise to other sets of vibrations.

Professor J. J. Thomson attributes the spectral lines to the vibrations of "corpuscles" much smaller than the chemical atom, and he believes that the chemical elements are different aggregations of the same kind of material. Possibly the original uniformly diffused matter of the universe was protyle, and we have the evolution of the chemical elements going on and at different stages in the different nebulæ and stars.

Sir Norman Lockyer maintains that the differences between our terrestrial spectra and those of the sun and stars can only be explained by assuming that our elements are at stellar temperatures dissociated into finer forms of matter, and that "if the terrestrial elements exist at all in the sun's atmosphere, they are in process of formation in the cooler parts of it." This would account for the absence of some of our elements, if in the intense solar heat they are dissociated into simpler forms the spectra of which we do not recognize.

At the same time there are observations which lead to a different conclusion. Professor Rowland did not find any lines common to several elements, or where there appeared to be such coincidence more accurate measurement showed some slight difference in wavelength, or revealed the presence of a common impurity. Sir William Huggins has investigated the spectrum of calcium and magnesium under varying conditions, and his experiments seem to show that variations in density or in the relative abundance of material have an important influence on the relative behaviour of the different lines of a spectrum. Sir William says:—

"In the laboratory, as well as in the stars, one strongly marked feature which distinguishes some conditions of the spectrum of calcium is the relative behaviour of a line in the blue at 4227, and the lines known in the solar spectrum as H and K. As this relative behaviour is usually different in the spectrum of the arc as compared with that of the spark, the condition of relative feebleness of the blue line, which is characteristic in the latter case, has been regarded as a criterion of a higher temperature. As this view led to the improbable conclusion that the temperature in the highest regions of the solar atmosphere, notwithstanding that the temperature-gradient must be extremely rapid near the solar surface, was very much greater than lower down, and just above the photosphere, we were induced to make in 1897 a series of experiments which showed clearly that the relative behaviour of the blue line to the lines H and K, which had been attributed to an exalted temperature, could be brought about by reducing the density of the calcium vapour.

"This view at once brought the interpretation of the solar phenomena into agreement with our knowledge, from other sources, of the probable physical conditions existing near the sun's limb.

"We are furnished, too, by this interpretation of the relative behaviour of the blue calcium line and the H and K lines of the same substance, with an important criterion which we can apply to stellar spectra, since we meet with these lines of calcium in different conditions, as a marked feature in the gradual transition of stars from the white to the solar type.

"What the spectroscope immediately reveals to us are the waves which are set up in the ether. As a rule it is only when a body is gaseous and sufficiently hot that the motions within its molecules can produce bright lines. The spectra of the heavenly bodies are to a great extent absorption-spectra, but we have to study them through the corresponding emission-spectra of bodies brought into the gaseous form and rendered luminous by means of flames or of electric discharges. There does not appear to be any direct relation between the luminous radiation as shown in the spectroscope and the temperature of the flame, or of the gaseous contents of the vacuum-tube, that is, in the usual sense of the term as applied to the mean motion of all the molecules. In both cases, the vibratory motions within the molecules to which their luminosity is due are almost always much greater than would be produced by encounters of molecules having motions of translation no greater than the average motions which characterize the temperature of the gases as a whole. The temperature of a vacuum-tube through which an electric discharge is taking place may be low as shown thermometrically, but the vibrations of the luminous molecules must be violent, and it is to the fierce encounters of the few molecules which carry the discharge that the luminosity is due; if all the molecules had similar motions the temperature of the gas would be very high.

"So in flames where chemical changes are in progress, the vibratory motions of the molecules which are luminous may be very different from those corresponding to the mean temperature of the flame.

"Very great caution is therefore called for when we attempt to reason by the aid of laboratory experiments to the temperature of the heavenly bodies from their radiation, especially on the reasonable assumption that in them the luminosity is not ordinarily associated with chemical changes, or with electric discharges, but is due to a simple glowing from the ultimate conversion into molecular motion of the gravitational energy of shrinkage.

"The presence in the solar spectrum of lines which we can only produce electrically is, however, an indication of the high temperature of the sun."

Doppler's Principle.

If a radiating body, emitting vibrations of a certain definite frequency, is in rapid motion towards or from the observer, the frequency will be altered to the observer in consequence of the change in the velocity relative to the observer. Thus, a vessel moving in a direction at right angles to the waves will encounter more waves in a given time if she is moving against the waves than she will if moving in the same direction as the waves. The same thing is true of waves of sound and of light. When a railway engine, whistling, passes an observer at full speed, he notices that the pitch of the whistle is higher when the engine is approaching, and lower when it is receding, than the true note of the whistle. If the velocity of sound in air is 1100 feet per second, then an open organ-pipe of two feet in length will give a note of $\frac{1100}{4}$, or 275, vibrations per second. If this note be sounded on an engine travelling 40 miles an hour, or 59 feet per second, then, when the engine is approaching,

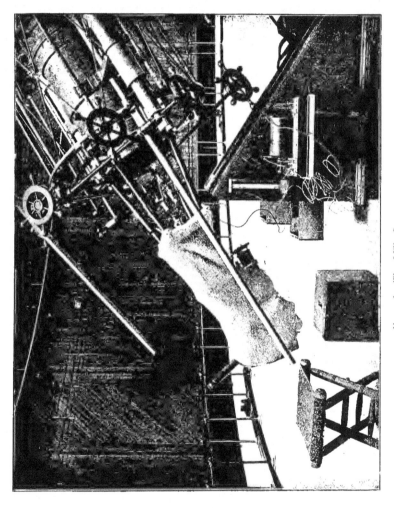

FIG. 76.—The Mills Spectrograph. (*From the Astrophysical Journal.*)

the observer will hear a note of $\frac{1159}{4}$, or 289, vibrations per second, and if the engine is receding the note will be $\frac{1041}{4}$, or 260, vibrations per second; which is an alteration of the note by about a semitone, up or down. If, then, the exact alteration of note can be measured, the velocity of the engine can be calculated from the known velocity of sound. The same reasoning applies to light, only here we are dealing with an enormously greater velocity. The velocity of light being known to be 300,400,000 metres, or 186,000 miles, per second, if the exact amount of shifting of the lines of a spectrum can be determined, then the velocity of approach or of recession between the source of light and the observer can be calculated. The displacement of known lines in the spectrum at the edge of the sun, or in sun-spots, indicates rapid motion of the radiating gas to or from the earth of 50 miles a second or more; in other words, we have here evidence of violent storms upon the sun.

Huggins was the first to apply Doppler's principle to the measurement of the velocity of stars in the line of sight. His observations showed that Sirius and α Orionis are approaching us with a velocity of about 20 miles a second, and that Arcturus and α Lyræ are receding from the earth with a velocity of 40 or 50 miles a second. But more exact measurements have been obtained by the application of photography. During the last ten years exact measurements of the velocities of stars in the line of sight have been made in the observatories at Potsdam and at Greenwich, as well as in America. At the Lick Observatory a special solidly built instrument—the Mills spectrograph, which is shown in Fig. 76—is employed for these measurements, with the great refractor of 36 inches. It consists of a collimator of $1\frac{1}{2}$ inch aperture and $28\frac{1}{2}$ inches focal length, and a camera, rigidly mounted with their axes parallel. The light from the star after entering the slit is dispersed by a train of three glass prisms rigidly clamped for the minimum deviation of the hydrogen line F. A comparison spectrum from a hydrogen vacuum-tube, or from an iron spark, is photographed upon the same plate, so that the resulting photograph shows the spectrum of the star lying between two comparison spectra, the lines of which serve as standards to determine the displacement of the lines.

CHAPTER VIII.

THE SUN, ITS PHOTOSPHERE, CHROMOSPHERE, CORONA, SUN-SPOTS, AND PROMINENCES.

THE nature of the sun's spectrum indicates that there is a central body from which we get a continuous spectrum, and that surrounding this there is an absorbing atmosphere giving rise to the dark lines. By observations made during total eclipses of the sun, and in other ways, we become aware that outside the reversing layer there is an atmosphere of incandescent hydrogen called the chromosphere, and

FIG. 77.

beyond this again a much more extended halo known as the corona. The central portion of the sun which gives rise to the continuous spectrum—sometimes called the photosphere—need not necessarily be solid, for a sufficiently thick layer of gas under pressure would produce a continuous spectrum like a solid or liquid does. The heated gases must be in a state of violent motion, convection currents carrying the substances up into the cooler portions of the atmosphere there to condense and fall back again into the hotter regions, where they are again vaporized. As a consequence of these violent motions the incandescent gas is projected into enormous "red

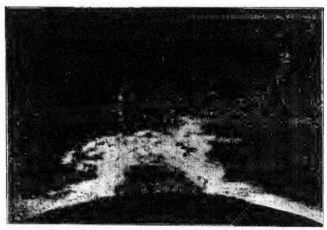

FIG. 78.—Quiescent prominence, photographed in full daylight by Professor G. E. Hale.
(*From the Astrophysical Journal.*)

FIG. 79.—Eruptive prominence, photographed by Professor G. E. Hale.
(*From the Astrophysical Journal.*)

flames," or prominences, which are best seen during a total solar eclipse, when the body of the sun is hidden by the moon. They vary in form and in height, sometimes extending as much as 70,000 miles beyond the sun's disc. Fig. 77 gives a representation of the prominences as seen during the total eclipse of 1869.

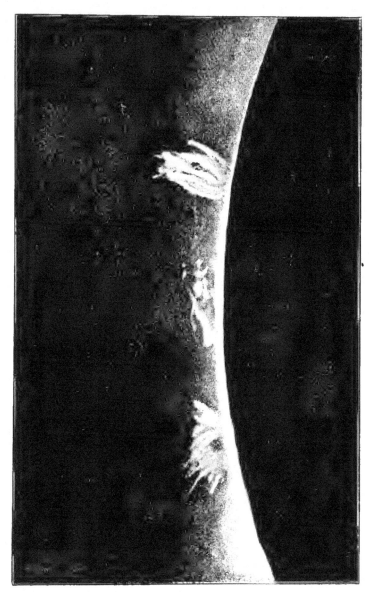

FIG. 80.—Group of Prominences. Total eclipse, May 28, 1900.
(*From the Astrophysical Journal.*)

The Sun—its Corona. 99

FIG. 81.—The Corona. Total eclipse, May 28, 1900.
(*From the Astrophysical Journal.*)

A method of observing the prominences at any time, and not only during an eclipse, was discovered independently by Janssen and Lockyer, which consists in so weakening the white light of the sun by passing it through a long train of prisms that the monochromatic

FIG. 82.

images of the prominences become visible, and by the adoption of such methods it is now possible to see and to photograph the prominences round the sun at any time. Figs. 78 and 79 are copies of photographs of prominences made at the Kenwood Observatory,

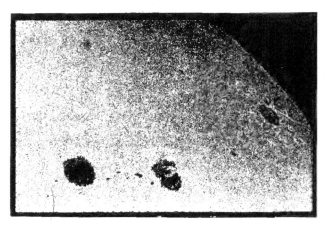

FIG. 83.
(*From Thornton's "Advanced Physiography."*)

Chicago, and Fig. 80 is a copy of a beautiful photograph taken at the eclipse of 1900. Fig. 81 shows a drawing of the corona at this same eclipse made from photographs (copied by permission from the *Astrophysical Journal*).

The telescope shows on the surface of the sun dark spots, varying

greatly in number and size, and often large enough to be seen with the naked eye, or with the aid of an opera-glass. They share in the general motion of the sun's surface, which is due to a rotation of the sun on its axis in about $27\frac{1}{2}$ days, but they have also motions of their own; they open out or close up and disappear, to be succeeded by new spots. The spots are more abundant in two zones parallel to the sun's equator, between the latitudes 5° and 40°, as shown in Fig. 82.

The bright surface of the sun is seen in a telescope not to be uniformly bright, but to present a mottled appearance. The brighter portions of irregular shape are called faculæ. Fig. 83 shows the appearance of a portion of the sun, showing spots and faculæ. Fig. 84 shows the comparative size of the earth and of the great spot of

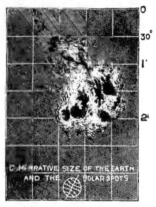

FIG. 84.—The great sun-spot of April 19, 1892; area, about 1,093,500,000 square miles. (*From Morgan's " Advanced Physiography."*)

April, 1882. A spot appeared in 1851, which was 140,000 miles in diameter.

If, using a spectroscope attached to a telescope, the image of a spot is made to fall across the slit of the spectroscope, the Fraunhofer lines are seen to be darker in the spot than elsewhere, but they are also seen to be thickened and distorted, as shown in Figs. 85 and 86.

FIG. 85.—Thickening of D lines in the spectrum of a spot.
(*From Thornton's " Advanced Physiography."*)

It will easily be understood that these distortions are the result, in accordance with Doppler's principle, of rapid motions in the absorbing material in the line of sight, *i.e.* of an uprush or a downrush of gas, and from the amount of disturbance of the lines the velocities of these motions can be calculated. The velocities measured amount to 50 or more miles per second; and prominences have been seen to form with a velocity of 250 miles a second.

When the slit of the spectroscope is placed on the edge of the sun, the dark lines are seen to give place to the bright lines of the chromosphere and prominences, and these bright lines are also seen

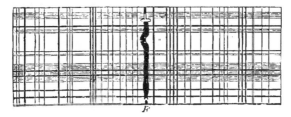

FIG. 86.

to be distorted in consequence of the violent motion of the gases to which they are due. Such contortions of the hydrogen F-line are shown in Fig. 87.

FIG. 87.

Although we speak of the spots as dark, this is only by comparison with the brightness of the rest of the sun's surface. The darkest part of a sun-spot has really a brightness exceeding that of the limelight. Surrounding the darkest central portion of a spot is a less dark margin, known as the penumbra. The entire spectrum across a spot is darkened, but irregularly. Besides the widening of most of the lines, some are seen to be reversed, that is, instead of a dark line we have a bright one, as shown in Fig. 88. This reversed

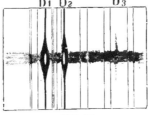

FIG. 88.

104 *An Introduction to the Study of Spectrum Analysis.*

line is also frequently curved and displaced, showing rapid motion in the gas producing it. It is further to be remarked that all the lines

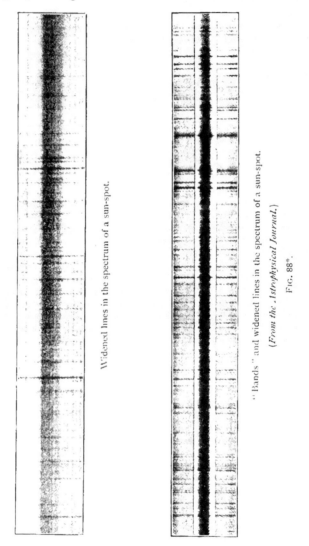

Fig. 88*.
(*From the Astrophysical Journal.*)
Widened lines in the spectrum of a sun-spot.
"Bands" and widened lines in the spectrum of a sun-spot.

of the same substance are not equally displaced. Fig. 89 shows the new Potsdam spectrograph.

The chromosphere, when quite quiescent, gives the bright lines of hydrogen and the bright yellow line D_3 due to helium. The chromosphere is, however, disturbed by prominences, and by the slow formation of "domes," which may last for weeks, and may be due

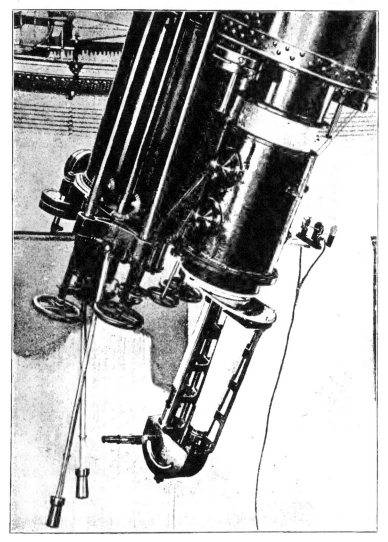

Fig. 89.—New Potsdam Spectrograph.
(*From the Astrophysical Journal.*)

to the welling up of vapours from beneath. Professor Young, observing on Mount Sherman, has catalogued over 200 lines of the chromosphere, due chiefly to calcium, iron, sodium, and magnesium.

The great prominences seem to be formed over the spot-zones, the equatorial and polar regions being apparently regions of less activity. Respighi remarks that "there is a great difference in the duration of prominences. Some develop and disappear in a few minutes; others remain visible for several days. They originate, generally, in rectilinear jets, either vertical or oblique, very bright and well defined. These rise to a great height, often to a height of at least 80,000 miles, and occasionally to double that height; then, bending back, fall again upon the sun like the jets of a fountain. Then they spread into figures resembling gigantic trees, more or less rich in branches."

Since 1869, when the spectroscope was first used for its investigation, there has been much discussion as to the nature of the corona. During the eclipses of 1869 and 1870, it was shown that the spectrum of the corona was discontinuous, and characterized by a bright green line 1474 on Kirchhoff's scale. In the eclipse of 1871 it was conclusively shown by photography that the corona belongs to the sun, and that the appearance is not produced by our own atmosphere, as had been maintained by some observers. The corona was found to be not simply a soft effulgence of light, but to have a certain structure. It exhibits rays, compared to those produced by searchlights through a fog; from the polar regions the rays appear sometimes curved, bending away from the axial line.

The spectrum of the corona is found to be a faint continuous spectrum crossed by bright lines, the most noticeable being the line 1474 of wave-length 5317. A later measurement of this line in the corona by Lockyer gives the wave-length 5303; its origin is unknown, but it has been attributed to a hypothetical substance, "Coronium." Other bright lines are 4230 and 4290, and others belonging to helium, hydrogen, and calcium.

CHAPTER IX.

NEW STARS.—DOUBLE STARS.—COMETS.

ONE of the most remarkable phenomena of the heavens is the occasional appearance of a new star. The earliest recorded instance is that of a star which appeared suddenly in the constellation Cassiopeia in 1572, and which was as bright as Jupiter. It increased in brilliancy so as to be visible even in the daytime; its brilliancy gradually diminished for a year or more, and it has never since been seen. In 1866 a star of the ninth magnitude in the constellation Corona Borealis suddenly flashed up into a star of the second magnitude, and lasted for some weeks. Its spectrum was nearly continuous, but showed also bright lines of hydrogen; this is represented in Fig. 90.

FIG. 90.—Spectrum of τ Coronæ Borealis.

In 1876 a new star appeared in Cygnus which had never been seen before. It was of the third or fourth magnitude and of a deep gold-red colour. Its spectrum was like that of τ Coronæ Borealis, but the continuous spectrum faded and the bright lines remained longest; one line at 4990 is one of the lines characteristic of nebulæ (Fig. 91).

In 1885 a new star appeared in the midst of the great nebula in Andromeda. It reached the seventh magnitude and then faded.

In 1892 a new star appeared in Auriga. Its spectrum showed the bright lines of hydrogen and lines at 5750, 5010, 4960, and 4360, which have been observed in the spectra of some nebulæ.

Nova Sagittarii appeared in 1899 as a star of the eleventh magnitude. Examined with the spectroscope, it showed a faint continuous spectrum crossed by nine bright lines, the same as seen in Nova Aurigæ and in the nebulæ.

Nova Aquilæ appeared in July, 1900. Its spectrum was a faint

108   *An Introduction to the Study of Spectrum Analysis.*

continuous one with three bright bands agreeing in position with the three brightest lines in the spectra of the nebulæ.

On February 21, 1901, Dr. Anderson discovered a new star in

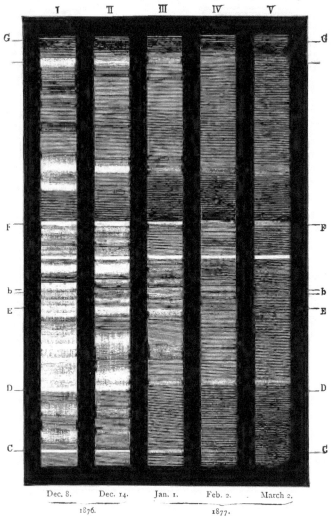

FIG. 91.—Spectrum of new star in Cygnus.

the constellation Perseus of the second or third magnitude. On February 23 it had become brighter than Aldebaran; it then declined in brightness, but increased at the end of March, and then

New Stars.—Double Stars.—Comets.

declined again till it became about equal to a star of the tenth or eleventh magnitude. Its colour—at first white—changed through claret-red to dull orange-red. At first its spectrum strongly resembled

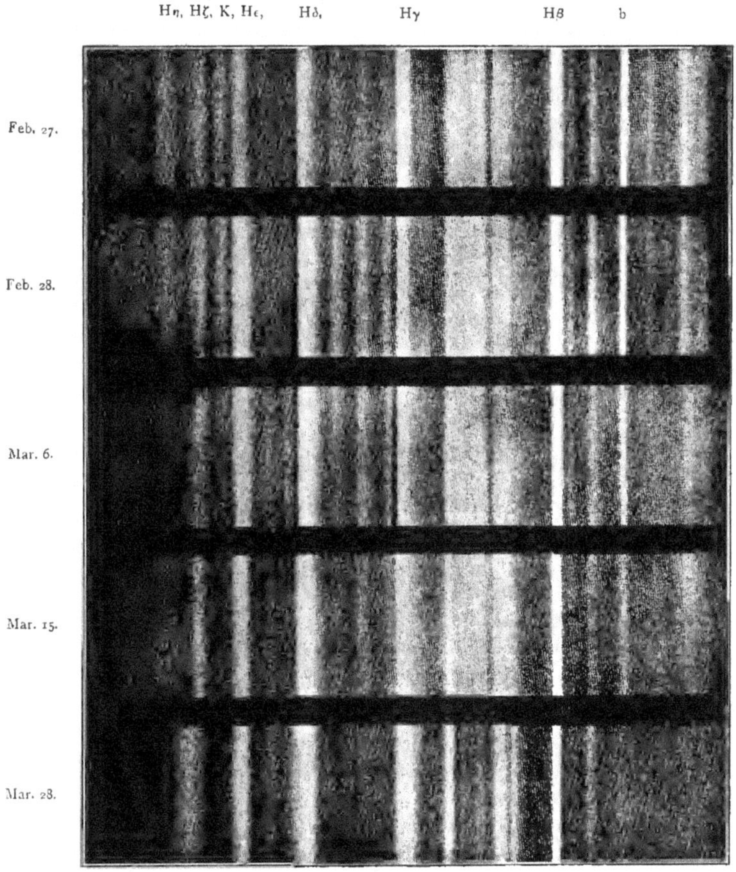

Hη, Hζ, K, Hε,   Hδ,   Hγ   Hβ   b

Feb. 27.

Feb. 28.

Mar. 6.

Mar. 15.

Mar. 23.

FIG. 92.—Spectrum of Nova Persei.
(*From the Astrophysical Journal.*)

that of Nova Aurigæ, a continuous spectrum with dark lines and a spectrum of bright lines; the bright-line spectrum increased in brilliancy, and the continuous spectrum faded. The principal bright

110 *An Introduction to the Study of Spectrum Analysis.*

lines were of considerable width, and the hydrogen lines were especially brilliant. The displacement of the dark lines indicated a relative motion of something like 500 miles per second. Velocities nearly as great have been observed in the solar explosions which give rise to the great prominences.

Fig. 92 shows the spectrum as photographed on five occasions, from February 27, 1901, to March 28, 1901, at the Yerkes Observatory with the great telescope.

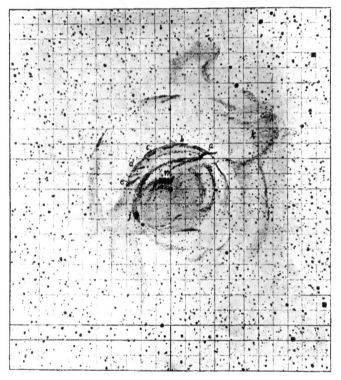

FIG. 93.—Nebulosity about Nova Persei, September 20, 1901.
(*From the Astrophysical Journal.*)

The spectrum is very similar to the first spectrum of Nova Aurigæ, the hydrogen lines are bright and broad, and accompanied on the more refrangible side by dark lines, as in Nova Aurigæ. If the appearance of a "Nova" is due to an outburst of hot gas, which cools as it recedes from the star, the cooler gases approaching us would give a spectrum of dark lines slightly shifted towards the blue, and the hotter gases on the side of the star remote from us would give bright lines slightly shifted towards the red. This is exactly what occurred.

Most remarkable changes seem to have taken place in the spectrum of this Nova, as may be gathered from a study of the photographs reproduced in Fig. 92. In the photograph of February 27, the H and K lines are bright, crossed by fine dark H and K lines. The band H is, no doubt, due to the superposition of the calcium and hydrogen

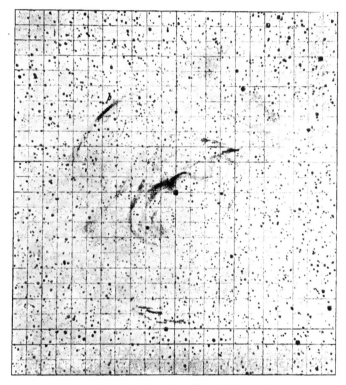

FIG. 94.—Nebulosity about Nova Persei, February 8, 1902.
(*From the Astrophysical Journal.*)

bands. In the photograph of March 15, the K band has disappeared, but the fine H and K lines remain. There are helium lines at 5876, 4713, and 4472. H ζ, in the photograph of March 28, seems to have expanded towards the violet, and has thus apparently altered its position. But in a photograph of April it has resumed its original position and width, although much less intense; C has disappeared.

Photographs of the stars in the region containing the Nova show a spiral nebula surrounding the Nova, which has exhibited remarkable changes, as can be seen from Figs. 93 and 94.

This nebulosity is found to be expanding with the incredible velocity of something like 11 minutes of arc per annum. These astonishing changes can be studied by a comparison of the two photographs, Figs. 93 and 94, taken on September 20, 1901, and February 8, 1902, with the two-foot reflector of the Yerkes Observatory. It has been suggested by Kapteyn that the changes seen are due to changes of illumination of stationary nebular matter. If this theory is correct, and if the successive illumination of portions of nebular matter further away from the centre of disturbance is to be explained as due to the time taken by the light of the central explosion to travel out to these outlying portions of matter, then we may draw some conclusions as to the distance of this Nova from the earth. Light travelling with a velocity of 186,000 miles per second, or $365 \times 24 \times 60 \times 60 \times 186,000$ miles a year, we have to calculate at what distance from the earth this number of miles would subtend an angle of 11 minutes of arc. This would give the distance of the Nova as about 1,833,160,000,000,000 miles. It would take light about 317 years to traverse this distance, so that the explosion which was seen on the earth in 1901 must have taken place in 1584, in the reign of Queen Elizabeth.

On March 16, 1903, a new star was discovered in the constellation Gemini. It was of a red colour, and its spectrum showed bright lines on a faint continuous spectrum, the red hydrogen line being especially bright; it corresponds pretty nearly with the spectra of Nova Aurigæ and Nova Persei in their later stages.

Spectroscopic Binaries.

The telescope enables us to see that some stars which appear as one to the naked eye are really double. This may be either that the two stars happen to be nearly in the same line of sight as seen from the earth, or because the two stars have some physical connection, the line joining them being perceived to change its position, indicating that the two stars form a system revolving round each other in a certain definite time. Sir William Herschel observed about 2400 double stars, and many more have since been added to the list. In some cases the time of a complete revolution occupies many years, in other cases only a few days or hours. The star Mira (o Ceti) has a period of eleven months. For two-thirds of this time it is a faint star of the ninth magnitude; it then becomes brighter, and is seen as a star of the second magnitude for ten or twelve days. Algol (β Persei) has a period of sixty-nine hours. Ordinarily of the second magnitude, it decreases gradually to the fourth magnitude, remains so for twenty minutes, and then gradually recovers its original brightness. In many cases the second star of the double cannot be seen, and its presence is inferred from the variation in brightness. The variability of Algol is supposed to be caused by a temporary eclipse of the light of the star by the passage in front of it of a dark component of the system.

The introduction of the spectroscope has made possible the recognition as binary systems of many stars which could not be recognized as such even by the most powerful telescopes. The telescope can detect a system, like that of Algol, only in the exceptional case when the plane of the orbit which one component describes round the other passes nearly through the sun, so that one component seems to pass over the other, and so causes an eclipse. Unless the plane of the orbit is nearly at right angles to the line of sight, the motion to or from the observer at the spectroscope will give rise to a displacement of the lines of the spectrum. If only one of the two components is luminous, there will be a periodic displacement of the lines; if both are luminous the lines will be periodically doubled. When they are in conjunction the spectrum shows nothing unusual, but when one component is moving away and the other is approaching us, the lines will be displaced in opposite directions, and all lines strong enough to be seen in both spectra will appear to be doubled. Binary systems which have been discovered in this way by means of the spectroscope are known as "spectroscopic binaries."

The bright star Capella (α Aurigæ) was discovered in 1899 to be a spectroscopic binary; the spectrum of the principal component is of the solar type, and that of the secondary component is of the Sirian type. Photographs taken in 1896 show that the principal component had a velocity towards the earth of 34 kilometres per second on August 31; 54 kilometres on September 16; 44 kilometres on October 5; and only 4 kilometres on November 12. The period seems to be 104 days.

The pole star has been found to be a spectroscopic binary with a period of four days.

Fig. 62 shows the spectra of the two components of β Cygni—a blue star, much the brighter of the two with a spectrum similar to that of α Lyra, and a feebler companion of a yellow colour.

Spectra of Comets.

One of the most interesting applications of spectrum analysis in astronomy is to the determination of the nature of comets. Many hundreds of these mysterious bodies have been observed, some periodic, returning time after time; others are seen once and never seen again. From successive observations of the position of a comet, its orbit can be determined. If the orbit is a parabola, the comet is seen once when it circles round the sun, and never again; but if the orbit is an ellipse, the comet may be expected to make its reappearance after the lapse of a definite number of years. Fig. 95 shows the orbit of Halley's comet. This comet was discovered in 1682 by Halley, the Astronomer Royal of the time. He found its orbit to be an ellipse, and its periodic time to be seventy-five or seventy-six years, and therefore predicted its return in 1758; it returned punctually in 1758 and 1833, and should reappear in 1910.

One of the most remarkable comets of the last fifty years was that known as Donati's comet, which was seen in 1858. The orbit of this comet is shown in Fig. 96. It attained its fullest development and greatest brilliancy in October. The tail extended 40° across the sky, but besides the principal tail it developed two smaller, nearly

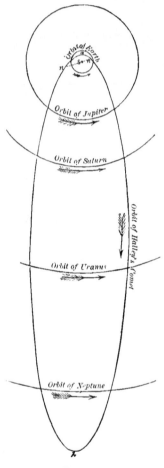

FIG. 95.

straight ones, as shown in Fig. 97. It appears as if the tail of a comet were formed of matter driven off from the head by some repulsive force—possibly electrical—emanating from the sun. Unfortunately there were no spectroscopes waiting for the comet in 1858, and Donati's comet will not return for 2000 years.

New Stars.—Double Stars.—Comets.

Biela's comet was discovered in 1772; it was observed in 1805 and 1826, and found to have a period of 6·6 years. It was seen again in 1832, but at its return in 1846 it was found to have broken up into two portions, each with a tail and nucleus, and when next seen, in 1852, the two portions had become widely separated. Since then it has never been seen, and probably never will be seen again.

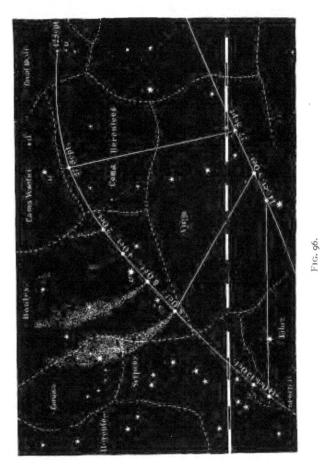

FIG. 96.

The rapid changes which may take place in a comet are shown in Figs. 98 and 99, which are from photographs taken on two successive nights of a comet which appeared unexpectedly in March, 1892, known as Swift's comet. No less than thirty-six unexpected comets appeared in the ten years from March, 1890, to March, 1899.

The first application of the spectroscope to the study of comets

116 *An Introduction to the Study of Spectrum Analysis.*

FIG. 97.
(*From Morgan's "Advanced Physiography."*)

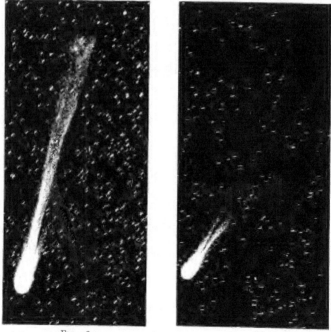

FIG. 98.   FIG. 99.
(*From Morgan's "Advanced Physiography."*)

New Stars.—Double Stars.—Comets.

was made by Sir William Huggins in 1866. Sir William Huggins thus describes his observation of the comet of 1868:—

"I had myself, in the case of three faint comets in 1866, in 1867, and in January, 1868, discovered that part of their light was peculiar to them, and that the light of the last one consisted mainly of three bright flutings. Intense, therefore, was the expectancy with which I directed the telescope, with its attached spectroscope, to the much brighter comet which appeared in June, 1868.

"The comet's light was resolved into a spectrum of three bright bands or flutings, each alike falling off in brightness on the more refrangible side. On the evening of the 22nd, I measured the positions in the spectrum of the brighter beginnings of the flutings on

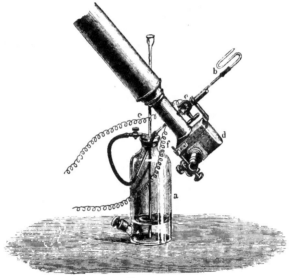

FIG. 100.

the red side. I was not a little surprised the next morning to find that the three cometary flutings agreed in position with three similar flutings in the brightest part of the spectrum of carbon. Some time before, I had mapped down the spectrum of carbon from different sources, chiefly from different hydrocarbons. In some of these spectra the separate lines, of which the flutings are built up, are individually more distinct than in others. The comet bands, as I had seen them on the previous evening, appeared to be identical in character in this respect, as well as in position in the spectrum, with the flutings as they appeared when I took the spark in a current of olefiant-gas. I immediately filled a small holder with this gas, arranged an apparatus in such a manner that the gas could be attached to the end of the telescope, and its spectrum, when a spark was taken in it, seen side by side with that of the comet (Fig. 100).

"Fortunately, the evening was fine; and on account of the exceptional interest of confronting for the first time the spectrum of an earthly gas with that of a comet's light, I invited Dr. Miller to come and make the crucial observation with me. The expectation which I had formed from my measures was fully confirmed. The comet's spectrum, when seen together with that from the gas, agreed

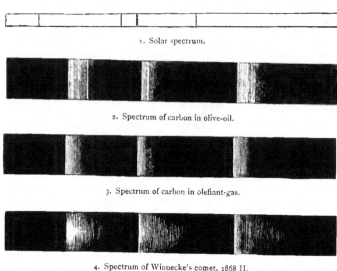

1. Solar spectrum.

2. Spectrum of carbon in olive-oil.

3. Spectrum of carbon in olefiant-gas.

4. Spectrum of Winnecke's comet, 1868 II.

5. Spectrum of Brorsen's comet, 1868 I.

FIG. 101.

in all respects precisely with it. The comet, though 'subtle as Sphinx,' had at last yielded up its secret. The principal part of its light was emitted by luminous vapour of carbon (Fig. 101).

"This result was in harmony with the nature of the gas found occluded in meteorites. Odling had found carbonic oxide as well as hydrogen in his meteorite. Wright, experimenting with another type of meteorite, found that carbon dioxide was chiefly given off. Many meteorites contain a large percentage of hydrocarbons. From one of such sky-stones, a little later, I observed a spectrum similar to that of the comet. The three bands may be seen in the base of a candle-flame.

New Stars.—Double Stars.—Comets.

"In 1881, for the first time since the spectroscope and also suitable photographic plates had been in the hands of astronomers, the coming of a bright comet made it possible to extend the examination of its light into the invisible region of the spectrum at the blue end. On June 22, I was able to obtain, with an exposure of one hour, a good photograph of the head of the comet. It was under a great tension of expectancy that the plate was developed, so that I might be able to look for the first time into a virgin region of nature, as yet unexplored by the eye of man.

"The plate contained an extension and confirmation of my earlier observations by eye. There were the combined spectra of two kinds of light—a faint, continuous spectrum, crossed by Fraunhofer lines, which showed it to be reflected solar light. Upon this was seen a second spectrum of the original light emitted by the comet itself. This spectrum consisted mainly of two groups of bright lines, characteristic of the spectra of certain compounds of carbon. It will be remembered that my earlier observations revealed the three principal flutings of carbon as the main feature of a comet's spectrum in the visible region. The photograph brought a new fact to light. Liveing and Dewar had shown that one of these bands consisted of lines belonging to a nitrogen compound of carbon. We gained the new knowledge that nitrogen, as well as carbon and hydrogen, exists in comets. Now, nitrogen is present in the gas found occluded in some meteorites. At a later date, Dr. Flight showed that nitrogen formed as much as 17 per cent. of the occluded gas from the meteorite of Cranbourne, Australia."

Comet 1898 I (Perrine) was observed by Professor Wright to have a spectrum of the usual type, the three characteristic bands superposed upon a relatively strong continuous spectrum.

Comet 1898 VII (Coddington) showed the same spectrum.

Comet 1898 X (Brooks) showed the three bands, the one in the green being much brighter than usual, with a weak continuous spectrum.

Comet 1899 a (Swift) had a spectrum resembling that of Brook's comet of 1898; it was photographed, and gave the following results:—

```
4883  bright line.
472   blue band, agrees with the fourth carbon band.
440 ⎫
435 ⎬ violet band,  ,,    ,,    ,,   fifth carbon band {438.
                                                       {436.
4313              ,,    ,,    ,,   carbon band (f) at 4313.
421   faint band, ,,    ,,    ,,   cyanogen band at 4216·1.
413   faint band, ,,    ,,    ,,        ,,        ,,  4128·1.
4100
4074  bright.
4052  bright.
4042  bright.
4019 ⎫
4014 ⎬ bright.
3987  faint.
3879  bright, agrees with cyanogen 3883·5.
3869  very bright, agrees with cyanogen 3871·5.
```

CHAPTER X

THE CONCAVE GRATING.—PHOTOGRAPHY OF THE SPECTRUM.

THE great advance in accuracy in recent measurements of spectra is undoubtedly due to Rowland's invention of the concave grating. In order to attain accuracy Professor Rowland had first to devise a method of cutting a sufficiently accurate screw. The method he adopted for this purpose will be found described in the "Encyclopædia Britannica" in the article "Screw." In order to produce an accurate screw, the screw, having been cut, is ground by means of a grinding-nut as long as the screw, the two halves of which can be tightened together as required. It is excessively difficult to avoid all periodic error in the screw, and that due to error in the centring and graduation of the divided head. The dividing engine constructed by Professor Rowland is capable, when maintained at a constant temperature, of making a scale of six inches in length, with errors at no point exceeding one hundred-thousandth of an inch. To make a grating of that length with 14,000 lines to the inch requires four days and nights of continuous labour, and the result is seldom perfect, on account, possibly, of wear of the machine or change of temperature. The grating is ruled on a concave spherical surface of polished speculum metal. The lines are the intersections of a series of parallel planes, one of which passes through the centre of the sphere. The relationship between the number ω of lines (and spaces) in a grating and the wave-length λ of the light by which a diffracted image is formed in a spectrum of the order N, is given by the formula

$$N\lambda = \omega (\sin \iota \pm \sin \theta);$$

where i and θ are the angles made by the incident and refracted light with the normal to the surface of the grating. This formula applies to either plane gratings or curved ones. (The lower negative sign is to be taken if the incident and diffracted rays are on opposite sides of the normal.) If the radius of curvature of the grating be taken as a diameter on which a circle is described, then it may be shown that a luminous point anywhere on this circle will have its image somewhere on the same circle. Rowland adopts the mounting shown in Fig. 102. SE and SG are two heavy wooden beams on

The Concave Grating.—Photography of the Spectrum.

which are rails fixed at right angles to each other. GE is a tubular iron girder equal in length to twice the radius of curvature of the grating. It is supported by carriages at G and E, which run on the rails GS and ES. In all positions, then, S will be on the circle of which GE is the diameter. The grating being at G, and the slit at S, and the camera or eye-piece at E, the image of the slit will always be in exact focus at E. Since GE passes through the centre of curvature of the grating, $\theta = 0$, and the formula given above becomes

$$N\lambda = \omega \sin i.$$

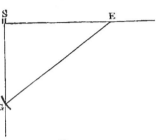

FIG. 102.

The resolving power of a spectroscope or its capacity for separating lines which differ little in wavelength must be carefully distinguished from its dispersive power. The dispersion of a grating depends chiefly upon the number of lines ruled in a unit of length and upon the order of the spectrum observed. The resolving power depends upon the total number of lines, on their exact equality of distance, and on the order of the spectrum. The resolving power may be defined as the ratio of the mean wave-length of two lines, which can just be seen as separate, to their difference in wave-length. The mean wave-length of the two sodium lines is 5893, and their difference of wave-length is 5·97. To separate them a spectroscope must have a resolving power of 988. The most powerful gratings have a resolving power of between 100,000 and 200,000. If a grating has altogether n lines, and we employ the spectrum of the Nth order, then the resolving power is proportional to Nn. We thus attain the same result by using a spectrum of a higher order with a smaller number of lines. Gratings of 15,000 or 20,000 lines to the inch are used, but there is little advantage in having a larger number of lines to the inch than this. Fig. 54 shows Mr. Higgs's apparatus for photographing with a Rowland concave grating. Figs. 51, 53, 55, and 56 show (imperfectly) the quality of the photographs produced. Most gratings give a brighter spectrum at one side than the other. It may happen that, in consequence of some peculiarity in the shape of the grooves, most of the light is concentrated in the spectrum of one particular order on one side or the other. The rail SE may be graduated in equal divisions representing wave-lengths, so that the camera may be set to any particular wave-length which it is desired to photograph. The radius of curvature of the grating is usually $21\frac{1}{2}$ feet, and the photographic plates are 19 inches long and 2 inches wide.

Professor Rowland says: "We put in the sensitive plate and move to the part we wish to photograph. Having exposed that part we move to another position and expose once more. We have no thought for the focus, for that remains perfect, but simply refer to the table giving the proper exposure for that portion of the spectrum, and so have a perfect plate. Thus we can photograph the whole spectrum on one plate in a few minutes from the F line to the extreme violet, in several strips, each twenty inches long, and we may photograph in the red rays by prolonged exposure. Thus the work of days with any other apparatus becomes the work of hours with this. Furthermore, each plate is to scale, an inch on any one of the strips representing *exactly* so much difference of wave-length. The scales of the different orders are exactly proportional to the order. Of course, the superposition of the spectra gives the relative wave-length. One important property of the concave grating is its astigmatism, *i.e.* that

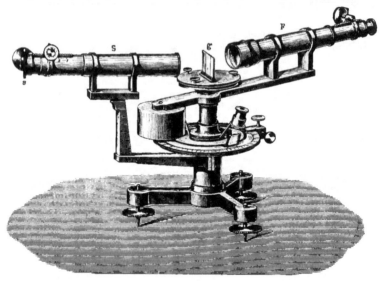

FIG. 103.

the image of a point of light at the slit is a short line. Thus a small spark gives a spectrum of sensible width; there are no longitudinal lines due to dust on the slit, since these are brought to a different focus."

Fig. 103 represents a spectrometer and plane grating arranged for the measurement of wave-lengths. This method involves the accurate measurement of the angular deviation of the ray observed, and the determination of the exact value of the grating space. The grating space is never exactly the same throughout the whole ruled surface. Regular or periodic variations give rise to the so-called "ghosts," or false lines, first described by Quincke and carefully investigated by Pierce, and to differences in focus of the spectra on opposite sides, as investigated by Cornu; or a portion of the grating may be altogether abnormal, having a ruling peculiar to itself. If this abnormal ruling be confined to a few hundred lines, the effect will only be to diffuse a certain proportion of the light without producing false lines or sensibly injuring the definition, but an error will be introduced into the estimate of the grating space if this be determined by counting the number of lines and dividing this into the total length of the grating. The abnormal ruling is more likely to occur at the commencement of the ruled space, and if it can be detected it should be covered up.

Professor Hartley, in Thorpe's "Dictionary of Applied Chemistry," gives the following account of his method of photographing the spectrum:—

"In photographing spectra ranging from 4000 to 2000 tenth-metres the most suitable prisms are of quartz, as first used by M. Cornu; they are cut perpendicular to the axis, one of right-handed, the other of left-handed rotation, each of an angle of thirty degrees. They may be cemented together, back to back, by a drop of glycerin,

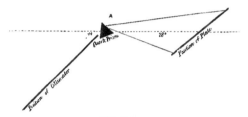

Fig. 104.
(*From Thorpe's " Dictionary of Applied Chemistry."*)

or the one may be fitted to the collimator close to the lens, and the other in a similar manner in front of the telescope or camera lens. The lenses are of similar thickness, and of right- and left-handed crystals. Instead of a telescope, a photographic camera of somewhat unusual construction is employed, the plate carrier of which is so inclined to the direction of the mean ray of the spectrum that it makes an angle therewith of nineteen degrees to twenty-four degrees (Fig. 104). By such means all the rays, inclusive of the wave-lengths given above, are focussed with accuracy on one plate, and a magnifying power of twenty-five diameters may be employed with advantage in examining the photographs. The camera back is constructed so that the normal position is angular, but it is also made to swing on a vertical pivot situated at its centre, the centre of the pivot being in the same vertical plane as the centre and front of the surface of the focussing screen. The collimator should be fitted with a graduated draw-tube and rack and pinion. A connection between this and the front half of the camera is made of leather, folded bellows fashion. This admits of a certain degree of 'side-swing,' with to-and-fro motion for focussing. The camera should be mounted on an iron frame, which falls into position on an iron table to which the collimator is fixed. No matter what be the length, of the collimator, it should be supported for at least one-half of its length, and admit of being fixed at the minimum angle of deviation for the mean ray. An opening is cut in the collimator-tube of about one-third of its circumference in width, and two inches in length, which may be closed by a sliding cover. This enables the experimenter to judge in which direction to move the electrodes, so that the rays of the spark may fall exactly upon the slit and pass along the axis of the collimator. This is done by means of a card, which fits just inside the opening, and has a vertical line ruled at a point coinciding with the centre of the tube. When the spark is properly adjusted, a spindle-shaped bundle of rays strikes the centre of the card. The slit should be $\frac{1}{500}$ to $\frac{1}{1000}$ of an inch in width, and it is well to protect it from dust by a plate of quartz. The source of illumination, if

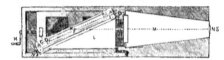

FIG. 105.
(*From Thorpe's " Dictionary of Applied Chemistry."*)

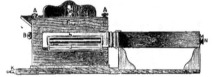

FIG. 106.
(*From Thorpe's " Dictionary of Applied Chemistry."*)

FIG. 107.
(*From Thorpe's " Dictionary of Applied Chemistry."*)

absorption spectra are to be studied, should be condensed sparks from metals affording lines of known wave-lengths, and so numerous that they practically serve the purpose of a continuous spectrum.

"Details of construction of the camera will be understood from Figs. 105 and 106, which show the instrument in plan and elevation, while Fig. 107 shows the back of the camera with the dark slide in position, and the shutter in front slightly raised. M is a rigid shallow box, in front of which is the lens in its fitting N. L, which is a continuation of M, is triangular in form, and is movable in two directions. It moves to and fro by means of the screw K, and makes a greater or lesser angle with the mean ray XN by turning on the pivot situated at X. The screws A A serve to clamp the 'swing-back' in position. The camera back is constructed to carry plates capable of taking several photographs, and the dark slide is moved up or down by the thumb screws B B acting on a pinion which works the rack on the

The Concave Grating.—Photography of the Spectrum. 125

front edge of the dark slide DD. CC is the movable frame for the dark slide. The interior edge of the dark slide is shown in shadow by GG, while H is the slit in the camera back through which the spectrum is projected. E and F represent the door at the back and the sliding front respectively. In the elevation (Fig. 106) is seen the body of the camera, and door to the same, J, through which is seen the slit by which the spectrum passes to the sensitive plate. In the act of focussing a glass plate covered with some fluorescent material is placed in the dark slide, and the lines of the spectrum are viewed by reflection.

"Some care is required to secure a proper adjustment of the instrument and obtain good photographs. The battery power, size of coil, and condensing surface must all be proportional to the distance between the electrodes, in order that the rapidity of the passage of the sparks should render the light almost continuous. The coil should give a six-inch spark in air, and it is better to excite it with three storage cells than with five cells of Groves battery. The electromotive force of the cells should be 1·8 volts. The current required to work such a coil is from $7\frac{1}{2}$ to 8 ampères; three storage cells yield $15\frac{1}{2}$ ampères, but with a resistance of $\frac{1}{4}$ ohm in circuit, the current is conveniently reduced. Electric light carbons have been used for the resistance. The smallest condenser to be of any use has 72 square inches of tin-foil on each side of a glass plate, and a margin of 3 inches. It is fixed in a wooden frame, with binding screws attached to the wood. Special methods have been adopted for examining the emission spectra of solutions, and for observing absorption spectra. Two materials have been commonly used for solutions, namely, electrodes of graphite and gold. Wicks of gold wire are made to pass just above the surface of the solution, which is contained either in a porcelain crucible or in a small U-tube, one limb being longer than the other (Fig. 108).

FIG. 108.
(*From Thorpe's "Dictionary of Applied Chemistry."*)

"Graphite electrodes for the same purpose are cut to the shape of wedges, about $\frac{1}{4}$ inch in length and $\frac{1}{8}$ inch in width. The wedges are attached to platinum wires, and are fixed in glass tubes as shown in the figure; the lower wedge dips into the solution, which is carried to its upper edge by deep grooves or scratches. Capillary attraction keeps the lower electrode moist at its upper surface. Generally speaking, there are only two lines of any other element than carbon visible in the spectrum of good graphite, and these are the first and third of the quadruple group in the magnesium spectrum, wave-lengths 2794·4 and 2801·1. The second and fourth are very faintly seen, wave-lengths 2796·9 and 2789·6. Impure graphite is apt to show the spectrum of iron.

In order to secure fine definition, a condensing lens in front of the slit is necessary. It should be of quartz, of 3 inches diameter and 3 inches focal length. The spark is best if very brilliant and not exceeding $\frac{3}{16}$ inch in length. It should pass upwards—that is to say, the lower electrode must be the negative pole. When this is the case, splashes of liquid are carried up, and the noise of the spark is louder.

"The best gelatino-bromide emulsion plates are used for photographing. The image is developed by pyrogallol, or hydroquinone and ammonia. Hydroxylamine hydrochlorate, and caustic soda with a little potassium bromide, is also a good developer."

The sensitiveness of the ordinary gelatino-bromide plate only begins in the green about the b lines, although it extends into the

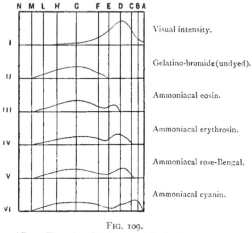

FIG. 109.
(*From Thorpe's " Dictionary of Applied Chemistry."*)

spectrum far beyond the visible violet. Of the yellow and red lines no trace is obtained. If it is desired to photograph in this region, special plates must be employed, made by staining the plate with some dye. Fig. 109 shows the effect of various dyes in extending the sensitiveness of the plate into the yellow and red.

By the use of coloured transparent screens, to reduce the action of the blue part of the spectrum, it is possible to photograph as far as the line C on ordinary unstained plates with a long exposure.

No single staining material is known which will give a correct representation of all the colours of the spectrum, but by the simultaneous use of stained plates and properly chosen screens, a very fair approximation to the desired result can be attained. Vogel first, in 1873, employed aniline dyes to render the plates sensitive to the green, yellow, and red rays. Plates stained with cœrulein,* and used with a screen of chrysoidin (a thickness of 11 mm. of an alcoholic solution of the strength 1 : 12000), enables the whole spectrum, from the ultra-violet O up to the red line A, to be photographed.

Erythrosine † plates are sensitive to the whole of the spectrum from D to H. These are the ordinary "orthochromatic" plates. They are especially sensitive to the green and yellow light.

Cyanin ‡ increases the sensitiveness of the plate to orange and red in a marked degree; whilst the plate possesses less sensitiveness to green. These plates are also useful with longer exposure for the ultra-violet rays. The cyanin bath is made by taking 2 c.c. of an alcoholic solution (1 : 400) of cyanin with 100 c.c. water and $\frac{1}{2}$ c.c. ammonia. The plates should be prepared and developed in absolute darkness.

Congo-red and benzo-purpurin increase the sensitiveness for the region from the green line E to the orange beyond D. The bath is made by adding to 100 c.c. water 1 c.c. ammonia and 2 c.c. aqueous solution of the dye (1 : 400).

Of plates which may be purchased ready dyed may be mentioned the Cadett "Spectrum plates." These must be developed as far as possible in absolute darkness; metol is recommended as the best developer. There are also the plates prepared by the Lumière Company, which are of three kinds: the A orthochromatic plates, sensitive to green and yellow; the B orthochromatic, sensitive to yellow and red; and the C orthochromatic, or panchromatic, plates, sensitive to green, yellow, and red. These last must be developed in darkness; the A plates may be developed by feeble red light, and the B plates may be developed by feeble green light.

It may be noted that the dye substances used to extend the sensitiveness of the plate towards the red also not unfrequently improve the qualities of the plate for the blue and ultra-violet portion of the spectrum, inasmuch as the sharpness of the lines is increased. If intended for photographing the blue portion, the quantity of the dye (cœrulein, for example) may be increased.

The fullest information on the subject of dyeing plates for spectrum photography will be found in the valuable researches of Eder and Valenta, entitled "Beiträge zur Photochemie und Spectralanalyse."

In Fig. 110 are shown the spectra of cadmium, zinc, lead, thallium, and tin, from about 2770 to 1940, as photographed by Professors Eder and Valenta, copied by permission from their "Beiträge zur

---

* Cœrulein is the colouring substance obtained by heating gallein with sulphuric acid; it does not dissolve readily, and is best used in the form of the compound cœrulein-sodium-bisulphite, which is soluble in water. The plates are stained by bathing them for three or four minutes in a solution of 0·02 grms. of the cœrulein-bisulphite.in 100 c.c. of water with 8 drops of ammonia, and allowing the plates to dry.

† Erythrosine, or iodo-eosine, is the potassium compound of tetraiodo-fluoresceine. The bath must be highly dilute (one in ten thousand) and ammoniacal.

‡ Cyanin is chinoline blue.

128 *An Introduction to the Study of Spectrum Analysis.*

Photochemie und Spectralanalyse." These photographs are of the spark-spectrum obtained with a large Rowland concave grating. In the cadmium spectrum the strong line on the left has the wave-length 2748, the next strong line is 2573, then three lines at 2329, 2321,

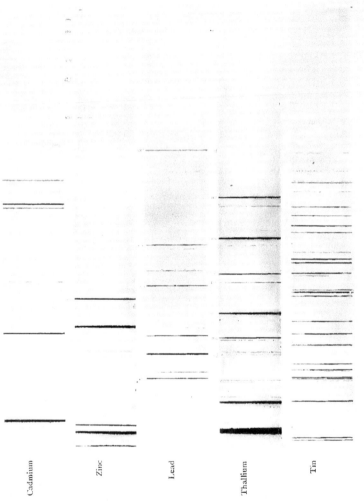

Fig. 110.

and 2313, two lines at 2288 and 2265, and then two at 2194 and 2144. The original photographs show many more lines, hardly to be discerned in the reproductions.

In the zinc spectrum the lines to which numbers are attached are

The Concave Grating.—Photography of the Spectrum. 129

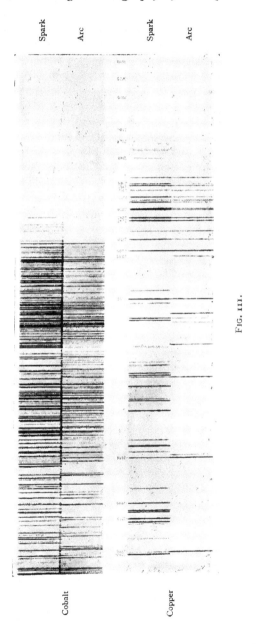

Fig. 111.

2771, 2756, 2658, 2502, 2138, 2064, 2061, 2025, 1967, and 1947, of which the first four are strong lines.

In the lead spectrum we have marked 2663, 2614, 2577, 2476, 2393, 2203, and in the thallium spectrum 2768, 2709, 2580, 2530, 2469, 2452, 2379, double 2298 and 1964.

Fig. 111 shows the spark- and arc-spectra of cobalt and copper. In the spark spectrum of copper the lines marked are 2769, 2766, 2713, 2689, 2618, 2369, 2303, 2294, 2276, 2247, 2242, 2228, 2210, 2199, 2192, 2189, 2149, 2123, 2104, 2055, 2025, and 1999.

In Fig. 112 we have the spark- and arc-spectra of iron and nickel; these photographs show the accuracy with which an enormous number of closely packed fine lines can now be recorded by the photographic method. In the iron spectrum the lines whose wave-lengths are marked are 2767, 2747 and 2746, 2720, 2689, 2664, 2628, 2611, 2599 and 2598, 2585, 2563, 2534 and 2533, 2493, 2454, 2439, 2413, 2399, 2368, 2373, 2332, 2327, and 2280.

In the nickel spectrum the lines marked are 2593, 2576, 2511, 2484, 2473, 2437, 2416, 2375, 2287·7 and 2287·2, 2270, and 2264.

Absorption Spectra.

It has already been remarked that some substances are best recognized by observation of their absorption spectra. All so-called transparent substances absorb some light, even air and colourless glass, and, as we have seen, the photography of the spectrum is interfered with by this absorption. But in the case of these colourless substances, the absorption may be said to be general, as opposed to the selective absorption of such substances as those of which the spectra are shown in Figs. 32 and 33. These are obtained by placing the solution to be examined in a wedge-shaped glass trough in front of the slit of the spectroscope, and using daylight or some other source of white light. The thickness of the solution increasing in a regular manner from the edge of the glass cell, we obtain a series of spectra corresponding to different thicknesses of the absorbing material, and we observe that certain colours of the spectrum are acted on more quickly than others. Thus, a solution of chromium sesquichloride, if dilute, is of a green colour, but a strong solution, or a greater thickness of solution, transmits only purple or red light. In the same way glass coloured with cobalt oxide is blue in a small thickness, but if many pieces of glass are placed together only red light can make its way through.

A very dilute solution of potassium permanganate shows five dark absorption bands in the green, as shown in Figs. 27 and 32. But a very slight increase in the thickness of the layer of liquid or in the strength of the solution obliterates these bands, and only a broad band of blue light and a narrow band of red light are transmitted; a further increase in thickness extinguishes the blue band, and only deep red light passes.

The Concave Grating.—Photography of the Spectrum.

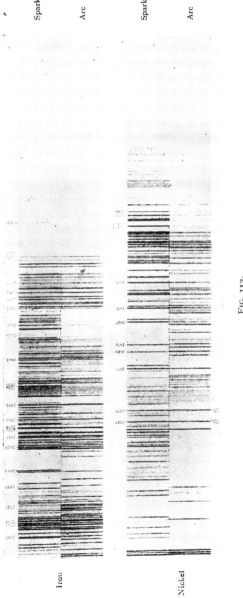

FIG. 112.

132 *An Introduction to the Study of Spectrum Analysis.*

Fig. 113 shows the absorption spectra of chlorophyll (No. 2) (the green colouring matter of leaves), of blood (No. 3), and of the coloured vapours of iodine (No. 4), and of nitrogen peroxide (No. 5) (nitrous acid). These two gases, as well as other coloured gases, such as bromine vapour, chlorine, and others, are remarkable for the regularity and intricacy of the banded spectra which they give by absorption at low temperatures. The absorption spectrum of iodine vapour is altogether different from the emission spectrum shown in Fig. 27. These differences are no doubt due to different complexity of the molecules in the different states of the same absorbing substance. Iodine dissolves in

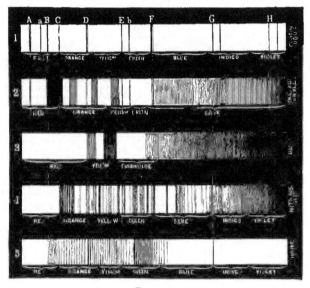

Fig. 113.

carbon disulphide or chloroform to form a violet solution of nearly the same colour as the vapour, but these solutions do not give the same banded absorption spectrum as that of the vapour. The molecule of iodine in the solution is, no doubt, more complex than the molecule in the cool vapour, and this, again, is not so simple as the molecule in the electric discharge. Blood possesses so distinct an absorption spectrum, that it is possible to determine with certainty that a reddish fluid, or the stain produced by it, is really blood, even when the microscope fails to give certain evidence. Blood owes its red colour to a substance called hæmoglobin, which is a compound of an albuminoid substance with a red colouring substance containing iron, known as hæmatin. In arterial blood hæmoglobin is loosely combined with oxygen, which is easily removed by treating the blood with reducing agents, such as ammonium sulphide. In cases of poisoning by carbon monoxide (*e.g.* from water-gas), the hæmoglobin enters into combination with carbon monoxide instead of oxygen, and this compound—as will be seen—possesses its own characteristic absorption spectrum.

Even a very dilute solution of blood gives two characteristic absorption bands between D and E, whose wave-lengths are 5774 and 5390. On addition of ammonium sulphide, two strong bands of reduced hæmatin at 5570 and 5240 are produced; the second of

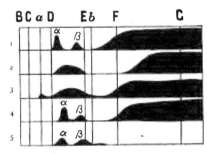

FIG. 114.
(*From Thorpe's " Dictionary of Applied Chemistry."*)

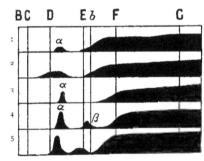

FIG. 115.
(*From Thorpe's " Dictionary of Applied Chemistry."*)

these, it may be noted, is between E and *b*, whereas the oxyhæmoglobin band is between E and D. On shaking up the liquid with air the bands disappear, but a further addition of ammonium sulphide restores them.

Blood which has absorbed carbon monoxide shows two bands between D and E, but nearer to E than the bands of unpoisoned blood. Their wave-lengths are 5735 and 5380. *These bands are not affected by ammonium sulphide.*

The spectroscope may be combined with the microscope for the

Fig. 116.

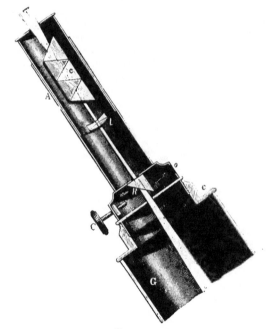

Fig. 117.

The Concave Grating.—Photography of the Spectrum. 135

examination of small objects. Figs. 116 and 117 show such a micro-spectroscopic eye-piece. The prism is contained in the tube A. Below the prism is an achromatic combination, having an adjustable slit between the two lenses, the upper lens being furnished with a screw-motion to focus the slit. C and H are milled heads which adjust the slit. D is an arrangement for holding a small tube, so that the spectrum of its contents may be compared with the spectrum of the object on the stage of the microscope. I is a mirror for throwing light through this, and E a screw regulating the amount

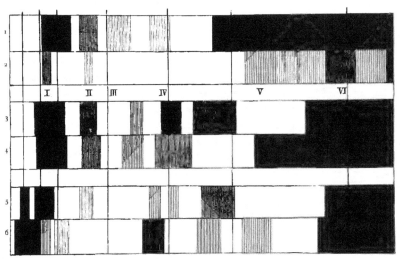

FIG. 118.
(*From Watts's "Dictionary of Chemistry."*)

I. Absorption spectrum of chlorophyll—strong solution.
II. ,, ,, chlorophyll—weak solution.
III. ,, ,, phyllocyanin.
IV. ,, ,, phylloxanthin.
V. ,, ,, a phylloxanthin derivative.
VI. ,, ,, an ethyl compound of the preceding.

of light which is admitted to form this second spectrum. The exact focussing on the lines of the spectrum is done by means of the milled head B.

Chlorophyll is insoluble in water but soluble in alcohol. A solution made by digesting green leaves with alcohol, if strong, absorbs nearly all the spectrum—only red light being transmitted; but with a more dilute solution absorption bands are developed in the green. Addition of acid changes the colour to dull yellowish green or olive, and from this acid solution Fremy has separated two other colouring substances, which are called phyllocyanin and phylloxanthin. Phyllocyanin form a blue solution in hydrochloric acid which gives a spectrum with five absorption bands. Phylloxanthin is yellow, and has a spectrum with four absorption bands. These spectra are shown in Fig. 118.

The spectroscope is often of value in identifying particular dyes or colouring substances and in tracing them even when mixed with

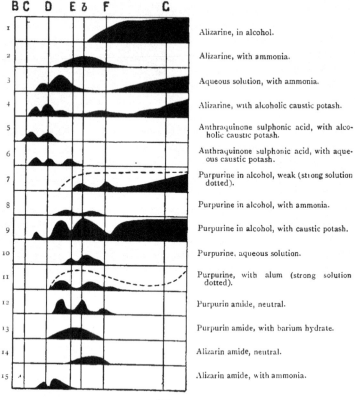

FIG. 119.
(*From Thorpe's " Dictionary of Applied Chemistry."*)

other coloured substances, and thus in detecting adulteration. The colouring substances in madder, or obtained from madder, have characteristic spectra, of which the most important are alizarine and purpurine, both now manufactured artificially from the hydrocarbon anthracene. From anthracene, anthraquinonedisulphonic acid is made, and this by treatment with caustic potash gives dioxyanthraquinone, or alizarine. The absorption spectrum of alizarine is marked by two bands, one about D and the other near C; and purpurine is marked by different bands in the neighbourhood of F and E.

The genuine red colouring substance of wine, derived from the skin of the grape, has a spectrum quite different from that of magenta or other dyes sometimes used in sophisticating "wine." The

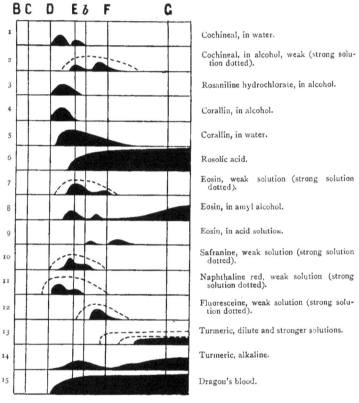

FIG. 120.
(*From Thorpe's "Dictionary of Applied Chemistry."*)

detection of such adulterations does not depend only on the differences between the spectra themselves, but also upon the series of alterations in the spectrum brought about by treatment with various reagents. Cubes of glycerine jelly soaked in the wine to be tested are not much stained if the wine is genuine, but many of the dyes penetrate the jelly throughout, and a slice cut from the cube may be used to give the absorption spectrum. Indigo and logwood may be detected in this way.

CHAPTER XI.

RELATIONSHIPS BETWEEN THE DIFFERENT LINES OF A SPECTRUM, AND BETWEEN LINES OF THE SPECTRA OF ALLIED ELEMENTS.

ONE of the most interesting subjects of speculation is the inquiry into the existence of relationships between the different lines of the same spectrum, and of relationships between lines of the spectra of allied elements. One cannot but be impressed by the beautiful rhythmical arrangement of the lines forming such groups as those of the carbon spectrum (Fig. 16), of cyanogen (see Fig. 51, lower strip, between 7 and 8), and of the groups A and B in the solar spectrum (see Figs. 56 and 57), which seem to be repetitions of each other. The lines we observe are due to vibrations in the ether of definite period, and the period is in some way determined by the particular atoms or molecules of the substance, which—as we say—"give that spectrum."

Even in the early days of spectrum analysis it was felt that there must be some connection between the vibrations to which the different lines of a glowing gas are due, and the earlier attempts at tracing this connection were based upon analogy with music. A pianoforte string, for example, is capable of giving not only its fundamental or lowest note but also a series of overtones; the octave, of just twice the frequency; the twelfth, or fifth of the octave, of just three times the frequency, and so on. In Fig. 25 we have shown the spectrum of hydrogen in a vacuum tube of four lines, known as $H\alpha$ in the red, $H\beta$ in the green, and $H\gamma$ and $H\delta$ in the blue; and in the spectra of the stars (see Fig. 73) we have a continuation of the spectrum, so that the complete spectrum is made up of a series of lines getting closer and closer together as we advance into the ultra-violet. Professor Johnstone Stoney endeavoured to explain this rhythmical arrangement of lines on the theory that they were due to overtones of a low fundamental vibration, and he showed that $H\alpha$, $H\beta$, and $H\delta$ might be the twentieth, twenty-seventh, and thirty-second harmonics of a fundamental vibration of wave-length 131277 $\cdot$ 4. But there was no place found for $H\gamma$ in this arrangement, nor does it explain the series of stellar lines of hydrogen. It is now generally admitted that such theories will not account for the facts, and a definite end was put to such speculations by Professor Schuster, who showed that the coincidences observed were not more numerous than ought to be the case as the result of chance, as we are taught by the theory of probabilities. The first striking success in the attempt to explain these regularities in spectra was obtained with the hydrogen spectrum by Professor Balmer, in the year 1885, who showed that the wave-lengths of the hydrogen lines could be calculated by a very simple formula, viz. the oscillation frequency

$$\frac{1}{\lambda} = 27418 \cdot 75\left(1 - \frac{4}{m^2}\right)^*$$

where m is to have given to it the values 3, 4, 5, 6, 7, 8, 9, etc., in succession. The spectrum of hydrogen is given in the accompanying table, from which may be seen the remarkable agreement between observed and calculated values. It will be noticed that the lines for which values are calculated from the formula are the brightest lines, but there are many other lines of less intensity which do not fall into this series. These belong to what is called the secondary or "compound-line-spectrum" of hydrogen. It should be noted that Professor Trowbridge is of opinion that the "four-line" spectrum of hydrogen is really due to water-vapour and not to the element hydrogen, and that the true spectrum of hydrogen is to be found in this compound spectrum.

HYDROGEN (VACUUM TUBE AND STELLAR SPECTRA).

Wave-length (Rowland).	Intensity.	m.	Oscillation frequency in vacuo.	
			Observed.	Calculated.
C α 6563·042		3	15232·7	15232·6
5084·9				
5055·2				
5013·15				
4973·3	6			
4928·8	6			
4876·1	4			
F β 4861·49	20	4	20564·1	20564·1
4838·3	4			
4797·9	4			
4764·0	3			
4719·2	5			
4683·95	5			
4634·15	6			
4580·1	4			

* Or otherwise written $\frac{1}{\lambda} = 27418 \cdot 75(1 - 4m^{-2})$.

HYDROGEN (VACUUM TUBE AND STELLAR SPECTRA)—*continued*.

Wave-length (Rowland).	Intensity.	m.	Oscillation frequency in vacuo.	
			Observed.	Calculated.
4534·8	2			
4498·75	4			
4461·1	5			
4447·85	3			
4412·35	5			
G' γ 4340·66	15	5	23031·6	23031·7
4212·65	7			
4205·2	8			
4195·9	6			
4177 25	8			
4171·35	7			
h δ 4101·89	10	6	24372·2	24372·3
4079·0	5			
4069·75	7			
4067·0	7			
4062·6	6			
3997·25	4			
3992·0	4			
3990·15	6			
3987·0	3			
3982·75	4			
H ε 3970·25	8	7	25180·2	25180·5
3963·3	3			
3962·4	2			
3944·5	3			
3924·5	3			
3889·3	4			
ζ 3889·15	7	8	25705·3	25705·1
3879·7	3			
3872·45	4			
3871·8	5			
3867·2	4			
3863·3	5			
3861·7	4½			
3858·85	4			
3836·6	3			
η 3835·6	n	9	26064·2	26064·8
3804·9	6			
3803·2	4			
θ 3798·0	n	10	26322·3	26322·0
3797·7	4			
3796·8	5			
3771·7	3			
ι 3770·7	<1:n	11	26512·8	26512·4
3770·3	2			
κ 3750·15	<1	12	26658·1	26657·1
3741·3	2			
λ 3734·15	<1	13	26772·3	26769·8
3732·2	3			
3722·2	2			
μ 3722·0	<1	14	26859·7	26859·2
3716·05	1			
ν 3712·0	?	15	26932·1	26931·3

Relationships in Spectra.

HYDROGEN (VACUUM TUBE AND STELLAR SPECTRA)—*continued*.

Wave-length (Rowland).	Intensity.	m.	Oscillation frequency in vacuo.	
			Observed.	Calculated.
ξ 3703·99	Measured in stellar spectra.	16	26990·3	26990·3
ο 3697·22		17	27039·8	27039·3
π 3691·71		18	27080·1	27080·3
ρ 3687·05		19	27114·4	27114·9
σ 3682·93		20	27144·7	27147·3
τ 3679·48		21	27170·1	27170·1
υ 3676·43		22	27192·6	27192·2
φ 3673·81		23	27212·0	27211·4
χ 3671·53		24	27228·9	27228·3
ψ 3669·52		25	27243·8	27243·3
ω 3667·70		26	27257·3	27256·5
3666·15		27	27268·9	27268·3
3664·71		28	27279·6	27278·9
3663·40		29	27289·3	27288·3
3662·14		30	27298·7	27296·9
3661·16		31	27306·0	27304·6

In the column headed "Intensity," 20 denotes the strongest line, "n" signifies "nebulous."

It will be seen that—according to this formula of Balmer's—the hydrogen lines run closer and closer together, the series ending at 27418·75, which is called "the convergence frequency." Professor Pickering has, however, observed in the spectrum of the star ζ Puppis, besides this hydrogen series, a number of lines which do not fall into this series, and which probably constitute a new series of hydrogen lines. They can be calculated by the modified formula $\frac{1}{\lambda} = 27559\left(1 - \frac{4·864}{m^2}\right)$. This series would end at 27559, nearly the same place as the first series. Now, Kayser and Runge have found series in a large number of elements, and generally two series, ending at nearly the same point. Professor Kayser, therefore, thinks it probable that hydrogen also has two series. He remarks "that this series, which has never been observed before, can perhaps be explained by insufficient temperature in our Geissler tubes and most of the stars."

The formula of Balmer is a simpler form of the general equation $\frac{1}{\lambda} = A - Bm^{-2} - Cm^{-4}$, or $\frac{1}{\lambda} = A\left(1 - \frac{B}{A}m^{-2} - \frac{C}{A}m^{-4}\right)$. This is the general formula of Kayser and Runge; it reduces to Balmer's formula by putting $C = 0$.

The number of lines in the spectra of the elements varies very greatly. In some we have only a few lines or groups of lines, obviously distributed with some regularity, so that they suggest the existence of some law. In other spectra we have an enormous number of lines, so that it becomes very difficult for the eye to trace any connection. It is generally easier to trace such regularities in the ultra-violet portion of a spectrum, because with decreasing wavelength the lines of a series approach continually closer together, and thus their character of symmetry strikes the eye more easily. Again, we can hardly expect all the lines of a spectrum, or indeed any large proportion, to fall under any one formula, for in a luminous gas we have—no doubt—molecules of very different degrees of complexity. A particular spectrum, probably, does not correspond to a definite temperature, but is a mixture of the spectra of different temperatures, in which the spectrum of the mean temperature predominates. We cannot assume that all the atoms of a molecule vibrate in precisely the same manner, and if they do not, then each atom may give rise to a separate series, which will require a separate formula for its representation. Again, of lines belonging to temperatures far removed from the mean temperature, only the most intense may be visible, and it will not be possible to find any formula connecting them. Thus in the spectrum of hydrogen it is only the strongest which can be represented by Balmer's formula.

In the case of some elements, such as the metals of the alkalies, the spectrum seems to change little with change of temperature, and these are therefore the easiest to deal with.

In the arc-spectrum of lithium twenty lines have been observed, and Kayser and Runge find it possible to account for all of the lines by means of formulæ. The lines fall into three series, which are called respectively the principal series, the first subordinate series, and the second subordinate series. The formulæ for the three series are:—

Principal series . . . . $10^8\lambda^{-1} = 43584·73(1 − 3·06688m^{-2} − 25·24012m^{-4})$
First subordinate series . $10^8\lambda^{-1} = 28586·74(1 − 3·83479m^{-2} − 0·0646096m^{-4})$
Second subordinate series $10^8\lambda^{-1} = 28666·69(1 − 4·26945m^{-2} − 8·08255m^{-4})$

The following table shows the agreement between the results of calculation and the observed wave-lengths of the lines in the spectrum of lithium:—

Value of m and series.	Calculated wave-length.	Observed wave-length.
P3	6600·08	6708·2
A3	6103·77	6103·77
B4	4972·11	4972·11
A4	4602·37	4602·37
B5	4273·44	4273·44
A5	4132·44	4132·44
B6	3985·94	3985·94
A6	3915·40	3915·2
B7	3835·47	3838·3
A7	3795·24	3794·9
A8	3721·15	3718·9
A9	3672·01	3670·6
P4	3232·77	3232·77
P5	2741·39	2741·39
P6	2562·60	2562·60
P7	2475·33	2475·13
P8	2425·56	2425·55
P9	2394·25	2394·54
P10	2373·15	2373·9
P11	2358·22	2359·4

In this table the principal series is marked P, the first subordinate series A, and the second subordinate series B. The wave-lengths in italics are those used in calculating the constants of the formulæ. The agreement between calculated and observed values is very satisfactory except for the red line. It is observed that the lines of any one series agree in character; thus the lines of the principal series are sharp and easily reversed, those of the first subordinate series are diffuse and reversible, and those of the second subordinate series are diffuse on the red side, and are not reversible. Further, it is to be observed that the intensity of the lines of any one series decreases regularly with increasing values of m.

Probably the lines which belong to any one series result from the vibrations of the same molecule; the principal series belonging to the simplest molecule, for it appears particularly at high temperatures, and embraces especially the ultra-violet lines. The diffuseness of the lines of the secondary series seems to indicate that they are due to the vibrations of more complicated molecules, belonging to a lower temperature. We may expect a whole series to be absent as the result of dissociation under particular circumstances, but it is not likely that we shall have some lines of a series while the brighter lines of that series are absent.

In the spectra of the other metals of the alkalies, viz. sodium, potassium, rubidium, and cæsium, similar relationships are found; the lines in each case being divisible into a principal series and two subordinate series, in one of which the lines are sharp, and in the other diffuse. There is, however, this difference between these spectra and that of lithium, that instead of single lines, as in lithium, we have pairs of lines in sodium, potassium, rubidium, and cæsium. The arrangement into series in the case of sodium is shown in Fig. 121,

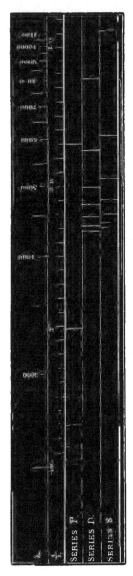

FIG. 121.

(*From Watts's "Dictionary of Chemistry."*)

144   *An Introduction to the Study of Spectrum Analysis.*

where P denotes the principal series, D the diffuse, and S the sharp subordinate series. The formulæ are as follows :—

Principal series . . $10^8\lambda^{-1} = 41536\cdot81(1 - 3\cdot12939m^{-2} - 19\cdot33950m^{-4})$
Subordinate sharp series $\begin{cases} 10^8\lambda^{-1} = 24549\cdot12(1 - 4\cdot91774m^{-2} - 8\cdot06103m^{-4}) \\ 10^8\lambda^{-1} = 24565\cdot83(1 - 4\cdot91485m^{-2} - 8\cdot05882m^{-4}) \end{cases}$
Subordinate diffuse series $\begin{cases} 10^8\lambda^{-1} = 24476\cdot72(1 - 4\cdot49905m^{-2} - 0\cdot146997m^{-4}) \\ 10^8\lambda^{-1} = 24496\cdot26(1 - 4\cdot49905m^{-2} - 0\cdot119447m^{-4}) \end{cases}$

The Fraunhofer D lines correspond to $m = 3$ in the principal series. It appears that the double lines of the principal series get closer and closer together as the value of m increases, but that in the two subordinate series the double lines are always at about the same distance apart. The same rule applies to the double lines in the spectra of the other alkali metals. These formulæ account for all the lines in the arc-spectrum of sodium with the exception of a pair at $5675\cdot92$, $5670\cdot40$.

Similar relationships are found to hold in the case of potassium; there is a principal series of pairs of lines extending far into the ultra-violet, and two subordinate series, also of pairs of lines, in the visible portion of the spectrum. The red and blue lines of the flame-spectrum belong to the principal series, and correspond to $m = 3$ and $m = 4$. The formulæ given by Kayser and Runge for potassium are as follows :—

Principal series . . $\begin{cases} 10^8\lambda^{-1} = 35086\cdot55(1 - 3\cdot16914m^{-2} - 17\cdot82216m^{-4}) \\ 10^8\lambda^{-1} = 35085\cdot90(1 - 3\cdot61692m^{-2} - 17\cdot71746m^{-4}) \end{cases}$
First subordinate series $\begin{cases} 10^8\lambda^{-1} = 22021\cdot83(1 - 5\cdot42157m^{-2} - 2\cdot83837m^{-4}) \\ 10^8\lambda^{-1} = 22077\cdot11(1 - 5\cdot40216m^{-2} - 2\cdot89807m^{-4}) \end{cases}$
Second subordinate series $\begin{cases} 10^8\lambda^{-1} = 21991\cdot24(1 - 5\cdot20434m^{-2} - 5\cdot05410m^{-4}) \\ 10^8\lambda^{-1} = 22050\cdot32(1 - 5\cdot19167m^{-2} - 5\cdot04922m^{-4}) \end{cases}$

An inspection of these formulæ would suggest that probably, in the two subordinate series, the coefficients of m^{-2} and m^{-4} should have the same values for the two lines of a pair, which would give the succession of pairs of lines at the same distance apart; while in the principal series, if the first and second coefficients had the same value, then the width of the lines apart would depend on the difference between the values of the coefficients of m^{-4}. The distance apart of the lines of the pairs would then decrease with increasing values of m, and would be inversely proportional to the fourth power of m, which is what is found to be very nearly the case. All the forty-one lines of the arc-spectrum of potassium are accounted for by the above formulæ, with only small differences between the calculated values and those observed, but the formulæ do not give accurately the wave-lengths of the infra-red lines observed by Becquerel and by Snow.

Rydberg prefers another formula, viz. $10^8\lambda^{-1} = a - \dfrac{N}{(m + \mu)^2}$, where a stands for the convergence frequency, and N has the value $109721\cdot6$ and $\mu = 0\cdot254$. Over a certain range of spectrum the two formulæ, Rydberg's and that of Kayser and Runge, agree with the observations about equally well, but neither will fit the whole range

Relationships in Spectra. 145

from infra-red into the ultra-violet. Rydberg thinks that the value of N in his formula is the same for all elements (or that the product A × B, in Kayser and Runge's formula, has always the same value), and that the two subordinate series in each element end exactly at the same point. This does not appear to be exactly true, though it is very nearly so.

In rubidium we have a principal series, consisting of pairs of lines closer together as we pass into the ultra-violet, and two subordinate series in the visible spectrum, which are probably pairs, although all have not been actually seen as such. The formula for the principal series is—

$$10^8\lambda^{-1} = 33762\cdot11(1 - 3\cdot71781m^{-2} - 16\cdot65343m^{-4})$$
$$10^8\lambda^{-1} = 33765\cdot38(1 - 3\cdot71478m^{-2} - 16\cdot13129m^{-4})$$

For the two subordinate series we have—

$$10^8\lambda^{-1} = 20939\cdot39(1 - 5\cdot78780m^{-2} - 6\cdot42884m^{-4})$$
$$10^8\lambda^{-1} = 21179\cdot38(1 - 5\cdot73303m^{-2} - 6\cdot22299m^{-4})$$

Again it seems that all the lines of rubidium can be accounted for by means of such formulæ.

With cæsium we have quite similar relationships: a principal series extending into the ultra-violet and two subordinate series. The formulæ are—

Principal series . . . . . $\begin{cases} 10^8\lambda^{-1} = 31501\cdot56(1 - 3\cdot97050m^{-2} - 15\cdot55107m^{-4}) \\ 10^8\lambda^{-1} = 31465\cdot78(1 - 3\cdot91498m^{-2} - 14\cdot76461m^{-4}) \end{cases}$

First subordinate series . . $10^8\lambda^{-1} = 19743\cdot25(1 - 6\cdot22335m^{-2} - 15\cdot4902m^{-4})$

Second subordinate series . . $10^8\lambda^{-1} = 20295\cdot22(1 - 6\cdot05517m^{-2} - 15\cdot6010m^{-4})$

The spectra of magnesium, zinc, and cadmium are characterized by the presence of triplets, repeated over and over again; close triplets in magnesium, wider in zinc, and still wider in cadmium. The Fraunhofer b group is one of these magnesium triplets, shown in Fig. 51, and in Fig. 23 the same is seen at 75, and in the zinc spectrum a triplet at 95, 100, and 102; and in the cadmium spectrum a triplet at 80, 95, and 103.

Kayser and Runge arrange the triplets of magnesium in two series, which they think to be both subordinate series, and find that the oscillation frequencies can be calculated very nearly by means of the following formulæ:—

First series . . $\begin{cases} 10^8\lambda^{-1} = 39796\cdot10 - 130398m^{-2} - 1432090m^{-4} \\ 10^8\lambda^{-1} = 39836\cdot79 - 130398m^{-2} - 1432090m^{-4} \\ 10^8\lambda^{-1} = 39857\cdot00 - 130398m^{-2} - 1432090m^{-4} \end{cases}$

Second series . $\begin{cases} 10^8\lambda^{-1} = 39836\cdot74 - 125471m^{-2} - 518781m^{-4} \\ 10^8\lambda^{-1} = 39877\cdot95 - 125471m^{-2} - 518781m^{-4} \\ 10^8\lambda^{-1} = 39897\cdot91 - 125471m^{-2} - 518781m^{-4} \end{cases}$

By means of these formulæ, 39 lines out of the 56 lines in the arc-spectrum of magnesium are accounted for, with very small differences between the calculated and observed values, except in the red, where the differences amount to 1 per cent. It will be seen that, according to these formulæ, since the coefficients of m^{-2} and m^{-4} are the same for the three lines of the triplets in each series, the spacing of the lines in the successive triplets will be always the same.

In the spectrum of calcium, 36 lines out of 106 are accounted for by the formulæ—

First series $\begin{cases} 10^8\lambda^{-1} = 33919\cdot51 - 123547m^{-2} - 961696m^{-1} \\ 10^8\lambda^{-1} = 34022\cdot12 - 123547m^{-2} - 961696m^{-1} \\ 10^8\lambda^{-1} = 34073\cdot82 - 123547m^{-2} - 961696m^{-1} \end{cases}$

Second series $\begin{cases} 10^8\lambda^{-1} = 34041\cdot17 - 120398m^{-2} - 346097m^{-1} \\ 10^8\lambda^{-1} = 34146\cdot95 - 120398m^{-2} - 346097m^{-1} \\ 10^8\lambda^{-1} = 34199\cdot09 - 120398m^{-2} - 346097m^{-1} \end{cases}$

For strontium, Kayser and Runge find only one series, but Lehmann has discovered a second series. The formulæ are—

First series $\begin{cases} 10^8\lambda^{-1} = 31030\cdot64 - 122328m^{-2} - 837473m^{-1} \\ 10^8\lambda^{-1} = 31424\cdot67 - 122328m^{-2} - 837473m^{-1} \\ 10^8\lambda^{-1} = 31610\cdot58 - 122328m^{-2} - 837473m^{-1} \end{cases}$

Second series $\begin{cases} 10^8\lambda^{-1} = 31226 - 120300m^{-2} - 301000m^{-1} \\ 10^8\lambda^{-1} = 31618 - 120300m^{-2} - 301000m^{-1} \\ 10^8\lambda^{-1} = 31806 - 120300m^{-2} - 301000m^{-1} \end{cases}$

In the spectrum of barium, with 162 lines, Kayser and Runge did not succeed in finding any formula.

In the spectrum of zinc, Kayser and Runge find two series of triplets which can be represented by the formulæ—

First series $\begin{cases} 10^8\lambda^{-1} = 42945\cdot32 - 131641m^{-2} - 1236125m^{-1} \\ 10^8\lambda^{-1} = 43331\cdot71 - 131641m^{-2} - 1236125m^{-1} \\ 10^8\lambda^{-1} = 43521\cdot48 - 131641m^{-2} - 1236125m^{-1} \end{cases}$

Second series $\begin{cases} 10^8\lambda^{-1} = 42954\cdot59 - 126919m^{-2} - 632850m^{-1} \\ 10^8\lambda^{-1} = 43343\cdot65 - 126919m^{-2} - 632850m^{-1} \\ 10^8\lambda^{-1} = 43533\cdot32 - 126919m^{-2} - 632850m^{-1} \end{cases}$

These formulæ account for 36 lines out of the 73 lines in the arc-spectrum. The zinc spectrum shows an extraordinarily strong line at 2138·3, of which Professor Crew remarks that it is "the most characteristic single line of the spectrum." This line, and several other strong lines, are not accounted for by the formulæ, so that the whole spectrum is far from being reduced under any one law, as was the case with the simpler spectra of the metals of the alkalies.

For cadmium the formulæ are—

First series $\begin{cases} 10^8\lambda^{-1} = 40755\cdot21 - 128635m^{-2} - 1289619m^{-1} \\ 10^8\lambda^{-1} = 41914\cdot60 - 128635m^{-2} - 1289619m^{-1} \\ 10^8\lambda^{-1} = 42456\cdot64 - 128635m^{-2} - 1289619m^{-1} \end{cases}$

Second series $\begin{cases} 10^8\lambda^{-1} = 40797\cdot12 - 126146m^{-2} - 555137m^{-1} \\ 10^8\lambda^{-1} = 41968\cdot80 - 126146m^{-2} - 555137m^{-1} \\ 10^8\lambda^{-1} = 42510\cdot58 - 126146m^{-2} - 555137m^{-1} \end{cases}$

These formulæ account for 36 lines out of the 74 lines in the arc-spectrum of cadmium. We have again several strong lines unaccounted for, *e.g.* one at 2288·10.

The spectrum of mercury appears to be more complicated than those of zinc and cadmium. Kayser and Runge account for 25 lines out of some 92 lines in the arc-spectrum by the following formulæ:—

First series $\begin{cases} 10^8\lambda^{-1} = 40159\cdot60 - 127484m^{-2} - 1252695m^{-1} \\ 10^8\lambda^{-1} = 44792\cdot87 - 127484m^{-2} - 1252695m^{-1} \\ 10^8\lambda^{-1} = 46560\cdot78 - 127484m^{-2} - 1252694m^{-1} \end{cases}$

Second series $\begin{cases} 10^8\lambda^{-1} = 40217\cdot98 - 126361m^{-2} - 613268m^{-1} \\ 10^8\lambda^{-1} = 44851\cdot01 - 126361m^{-2} - 613268m^{-1} \\ 10^8\lambda^{-1} = 46618\cdot44 - 126361m^{-2} - 613268m^{-1} \end{cases}$

In the mercury spectrum, as in those of cadmium and zinc, there are some strong lines not accounted for, in particular the strong line at 2536·72. The arrangement of lines in series in the spectra of magnesium, calcium, strontium, zinc, cadmium, and mercury is shown in Fig. 122.

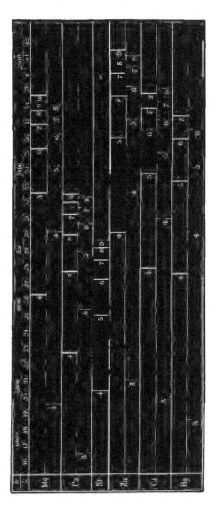

Fig. 122.
(From Watts's "Dictionary of Chemistry.")

In the spectra of copper and silver, Kayser and Runge find that the lines occur in pairs with a constant difference in oscillation frequency, as shown in Fig. 123. They find that there are in each case two series of pairs, for which the formulæ are, for copper—

First series . . $\begin{cases} 10^8\lambda^{-1} = 31591\cdot6 - 131150m^{-2} - 1085060m^{-4} \\ 10^8\lambda^{-1} = 31840\cdot1 - 131150m^{-2} - 1085060m^{-4} \end{cases}$

Second series . $\begin{cases} 10^8\lambda^{-1} = 31591\cdot6 - 124809m^{-2} - 440582m^{-4} \\ 10^8\lambda^{-1} = 31840\cdot1 - 124809m^{-2} - 440582m^{-4} \end{cases}$

and for silver—

First series . . $\begin{cases} 10^8\lambda^{-1} = 30712\cdot4 - 130621m^{-2} - 1093823m^{-4} \\ 10^8\lambda^{-1} = 31633\cdot2 - 130621m^{-2} - 1093823m^{-4} \end{cases}$

Second series . $\begin{cases} 10^8\lambda^{-1} = 30696\cdot2 - 123788m^{-2} - 394303m^{-4} \\ 10^8\lambda^{-1} = 31617\cdot0 - 123788m^{-2} - 394303m^{-4} \end{cases}$

These formulæ only account for very few of the large number of lines in the spectra of copper and silver.

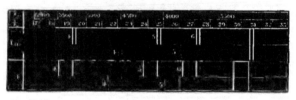

FIG. 123.
(*From Watts's " Dictionary of Chemistry."*)

In the spectra of the elements aluminium, indium, and thallium, Kayser and Runge find in each case two subordinate series of pairs of lines. Their formulæ are, for aluminium—

First series . . $\begin{cases} 10^8\lambda^{-1} = 48308\cdot2 - 156662m^{-2} - 2505331m^{-4} \\ 10^8\lambda^{-1} = 48420\cdot2 - 156662m^{-2} - 2505331m^{-4} \end{cases}$

Second series . $\begin{cases} 10^8\lambda^{-1} = 48244\cdot5 - 127527m^{-2} - 687819m^{-4} \\ 10^8\lambda^{-1} = 48356\cdot5 - 127527m^{-2} - 687819m^{-4} \end{cases}$

indium—

First series . . $\begin{cases} 10^8\lambda^{-1} = 44515\cdot4 - 139308m^{-2} - 1311032m^{-4} \\ 10^8\lambda^{-1} = 46728\cdot6 - 139308m^{-2} - 1311032m^{-4} \end{cases}$

Second series . $\begin{cases} 10^8\lambda^{-1} = 44535\cdot0 - 126766m^{-2} - 643584m^{-4} \\ 10^8\lambda^{-1} = 46748\cdot2 - 126766m^{-2} - 643584m^{-4} \end{cases}$

thallium—

First series . . $\begin{cases} 10^8\lambda^{-1} = 41542\cdot7 - 132293m^{-2} - 1265223m^{-4} \\ 10^8\lambda^{-1} = 49337\cdot6 - 132293m^{-2} - 1265223m^{-4} \end{cases}$

Second series . $\begin{cases} 10^8\lambda^{-1} = 41506\cdot4 - 122617m^{-2} - 790683m^{-4} \\ 10^8\lambda^{-1} = 49301\cdot3 - 122617m^{-2} - 790683m^{-4} \end{cases}$

For the spectra of tin, lead, arsenic, antimony, and bismuth, no formulæ have been discovered, but certain regularities have been noted. In the spectrum of tin the lines 3801·16, 3330·71, 2850·72, 2813·66, 2785·14, 2779·92, 2594·49, 2571·67, 2524·05, 2495·80, 2408·27, 2358·05 and 2317·32 are repeated in the lines 3175·12, 2840·06, 2483·50, 2455·30, 2433·53, 2429·58, 2286,79, 2269·03, 2231·80, 2209·78, 2141·1, 2100·9, 2068·7, that is to say, the first thirteen lines are respectively at the same distances from the second thirteen lines when reckoned on the scale of oscillation frequency, and again the first five of these; the seventh, ninth, and eleventh occur again further on. In lead also ten lines are repeated with a constant difference, and eight of these are repeated again. The same occurs with eight lines in the spectrum of arsenic, and in antimony a set of lines seems to be repeated no less than five times.

Another subject of inquiry of much interest and importance is that of a possible connection between the spectra of allied elements. The study of chemistry leads us to associate certain elements as forming natural families; *e.g.* fluorine, chlorine, bromine, and iodine form a well-marked group, so also lithium, sodium, potassium, rubidium, and cæsium; calcium, strontium, and barium; magnesium, zinc, and cadmium; phosphorus, arsenic, and antimony, and so on. Mendelejeff's periodic law is an attempt to connect the properties of the elements with their atomic weights—that is, of the smallest masses of the elements *known to the chemist*.

Groups	1	2	3	4	5	6	7	8	
Series				RH_4	RH_3	RH_2	RH	(R_2H)	Hydrogen Compounds
	R_2O	R_2O_2 or RO	R_2O_3	R_2O_4 or RO_2	R_2O_5	R_2O_6 or RO_3	R_2O_7	R_2O_8 or RO_4	Higher Oxygen Compounds
1	1 H	—	—	—	—	—	—	—	
2	Li 7	Be 9	B 11	C 12	N 14	O 16	F 19	Ne 20	
3	23 Na	24 Mg	27 Al	28 Si	31 P	32 S	35·5 Cl	A 40	
4	K 39	Ca 40	Sc 44	Ti 48	V 51	Cr 52	Mn 55	Fe 56. Co 59. Ni 59	
5	63 Cu	65 Zn	69 Ga	72·5 Ge	75 As	78 Se	80 Br	Kr 81	
6	Rb 85	Sr 87	Yt 89	Zr 90	Nb 94	Mo 96	—	Ru 102. Rh 103. Pd 106	
7	107 Ag	112 Cd	114 In	118 Sn	120 Sb	—	126 I	Te 126·6. X 128	
8	Cs 133	Ba 137	La 138	Ce 140	Nd 142·5	—			
9	Gd 155	—	159 Tb	—	—	—	—	Os 190. Ir 193. Pt 196	
10	—	—	Yb 172	—	Ta 182	W 183	—		
11	197 Au	200 Hg	204 Tl	—	208 Bi	—	—		
12	—	Ra 225	—	—	—	U 237	—		

The arrangement of the elements according to the periodic law is shown in the above table, in which the elements are represented by their symbols, and the significance of the symbols and the most accurate determinations of the atomic weights are given in the following table:—

INTERNATIONAL ATOMIC WEIGHTS.

		O = 16.	H = 1.			O = 16.	H = 1.
Aluminium	. Al	27·1	26·9	Molybdenum .	. Mo	96·0	95·3
Antimony .	. Sb	120·2	119·3	Neodymium .	. Nd	143·6	142·5
Argon . .	. A	39·9	39·6	Neon . .	. Ne	20·0	19·9
Arsenic . .	. As	75·0	74·4	Nickel . .	. Ni	58·7	58·3
Barium . .	. Ba	137·4	136·4	Nitrogen .	. N	14·04	13·93
Bismuth .	. Bi	208·5	206·9	Osmium . .	. Os	191·0	189·6
Boron . .	. B	11·0	10·9	Oxygen . .	. O	16·0	15·88
Bromine .	. Br	79·96	79·36	Palladium .	. Pd	106·5	105·7
Cadmium .	. Cd	112·4	111·6	Phosphorus .	. P	31·0	30·77
Cæsium . .	. Cs	133·0	132·0	Platinum . .	. Pt	194·8	193·3
Calcium .	. Ca	40·1	39·8	Potassium .	. K	39·15	38·86
Carbon . .	. C	12·00	11·91	Praseodymium	. Pr	140·5	139·4
Cerium . .	. Ce	140·0	139·0	Radium . .	. Ra	225·0	223·3
Chlorine .	. Cl	35·45	35·18	Rhodium . .	. Rh	103·0	102·2
Chromium .	. Cr	52·1	51·7	Rubidium .	. Rb	85·4	84·8
Cobalt . .	. Co	59·0	58·56	Ruthenium .	. Ru	101·7	100·9
Columbium (Niobium)	. Nb	94·0	93·3	Samarium .	. Sm	150·0	148·9
				Scandium .	. Sc	44·1	43·8
Copper . .	. Cu	63·6	63·1	Selenium . .	. Se	79·2	78·6
Erbium . .	. E	166·0	164·8	Silicon . .	. Si	28·4	28·2
Fluorine .	. F	19·0	18·9	Silver . . .	. Ag	107·93	107·12
Gadolinium .	. Gd	156·0	155·0	Sodium . .	. Na	23·05	22·88
Gallium .	. Ga	70·0	69·5	Strontium .	. Sr	87·6	86·94
Germanium .	. Ge	72·5	71·9	Sulphur . .	. S	32·06	31·83
Glucinum (Beryllium)	. Be	9·1	9·03	Tantalum .	. Ta	183·0	181·6
				Tellurium .	. Te	127·6	126·6
Gold . . .	. Au	197·2	195·7	Terbium . .	. Tb	160·0	158·8
Helium . .	. He	4·0	4·0	Thallium . .	. Tl	204·1	202·6
Hydrogen .	. H	1·008	1·0	Thorium . .	. Th	232·5	230·8
Indium . .	. In	114·0	113·1	Thulium . .	. Tm	171·0	169·7
Iodine . .	. I	126·85	125·90	Tin . . .	. Sn	119·0	118·1
Iridium . .	. Ir	193·0	191·5	Titanium . .	. Ti	48·1	47·7
Iron . . .	. Fe	55·9	55·5	Tungsten . .	. W	184·0	182·6
Krypton .	. Kr	81·8	81·2	Uranium . .	. U	238·5	236·7
Lanthanum .	. La	138·9	137·9	Vanadium .	. V	51·2	50·8
Lead . . .	. Pb	206·9	205·36	Xenon . . .	. X	128·0	127·0
Lithium . .	. Li	7·03	6·98	Ytterbium .	. Yb	173·0	171·7
Magnesium .	. Mg	24·36	24·18	Yttrium . .	. Yt	89·0	88·3
Manganese .	. Mn	55·0	54·6	Zinc . . .	. Zn	65·4	64·9
Mercury .	. Hg	200·0	198·5	Zirconium .	. Zr	90·6	89·9

Mitscherlich, so long ago as 1864, pointed out the similarity in the spectra of the chloride, bromide, and iodide of barium, and endeavoured to trace a connection with the molecular weights of these compounds. A comparison of the spectra of these compounds in Fig. 16 shows that the iodide lines are nearer the red than the bromide lines, and that these again are nearer the red than the lines of the chloride, roughly according to the increase in the atomic weight. M. Lecoq de Boisbaudran, in 1869, called attention to the spectra of the metals of the alkalies and alkaline earths, remarking that the spectrum of cæsium is like that of potassium shifted bodily towards the red. Hartley, in 1890, showed that three triplets in the spectrum of zinc corresponded with three triplets in the spectrum of cadmium, and that in each of these spectra the triplets have their lines equally spaced if mapped on the scale of oscillation frequency. Kayser and

Runge, in 1891, confirmed this statement, and pointed out many more triplets connected by the formula already given. They further call attention to the fact that the differences in oscillation frequency in the corresponding lines of the triplets increase with increase of atomic weight, and that they are nearly as the squares of the atomic weights. They also remark that in the spectra of potassium, rubidium, and cæsium, the differences in oscillation frequency between the close pairs of the subordinate series are nearly proportional to the squares of the atomic weights. These relationships are most clearly exhibited by plotting squares of atomic weights as ordinates and oscillation frequencies as abscissæ, that is, by making a diagram on squared paper (like Fig. 46), marking off a scale of oscillation frequencies on the bottom edge of the paper and a scale of squares of atomic weights along the left-hand edge, and marking down the positions of the lines of the spectra. Ramage, who has discussed these relationships in a paper communicated to the Royal Society (*Proc. Roy. Soc.*, 1901), has given such a diagram. He points out that the lines connecting corresponding points are nearly straight in the case of potassium, rubidium, and cæsium; and that the straight lines drawn through corresponding members of doublets and triplets in such cases as those of zinc and cadmium intersect on the line of zero atomic weight.

In cases where this law holds good we can, then, determine the atomic weight of an element from that of another, or from those of two others, if only we can be sure that the lines chosen are really homologous, or do really correspond to each other. Thus, for example, we may calculate the atomic weight of zinc from that of cadmium (112·4) by means of the corresponding triplets in the spectra of these two metals. The differences between the first and third lines of the triplets are as follows:—

	Cadmium.	Zinc.
3†	1713·0	578·7
4*	1701·3	571·0
4†	1711·2	578·5
5*	1699·3	575·8
5†	1713·0	578·6
6*	1704·0	576·4
6†	1713·2	579·2
7*	1704·7	579·2
7†	1664·9	586·4
8*	1639·4	546·3
8†	1700·5	578·1

We thus obtain the following values for the atomic weight of zinc:—

3†	65·33	6†	65·35
4*	65·12	7*	65·52
4†	65·35	7†	66·71
5*	65·43	8*	64·88
5†	65·32	8†	65·54
6*	65·37		

the mean of which is 65·45. The accepted value is 65·4.

A similar relationship holds—though not so exactly—between the pairs of lines in the subordinate series in the spectra of sodium, potassium, rubidium, and cæsium. The mean differences between the pairs are given by Kayser and Runge as follows:—

	Sodium.	Potassium.	Rubidium.	Cæsium.
Differences	172	568	2344	5450
Square roots	13·5	23·8	48·4	73·8

By multiplying these last numbers by 1·706 we obtain the numbers—

	23·0	40·6	82·6	126
Atomic weights . . .	23·05	39·15	85·4	133

If in the diagram drawn with atomic weights squared as ordinates, and oscillation frequencies as abscissæ, we join the corresponding lines of the spectra of potassium, rubidium, and cæsium, we see that these connecting lines are straight, or nearly so, and also that they are nearly parallel. If the lines *are* straight, we can calculate the atomic weight of one of three elements from those of the other two. For example, taking the convergence frequencies of the three elements mentioned (in the principal series) as being corresponding points, viz. 35085·9 for potassium, 33765·4 for rubidium, and 31465·8 for cæsium, we calculate from the atomic weight of potassium, 39·15, and that of cæsium, 133, what must be the atomic weight of rubidium, and find 86·17 : the correct value is 85·4.

Similar calculations can be made with calcium, strontium, and barium. The following lines in the arc-spectra lie on straight and nearly parallel lines :—

	Barium.	Strontium.	Calcium.
(a) . .	15387·0 (6r)	19387·7 (10)	21616·6 (1n)
(b) . .	17872·7 (4n)	22061·0 (6)	24390·0 (4n)
(c) . .	21951·2 (10r)	26975·9 (6n)	29735·8 (8n)
(d) . .	22979·0 (8r)	28176·9 (6n)	30991·1 (4n)
(e) . .	24200·7 (8r)	29399·4 (1n)	32228·6 (1n)

Taking the atomic weights of calcium and strontium as 40·1 and 87·6, we calculate the atomic weight of barium on the assumption that the points assumed to correspond in the three spectra have some physical connection, and that they do actually lie upon straight lines. We thus get by calculation for the atomic weight of barium—

From (a) 136·90
(b) 136·97
(c) 137·51
(d) 138·06
(e) 137·85

Mean, 137·46

The accepted value is 137·4.

Rydberg and Schuster's Rule.

A relationship existing between the convergence frequencies of the principal series and of the subordinate series was noticed independently by Professor Rydberg and by Professor Schuster. If we call the slowest vibration of a series the "fundamental" vibration, *i.e.* the one for which the value of n in Kayser and Runge's formulæ is 3, the convergence frequency of the principal series can be calculated—approximately, at least—from the fundamental vibration and from the convergence frequency of the subordinate series. The convergence frequencies of the two subordinate series are nearly the same; in the case of lithium they are 28586·7 and 28666·7. If to the mean of these numbers, viz. 28626·7, we add the fundamental oscillation frequency 14907·1, we obtain 43533·8, which is nearly the value of the observed convergence frequency of the principal series, viz. 43584·7. The rule may conveniently be expressed thus:—
$CF_p = CF_s + OF_r$, where CF_p means the convergence frequency of the principal series, CF_s the mean convergence frequency of the subordinate series, and OF_r the oscillation frequency of the fundamental vibration.

The following numbers for the metals of the alkalies show how far the law is accurate:—

Lithium . 28626·7+14907·1=43533·8   Observed CF_p 43584·7   Difference 50·9
Sodium . 24521·2+16968·8=41490·0   ,,   41536·8   ,,   46·8
Potassium 22035·1+13016·7=35051·8   ,,   35086·2   ,,   34·4
Rubidium 21059·4+12691·0=33750·4   ,,   33763·5   ,,   13·1

We cannot make the calculation in the case of cæsium, because the fundamental vibration lies in the infra-red, where no lines had been observed in 1896 when this rule was enunciated; but Professor Schuster ventured upon the prediction that infra-red lines of cæsium would be found with wave-lengths 8908 and 8518: possibly these are the lines since observed by Lehmann at 8949·9 and 8527·7. It will be noticed that the differences between the calculated and observed values decrease with increasing atomic weight.

No principal series is known in the other elements, but calculating from this rule we may form some idea as to whereabouts the principal series would terminate, and we find that in many cases it would lie far in the ultra-violet. Using the first lines of the triplets in magnesium, calcium, zinc, etc., we obtain the following approximate values of the convergence frequency of the principal series:—

Magnesium 59127
Calcium 50268
Zinc 63731
Cadmium 60459
Mercury 58530

A consideration of these numbers seems to show that magnesium will not go with zinc, cadmium, and mercury, but that it fits in best with calcium, strontium, and barium; and that lithium and sodium go together, but not with potassium, rubidium, and cæsium.

We have seen that in the case of the metals of the alkalies, and in the case of zinc and cadmium, the distances apart of corresponding lines are nearly as the squares of the atomic weights. But this rule certainly does not hold universally. It may be, however, that in other groups of related elements the distances apart of the lines of a pair (or triplet) are proportional to the atomic weight raised to some other power than *two* exactly. Thus for copper and silver the power would be about 2·4765, for magnesium, calcium, strontium, and barium, 1·6214, and for aluminium, gallium, indium, and thallium, 2·1127.

Runge and Precht express this by plotting as ordinates the logarithms of the atomic weights, and the logarithms of distances apart as abscissæ; then the points representing chemically related elements lie on the same straight line. This appears to be nearly (but again only *nearly*) true in many cases, and from this relationship we can obtain a formula for calculating the atomic weight from the separation of the lines of a pair (which we will call x).

Thus for the aluminium group we have the formula—the atomic weight is the number whose logarithm is the number we obtain by multiplying the logarithm of the separation by 0·47327 and adding 0·47185; or we may write the formula—atomic weight $= \log^{-1}(0·47185 + 0·473327 \log x)$. We thus obtain the following calculated values for the atomic weights:—

Boron	10·83	instead of	11
Aluminium	27·65	,,	27·1
Gallium	71·23	,,	70·0
Indium	113·54	,,	114·0
Thallium	206·04	,,	204·1

For the zinc and cadmium group the formula is—

Atomic weight $= \log^{-1}(0·54057 + 0·49285 \log x)$

This gives—

Beryllium	8·8	instead of	9·1
Zinc	65·4	,,	65·4
Cadmium	112·4	,,	112·4
Mercury	222·5	,,	200·0

For the magnesium calcium group the formula—

Atomic weight $= \log^{-1}(0·45705 + 0·57223 \log x)$

gives—

Beryllium	8·43	instead of	9·1
Magnesium	23·89	,,	24·36
Calcium	40·58	,,	40·1
Strontium	87·56	,,	87·6

For the copper silver group the formula—

Atomic weight $= \log^{-1}(0·83405 + 0·40378 \log x)$

gives—

Lithium	6·82	instead of	7·03
Copper	63·6	,,	63·6
Silver	107·93	,,	107·95
Gold	196·7	,,	197·2
Mercury	206·2	,,	200·0

Relationships in Spectra.

Mercury seems to fit in here better than with zinc and cadmium; lithium is included by putting log $x = 0$ on the supposition that the lines of lithium are doubles with an infinitesimal separation.

For the metals of the alkalies the formula—

$$\text{Atomic weight} = \log^{-1}(0.65284 + 0.53869 \log x)$$

gives—

Sodium	20·82 instead of	23·05
Potassium	39·62 ,,	39·15
Rubidium	85·02 ,,	85·4
Cæsium	133·94 ,,	133·0

Lithium would come out only 4·5.

These results would seem to confirm our previous conclusion that lithium and sodium will not go with potassium, rubidium, and cæsium; and that magnesium must be placed with calcium and strontium and not with zinc and cadmium.

Effect of Variations in Pressure and in Density of the exact Wave-lengths of Lines.

A comparison of the accurately measured wave-lengths of the same lines, as observed in the solar spectrum, and as produced in the spark and arc, reveals in nearly every case a slight difference, the lines in the arc and spark having a slightly greater wave-length than their corresponding reversals in the solar spectrum. The difference is in most cases extremely small, but there can be no doubt of its reality, and the matter becomes one of importance in view of the use of the Fraunhofer lines as standards of wave-length. If we use a line in the spark- or arc-spectrum for the purpose of comparison, and as a standard to measure other lines by, it is most important to know if its wave-length differs, even in the smallest degree, from that of the same line seen as a Fraunhofer line; and it may become necessary to look to the vacuum tube for lines of unalterable wave-length to serve as standards for the future. The following table showing the wave-lengths of some calcium lines in the arc, in the spark, and in the sun, will show the amount of difference which may exist :—

In the sun.	In the arc.	In the spark.
3737·06	3737·08	3737·25
	3706·18	3706·25
3181·39	3181·39	3181·51
3179·45	3179·48	3179·60
3159·00	3158·99	3159·11

It is clear, therefore, that the exact oscillation frequency (and consequently the wave-length) of a line depends upon the exact conditions under which the vibration takes place, an increase in density or an increase in pressure giving rise to slower vibrations, thus increasing the wave-length of the line.

The papers by Sir William and Lady Huggins, reprinted in the Appendix, show how greatly the appearance of the spectrum may be altered by changes in the amount of material present in the arc. An increase in the density of the vapour producing the lines in general increases their width: some broadening symmetrically, others more on the one side or the other, but generally most towards the red. Again, some lines easily become reversed; others are reversed with difficulty or not at all.

The effect of pressure upon the exact position of lines has been put to the test of direct experiment by Humphreys, by producing the arc in an enclosed space, into which air was pumped so as to obtain high pressure up to 13 or 14 atmospheres. The result of these experiments was to show that increase of pressure in almost every case caused a shift of the line towards the red end of the spectrum, the amount of which was proportional to the increase of pressure and to the wave-length, but that the amount of shift was very different for different elements, and even different for different sets of lines in the spectrum of one and the same element; thus in the alkalies the lines of the principal series and of the subordinate series are unequally shifted; these shifts (for equal wave-lengths) are to each other approximately as 1 : 2 : 4 for the principal, first subordinate, and second subordinate series respectively.

The calcium lines H and K are found to be affected by pressure only about half as much as the g calcium line at 4226·9; the metals cadmium and indium show the largest shift. The lines of banded spectra, such as those of cyanogen and of alumina, do not seem to be affected by pressure. The displacement of lines in the spark-spectrum towards the red is believed to be due to a high pressure in the metallic vapours thrown off from the electrodes with a high velocity in each discharge—a velocity estimated by Professor Schuster to be as high as 2000 metres per second. To account for the displacement of the spark lines on the basis of the measurements of pressure in the arc just described, a pressure of from 24 to 30 atmospheres must exist in the metallic vapours in the path of the spark. That a stream of sparks in a partially exhausted space does cause a sudden increase of pressure was shown directly by De la Rue and Miller so long ago as 1879.

The possibility of any difference between the wave-length of a line as produced in the arc, and that of the corresponding Fraunhofer line, was not taken into account by the late Professor Rowland in constructing his "Table of Standard Wave-lengths," which is given in the Appendix. Any such differences were supposed by him to be due to accidental movement of the apparatus when changing from the spectrum of the sun to that of the arc, and the wave-lengths of metallic lines read off on the "arc" photographs were corrected by means of the strong iron lines on the plate, so as to bring them into agreement with the measurements made in the solar spectrum. This is probably, in part, the explanation of certain differences between the numbers obtained for some bright cadmium and mercury lines by Messrs. Michelson and Fabry and Perot by the use of methods of interference not employing the concave grating, and Rowland's

Effects of Pressure and Density.

measurements of the same lines. By counting the number of interference fringes in the length of the standard metre at the Bureau des Poids et Mesures in Paris, formed in the red cadmium line and also in the green and blue lines, Michelson has obtained results which are probably correct to a few units in the thousandth place, and his result is thus more accurate than the best determination of wave-length made with any grating. Michelson's values for these three lines are 6438·472, 5085·824, and 4799·911; whereas Rowland's values are 6438·680, 5086·001, and 4800·097.*

It would appear that the values given in Rowland's Table for the standard lines in the arc have been "corrected" in a manner which cannot now be followed.

Messrs. Fabry and Perot have measured with their apparatus the wave-lengths of thirty-three solar lines. Their results are given in the following table, and Rowland's values for the same lines:—

Fabry and Perot.	Rowland.	Difference.	Ratio.
6471·666	6471·885	0·219	1·0000338
6408·027	6408·231	0·204	321
6335·346	6335·550	0·204	328
6322·700	6322·912	0·212	327
6230·746	6230·946	0·200	316
6065·506	6065·708	0·202	335
6016·650	6016·856	0·206	351
5987·081	5087·286	0·205	349
5934·666	5934·883	0·217	362
5862·368	5862·580	0·212	365
5763·004	5763·215	0·211	371
5715·095	5715·309	0·214	373
5506·794	5507·000	0·206	374
5497·536	5497·731	0·195	362
5434·544	5434·742	0·198	370
5409·800	5410·000	0·200	343
5367·485	5367·670	0·185	302
5171·622	5171·783	0·161	328
5080·787	5090·959	0·172	333
4923·943	4924·109	0·166	350
4859·758	4859·934	0·176	340
4783·449	4783·601	0·152	349
4643·483	4643·645	0·162	

If for any particular purpose it is important to have the true absolute wave-length of a line, then Rowland's numbers must be increased by from 0·15 to 0·2, but as in most work we want only relative values of the wave-lengths, the numbers of Rowland's Table given in the Appendix will still form the basis of reference. A comparison of the "ratios" given in the table shows that the *relative*

---

* M. Fabry points out (*Astrophysical Journal*, xix. p. 117, March, 1904) that the green cadmium line measured by Michelson in a cadmium vacuum tube *with electrodes* is a close doublet, but that in the tube *without electrodes* used by Hamy (*Comptes Rendus*, cxxx. p. 490, 1900), it appears as a triplet, and that these two observers have measured different lines.

values may be trusted to about 0·02, and when we require greater accuracy than this, it becomes necessary to take into account variations due to pressure, density, and other conditions of the source of light. It seems to be even more important to have a generally accepted standard than to have great accuracy in the absolute values.

We have seen that the spectrum of any particular metal is liable to considerable variation, according to the mode of its production, the temperature, and pressure of the luminous gas, the quantity of material present, or the density of the luminous gas, etc. Fig. 20 shows the different lengths of the lines of strontium, calcium, and aluminium in the arc-spectrum. It must be clearly understood that the *longest* lines are not necessarily the *strongest* lines. For example, the magnesium line 4481 is strong but short in the spark, and is absent from the arc (see Fig. 135); the blue lithium line at 4602·4 is strong but short. In the spark-spectrum of lead, the line 4058 is one of the longest lines, but quite faint; it is, however, the strongest line in the oxyhydrogen flame-spectrum, and one of the strongest lines in the arc-spectrum, and the reader can easily find other examples. If instead of taking the spark between electrodes of the metal, we use electrodes of platinum moistened with solutions of salts of the metals, we have generally a smaller number of lines, and it is observed that it is the short lines which are missing: those which persist are not the brightest lines, but the longest. The same thing is observed in using electrodes made of an alloy; the spectrum of a metal present in very small quantity, perhaps only as an impurity, is reduced to one or two of the longest lines. Thus cadmium, as an impurity in other metals, will be detected by the presence of the line 5086, the longest line in the spark-spectrum of cadmium.

When lines are reversed, it is always the longest lines which are reversed first. The two aluminium lines between H and K, shown in Fig. 20, are the longest, but not the strongest, lines in the spark-spectrum. They are the only aluminium lines reversed in the sun.

These observations show that the character of particular lines of a spectrum may be modified by the mere presence of other substances, without chemical action. The dilution of a gas with a large proportion of some other gas has the same effect as reducing the pressure, making the lines due to the first gas sharper, and, on the other hand, an increase in pressure or in quantity of material has the effect of expanding the lines. This may be easily observed with the spectrum of sodium in a Bunsen flame. In a mixture of gases, the molecules of any one gas come into collision with like molecules less frequently, and the effect is the same as if the gas were observed under conditions of reduced temperature or quantity of material. For further illustration of these points the reader is referred to the interesting papers by Sir W. Huggins reprinted in the Appendix.

When we compare together the spark and arc we see that in the middle of the spark we have only the longest lines, and at each pole, where the temperature is the highest and the density of the metallic vapours the greatest, we have the short lines, whereas in the middle

Nature of the Spark-discharge.

of the arc the density is greatest and the temperature highest. Consequently we get the long lines from the poles and the short lines from the centre of the arc.

The method of long and short lines cannot be used with the concave grating in consequence of its astigmatism—that is, that each point of the luminous object has for its image a line. The method is only available with prisms and plane gratings.

It was observed by Kirchhoff and by Thalen that certain changes could be produced in spark-spectra by inserting a wet string in the circuit containing the Leyden jar and spark-gap, so as to increase its resistance, or by causing the spark discharge to pass through the coils of an electro-magnet, which increases its self-induction.

The spark is a complicated phenomenon. When the difference of potential between the electrodes becomes great enough, there occurs a first brilliant flash, giving the air-spectrum; then the space between the electrodes becomes filled with metallic vapour, through which a series of oscillatory discharges takes place, giving rise to the metallic spectrum. Schenck, studying the effect of introducing self-induction into the circuit upon the lines of the cadmium spark, finds three sets of lines which behave differently. One set of lines (C), extending only a short distance from the poles, disappeared on the introduction of self-induction; they are none of them reversed, and they are absent from the arc-spectrum. The second set of lines (B) includes the rest of the "spark" lines—that is, lines absent from or weak in the arc-spectrum, though prominent in the spark-spectrum. Some of them extend right across the spark-gap, but they are only strong close to the poles. The effect of self-induction upon them is to cause them to shorten or disappear. The third set of lines (A) consists of the so-called arc-lines, including most of the lines which are common to both arc and spark. Some are extremely weak or absent in the spark, but strong in the arc. The effect of self-induction upon these lines is to make them approach more nearly to the condition in the arc. They extend right across the spark-gap with a self-induction which shortens the lines of group B close up to the poles, and are no doubt due to metallic vapour. The lines of groups A and B are due to the oscillatory discharge, the lines of group A, while partly due to the oscillations, are also caused by the metallic vapours filling up the gap, which retain their luminosity after the oscillations have ceased. By photographing with a revolving mirror, Schenck succeeded in showing that the "arc" lines in the spark persisted about twice as long as the "spark" lines, viz. about 0·00004 of a second.

CHAPTER XII.

BAND-SPECTRA.—SPECTRA OF COMPOUNDS.

WE have seen that the spectra of the elements usually consist of lines, and that there are some spectra—both emission and absorption spectra—which appear to be due to compounds; the diagrams of Fig. 16 show that the flame-spectra of the chlorides of barium, strontium, and calcium are complex, being made up partly of bands due to the undecomposed chloride, partly to the oxide of the metal, with only one or two lines which can be traced to the metal itself. In Fig. 26 we have a band-spectrum and a line-spectrum of sulphur, and we have many other examples. The spectra of " fluted bands," or " channelled spaces," when seen with small dispersion, are generally made up of bands sharply defined on the one side and gradually fading away upon the other. When seen with greater dispersion, each band is seen to be made up of a large number of very fine lines which come closer together as the sharp edge is approached. Of spectra in which the bands are sharp on the side towards the red (or least refracted side) and fade away towards the blue, we have examples in the spectrum of the Bunsen flame (the " Swan " spectrum), Fig. 16 (9), the nitrogen vacuum tube spectrum, Fig. 27 (1), the beautiful green band seen in the spectrum of burning magnesium, Fig. 23 (3), at 89, the bands of cyanogen, one of which is shown in the lower spectrum of Fig. 51 opposite the number 78 of the scale.

Band-spectra which show the opposite character, of sharp edges towards the violet and bands fading away towards the red, are more common; we have examples in copper oxide, Fig. 17 (1), manganese oxide, Fig. 17 (4), sulphur, Fig. 26 (2), aluminium oxide, bismuth oxide, chromium chloride, copper chloride, gold chloride, lead oxide, and the terrestrial bands in the solar spectrum due to oxygen and water vapour, Figs. 56 and 57, the absorption spectra of bromine, iodine vapour, iodine monochloride, and nitrogen peroxide.

It seems reasonable to suppose that band-spectra are due to more complex molecules than line-spectra. We know that sulphur vapour at a low temperature has a higher specific gravity than when it is raised to a much higher temperature, and that consequently at the low temperature the molecule is more complex, and also that at very high temperatures the molecules of iodine vapour become dissociated.

Many attempts have been made to discover some law of the distribution of the lines which make up these band-spectra. That there is *some* law underlying the arrangement no one who studies such photographs as those of the Fraunhofer groups A and B in Figs. 56 and 57 can possibly doubt. In the same way as the lines of one of Kayser and Runge's series approach closer and closer together up to the convergence frequency, so the lines of a band seem to get closer and closer together till they combine to form the bright edge of the band. Deslandres has proposed a formula of the form $\lambda^{-1} = A + Bm^2$, where m has in succession the values 0, 1, 2, 3, 4, 5, etc., and Kayser and Runge have found such a law verified in their measurements of the lines of the cyanogen spectrum forming the bands beginning at 4606·3, 4216·1, and 3883·5 (see Fig. 51).

Thiele [*] has undertaken a very laborious research with the object of finding a satisfactory formula, and adopts $\lambda = f[(n + c)^2]$, where c is the same for any series ("the phase"), and n has the values 1, 2, 3, 4, 5, etc. f is some function of $(n + c)^2$, and if n be given successively all real integral values will have a maximum value at $\lambda = f(0)$, where the lines unite to form an edge, or "head," and a minimum value at $\lambda = f(\infty)$, where there should be a crowding of lines together to form a "tail."

Professor Thiele has tested his formula on the brightest band of the "Swan" spectrum, that shown at 76 in Fig. 16 (9), with "heads" at 5165·3, 5129·4, 5100(?), 5067, and 5050, and regards the correspondence between calculated and observed values as satisfactory. Professor King [†] by long exposure on an arc between poles of pure carbon has discovered some new cyanogen bands at 3465·7 and 3203·8, which appear to be really the "tails" corresponding to the heads at 3883·55 and 3590·52 respectively.

The history of the "Swan" spectrum is interesting. It was first observed by Wollaston in 1802, but first described by Swan in 1857, and was considered by him to be due to a hydrocarbon. Plücker and Hittorf give a fine coloured representation of it in the Philosophical Transactions of 1865. Attfield came to the conclusion that the spectrum was that of carbon, since it was common to compounds of carbon with hydrogen, nitrogen, oxygen, and sulphur.

Morren undertook experiments to prove that Attfield was wrong, but became convinced that he was right. Morren particularly describes the brilliant spectrum produced by burning cyanogen with oxygen. Dibbits arrived at the same conclusion. In answer to the objection raised that carbon in the state of vapour could not exist in the flame of a candle or that of a Bunsen burner, Dibbits argues that carbon exists in combination with hydrogen in the gas which is burnt, and after the combustion that carbon is in combination with oxygen, and during the chemical change it may have existed as uncombined carbon; a flame of carbonic oxide does not show the spectrum because the carbon was already combined with oxygen.

In the case of cyanogen the carbon is at first combined with

---

[*] *Astrophysical Journal*, vi. p. 65 (1897).　[†] *Ibid.*, xiv. p. 322 (1901).

nitrogen, and after the combustion it is combined with oxygen, and so the same explanation applies. This spectrum is obtainable not only from flames but also by means of the spark in different gases containing carbon, either at atmospheric pressure or under reduced pressure in vacuum tubes. Thus it is given by the spark discharge in cyanogen, carbonic oxide, naphthalin, carbon disulphide, carbon tetrachloride, olefiant-gas, coal-gas, benzene, chloroform, aniline, ethylene dibromide, ethyl bromide, etc. These substances have only carbon in common, and unless the experiments are vitiated by impurities, the conclusion is irresistible that the spectrum in question is due to carbon itself, and not to any compound of carbon. In 1875 a paper by Ångström and Thalén was published, in which they maintained that the spectrum was due to a hydrocarbon. They seem to have been led to this conclusion by the resemblance of the spectrum to the spectra of metallic oxides. Their theory was adopted and maintained by Professors Liveing and Dewar, who observed the electric arc between carbon poles in various gases, such as air, hydrogen, nitrogen, chlorine, carbonic oxide, nitric oxide, and ammonia. They found the Swan spectrum well seen in the arc in hydrogen, but less strong when the arc was taken in chlorine or nitrogen, but it seemed to be *present whatever the atmosphere*. They account for this by the difficulty of completely removing all traces of hydrogen from the carbon electrodes.

Lockyer, observing the electric discharge in the vapour of carbon tetra-chloride, found that it gave the Swan spectrum brightly, although there was no sign of the hydrogen lines. Liveing and Dewar found that the Swan spectrum was always to be seen in the spark between electrodes close together in the saturated vapour freed from moisture and air. Professors Liveing and Dewar, later on, and in consequence of their own further experiments, abandoned the view that the Swan spectrum depended upon the presence of hydrogen. The temperature of the arc is supposed to be about 3500° C., and Moissan has shown that carbon is distinctly volatile at that temperature. The flame of cyanogen in oxygen is the hottest flame known (except perhaps the flame of cyanogen in nitric oxide), and is far above 3500°, and Liveing and Dewar admit that carbon vapour may exist in a cyanogen flame.

Those who attribute the Swan spectrum to carbon, after having had to contend against the hypothesis that it is due to a compound with hydrogen—an hypothesis abandoned by the very chemists who supported it so strongly—now find themselves called upon to contend against a new theory advanced by Professor Smithells (on the suggestion of the late Sir G. G. Stokes), that the spectrum under discussion is due to a compound of carbon and oxygen. Professor Smithells has, with much skill, constructed a defence of his position, based for the most part upon a study of the phenomena of flames. He seeks to set aside the natural conclusion to be drawn from the repeated observations of the Swan spectrum in carbon compounds not containing oxygen, by the suggestion that it is impossible to free these substances from impurities, water, etc., containing oxygen. He is "distrustful of conclusions based upon the supposed purity of the substances submitted to examination in highly exhausted Plücker tubes. The difficulty of removing films of air or moisture from glass, the occlusion of gases by electrodes, the oxidizing character of glass itself, all form well-recognized difficulties quite apart from the purely chemical difficulties in obtaining pure materials," and in this distrust all spectroscopists will share. It is true that sometimes in vacuum tubes the brightest part of the spectrum may be due to some substance present in very small quantity, as, for example, mercury in any tube exhausted by means of a mercury pump, but it would seem that the circumstances are altogether different when the spark is taken in gases at ordinary pressure, and still more so in the spark taken in liquids.

To assume that in these cases the spectrum seen is always due to the substance present in the smallest quantity seems a rather extreme hypothesis, and the number of carbon compounds which do not contain oxygen (or which ought not to contain oxygen), and which still give the Swan spectrum more brightly than anything else, is so large, that the conclusion naturally to be drawn from this accumulation of evidence will seem to most people to be that first drawn by Attfield.

Some recent unpublished observations by the author on the spark in liquids seem to him to confirm the conclusion. Most of these liquids offer so much resistance to the passage of the spark that it is only possible to employ a very minute spark; but when platinum electrodes, only a fraction of a millimetre apart, are used, there is no difficulty in obtaining a spectrum, the discharge being attended by rapid decomposition with separation (in most cases) of carbon, so that there is sometimes only a very brief time in which the spectrum can be seen.

Thus the spark in chloroform (the purest that could be obtained) rapidly decomposes it with separation of solid carbon and evolution of torrents of hydrochloric acid. The carbon so rapidly obscured the spectrum that it was found better to arrange a continuous flow of fresh chloroform, which carried the carbon with it. The electrodes were heated red-hot inside the liquid before the observation was made, but although the experiment was made many times, nothing but a brilliant Swan spectrum was ever observed. The same spectrum was obtained from the spark in the following liquids, in each case as pure as could be obtained:—benzene, naphthalene, aniline, ethylene dibromide, ethyl bromide. In these cases we see the decomposition of the liquid into carbon and something else going on all the time, and it seems impossible to resist the conclusion that the spectrum which they all give is that of the only element common to all, that is, carbon.

By the Swan spectrum in these experiments is meant the spectrum shown in Fig. 16 (9), but in certain cases, more particularly when cyanogen is used, or when the arc is taken in air or nitrogen, certain other bands appear which are generally admitted to be due to a compound of carbon and nitrogen. These are—in the visible spectrum—a band of seven edges from 4600 to 4500, which we will call ζ, a band of six edges from 4216 to 4158, which we will call θ, a band of four edges from 3884 to 3855, which we will call ι, and in the ultra-violet other bands observable in photographs at 3590·5, 3361. An interesting experiment which shows the dependence of some of these bands on the presence of nitrogen may be made by taking a very short spark in liquid absolute alcohol. This yields the Swan spectrum brilliantly, but the groups ζ and θ are not seen. On adding a little strong ammonia the group θ comes out very bright and also ζ less brilliantly.

There are two other spectra given by carbon compounds under certain circumstances. One of these is generally admitted to be the spectrum of an oxide of carbon. It is given by a vacuum tube containing carbon monoxide, carbon dioxide, olefiant-gas, coal-gas, or benzene, if no special precautions are taken to exclude oxygen. It consists of about six bands at about 6060, 5610, 5198, 4837, 4509, and 4395. A vacuum tube filled with purified benzene, and containing pieces of bright metallic sodium, showed this spectrum at first, but after heating the sodium the spectrum had completely disappeared, and the tube showed the spectrum of hydrogen. On introducing a little oxygen into the tube, by heating a fragment of potassium chlorate wrapped up in platinum foil which had been previously introduced into the tube, this spectrum of carbon oxide at once comes out.

The third spectrum is produced by the spark with jar in carbon monoxide or carbon dioxide at the ordinary pressure. It is not unlike the spectrum of air shown in Fig. 17 (9), but the lines are quite different. The chief features of the spectrum are a double red line close to the red hydrogen line, a double green line at 5152 and 5145, and a strong broad line in the violet at 4267, besides some lines in the ultra-violet. This spectrum is, no doubt, the *line* spectrum of carbon.

Since the Swan spectrum and the spectrum of cyanogen have been observed in comets and in some stars, the question of their chemical parentage becomes one of cosmical importance.

CHAPTER XIII.

THE SPECTROHELIOGRAPH-ELECTRO-MAGNETIC THEORY OF LIGHT.—THE "ZEEMAN EFFECT."

An important achievement of recent years is the taking of photographs of the Sun's disc at any time by means of the monochromatic light of any given substance, *e.g.*, of calcium or of hydrogen. This is accomplished by means of the spectroheliograph. This instrument, the invention of Professor Hale of the Yerkes Observatory, was first used at the Kenwood Observatory in 1891, with a 12-inch equatorial refractor, but a much larger instrument has been made for the great 40-inch telescope of the Yerkes Observatory, which gives an image of the Sun seven inches in diameter, and with this instrument Professor Hale now photographs the Sun, with all its spots and faculæ and surrounded by all its prominences, in a few minutes at any time, whereas formerly we had to wait for the rare occurrence of a total eclipse in order to see or to study the prominences. Other instruments of the kind are those of M. Deslandres at the Observatory of Meudon, of Dr. Kempf at the Potsdam Observatory, and at the South Kensington Observatory under the charge of Sir Norman Lockyer, and other important observatories will shortly be supplied with similar instruments. The principle of the method may be explained thus :—Across the image of the Sun formed by the telescope a slit is made to travel at a uniform rate by means of an electric motor, and an image of the light passing through this slit is formed by a spectroscope and thrown on a photographic plate, in front of which a second slit is made to travel at the same rate as the first, being driven by the same motor. If we suppose the first slit to be illuminated by monochromatic light, then in passing through the spectroscope it would suffer no deviation, we should simply get an image of the first slit on the plate ; and if the second slit is adjusted in the right position, we should get a photograph of the Sun's disc taken in successive slices. Of course, the first image is *not* monochromatic, but the spectroscope sends all the light not of the exact wave-length for which the instrument is adjusted elsewhere than through the second slit, and it is not admitted to the plate. If the adjustment has been made for the H or K line, we obtain a photograph of the incandescent calcium vapour forming part of the Sun's surface, and so for any other substance or line which is selected.

166   *An Introduction to the Study of Spectrum Analysis.*

The ordinary visual spectrum of the faculæ shows the H and K bands reversed by a thin bright line running down the centre of each. This indicates the presence at a high level of calcium vapour at a higher temperature than that of the reversing layer below.

Fig. 124 shows the spectroheliograph of the Yerkes telescope, and Fig. 125 is a copy of a photograph of a sun-spot made by means of it.

In Fig. 121 we have a photograph showing the bands and widened lines in the spectrum of a sun-spot; the most conspicuous group in Fig. 1 is the "little *b*" group, as may be seen by a comparison of this photograph with Fig. 51.

FIG. 124.—Spectroheliograph attached to 40-inch Yerkes refractor.

In February, 1894, a most remarkable disturbance of the usual conditions of the Sun's reversing layer was recorded accidentally in a series of photographs reproduced in Fig. 126, in which the broad shading of the H and K lines usually attributed to calcium actually disappeared for a short time. In photograph No. 1 the dark streak is the spectrum of a spot, in which the H and K lines may be seen to be reversed on the spot-band. A few moments later the spectrum had changed to that shown in No. 2, the broad shading of H and K has almost disappeared, the spot-streak is very faint in their neighbourhood, there are two very conspicuous bright lines at 3884·64 and 3896·21, and there are other changes. After a very short time the spectrum had returned to its normal condition, as shown in

No. 4. Such an extraordinary change involves an area of the Sun's surface round the spot of a diameter of one-eighth of the Sun's diameter, and there does not appear to be any record of any similar occurrence.

Electro-magnetic Theory of Light—the "Zeeman Effect."

Light is now known to be closely connected with electricity and magnetism. The first experimental observation of such a connection was made by Faraday so long ago as 1845, when he showed that a cube of a certain heavy glass (lead borate) when placed

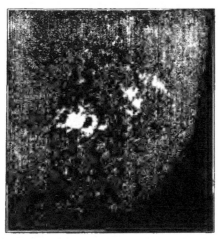

FIG. 125.—Sun-spot of March 6, 1900.
(*Photographed with the Yerkes spectroheliograph.*)

between the poles of a powerful electro-magnet and examined by means of polarized light sent through it, rotated the plane of polarization of the light when the magnet was excited, the direction of the rotation being the same as the direction of the electric current which excited the magnetism.*

According to the electro-magnetic theory of light of Clerk Maxwell, put forward in 1867, the waves of light are not due simply to mechanical vibrations of the ether, but depend upon electrical and magnetic vibrations at right angles to each other, and at right angles to the direction of propagation of the light-wave. Faraday's experiment of the rotation of the plane of polarization in a transparent

* It is worthy of record that Faraday thought it possible that the bright lines of a spectrum might be affected by a magnetic field, and in the last experimental research that he made he tried the effect on the sodium lines in a flame placed between the poles of an electro-magnet, but without observing any change.

diamagnetic medium implies the molecular rotation of the ether. Plane polarized light may be resolved into two components of circularly polarized light, one rotating *with*, the other *against* the ether. If the diamagnetic medium absorbs only one wave-length, thus producing a single dark line, then when the magnetic field is excited the absorption of the one component will be of a wave-length *greater*, and of the other component of a wave-length *less*, than if the magnetic field did not exist. The dark line thus becomes split up into two. This is known as the "Zeeman effect," as first observed by Professor Zeeman in 1896. To observe these effects very powerful magnetic fields are necessary, and also a spectroscope of great dispersion. The most efficient form of spectroscope is the "echelon" grating, to be presently described. The appearance of the lines will be different according as they are seen in the direction of the lines of force, or at right angles to them. Since the effect of the magnetic field is an acceleration in the one direction, and a retardation in the other, round the lines of force, when viewed in the direction of the lines of force the result will be that the two components are circularly polarized in opposite directions, and if they then pass through a quarter-wave plate to convert them into plane polarized light, and then through a Nicol's prism, the spectroscope will show a displacement in the issuing light on turning on the current. The direction of rotation of the accelerated component is the same as that of the magnetizing current, because in the magnetic field the molecules are rotated round the lines of force in this direction. If light consists in the motion of electrically charged particles about a position of equilibrium, their motion can be resolved into three components, one in the direction of the lines of force, and two others at right angles to the lines of force, and these last can be resolved either into right-handed or left-handed rotations. The magnetic field acts only on these last, and according to the direction of their motion and the nature of the charge, whether positive or negative, they are pressed towards or drawn from the position of equilibrium, and there results either an increase or decrease in oscillation frequency. The observation that the accelerated component has the same direction of rotation as the magnetizing current leads to the conclusion that the particles are negatively charged. At right angles to the lines of force the edges of the bands are plane polarized, the plane of polarization being parallel to the lines of force, since the vibrations are at right angles to the lines of force. Zeeman concludes that, seen at right angles to the lines of force, a line in the spectrum should be resolved into a triplet, the central component of the triplet corresponding to vibrations in the same direction as the lines of force, while the two outer components correspond to the vibrations at right angles to the lines of force, and he actually observed this to happen with the sodium D lines, in 1896. Zeeman, in 1898, observed that the splitting up of the different lines in the same spectrum is very different in the same magnetic field. In the zinc spectrum the components of the lines marked † are

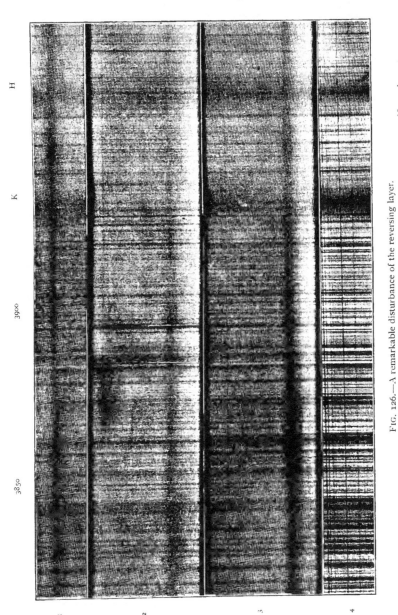

Fig. 126.—A remarkable disturbance of the reversing layer. 1. Spectrum just before the disturbance. 2. "Abnormal" spectrum. 3. "Intermediate" spectrum. 4. Normal spectrum.

widely separated, whilst those of the lines marked * are hardly perceptibly divided.

Upon further examination it appeared that the phenomena were more complicated than at first supposed. Michelson showed that the middle component of the triplet into which any spectral line becomes resolved in a magnetic field was itself a symmetrical triplet, that the relative intensity of the components varies for different substances and for different lines of the same substance, so that the appearance may be that of a single line, a double line, or a triplet; the outer lines are unsymmetrical, but symmetrically placed with respect to the central line; their intensities vary so that the outer groups may present the appearance of single, double, or multiple lines. In the sodium spectrum the least refrangible of the yellow lines is split up into four components, and the most refrangible line into six components; in the first case the central line of the normal triplet becomes doubled, and in the second case each line of the triplet becomes doubled.

Still more complicated effects have been observed in the spectra of mercury, zinc, cadmium, magnesium, etc. It is a most interesting fact that the homologous lines of related elements whose wave-lengths can be calculated from the formulæ of Kayser and Runge seem, generally, to be affected in the same way by the magnetic field, and that in the same spectrum the lines of the first subordinate series are affected differently from those of the second subordinate series. The different behaviour of some lines of mercury is shown in Fig. 127, reproduced by the kind permission of Professors Runge and Paschen. The line 5461·0 is seen to be resolved into nine lines, of which the three in the centre are polarized in one plane, and the outer six are polarized in a plane at right angles to the first three. This is the first line of the triplet in the second subordinate series for which $n = 3$. The second line of this triplet, 4358·6, is resolved into four lines; the line 4046·8 is not one of the series lines, it is resolved simply into three lines.

Preston has observed that the separation of the components bears the same ratio to the square of the wave-length in the corresponding series-lines in the same element, and that this remains the same for corresponding lines in the homologous spectra of allied elements.

The pairs of lines in copper and silver show the same behaviour as the two sodium D lines, except that it is the line of *less* wave-length which is split up into four like D_1, and the other line of the pair which is split up into six like D_2.

The wave-lengths of the components of D_1 are 5898·01, 5897·09, 5895·26, and 5894·28 in a certain field, and the components of D_2 in the same field, 5892·55, 5891·54, 5890·66, 5889·72, 5888·76, and 5887·91.

In the case of the mercury line, 5461, shown in Fig. 127 in a field of about 24600 C.G.S. units, the components had the wave-lengths 5461·61, 5461·45, 5461·29, 5461·13, 5460·97, 5460·81, 5460·65, 5460·48, and 5460·32. There appears to be no splitting up

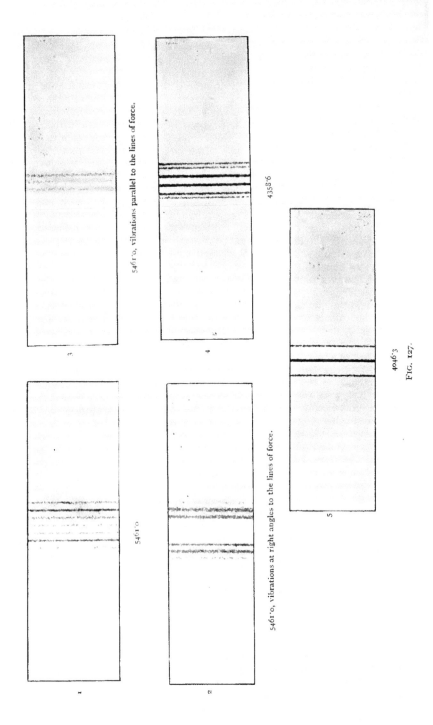

5461·0, vibrations parallel to the lines of force.

4358·6

5461·0

5461·0, vibrations at right angles to the lines of force.

4046·3

FIG. 127.

of the *bands* of mercury or of those of nitrogen or of cyanogen in the magnetic field.

Professor Lorentz has given a theory which goes far towards explaining the Zeeman effect. He assumes that in the luminous gas minute electrically charged particles of definite mass and charge are present, and that the vibrations of the light emitted are determined by the vibrations of these particles. The assumption that every molecule of a source of light contains one such electron vibrating about a position of equilibrium, and always driven back to that position by a force proportional to the displacement, leads to the conclusion that a single line will be tripled by the action of a magnetic field if viewed at right angles to the lines of force, and will be doubled if viewed along the lines of force, and further, that the components will be polarized in the manner observed. Professor Zeeman gives the following account of the theory:—
" Imagine an observer looking at a flame placed in a magnetic field in a direction such that the lines of force run towards or from him. Let us suppose that the observer could see the actual ions as they are revolving; then the following will be remarked: There are some ions moving in circles and hence emitting circularly polarized light; if the motion is round in the positive direction, the period will be longer than with no magnetic field; if in the negative direction, shorter. There will also be ions seemingly stationary and really moving parallel to the lines of force with unaltered period. In the third place there are ions which seem to move in slowly rotating elliptical orbits."

But this original theory of Lorentz does not account for the more complicated phenomena which have since been observed, and in a later paper Lorentz modifies the theory by substituting for the single electron a system of electrically charged particles having more than three degrees of freedom, viz. as many as the components observed in the magnetic field.

CHAPTER XIV.

THE MICHELSON ECHELON DIFFRACTION GRATING.

THE echelon diffraction grating was the result of endeavours on the part of its inventor to obtain means of higher resolution of the spectrum than were at the time available. Trains of prisms have, of course, long been superseded where high resolving power was desired, recourse being had to ruled diffraction gratings, of which those ruled on Professor Rowland's engine hold a monopoly of the field.

The resolving power of a spectroscope must be clearly distinguished from its dispersion. The latter is a measure of the angular separation produced between two given monochromatic rays, while the former is a measure of the number of monochromatic rays which it is possible to distinguish as separate between two given monochromatic rays, and is the really important criterion of the power of the instrument. For it must be remembered that the image produced by a telescope—the termination of every spectroscope—is not the indefinitely thin line given by the construction of geometrical optics, but one of appreciable breadth, shading off to darkness on each side. The smaller the aperture of the telescope (as limited either by the diameter of its own object glass or by the width of the beam of light from the prism or grating system) the broader do the lines become. If then the wave-lengths of two rays differ by so little that these lines overlap with a particular aperture, an increase of aperture alone, provided it be sufficiently great, is sufficient to separate these rays.

The resolving power of a grating can then be indefinitely increased by ruling lines over a wider area without alteration in the number of lines to the millimetre, for the effective aperture being increased the spectral lines become finer and hence separable. The resolving power is in fact proportional to the length of ruling—that is, to the travel of the grating plate during the cutting.

Unfortunately the difficulties of cutting accurate gratings increase very rapidly as the length of ruling increases, so that gratings with 5 or 6-inch ruled surfaces are the biggest that can be obtained, and even these are very difficult to get.

There is another way of getting higher resolving power. The resolving power is given by the product $m\,n$, where m is the order

The Michelson Echelon Diffraction Grating.

of spectrum observed and n the number of elements of which the grating is composed—the number of divisions, that is, in the case of ruled gratings.

With the ordinary form of grating the intensity rapidly diminishes as the order is raised; but if a grating could be constructed to throw most of the light in one of the high orders the desired object would be attained.

The device which was first suggested by Michelson to obtain this result was as follows :—

Let a number of plates of silvered glass of equal thickness, t, be superposed, each projecting beyond the last by an equal amount in such a manner as to form a series of steps, as shown in Fig. 128.

If then a beam of "parallel" light be incident in the direction of the arrows, it will be reflected from the successive steps, and the reflected beam will consist of a number of beams reflected from the first, second, third, etc., plates, whose retardations behind that reflected

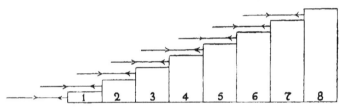

FIG. 128.—Reflection echelon.

from the first plate will be o, t, $2t$, $3t$, etc. They will, in fact, be in the requisite relation to produce, when brought to a focus by a lens, diffraction spectra of the light source.

If t be taken equal to 10 mm. the orders of spectra observed would be in the neighbourhood of the 34,000th, so that five plates would give a resolving power greater than that of a 10-inch grating in the first order.

It is, however, unnecessary to go into the analytical expressions for this form, as it has not yet been found possible to manufacture it. The accuracy required in the parallelism of the plates in order for the grating to perform in accordance with the theoretical expressions of its capabilities would be such, for one of ten plates, that no differences in thickness should exist among the different plates so great as one-twentieth of a wave-length of light, that is, so great as one-millionth of an inch. This, in itself, is not outside the limits of possible accuracy; it is, in fact, reached in some of the echelons made by Mr. Hilger. But the plates must lie on each other in perfect contact —no gap existing between even the extreme edges of successive plates of as much as the quantity stated above, and this is the difficulty which has not yet been surmounted.

The form which has been manufactured with success, and which is now well known as the echelon grating, is Professor Michelson's modification of his original idea, an account of which he published in the *Astrophysical Journal* for June, 1898, and subsequently in the *Journal de Physique*, 3rd series, tome viii., 1899.

It is from these sources that the following analytical investigations are taken.

The arrangement, which is illustrated in Fig. 129, consists, like that described above, of plates of parallel glass of equal thickness superposed in step form : but the glass is not silvered, and the beam of

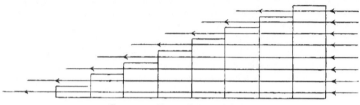

FIG. 129.—Transmission echelon.

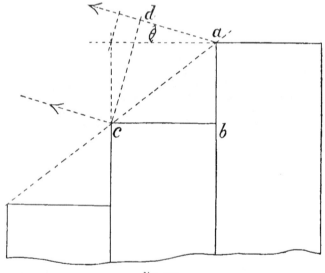

FIG. 130.

light passes through the mass, emerging at the exposed surfaces of the plates.

The beam of parallel light is produced by a collimator, and the light is received in a telescope.

The beams emerging from the various apertures will then be relatively retarded by successively equal amounts, and will produce spectra by interference in much the same way as in the case of the reflection form in Fig. 128.

Theory of the Echelon.

Suppose a beam of "parallel" homogeneous light be incident normal to the plates.

Let t = thickness of the plates ($b\,c$, Fig. 130).

s = width of the steps ($a\,b$, Fig. 130).

λ = wave-length of the light under consideration.

μ = refractive index of the glass for light of wave-length λ.

m = retardation in terms of λ between rays emerging at an angle of diffraction θ from corresponding points (such as a and c, Fig. 130) of successive elements.

n = number of elements.

Then (see Fig. 130)—

$$m\lambda = \mu t - ad$$
$$= \mu t - t\cos\theta + s\sin\theta$$

Since the values of θ which are of interest are very small, this may be written—

(1) $\qquad m\lambda = (\mu - 1)t + \theta s$

Differentiating with respect to λ, m constant, and rearranging the terms—

$$\frac{d\theta_1}{d\lambda} = \frac{1}{s}\left(m - t\frac{d\mu}{d\lambda}\right)$$

or, substituting for m its approximate value $(\mu - 1)\dfrac{t}{\lambda}$

(2) $\qquad \dfrac{d\theta_1}{d\lambda} = \dfrac{t}{s\lambda}\left[(\mu - 1) - \lambda\dfrac{d\mu}{d\lambda}\right]\;\cdot\;\cdot\;\cdot\;$ (*dispersion*)

$\qquad\qquad\quad = \dfrac{bt}{s\lambda}$

The value of the co-efficient b can be found for any wave-length from the optical constants for the glass used (it is between 0·5 and 1·0 for most glasses), and the equation (2) will then give the angular dispersion $d\theta_1$ between two homogeneous radiations whose wave-lengths differ by a small amount $d\lambda$.

Differentiating (1) with respect to m, λ constant, and rearranging the terms—

$$\frac{d\theta}{dm} = \frac{\lambda}{s}$$

Putting $dm = 1$, and representing the corresponding change in θ by $d\theta_2$, then—

(3) $\qquad d\theta_2 = \dfrac{\lambda}{s}\;\cdot\;\cdot\;\cdot\;$ (*separation of spectra*)

Equation (3) gives the angular separation between two successive orders of spectra.

Let $d\theta_3$ represent the angular limit of resolution of the echelon, *i.e.* the angular separation of two spectral lines when they are just distinguishable as separate in the eyepiece of the telescope. By the well-known rule (see Lord Rayleigh on Wave Theory, "Encyclopædia Britannica")—

$$(4) \quad d\theta_3 = \frac{\lambda}{\text{effective aperture of telescope object-glass}}$$
$$= \frac{\lambda}{ns} = \frac{d\theta_2}{n}$$

Let $d\lambda_3$ be the difference of wave-length corresponding to the angle $d\theta_3$.

Then from (2)—

$$\frac{d\theta_3}{d\lambda_3} = \frac{bt}{s\lambda}$$

or, substituting $\frac{\lambda}{ns}$ for $d\theta_3$ and rearranging terms—

$$(4a) \quad \frac{d\lambda_3}{\lambda} = \frac{\lambda}{bnt} \quad \cdots \quad (\textit{limit of resolution})$$

$d\lambda_3$ in the above represents the difference of wave-length corresponding to the angle $d\theta_3$, *i.e.* the difference of wave-lengths of the closest separable pair of homogeneous rays; and the ratio $\frac{\lambda}{d\lambda_3}$ is hence the resolving power of the echelon. This is, it will be seen, proportional to the total thickness of glass traversed, and for a given wave-length is independent of the thickness of plates or width of step.

The brilliancy of any line seen with the echelon depends not only on the intrinsic intensity of the radiation, but also on the angle of diffraction, θ. The co-efficient which depends on θ, and which may be called the intensity of illumination, is—

$$(5) \quad I = \left[\frac{\sin \pi \frac{s}{\lambda} \theta}{\pi \frac{s}{\lambda} \theta} \right]^2$$

Application of the Foregoing Expressions to an Actual Case.

The echelon whose performance will be investigated is one made by Mr. Hilger for Dr. Hauswaldt, of Magdeburg; the quantities being as follows:—

Thickness of plates, $t =$ about 10 mm.
Width of steps, $s =$ 1 mm.

The Michelson Echelon Diffraction Grating.

Refractive index of the glass—

$$\mu_c = 1{\cdot}5706$$
$$\mu_D = 1{\cdot}5746$$
$$\mu_F = 1{\cdot}5845$$
$$\mu_{G1} = 1{\cdot}5927$$

Whence $\dfrac{d\mu}{d\lambda}$ for wave-length 5890 (D) $= -7{\cdot}19 \times 10^{-6}$, λ being in 10^{-10} metres.

Number of elements, $n = 21$.

(It is to be noted that when a clear aperture of 1 mm. is left beyond the width of the largest plate, the number of apertures operative in the formation of the spectrum is one more than the number of plates. It is this number of apertures which is denoted by n.)

The Dispersion.

From (2), p. 177—

$$\frac{d\theta_1}{d\lambda} = \frac{bt}{s\lambda}, \text{ where } b = (\mu - 1) - \lambda\frac{d\mu}{d\lambda}$$

Substituting for μ, λ, and $\dfrac{d\mu}{d\lambda}$, their values for D,

$$b_D = 0{\cdot}575 + 0{\cdot}042$$
$$= 0{\cdot}617$$

Hence $\dfrac{d\theta_1}{d\lambda} = 0{\cdot}00105$ in the region of D.

Putting $d\lambda = 0{\cdot}1$, $d\theta_1 = 0{\cdot}000105$ radian, or $0{\cdot}37$ minute of arc.

This being, then, the dispersion between two rays which differ in wave-length by one-tenth of an Ångström unit.

The Separation of Successive Orders of Spectra.

From (3), p. 177, the angular separation of successive orders, denoted by $d\theta_2 = \dfrac{\lambda}{s}$

Hence for D—

$$d\theta_2 = 5{\cdot}89 \times 10^{-4} \text{ radians,}$$
or 2 minutes of arc.

The successive orders are, then, very close together, and an auxiliary spectroscope is necessary for preliminary analysis of the light; only a very restricted portion of the spectrum under observation being thrown on the slit of the echelon spectroscope.

The Angular Limit of Resolution.

From (4), p. 178, the angular separation of two lines which are just distinguishable as separate, denoted by $d\theta_3$, $= \dfrac{d\theta_2}{n}$.

Hence for D—

$$d\theta_3 = \frac{d\theta_2}{21} = \text{(for D) } 0\cdot 095 \text{ minute of arc}$$

From (4a), p. 178, the difference of wave-length necessary between two homogeneous radiations in order to distinguish them as separate, denoted by $d\lambda_3$,

$$= \frac{\lambda^2}{but} = \text{(for D)} \frac{5890^2}{0\cdot 617 \times 21 \times 10^8} \text{ Ångström units}$$

$$= 0\cdot 027 \text{ Ångström units}$$

It must be noted that one can determine the *displacement* of a single ray more readily than one can separate the components of a close doublet. In fact, a shift of a line of as little as one-tenth the angular limit of resolution can be detected. (See "Le Phénomène de Zeeman."—A. Cotton, p. 15.)

The Effect of Alteration of Dimensions of the Echelon.

These may be summarized as follows (see (2), (3), (4), (4a), pp. 177 and 178):—

Increase in thickness of plates increases the dispersion, and therefore the amount of detail distinguishable. The separation of spectra remains the same.

Increase of width of step decreases the separation of successive spectra; but the angular limit of resolution is reduced also, the amount of detail distinguishable remaining the same.

Increase of number of plates does not alter dispersion or separation of spectra; but it reduces the angular limit of resolution, the amount of detail distinguishable being thereby increased. In addition to this the amount of light is increased.

The Intensity Curve.

The curve in Fig. 131 has been plotted from the expression for the intensity in (5), p. 178.

It will be seen that $I = 0$ when $\theta = \dfrac{\lambda}{s}$. Now $\dfrac{\lambda}{s}$ is the angular separation of successive orders of the same line; hence if any spectral line be formed at $\theta = 0$, the two orders next it on each side are absent, and practically all the light is concentrated in the one line.

This fact should be well noted, as by a slight rotation of the echelon it is found that any desired line can be got into this position, and the property above mentioned is one of great importance in the practical manipulation of the echelon.

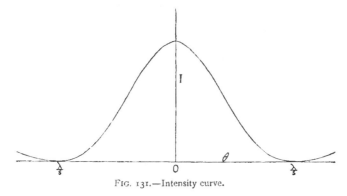

FIG. 131.—Intensity curve.

Mounting, etc.

Mr. Hilger, who has made echelons for many of the principal Universities of Europe, recommends the following dimensions as those which have been found most generally satisfactory, and which he always supplies when no contrary instructions are given in ordering:—

Thickness of plates . . . . 10 mm.
Width of step . . . . 1 ,,

FIG. 132.

The mounting adopted varies somewhat according to the number of plates. Fig. 132 shows the mounting of a small echelon, one of fourteen plates constructed for the University of Vienna. The largest plate of glass rests on an optically worked metal plate in which the aperture is cut, and the plates are clamped by steel rods with mill-head nuts. The plates are cleaned with the most scrupulous care, and when clamped in the above manner they make optical contact over the greater part of their surfaces.

By this means the great loss of light noticed by Professor Michelson (who did not clamp the plates of his echelons) is obviated to a surprising degree, and the more recently made echelons are remarkable for their brilliancy; while experience shows that, contrary to expectation, judicious clamping does not cause the slightest loss of definition. The smaller sizes of echelon can be adapted to almost any form of spectroscope, but owing to its peculiarity of being always used at direct vision, a special form becomes more convenient.

Such an echelon spectroscope, designed for a twenty-plate or larger echelon, is shown in Fig. 133 in conjunction with a special

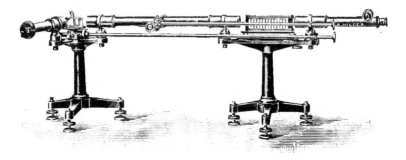

FIG. 133.

form of auxiliary spectroscope (known as the "Constant Deviation Spectroscope") which presents many advantages for the purpose, the chief of which is that neither collimator nor telescope is ever moved. Arrangements are provided by means of rods and bevel gear for the various adjustments that have to be made, such as the passing through the spectrum by rotation of the prism of the auxiliary spectroscope, the opening and shutting of the slit, the rotation of the echelon to get the line under observation into any desired position, and the moving of the echelon out of the field of view.

Hints on the Use of the Echelon.

It is well worth while spending a little time in carefully setting up the apparatus in the first instance, care being specially taken that the whole of the echelon is operative. To do this one should proceed as follows:—

Set the echelon and auxiliary spectroscopes up end to end as shown in Fig. 133, with the axis of each horizontal and at exactly the same height from the table. The eyepiece should, of course, be removed from the auxiliary spectroscope, and the distance from the end of its telescope tube to the focus of the telescope object glass being carefully measured beforehand, the auxiliary spectroscope should be put at such a distance from the slit of the echelon spectroscope as to bring the spectral lines to a focus on the slit. Set the telescope of the auxiliary and the collimator of the echelon spectroscope in one line as nearly as can be judged by the eye. Now put a sodium flame in front of the auxiliary slit, and turn the prism of the auxiliary spectroscope until D comes on to the "echelon" slit. Then on looking through the echelon spectroscope with the eyepiece removed, the object glasses should appear equally illuminated all over, except, perhaps, two slight black strips right and left, which, if present, should be perfectly symmetrical. When this is the case (and the setting is not right until it is so) the apparatus is ready.

If now the slit of the auxiliary spectroscope be closed to a convenient width and that of the echelon spectroscope be opened wide, the spectrum of any light placed in front of the slit of the auxiliary spectroscope will be seen in the eyepiece of the viewing telescope. Any particular line that it is desired to examine must then be got on to the fixed jaw of the slit, the slit closed to exclude all other lines, and the echelon introduced. Supposing the radiation to be homogeneous within the limit of resolution of the echelon, the following possible conditions may be observed in the eyepiece:—

1. There may be one bright single line visible, together with a series of very faint lines gradually diminishing in intensity as the distance from the central line is increased. This is the condition in which the two neighbouring orders to right and left are absent (see Fig. 131).

2. There may be two lines of equal intensity, which are successive orders of one and the same line, also with a series of very faint lines diminishing in intensity towards the edge of the field.

3. There may be any number of conditions intermediate between these two, with two lines visible, but of unequal brilliancy, and the series of very faint lines as before. The series of lines to right and left will not be found to interfere with the use of the instrument in the slightest degree—there are two points right and left which are *always dark* and which enclose a space equal to twice the separation of successive orders (see p. 181). It is on this region that the attention should be concentrated.

By a slight rotation of the echelon about a vertical axis any of the conditions above mentioned can be attained—indeed, one can pass a large number of orders through the field one after the other. There is one position of the echelon, however, at which, during rotation, the lines reverse the direction of their motion in much the same way as the lines in a prism spectrum when the prism is rotated through the position of minimum deviation. This is when the echelon plates are normal to the incident light, and this position, or near it, is the best to work at.

Uses of the Echelon.

As will be seen by reference to p. 179, the range of spectrum which can be observed at one time is very small; but with suitable means (see pp. 181 and 182) the passing from one line to another becomes very rapid and convenient. The purpose, then, for which the echelon is peculiarly suited is the analysis of minute details of structure or of variation of spectral lines. Such are, the determination of the effect of pressure on the nature of the radiations emitted by glowing gases, etc., the effect of motion of the light source relative to the spectroscope, and above all the observation of the interesting phenomenon known as the "Zeeman Effect."

It may be of interest to note the magnitude of these various effects in one or two cases.

The difference between the velocities of two opposite points on the sun's equator is 4 kilometres per second, and this produces a relative shift of the spectral lines of 0·075 Å.U. As in the grating investigated above a shift of 0·003 Å.U. would be perceptible, it seems probable that the echelon may form a valuable tool in the hands of astronomers.

The displacements towards the red end of the spectrum, due to a pressure of eleven atmospheres in various lines, have been given by Humphreys (from experiments made in Rowland's laboratory with the 6-inch reflection grating; see the *Astrophysical Journal*, October, 1897, p 169). The greatest among those observed vary from 0·02 to 0·50 Å.U.

In the case of the Zeeman effect, with fields of about 30,000 C.G.S. units, the separation of the components is of the order of 1·0 Å.U.

In conclusion it may be remarked that there is no difficulty in constructing echelons with plates considerably thicker than 10 mm. (Professor Michelson, in fact, made them with 20 mm. plates), and thus increasing the resolving power, should this be desired.

CATALOGUE OF SPECTRA.

TABLE OF STANDARD WAVE-LENGTHS (in air at 20° C. and 760 mm.).

[See Explanatory Note, p. 206.]

Rowland: "Astronomy" and "Astro-Physics," 1893, xii. 321.

Element.	Intensity and character.		Kind of standard.	Weight.		Wave-lengths.		Reduction to vacuo.		Oscillation frequency in vacuo.
	In arc.	In sun.		In arc.	In sun.	In arc (a).	In sun (b).	$\lambda +$	$\dfrac{1}{\lambda} -$	
? . . .		4			1		7714·686	2·09	3·5	12958·8
? . . .		7			1		7699·374	2·08	,,	12984·6
[A$_{11}$] { O .		7			3		7671·994	,,	,,	13030·9
O .		7			3		7670·993	,,	,,	13032·6
[A$_{10}$] { O .		8			3		7666·239	,,	,,	13040·7
O .		8			3		7665·265	,,	,,	13042·4
[A$_7$] { O .		14	III.		3		7660·778	2·07	,,	13050·0
O .		14	III.		3		7659·658	,,	,,	13051·9
[A$_2$] { O .		14	III.		3		7628·585	,,	,,	13105·1
O .		14	III.		3		7627·232	,,	,,	13107·4
[A$_1$] { O .		12	III.		4		7624·853	2·06	,,	13111·5
O .		12	III.		4		7623·526	,,	3·6	13113·7
[A*]	O .	10	II.		5		7621·277	,,	,,	13117·6
[A†]	O .				4		7594·059	,,	,,	13164·6
? . . .		3			1		7545·921	2·04	,,	13249·2
? . . .		6			3		7511·286	2·03	,,	13309·7
? . . .		6			3		7495·351	,,	,,	13338·0
? . . .		6			2		7462·609	2·02	,,	13396·5
? . . .		6			3		7446·038	,,	,,	13426·4
? . . .		6			2		7409·554	2·01	,,	13492·5
? . . .		7			2		7389·696	2·00	3·7	13528·7
? . . .		2			3		7331·206	1·99	,,	13636·6
? . . .		2			3		7321·056	1·98	,,	13655·5
wv ? . .		5″			4		7318·818	,,	,,	13659·7
wv ? . .		7			4		7304·475	,,	,,	13686·5
wv ? . .		4			3		7300·056	,,	,,	13694·8
wv ? . .		10″			3		7290·714	,,	,,	13712·4
wv ? . .		6			3		7287·689	,,	,,	13718·1
wv ? . .		8			4		7273·256	1·97	,,	13745·3
? . . .		3			2		7270·205	,,	,,	13751·1
wv ? . .		8			3		7265·833	,,	,,	13759·3
wv ? . .		8			3		7264·851	,,	,,	13761·2
wv ? . .		4			2		7247·461	1·96	,,	13794·2
wv ? . .		15	III.		4		7243·904	,,	,,	13801·0
wv ? . .		4			5		7240·972	,,	,,	13806·6
? . . .		8	III.		4		7233·171	,,	,,	13821·5
? . . .		3			3		7232·509	,,	,,	13822·8
? . . .		6			4		7227·765	,,	,,	13831·8
? . . .		8	III.		5		7223·930	,,	,,	13839·2
wv ? . .		6			4		7216·812	,,	,,	13852·8

* Single line at the beginning of the tail of A.   † Beginning of head of A, outside edge.

NOTE.—Unless otherwise stated, all wave-lengths are upon Rowland's scale in air of about 20° C. and 760 mm. pressure. All oscillation frequencies are in vacuo.

186 *An Introduction to the Study of Spectrum Analysis.*

TABLE OF STANDARD WAVE-LENGTHS—*continued.*

Element	Intensity and character. In arc.	Intensity and character. In sun.	Kind of standard.	Weight. In arc.	Weight. In sun.	Wave-lengths. In arc (*a*).	Wave-lengths. In sun (*b*).	Reduction to vacuo. $\lambda +$	Reduction to vacuo. $\dfrac{1}{\lambda} -$	Oscillation frequency in vacuo.
wv		10	III.		5		7201·468	1·95	3·8	13882·3
wv		10	III.		5		7200·753	,,	,,	13883·6
wv		7			3		7193·921	,,	,,	13896·8
wv ?		5″			6		7186·552	..	..	13911·1
wv ?		4			7		7184·781	,,	,,	13914·5
wv ?		3			6		7176·347	..	,,	13930·9
?		3			5		7168·191	1·94	,,	13946·7
?		7	II.		4		7148·427	,,	,,	13985·3
?		1			4		7147·942	..	,,	13986·2
?		6	II.		5		7122·491	1·93	,,	14036·2
?		4	II.		5		7090·645	1·92	,,	14099·3
?		4	III.		10		7040·058	1·91	,,	14200·6
?		2			6		7038·470	,,	,,	14203·8
?		6	II.		8		7035·159	,,	,,	14210·5
?		3			7		7027·726	,,	..	14225·6
?		1			1		7027·199	,,	,,	14226·6
?		3″	IV.		2		7024·988	1·90	,,	14231·1
?		3	IV.		7		7023·747	,,	,,	14233·6
?		4	IV.		1		7023·225	,,	,,	14234·5
wv ?		6	IV.		9		7016·690	,,	3·9	14247·8
wv ?		3	IV.		5		7016·279	,,	..	14248·7
?		3	III.		6		7011·585	,,	,,	14258·2
?		5	IV.		5		7006·160	,,	,,	14269·3
?		4	III.		3		7000·143	,,	,,	14281·5
wv ?		5″	IV.		6		6999·174	,,	,,	14283·5
wv ?		5	III.		7		6989·240	,,	,,	14303·8
wv		5	II.		10		6986·832	1·89	,,	14308·7
?		2			5		6978·655	,,	,,	14325·5
wv ?		6	III.		12		6961·518	,,	,,	14360·8
wv ?		3	III.		10		6959·708	,,	,,	14364·5
wv		8	I.		12		6956·700	,,	,,	14370·7
?		1 ⎱ ″ 2 ⎰	IV.		4		6953·838	,,	..	14376·6
wv ?										
wv ?		8	I.		10		6947·781	1·88	,,	14389·2
[B₁₂]	O O	1 1	III. III.		5 1		6935·530 6934·646	.. ..	.. ,,	14414·6 14416·4
[B₁₁]	O O	2 2	II. II.		8 5		6929·838 6928·992	.. ..	,, ,,	14426·4 14428·2
[B₁₀]	O O	3 3	I. I.		11 8		6924·420 6923·557	,, ,,	,, ..	14437·7 14439·5
[B₉]	O O	4 4	I. I.		9 5		6919·245 6918·363	,, ,,	.. ..	14448·5 14450·4
?		2	II.		5		6916·957	,,	,,	14453·3
Ni	5	3	II.		4		6914·819	,,	,,	14457·8
[B₈]	O O	5 5	I. I.		4 5		6914·328 6913·454	,, ,,	,, ,,	14458·8 14460·6
[B₇]	O O	6 6	I. I.		9 5		6909·675 6908·785	1·87 ..	.. ,,	14468·6 14470·4
[B₆]	O O	6 6	I. I.		5 5		6905·263 6904·358	,, ..	,, ,,	14477·8 14479·7
[B₅]	O O	6 6	I. I.		8 6		6901·113 6900·199	.. ,,	,, ,,	14486·5 14488·4
[B₁]	O O	6 6	I. I.		8 7		6897·195 6896·292	.. ,,	,, ,,	14494·7 14496·6

Catalogue of Spectra.

TABLE OF STANDARD WAVE-LENGTHS—continued.

Element.	Intensity and character.		Kind of standard.	Weight.		Wave-lengths.		Reduction to vacuo.		Oscillation frequency in vacuo.
	In arc.	In sun.		In arc.	In sun.	In arc (a).	In sun (b).	$\lambda +$	$\dfrac{1}{\lambda} -$	
[B₃] { O .		6	I.		5		6893·559	1·87	3·9	14502·4
{ O .		6	I.		5		6892·614	,,	,,	14504·4
[B₂] { O .		5	I.		5		6890·149	,,	,,	14509·6
{ O .		5	I.		5		6889·194	,,	,,	14511·6
[B₁] { O .		5	I.		12		6886·987	,,	,,	14516·2
{ O .		5	I.		12		6886·008	,,	,,	14518·3
[B] O . .		4	I.		13		6884·083	,,	,,	14522·4
Cr . . .	3	1	III.		5		6883·318	,,	,,	14524·0
Cr . . .	2	1	III.		5		6882·772	,,	,,	14525·1
Cr . . .	1	1	III.		5		6881·970	,,	,,	14526·8
[B] { O .		3	I.		11		6880·176	,,	,,	14530·6
{ O .		5	I.		11		6879·294	,,	,,	14532·5
[B] { O .		5	I.		7		6877·878	,,	,,	14535·5
{ O .		5	I.		7		6876·957	,,	,,	14537·4
{ O .		5	I.		9		6875·826	,,	,,	14539·8
[B] { O .		5	I.		5		6874·884	,,	,,	14541·8
{ O .		5	I.		5		6874·039	,,	,,	14543·6
[B] { O .		5	I.		4		6873·076	1·86	,,	14545·6
{ O .		5	I.		5		6872·493	,,	,,	14546·9
[B] { O .		5	II.		6		6871·527	,,	,,	14548·9
{ O .		5	II.		6		6871·179	,,	,,	14549·6
[B*] O .		{4} {4}″	I.		12		6870·186	,,	,,	14551·7
[B] { O .		4 ″	II.		5		6869·347	,,	,,	14553·5
{ O .		4	II.		5		6869·141	,,	,,	14554·0
{ O .		{3} {1}″	IV.		3		6868·779	,,	,,	14554·7
[B] { O .		6″	III.		2		6868·393	,,	,,	14555·5
{ O .		1	IV.		2		6868·124	,,	,,	14556·1
[B†] { O .		3	II.		11		6867·800	,,	,,	14556·8
{ O .		3	II.		11		6867·461	,,	,,	14557·5
Fe . . .		3	II.		10		6855·425	,,	,,	14583·1
Fe . . .		3	II.		5		6843·908	,,	,,	14607·6
Fe . . .		3	II.		6		6841·591	,,	,,	14612·6
Fe . . .		2	II.		7		6828·850	1·85	4·0	14639·7
Fe . . .		2	II.		5		6820·614	,,	,,	14657·4
Fe . . .		3	I.		8		6810·519	,,	,,	14679·2
Fe . . .		2	II.		6		6807·100	,,	,,	14686·5
Fe . . .		1	III.		5		6787·137	1·84	,,	14729·7
Ni . . .	2	3	II.		10		6772·565	,,	,,	14761·5
Ni . . .	5	4	I.		9		6768·044	,,	,,	14771·3
Fe . . .		2	II.		7		6752·962	1·83	,,	14804·3
Fe . . .		4	I.		12		6750·412	,,	,,	14809·9
Fe . . .		3	III.		7		6726·923	,,	,,	14861·6
? . . .		3	III.		10		6722·095	,,	,,	14872·3
Ca . . .	10	5	III.		10		6717·934	1·82	,,	14881·5
Li ‡ . . .	75		M.	3		6708·070		,,	,,	14903·4
? . . .		3	III.		12		6705·353	,,	,,	14909·5
? . . .		2	III.		10		6703·813	,,	,,	14912·9

* The principal line in the head of B, a difficult double.
† These two lines are at the beginning of the head of B. There is a fine line midway between them.
‡ A difficult triplet.

188 *An Introduction to the Study of Spectrum Analysis.*

TABLE OF STANDARD WAVE-LENGTHS—*continued.*

Element.	Intensity and character. In arc.	Intensity and character. In sun.	Kind of standard.	Weight. In arc.	Weight. In sun.	Wave-lengths. In arc (a).	Wave-lengths. In sun (b).	Reduction to vacuo. $\lambda +$	Reduction to vacuo. $-\frac{\tau}{\lambda}$	Oscillation frequency in vacuo.
Fe		5	I.	10			6678·232	1·81	4·0	14970·0
Fe		4 $\}''$	I.	6			6663·696	,,	4·1	15002·6
?		1 $\}$	I.	4			6663·525	,,	,,	15003·0
Ni	5	5	I.	10			6643·882	1·80	,,	15047·3
Fe		3	III.	7			6633·992	,,	,,	15069·8
Fe		4	I.	9			6609·345	,,	,,	15126·0
Fe		4	I.	12			6594·115	1·79	,,	15160·9
Fe		5	I.	11			6593·161	,,	,,	15163·1
Fe		4	IV.	7			6575·179	,,	,,	15204·6
?		2	III.	5			6574·477	,,	,,	15206·2
WV		1	III.	6			6572·312	,,	,,	15211·2
Fe		6	I.	13			6569·461	1·78	,,	15217·8
[C]H		30	I.	13			6563·054	,,	,,	15282·7
WV		2	III.	6			6552·840	,,	,,	15256·5
Fe		? $\}$ 6	I.	11			6546·486	,,	,,	15271·3
Ti		3 $\}$								
?		3	I.	12			6534·173	,,	,,	15300·1
WV		1	III.	7			6532·546	1·77	,,	15303·9
Fe		4	II.	10			6518·594	,,	,,	15336·6
?	6	4	III.	7			6516·315	,,	,,	15342·0
Ca	5	5	I.	10			6499·871	,,	4·2	15380·7
Fe		7	I.	9			6495·209	,,	,,	15391·8
Ca	8	6	I.	10			6494·001	1·76	,,	15394·6
?		4	I.	8			6482·099	,,	,,	15422·9
WV		1	III.	6			6480·264	,,	,,	15427·3
Ca	5	5	I.	7			6471·881	,,	,,	15447·2
Fe		? $\}''\}$	I.	9			6462·835	,,	,,	15468·9
Ca		10 $\}$9 $\}$								
Ca		6	I.	6			6450·029	1·75	,,	15499·6
Ca		10r 7	I.	11			6439·298	,,	,,	15525·4
Cd			M.	1		6438·680		,,	,,	15526·9
Fe		6	I.	10			6431·063	,,	,,	15545·3
Fe		6	III.	10			6421·569	,,	,,	15568·3
Fe		5	I.	8			6420·171	,,	,,	15571·7
Fe		7	I.	10			6411·864	1·74	,,	15591·9
Fe		6	I.	8			6408·231	,,	,,	15600·7
Fe		3	IV.	6			6400·509	,,	,,	15619·6
Fe		8	IV.	5			6400·200	,,	,,	15620·3
Fe		7	I.	9			6393·818	,,	,,	15635·9
Fe		4	I.	6			6380·951	1·73	,,	15667·4
Ni	5	2	IV.	2			6378·461	,,	,,	15673·6
Fe		6	I.	8			6358·902	,,	4·3	15721·7
Fe		5	III.	8			6355·259	,,	,,	15730·7
Fe		5	I.	6			6344·370	,,	,,	15757·7
Fe		6	I.	12			6337·042	1·72	,,	15775·9
Fe		6	I.	12			6335·550	,,	,,	15779·6
Fe		5	I.	13			6322·912	,,	,,	15811·2
Fe-(Ca)		6	I.	14			6318·242	,,	,,	15822·9
Fe		3	IV.	5			6315·541	,,	,,	15829·7
Ni	6	4	I.	7			6314·874	,,	,,	15831·3
Fe		7	I.	7			6301·719	1·71	,,	15864·4
O		3	I.	7			6296·144	,,	,,	15878·4
O *		3	III.	6			6293·152	,,	,,	15886·0

* Second line in the second pair of tail of **a**.

Table of Standard Wave-lengths—continued.

Element.	Intensity and character.		Kind of standard.	Weight.		Wave-lengths.		Reduction to vacuo.		Oscillation frequency in vacuo.
	In arc.	In sun.		In arc.	In sun.	In arc (a).	In sun (b).	$\lambda +$	$\dfrac{1}{\lambda} -$	
O* . . .		2	II.		5		6289·608	1·71	4·3	15894·9
O		2	II.		7		6281·374	,,	,,	15915·8
[α] O † . .		4″	I.		9		6278·289	,,	,,	15923·6
Fe . . .		3	I.		10		6270·439	,,	,,	15943·5
Fe . . .		5	I.		11		6265·347	1·70	,,	15956·5
Ti . . .	5	2	I.		9		6261·316	,,	,,	15966·8
Fe . . .	?	} 6	I.		8		6256·574	,,	,,	15978·9
Ni . . .	7									
Fe ‡ . . .		7	I.		9		6254·454	,,	,,	15983·8
Fe . . .		7	I.		9		6252·776	,,	,,	15988·6
Fe . . .		7	I.		9		6246·530	,,	,,	16004·6
? . . .		4	I.		8		6237·529	,,	,,	16027·7
Fe-Va . .	?-6	7	I.		12		6230·946	1·69	,,	16044·6
Fe . . .		6	I.		10		6219·493	,,	4·4	16074·1
Fe . . .		6	I.		9		6213·646	,,	,,	16089·2
Fe . . .		6	I.		10		6200·533	,,	,,	16123·2
Fe . . .		8	I.		10		6191·770	1·68	,,	16146·1
Ni . . .	4	6	I.		9		6191·397	,,	,,	16147·0
Fe . . .		6	I.		8		6180·419	,,	,,	16175·7
Ni . . .	5	6	I.		8		6177·028	,,	,,	16184·6
Fe . . .		6	I.		8		6173·554	,,	,,	16193·7
Ca . . .	7	7	I.		8		6169·775	,,	,,	16203·6
Ca . . .	6	6	I.		4		6169·260	,,	,,	16205·0
Ca . . .	15r	10	I.		9		6162·383	,,	,,	16223·1
Na . . .		5	I.		4		6160·970	,,	,,	16226·8
Na . . .		3	I.		5		6154·431	1·67	,,	16244·0
Fe-Ba . .	?-15	7	I.		9		6141·934	,,	,,	16277·1
Fe . . .		8	II.		9		6136·834	,,	,,	16290·6
Ca . . .	15r	9	I.		11		6122·428	,,	,,	16329·0
Fe . . .	5	6	I.		8		6116·415	1·66	,,	16345·0
Ni . . .	4	3	II.		8		6111·287	,,	,,	16358·8
Ni . . .	5	6	I.		8		6108·338	,,	,,	16366·7
Li . . .	20		M.	4		6103·812		,,	,,	16378·8
? } . . .		1	} IV.		8		6103·449	,,	,,	16379·8
Fe } . . .		4								
Ca . . .	10r	6	I.		9		6102·941	,,	,,	16381·1
Fe . . .		4	II.		4		6102·408	,,	,,	16382·6
Fe . . .		3	I.		12		6079·223	1·65	4·5	16445·0
Fe . . .		5	I.		13		6078·709	,,	,,	16446·4
Fe . . .		7	I.		13		6065·708	,,	,,	16481·6
Fe . . .		5	I.		9		6056·232	,,	,,	16507·4
Fe . . .		4	I.		8		6042·316	1·64	,,	16545·4
Fe . . .		4	I.		7		6027·265	,,	,,	16586·8
Fe . . .		6	I.		8		6024·280	,,	,,	16595·0
Mn . . .	10	5	I.		6		6022·017	,,	,,	16601·2
Fe . . .		5	} IV.		6		6020·347	,,	,,	16605·8
? . . .		3								
Mn . . .	10	6	I.		8		6016·856	,,	,,	16615·5
Mn . . .	10	6	I.		5		6013·717	,,	,,	16624·1
Fe . . .		6	I.		6		6008·782	,,	,,	16637·8

* First line of first pair in the tail of α.
† Chief line in the α group, a very close double.
‡ A difficult double.

190   An Introduction to the Study of Spectrum Analysis.

TABLE OF STANDARD WAVE-LENGTHS—continued.

Element.	Intensity and character.		Kind of standard.	Weight.		Wave-lengths.		Reduction to vacuo.		Oscillation frequency in vacuo.
	In arc.	In sun.		In arc.	In sun.	In arc (a).	In sun (b).	$\lambda +$	$\frac{1}{\lambda}$	
Fe		4	I.	3			6008·196	1·64	4·5	16639·4
Fe		6	I.	7			6003·245	1·63	,,	16653·2
Fe		6	I.	7			5987·286	,,	,,	16697·6
Fe		6	I.	6			5985·044	,,	,,	16703·8
wv		2	IV.	1			5977·254	,,	,,	16725·6
Fe		5	III.	13			5977·005	,,	,,	16726·2
Fe		4	I.	12			5975·576	,,	,,	16730·3
Fe		5	I.	12			5956·925	1·62	4·6	16782·6
Si		6	I.	14			5948·761	,,	,,	16805·6
Fe		6	I.	13			5934·883	,,	,,	16844·9
Fe		6	I.	14			5930·410	,,	,,	16857·6
wv		6	I.	12			5919·855	1·61	,,	16887·7
Fe		5	I.	16			5916·475	,,	,,	16897·4
? wv		5	} I.	17			5914·384	,,	,,	16903·3
Fe		4								
Fe		5	I.	15			5905·895	,,	,,	16927·6
Fe		1	} IV.	13			5901·681	,,	,,	16939·7
wv		5								
Fe?		1	} IV.	10			5898·395	,,	,,	16949·2
wv		3								
[D₁]N		10	I.	20			5896·154	,,	,,	16955·6
Ni*	3″	4	III.	14			5893·098	,,	,,	16964·4
[D₂]Na		15	II.	20			5890·182	1·60	,,	16972·8
w		3	IV.	8			5889·854	,,	,,	16973·7
w		4	} IV.	11			5884·048	,,	,,	16990·5
Fe		6								
[D₃]H							5875·982	,,	,,	17013·8
Fe		6	I.	16			5862·580	,,	,,	17052·7
Fe		6	I.	15			5859·810	,,	,,	17060·8
Ca	10	7	II.	14			5857·672	,,	,,	17067·0
Ba	10	5	I.	14			5853·903	1·59	,,	17077·9
Ni	3	3	II.	6			5831·832	,,	4·7	17142·6
Fe		6	IV.	14			5816·594	,,	,,	17187·5
Fe		5	I.	14			5809·437	,,	,,	17208·7
Ni	7	5	I.	7			5806·954	,,	,,	17216·0
Fe		5	I.	8			5805·448	1·58	,,	17220·5
?		4	I.	9			5798·400	,,	,,	17241·4
Fe } Cr }	10	7	I.	10 16			5798·087 5791·207	,, ,,	,, ,,	17242·4 17262·8
Cr	7	5	I.	13			5788·136	,,	,,	17272·0
Cr	6	4	I.	9			5784·081	,,	,,	17284·1
Cu? Co?		7	I.	9			5782·846	,,	,,	17289·3
Fe		5	I.	9			5775·304	1·57	,,	17310·4
Si		5	I.	6			5772·360	,,	,,	17319·2
Fe		7	IV.	8			5763·215	,,	,,	17346·7
? } Ni }		5	I.	9			5754·884	,,	,,	17371·8
Fe		5	I.	10			5753·342	,,	,,	17376·5
Fe		4	I.	10			5752·257	,,	,,	17379·8
Fe		3	III.	10			5742·066	,,	,,	17410·6
Fe		5	I.	10			5731·973	1·56	,,	17441·3

* An exceedingly close double.

Catalogue of Spectra.

TABLE OF STANDARD WAVE-LENGTHS—continued.

Element.	Intensity and character.		Kind of standard.	Weight.		Wave-lengths.		Reduction to vacuo.		Oscillation frequency in vacuo.
	In arc.	In sun.		In arc.	In sun.	In arc (a).	In sun (b).	λ +	$\frac{1}{\lambda}$	
Fe Ti } Ni }	3 5	} 5	I.		10		5715·309	1·56	4·8	17492·1
Mg *		6	M. III.	4		5711·374	5711·318	,,	,,	17504·3b
Ni	5	5	} III.		8		5709·760	,,	,,	17509·1
Fe		6	} III.		6		5709·616	,,	,,	17509·5
Si		5	I.		4		5708·620	,,	,,	17512·6
Fe	4	5	I.		8		5701·769	1·55	,,	17533·6
Na		6	I.		7		5688·434	,,	,,	17574·7
Na	3	4	I.		9		5682·861	,,	,,	17592·0
Fe	2	3	I.		8		5679·249	,,	,,	17603·2
Ti	3	2	III.		8		5675·648	,,	,,	17614·3
Fe	3	5	I.		9		5662·745	1·54	,,	17654·5
Yt ?	1	4	I.		9		5658·096	,,	,,	17669·0
Fe	2	4	II.		9		5655·707	,,	,,	17676·5
Si		2	III.		9		5645·835	,,	,,	17707·4
Fe	2	3	I.		10		5641·661	,,	,,	17720·5
Fe	2	3	I.		5		5634·167	,,	,,	17744·0
Fe-Va	5, 2	4	I.		14		5624·768	1·53	,,	17773·7
Fe	2	2	I.		12		5624·253	,,	,,	17775·3
Fe	2	6	II.		10		5615·879	,,	,,	17801·8
Fe	2	2	II.		10		5615·526	,,	,,	17803·0
Fe } Ca } † Fe }	5 6 2	5 3 2	} II.		10		5603·097	,,	4·9	17842·4
Ca	5	4	M. I.	2	4	5601·502	5601·501	,,	,,	17847·5b
Ca	7	4	II.	2	4	5598·712	5598·715	,,	,,	17856·3b
Fe	3	2	II.	1	2	5598·563	5598·555	,,	,,	17856·8b
Ca	7r	5	M. III.	2	5	5594·689	5594·695	,,	,,	17869·2b
Ca	5	4	M. I.	2	5	5590·352	5590·342	1·52	,,	17883·1b
Ca	10r	6	M. I.	2	9	5588·977	5588·980	,,	,,	17887·4b
Ca	6	4	M. I.	2	9	5582·204	5582·195	,,	,,	17909·2b
Fe	5	4	I.		7		5576·319	,,	,,	17928·1
Fe	6	5	I.		8		5569·848	,,	,,	17948·9
Fe	4	3	II.		8		5555·113	,,	,,	17996·5
Fe	3	2	I.		9		5544·158	1·51	,,	18032·1
Fe	3	2	I.		8		5543·418	,,	,,	18034·5
Fe		2	I.		8		5535·073	,,	,,	18061·7
Mg ‡	10	7	I.	4	8	5528·672	5528·636	,,	,,	18082·7b
Ca	5	3	III.	1	8	5513·127	5513·207	1·50	,,	18133·4b
Fe	5	4	I.		8		5507·000	,,	,,	18153·8
Fe	5	4	I.		8		5501·685	,,	5·0	18171·2
Fe	3	4	I.		8		5497·731	,,	,,	18184·3
Fe	2	3	II.		5		5487·968	,,	,,	18216·7
Ni	15r	4	I.		10		5477·128	,,	,,	18252·7
Fe	3	3	I.		10		5466·608	1·49	,,	18287·9
Fe	3	4	I.		10		5463·493	,,	,,	18298·3
Fe	3	4	I.		9		5463·174	,,	,,	18299·4

* Not recommended as a standard *in the arc*.
† Fe 5603·180
  Ca 5603·080
  Fe 5602·995
‡ In the arc this line is diffuse on one side. The solar line corresponds to the edge of the band-like line.

TABLE OF STANDARD WAVE-LENGTHS—*continued*.

Element.	Intensity and character.		Kind of standard.	Weight.		Wave-lengths.		Reduction to vacuo.		Oscillation frequency in vacuo.
	In arc.	In sun.		In arc.	In sun.	In arc (*a*).	In sun (*b*).	$\lambda+$	$\frac{1}{\lambda}-$	
Ni . . .	3	1	II.		7		5462·732	1·49	5·0	18300·9
Fe } . .	6	6	III.		1		5455·826	,,	,,	18324·0
			II.		8		5455·759	,,	,,	18324·3
Fe ? } . .		3	III.		1		5455·666	,,	,,	18324·6
Fe * . .	7	7	I.	1	9	5447·116	5447·130	,,	,,	18353·3*b*
Fe . . .	5	6	I.	1	9	5434·725	5434·742	1·48	,,	18395·1*b*
Fe } . .	5	} 7	I.		10		5424·284	,,	,,	18430·6
Va . . .	3									
Va . . .	4	} 6	I.		12		5415·421	,,	,,	18460·8
Fe . . .	4									
Cr . . .	10r	5	I.		7		5410·000	,,	,,	18479·3
Fe . . .	7	7	I.	1	14	5405·979	5405·987	,,	,,	18493·0*b*
Fe . . .	7	7	I.	1	12	5397·319	5397·346	1·47	5·1	18522·5*b*
Fe . . .	4	5	I.		11		5393·378	,,	,,	18536·2
Fe . . .	3	4	I.		11		5389·683	,,	,,	18548·9
Fe . . .	6	6	I.		11		5383·576	,,	,,	18569·9
Fe . . .	2	3	I.		9		5379·776	,,	,,	18583·0
Fe-Cr } ‡ .	9, 2	7	} IV.		8		5371·686	,,		18611·0
Ni }	2	2								
Fe . . .	1	6	I.		8		5370·165	,,	,,	18616·3
Fe . . .	1	6	I.		8		5367·670	,,	,,	18625·0
? . .	?	3	IV.		1		5363·056	1·46	,,	18641·0
Fe (Co) } .	1, 3	1	III.		5		5363·011	,,	,,	18641·1
? } .		2	III.		7		5361·813	,,	,,	18645·3
Fe-Ni . .	3, 3	4	IV.		8		5353·592	,,	,,	18673·9
Th ‡ . .	7·5		M.	2		5350·670		,,	,,	18684·1
Ca . . .	7	5	M. III.	1	4	5349·599	5349·623	,,	,,	18687·8*b*
Fe ? . .	3	4	II.		9		5333·092	,,	,,	18745·7
Fe . . .	9	8	I.		8		5324·373	1·45	,,	18776·4
Co ? . .	2	3	III.		1		5316·950	,,	,,	18802·7
[1174] } .		6	III.		7		5316·870	,,	,,	18803·0
Fe ? } §		1	III.		1		5316·790	,,	,,	18803·2
Fe . . .	3	4	I.		10		5307·546	,,	,,	18836·0
Cr . . .	2	3	I.		9		5300·918	,,	5·2	18859·5
Cr . . .	6r	4	I.		12		5296·873	,,	,,	18873·9
Fe . . .	2	2	I.		12		5288·708	1·44	,,	18903·0
Fe . . .	5	6	I.		11		5283·803	,,	,,	18920·6
Fe . . .	4	5	I.		11		5281·968	,,	,,	18927·1
Co . . .	3	1	} I.		11		5276·205	,,	,,	18947·8
Cr . . .	5	2								
? . .	?	2								
Fe } . .	3	3	I.		8		5273·554	,,	,,	18957·3
	6		II.		5		5273·443	,,	,,	18957·7
Fe } . .	3	3	I.		6		5273·344	,,	,,	18958·1
Fe	6	4	M. III.		3		5270·533	,,	,,	18968·2
[E₁] } .			I.		12		5270·495	,,	,,	18968·3
Ca } .	10	4	M. III.	2	3	5270·445	5270·448	,,	,,	18968·5*b*
E₂ Fe *	8	8	I.	1	16	5269·714	5269·722	,,	,,	18971·1*b*

* A difficult double.
† The red component, a difficult double.   ‡ A difficult triplet.
§ 1474 is a triplet, or rather a double, the red component of which has a weak side-line to the violet; probably the violet component is due to iron, and the weak line to cobalt, but the red is unknown.

Catalogue of Spectra.   193

TABLE OF STANDARD WAVE-LENGTHS—*continued*.

Element.	Intensity and character.		Kind of standard.	Weight.		Wave-lengths.		Reduction to vacuo.		Oscillation frequency in vacuo.
	In arc.	In sun.		In arc.	In sun.	In arc (*a*).	In sun (*b*).	$\lambda +$	$\frac{1}{\lambda}$	
[Fe]	6	6	I.	1	8	5266·733	5266·729	1·44	5·2	18981·9*b*
Cr (Ni?)	4r	}·2	III.		1		5265·884	,,	,,	18985·0
		5	III.		2		5265·789	,,	,,	18985·3
Ca	8	3	III.	1	2	5265·725	5265·727	,,	,,	18985·5*b*
Ca	6	3	M. III.	2	3	5264·408	5264·395	,,	,,	18990·3*b*
		6	I.		2		5264·371	,,	,,	18990·4
Cr	4r	3	III.		3		5264·327	,,	,,	18990·6
Ca	6	2	III.	2	5	5262·408	5262·394	,,	,,	18997·6*b*
?		1	M. IV.		1		5262·341	,,	,,	18997·7
Cr Ca	2 6	}3	III.	1	12		5261·880	,,	,,	18999·4
Ca	2	1	M. IV.	1	5	5260·556	5260·557	,,	,,	19004·2*b*
Fe	2	3	I.		12		5253·649	,,	,,	19029·2
Fe	3	3	I.		11		5250·825	1·43	,,	19039·4
Fe	2	2	I.		11		5250·391	,,	,,	19041·0
Fe	3	3	I.		10		5242·662	,,	,,	19069·1
Fe	7	8	I.		9		5233·124	,,	,,	19103·8
Fe	4	4	I.		8		5230·014	,,	,,	19115·2
Fe	2	2	I.		10		5225·690	,,	,,	19131·0
Fe	3	4	I.		10		5217·559	,,	,,	19160·8
Fe	3	4	I.		10		5215·352	,,	,,	19169·0
Ti	10r	3	M. I.	2	12	5210·549	5210·556	1·42	,,	19186·6*b*
Fe Cr	3 8r	3 4	} I.		10		5204·708	,,	5·3	19208·1
Fe ?	4 ?	3 2	} I.		11		5202·483	,,	,,	19216·3
Fe	3	4	I.		10		5198·885	,,	,,	19229·6
Ti	8	3	M. I.	2	8	5193·134	5193·139	,,	,,	19250·9*b*
Ca			M. I.	1	3	5189·019	5189·020	,,	,,	19266·2*b*
?	6	4	I.		7		5188·948	,,	,,	19266·4
Ti	2	4	I.		3		5188·863	,,	,,	19266·7
[*b₁*]Mg	40r	20	M. I.	2	11	5183·791	5183·792	,,	,,	19285·6*b*
Ti	10r	3	I.		11		5173·912	1·41	,,	19322·4
[*b₂*]Mg	35r	10	M. I.	2	9	5172·866	5172·871	,,	,,	19326·3*b*
Fe	5	5	I.		11		5171·783	,,	,,	19330·4
Fe	3	4	I.		3		5169·218	,,	,,	19340·0
[*b₃*]			I.		5		5169·161	,,	,,	19340·2
Fe	3	4	I.		3		5169·066	,,	,,	19340·5
Fe [*b₄*]	6	6	M. IV. III.	2	3 7	5167·664	5167·686 5167·572	,, ,,	,, ,,	19345·7*b* 19346·1
Mg	20r	8	M. IV.	2	3	5167·488	5167·501	,,	,,	19346·4*b*
Fe	2	2	I.		10		5165·588	,,	,,	19353·6
C*		1	M.	2	1	5165·241	5165·190	,,	,,	19354·9*a*
Fe	4	4	I.		13		5162·448	,,	,,	19365·4
Fe?		2	I.		11		5159·240	,,	,,	19377·4
Ni	6	2	I.		10		5155·937	,,	,,	19389·8
Ti? Co?		2	I.		10		5154·237	,,	,,	19396·2
Mn Fe	2 4	1 3	} III.		9		5151·026	,,	,,	19408·3
? Ni	? 5	}3	I.		10		5146·664	,,	,,	19424·8

* In the arc the first line of the first head of the green carbon band.

O

TABLE OF STANDARD WAVE-LENGTHS—*continued*.

Element.	Intensity and character.		Kind of standard.	Weight.		Wave-lengths.		Reduction to vacuo.		Oscillation frequency in vacuo.
	In arc.	In sun.		In arc.	In sun.	In arc (a).	In sun (b).	$\lambda +$	$\dfrac{1}{\lambda} -$	
Fe ⎱	3	4	⎧ IV.	2		5143·106		1·41	5·3	19438·2
Ni ⎰	5	2	⎨ IV.	5		5143·042		,,	,,	19438·4
Fe	2	3	⎩ IV.	1		5142·967		,,	,,	19438·7
Fe			I.	5		5141·916		,,	,,	19442·7
Fe ⎱			⎧ III.	4		5139·645		,,	,,	19451·3
	5	6	⎨ III.	4		5139·589		,,	,,	19451·7
Fe ⎰	4	6	⎩ III.	4		5139·437		,,	,,	19452·1
? ⎱	?	6	⎱ I.	12		5133·871		1·40	,,	19473·2
Fe ⎰	1									
Fe	4	4	I.	9		5127·530		,,	,,	19497·3
Co	3	2	I.	9		5126·369		,,	,,	19501·7
Fe ⎱	3	3	⎱ IV.	9		5121·797		,,	,,	19519·1
Ni ⎰	2	1								
Ni	5	.2	I.	9		5115·558		,,	5·4	19542·8
Fe ⎱	4	3	⎱ II.	11		5110·570		,,	,,	19561·9
? ⎰	?	2								
Fe	3	2	I.	11		5109·825		,,	,,	19564·7
Fe (Cu)	3?	3	I.	12		5105·719		,,	,,	19580·5
Fe	3	2	IV.	7		5097·176		1·39	,,	19613·3
Fe	3	2	I.	9		5090·959		,,	,,	19637·3
Cd		?	M.	1		5086·001		,,	,,	19656·4
Fe	4	3	I.	9		5083·525		,,	,,	19666·0
Fe	4	4	I.	14		5068·946		,,	,,	19722·6
Ti	10	3	II.	12		5064·833		,,	,,	19738·6
Fe	2	2	II.	15		5060·252		1·38	,,	19756·5
Fe	5	5	I.	12		5050·008		,,	,,	19796·5
Ca	3	2	M.	2	1	5041·867	5041·795	,,	,,	19828·5a
Ni ⎱	3	2	⎱ II.	8		5036·113		,,	,,	19851·2
Ti ⎰	6	3								
Ti	7	3	II.	8		5020·210		1·37	5·5	19914·0
Ti ⎱	5	4	⎱ M. II.	10		5014·412	5014·422	,,	,,	19937·5b
(Ni) Ti ⎰	?-10	3								
Mg b'd *			M.	3	10	5007·473		,,	,,	19964·6
Nebula						5007·05		,,	,,	19966·3
Fe ⎱	3	3	⎱ I.		10		5007·481	,,	,,	19964·8
Ti ⎰	10r	4								
Fe		6	I.		8		5006·303	,,	,,	19969·3
Fe	3	4	II.		10		5005·904	,,	,,	19970·9
Pb			M.	5		5005·634		,,	,,	19972·0
Ti-La	⎧ 10r ⎩ 10r	⎱ 4	M. III.		8	4999·668	4999·693	,,	,,	19995·7b
Fe	3	4	I.		7		4994·316	,,	,,	20017·3
Ti	10	4	III.	1	10	4981·893	4981·915	1·36	,,	20067·1b
? ⎱	?	1	⎱ III.		5		4980·362	,,	,,	20073·4
Ni ⎰	5	3								
Fe ⎱	3	3	⎱ I.		8		4978·782	,,	,,	20079·7
? ⎰		1								
Fe	3	⎱ 3	I.		10		4973·274	,,	,,	20102·0
Ti	1									
Nebula						4959·02				20159·8
Fe		8	M. IV.	3			4957·786	,,	,,	20164·8
Fe		6	M. IV.	3			4957·482	,,	,,	20166·0

* Commencement of the head of Mg band.

Catalogue of Spectra.

TABLE OF STANDARD WAVE-LENGTHS—continued.

Element.	Intensity and character.		Kind of standard.	Weight.		Wave-lengths.		Reduction to vacuo.		Oscillation frequency in vacuo.
	In arc.	In sun.		In arc.	In sun.	In arc (a).	In sun (b).	λ +	1/λ	
Ba*. . .	60	7	M. III.	1	10	4934·237	4934·247	1·35	5·6	20260·9b
Fe . . .	3	2	I.		12		4924·955	,,	,,	20299·2
Fe . . .	2	4	II.		13		4924·109	,,	,,	20302·6
Fe . . .	9	9	M. I.	1	7	4920·676	4920·682	,,	,,	20316·8b
Fe . . .	6	7	I.		4		4919·183	,,	,,	20323·0
Pb . . .			M.	1			4905·634	1·34	,,	20379·1
Fe } Cr } . .	5 2	6	} I.		14		4903·488	,,	,,	20388·0
Yt . . .		2	II.		11		4900·306	,,	,,	20401·3
Ti . . .	4	2	II.		11		4900·098	,,	,,	20402·1
Fe . . .	7	7	I.		11		4890·945	,,	,,	20440·3
[F]H . .		15	II.		5		4861·496	1·33	5·7	20564·1
Fe . . .	4	5	I.		14		4859·934	,,	,,	20570·8
Fe?. . .		4	I.		11		4824·325	1·32	,,	20722·6
Mn . . .	10	6	M. I.	1	12	4823·715	4823·697	,,	,,	20725·3b
Zn . . .		3	M. I.	1	1	4810·725	5810·723	,,	,,	20781·2b
Ti } ? } . .	1 ?	4 1	} IV.		3		4805·253	,,	,,	20804·8
Cd . . .		?	M.	3			4800·097	1·31	,,	20827·2
Mn . . .	10r	6	M. I.	1	1	4783·607	4783·601	,,	5·8	20898·9b
Mn . . .	15r	6	I.		11		4754·226	1·30	,,	21028·1
Mn } Fe } . .	7 2	3 4	} III.		11		4727·628	1·29	,,	21146·5
Zn . . .	4	4	M. I.	2	2	4722·339	4722·319	,,	,,	21170·1b
Ni . . .	9r	6″	M. III.	1	1	4714·598	4714·599	,,	,,	21204·9b
Ni . . .	3	3	I.		13		4703·986	,,	5·9	21252·7
Mg . . .	5	9	I.	1	11	4703·249	4703·180	,,	,,	21256·3b
Fe } Ti } . .	3 3	4 2	} IV.		11		4691·581	1·28	,,	21308·9
? . . .		4	II.		14		4690·324	,,	,,	21314·6
Ni . . .	4	4	I.		12		4686·395	,,	,,	21332·5
Fe . . .	2	3	I.		13		4683·743	,,	,,	21344·5
Zn . . .		2	M.	1		4680·319		,,	,,	21360·2
Fe . . .	3	6	II.		12		4679·028	,,	,,	21366·1
Cd . . .		4?	M.	3	3	4678·339	4678·353	,,	,,	21369·1b
Fe } ? } . .	3	5 2	} II.		11		4668·303	,,	,,	21415·2
Ni . . .	6r	3	M. III.	1	1	4648·833	4648·835	1·27	,,	21504·9b
Fe . . .	2	4	I.		17		4643·645	,,	,,	21528·9
Fe . . .	3	4	II.		14		4638·194	,,	,,	21554·2
Fe . . .	3	4	II.		14		4637·683	,,	,,	21556·6
Co } Ti } . .	5 4	} 5	II.		13		4629·515	,,	6·0	21594·5
Fe . . .	1	6	} IV.		11		4611·453	1·26	,,	21679·1
? } . .	?	2								
Sr } .	50r	2	M. II.	5	4	4607·506	4607·509	,,	,,	21697·7a
C† . . .						4606·6		,,	,,	21702·0
Li . . .	50c		M.	1		4602·25		,,	,,	21722·5
Fe . . .	2	4	I.		20		4602·183	,,	,,	21722·8
Ti? . . .		4	I.		15		4590·129	,,	,,	21779·9
Cr? . . .		4	I.		14		4588·384	,,	,,	21788·2
Ca Ti . .	3, 1	4	I.	1	14	4578·807	4578·731	1·25	,,	21834·1b

* A difficult double.   † First line in first head of blue cyanogen band (ζ).

TABLE OF STANDARD WAVE-LENGTHS—*continued*.

Element.	Intensity and character.		Kind of standard.	Weight.		Wave-lengths.		Reduction to vacuo.		Oscillation frequency in vacuo.
	In arc.	In sun.		In arc.	In sun.	In arc (*a*).	In sun (*b*).	$\lambda +$	$\dfrac{1}{\lambda} -$	
Ti . . .	5	6	I.		14		4572·157	1·25	6·0	21865·5
Mg . . .	3	5	I.	1	14	4571·281	4571·277	,,	,,	21869·7*b*
Ti . . .	4	6	I.		13		4563·939	,,	6·1	21904·8
Ba . . .	70r	7	M. I.	6	8	4554·212	4554·213	,,	,,	21951·6*b*
In . . .			M.	3		4513·883		1·24	,,	22147·8
In . . .			M.	4		4511·474		,,	,,	22159·6
Ti ? . .		4	I.		17		4508·456	,,	,,	22174·4
C . . .						4502·6		1·23	,,	22203·3
Ti . . .	6	5	II.		18		4501·444	,,	,,	22209·0
? }		1	II.		7		4499·315	,,	,,	22219·5
Mn }		2	I.		8		4499·070	,,	,,	22220·7
Zr }	2	1	} IV.							
Cr }	5	4		1	14		4497·041	,,	6·2	22230·7
Fe . . .		5	I.	2	18	4494·756	4494·735	,,	,,	22242·0
Ca . . .	1	1	M. IV.	5	2	4456·791	4456·793	1·22	,,	22431·5
Ca . . .	3r	2	M.	6	3	4456·055	4456·047	,,	,,	22435·2*a*
Ca . . .	6r	6	M. IV.	2	6	4454·949	4454·950	,,	,,	22440·7*b*
Fe . . .	8	5	I.	5	18	4447·912	4447·899	,,	,,	22476·3*b*
Ca . . .	4r	3	M. I.	5	6	4435·856	4435·852	,,	,,	22537·4*b*
Ca . . .	5r	4	M. III.	5	5	4435·133	4435·132	,,	,,	22541·0*b*
Ca . . .	5r	4	M. I.	9	7	4425·616	4425·609	1·21	6·3	22589·5*b*
Fe . . .	4r	4	M. III.	3	7	4415·298	4415·299	,,	,,	22642·2*a*
Cd . . .	6	6	M.			4413·181		,,	,,	22653·1
Fe }	3	3	} III.							
Va }	9r	2			19		4407·850	,,	,,	22680·5
Fe . . .	10r	8	M. III.	10	11	4404·928	4404·927	,,	,,	22695·6*b*
Ti }	1	1	} III.							
Fe }	2	3			14		4391·149	1·20	,,	22766·8
[d] Fe .	15r	10	M. II.	10	11	4383·721	4383·721	,,	,,	22805·4
Fe . . .	5	5	I.	1	17	4376·108	4376·103	,,	,,	22845·1*b*
Fe . . .	4	5	I.	1	14	4369·948	4369·943	,,	,,	22877·3*b*
Zr . . .	5	1								
Cr . . .	4	3	} III.		10		4359·778	,,	6·4	22930·5
Ni . . .	3	1								
Fe . . .	4	3	I.	1	17	4352·908	4352·903	1·19	,,	22966·8*b*
Fe }	2	2	} III.							
Cr }	2	1			11		4343·387	,,	,,	23017·1
[f] Fe .	10r	8	M. II.	8	15	4325·932	4325·940	,,	,,	23110·0*b*
Ca . . .	4r	3	M. I.	3	16	4318·816	4318·818	1·18	,,	23148·1*b*
Fe }	7r	5	III.	8	10	4308·072	4308·071	,,	6·5	23205·7*b*
[G] }			III.		3		4308·034	,,	,,	23205·9*b*
Ca . . .	4r	2	III.	3	3	4307·906	4307·904	,,	,,	23206·6*b*
Ti . . .	10r	4	M. III.	4	4	4306·071	4306·071	,,	,,	23216·5
Sr . . .	8	2	M.	1		4305·636		,,	,,	23218·9
Ca . . .	6r	4	M.	5	7	4302·690	4302·689	,,	,,	23234·8*b*
Ca . . .	3r	2	M. III.	3	5	4299·153	4299·152	,,	,,	23253·9*b*
? . . .		4	II.		14		4293·249	,,	,,	23285·9
Cr . . .	10r	4	M. III.	2	2	4289·884	4289·881	,,	,,	23304·2*b*
Ca . . .	4r	3	M. III.	3	5	4289·527	4289·523	,,	,,	23306·1*b*
Ca . . .	5r	3	M. III.	2	4	4283·175	4283·170	,,	,,	23340·7*b*
Cr . . .	15r	5	M. III.	1	2	4274·954	4274·958	1·17	,,	23385·5*b*
Fe . . .	10r	8	M. III.	8	9	4271·920	4271·924	,,	,,	23402·2*b*
? . . .	?	2	} III.		12		4267·958	,,	,,	23423·9

Catalogue of Spectra.

TABLE OF STANDARD WAVE-LENGTHS—*continued*.

Element.	Intensity and character.		Kind of standard.	Weight.		Wave-lengths.		Reduction to vacuo.		Oscillation frequency in vacuo.
	In arc.	In sun.		In arc.	In sun.	In arc (*a*).	In sun (*b*).	$\lambda +$	$\frac{1}{\lambda}$	
Fe . . .	6r	7	III.	4	3	4260·647	4260·638	1·17	6·5	23464·1*a*
Cr . . .	20r	7	M. I.	2	15	4254·494	4254·502	,,	,,	23498·0*b*
Fe . . .	5	7	II.	4	3	4250·949	4250·956	,,	6·6	23517·6*a*
Fe . . .	4	5	II.	1	1	4250·300	4250·290	,,	,,	23521·2*b*
[*g*]Ca . .	50r	10	M. III.	9	10	4226·898	4226·892	1·16	,,	23651·4*b*
Fe . . .	2	4	I.	1	22	4222·396	4222·381	,,	,,	23676·7*b*
C * . . .		1	M. III.	4	2	4216·133	4216·137	,,	,,	23711·8*a*
Sr } . .	40r	4	M. III.	{ 6	3	4215·688	4215·687	,,	,,	23714·3*a*
					18		4215·667	,,	,,	23714·4
Fe }	2	?2	III.	{	2		4215·616	,,	,,	23714·7
Fe . . .	8	5	II.	2	4	4202·187	4202·188	1·15	,,	23790·5*b*
Fe }	5									
Zr }	2	}5	I.	2	22	4199·257	4199·263	,,	6·7	23807·0*b*
C † . . .		1	M. III.	5	6	4197·256	4197·251	,,	,,	23818·4*b*
Fe . . .	4	3	I.		20		4185·063	,,	,,	23887·8
C . . .			M.			4158·2		1·14	,,	24042·2
Fe . . .	4	3	I.		17		4157·948	,,	,,	24043·6
Fe-Cr . .	3,1	3	II.		13		4121·968	1·13	6·8	24253·5
Co } + .	10r	3	} III.	1	12	4121·476	4121·481	,,	,,	24256·3*b*
Cr } + .	1	1								
Fe . . .	3	4	I.		14		4114·600	,,	,,	24296·9
Fe . . .	5	5	I.		12		4107·646	,,	,,	24338·0
Mn } . .	1	}6	I.		10		4103·101	,,	,,	24365·0
Si } . .	3									
Fe . . .	2	2	I.		8		4088·716	1·12	6·9	24450·7
Fe . . .	2	2	III.		7		4083·928	,,	,,	24479·3
Mn } . .	5	4	} III.		7		4083·767	,,	,,	24480·3
Fe } . .	2	2								
Sr . . .	50r	8	M. IV.	5	6	4077·876	4077·883	,,	,,	24515·6*b*
Fe . . .	4	4	I.		14		4073·920	,,	,,	24539·5
Fe . . .	10	10	M. IV.	7	9	4071·903	4071·904	,,	,,	24551·6*b*
Fe . . .	15r	15	M. IV.	7	7	4063·755	4063·756	,,	,,	24600·9*b*
Fe . . .	5	5	I.		8		4062·602	,,	,,	24607·9
Mn . . .	8	5	I.		13		4055·701	,,	,,	24649·7
Cr } . .	2									
Mn } . .	8	}6	III.		13		4048·893	1·11	7·0	24691·1
Zr } . .	1									
K . . .	40r	1?	M.	2		4047·373		,,	,,	24700·4
Fe . . .	20r	20	M. IV.	7	7	4045·975	4045·975	,,	,,	24708·9
K . . .	50r	1	M.	2	2	4044·301	4044·293	,,	,,	24719·2*b*
Mn . . .	7	3	M.		4	4035·88	4035·88	,,	,,	24770·7
Mn . . .	20r	5	M.	3	4	4034·642	4034·641	,,	,,	24778·2*b*
Mn . . .	25r	6	M.	3	4	4033·230	4033·225	,,	,,	24787·1*b*
Mn . . .	30r	7	M.	3	4	4030·919	4030·914	,,	,,	24801·3*b*
Zr } . .	2	}4	I.		10		4029·796	,,	,,	24808·1
Fe } . .	2									
Fe . . .		3	I.		7		4016·578	,,	,,	24889·8
Fe-? § .	10	10	III.		3		4005·305	1·10	,,	24959·9
Ce-Fe-Ti .	4,1,2	3	III.		9		4003·916	,,	,,	24968·5

* First line in first head of cyanogen band (*a*).
† First line in second head of cyanogen band (*a*).   ‡ Cobalt line measured.
§ Seven or eight lines, the brightest and most of the others due to Fe.

198 *An Introduction to the Study of Spectrum Analysis.*

TABLE OF STANDARD WAVE-LENGTHS—*continued.*

Element.	Intensity and character.		Kind of standard.	Weight.		Wave-lengths.		Reduction to vacuo.		Oscillation frequency in vacuo.
	In arc.	In sun.		In arc.	In sun.	In arc (a).	In sun (b).	$\lambda +$	$\frac{1}{\lambda} -$	
Co ⎫ Mn ⎬ ? ⎭	2 4 ?	⎫ 6 ⎬ ⎭	III.		4		3987·216	1·10	7·4	25073·0
Mn ⎫ ? ⎭	4 ?	1 7	⎫ III. ⎭		9		3986·903	..	..	25075·0
Fe ⎫ Cr ⎭	3 5	⎫ 6 ⎭	III.		9		3984·078	..	..	25092·8
Fe-Ti	6?	4	III.		14		3981·914	..	..	25106·4
Fe	5	4	I.		15		3977·891	..	..	25131·8
Ca *	5	3	M.	1	2	3973·881	3973·835	1·09	..	25157·5b
Fe	5	4	II.		11		3971·478	..	..	25172·4
H			M.			3970·05		..	..	25181·5
[H] Ca †	70r	200	M.	7	5	3968·617	3968·620	..	..	25190·6a
Al	30r	15	M. IV.	7	8	3961·680	3961·676	..	..	25234·7b
Fe	3	3	I.		11		3960·429	..	..	25242·7
Fe-Ca	5, 6	6	II.	1	2	3957·228	3957·180	..	..	25263·4b
Fe	2	2	II.		13		3954·001	..	7·2	25283·6
Yt	10	2	III.		13		3950·497	..	..	25306·1
Fe	4	4	I.		15		3950·101	..	..	25308·6
Ca	1	2	M.	1	2	3949·070	3949·034	..	..	25315·4b
Al ‡	20r	10	M. IV.	7	7	3944·165	3944·159	..	..	25346·7b
Fe ⎫ ? ⎭	5 ?	4 2	⎫ III. ⎭		15		3942·559	..	..	25357·0
Fe-Co	4, 4	5	III.	1	15	3941·034	3941·021	..	..	25366·9b
Fe	3	4	II.		8		3937·474	..	..	25389·8
[K] Ca +	75r	300	M.	6	5	3933·809 /	3933·809	1·08	..	25413·4
Fe	10r	8	M.	1	3	3928·060	3928·071	..	..	25450·6b
? ⎫ Fe ⎭	? 5	4 4	⎫ II. ⎭		12		3926·123	..	..	25463·2
Fe	3	4	III.		13		3925·792	..	..	25465·4
Va ⎫ Fe ⎭	2 1	⎫ 4 ⎭	II.		15		3925·345	..	..	25468·3
Ti	6	4	II.		15		3924·669	..	..	25472·7
Fe	3	3	II.	1	12	3916·886	3916·875	..	7	25523·4b
Si	10r	10	M.	4	4	3905·670	3905·666	..	7·3	25596·5b
Fe	3	4	II.		12		3897·599	..	..	25649·5
Fe	15r	9	M. IV.	7	6	3886·421	3886·427	1·07	..	25723·3a
Cr		1	III.		12		3883·773	..	..	25740·9
C §			M. IV.		8	3883·523	3883·548	..	..	25742·3b
C ‖		7	M. IV.	5	3	3883·479	3883·472	..	..	25742·8a
Va ⎫ ? ⎭		3	III.		15		3875·224	..	..	25797·7
C ¶		4	M.	4	4	3871·527	3871·528	..	..	25822·3b
C **		3	II.		8		3864·441	..	..	25869·7
Fe	10r	10	M. IV.	2	3	3860·050	3860·048	..	..	25899·1b
Fe	6	7	M.	1	2		3856·517	1·06	..	25922·8
Fe	4	5	III.		8		3843·406	..	..	26011·3
Fe	7r	7	M.	1	2	3840·589	3840·584	..	..	26030·4b
Mg	40r	20	M.		2		3838·430	..	..	26045·0

* Red component of double; the violet component is due to Fe.
† Solar line doubly reversed.   ‡ Red component of triplet.
§ Edge of first head of cyanogen band (*i*).
‖ First line of first head of cyanogen band (*i*).
¶ Second head of cyanogen band (*i*).   ** One of the lines in cyanogen band.

Catalogue of Spectra.

TABLE OF STANDARD WAVE-LENGTHS—continued.

Element.	Intensity and character.		Kind of standard.	Weight.		Wave-lengths.		Reduction to vacuo.		Oscillation frequency in vacuo.
	In arc.	In sun.		In arc.	In sun.	In arc (a).	In sun (b).	$\lambda +$	$\dfrac{1}{\lambda}-$	
C* . . .		5	M. IV.	1	1	3836·638	3836·652	1·06	7·3	26057·1b
? C . . .		4	III.		8		3836·226	,,	,,	26060·0
Mg . . .	30r	10	M.		2		3832·446	,,	,,	26085·7
Mg . . .	20r	8	M.		2		3829·505	,,	,,	26105·7
Fe . . .	8r	8	M.	1	1	3827·973	3827·973	,,	,,	26116·2
Fe . . .	20r	20	M. III.	4	4	3826·024	3826·024	,,	,,	26129·4
Mn (Cr) .	5, 1r	5	II.		10		3823·651	,,	,,	26145·7
Fe . . .	5	6	II.		10		3821·318	,,	,,	26161·7
Fe . . .	30r	30	M. III.	4	4	3820·566	3820·567	,,	·,	26166·8b
Fe . . .	20r	20	M. III.	4	3	3815·984	3815·985	1·05	7·4	26198·2a
Fe-Di . .	4, ?	6	I.		15		3805·487	,,	,,	26270·4
Fe . . .	2	3	I.		15		3804·153	,,	,,	26279·7
Fe . . .	8	8	III.		2		3799·698	,,	,,	26310·5
Fe . . .	7	7	III.		2		3798·662	,,	,,	26317·7
Fe . . .	8	8	M.	3	4	3795·148	3795·150	,,	,,	26342·0b
Fe-Cr . .	1, 1	3	III.		15		3794·014	,,	,,	26349·9
Fe . . .	7r	8	M. III.	3	3	3788·029	3788·032	,,	,,	26391·5b
Ni . . .	10r	6	III.		15		3783·674	,,	,,	26421·9
Fe . . .	2	3	II.		15		3781·330	,,	,,	26438·3
? . . .		4	II.		15		3780·846	,,	,,	26441·7
Th . . .	40r		M.	1		3775·869		1·04	,,	26476·6
Yt ? . .	6	3	M. III.	1	1	3774·478	3774·480	,,	·,	26486·3b
Fe . . .	3	4	III.		12		3770·130	,,	7·5	26516·8
Fe . . .	7r	8	M. III.	9	8	3767·342	3767·344	,,	,,	26536·4a
Fe . . .	9r	10	M.	9	8	3763·939	3763·942	,,	·,	26560·4a
Fe . . .	15r	15	M. III.	8	7	3758·380	3758·379	,,	·,	26599·7a
Fe . . .	2	2	II.		12		3756·211	,,	,,	26615·1
? } ? }		1 2	} III.		12		3754·664	,,	,,	26626·0
Fe . . .	20r	20	M. III.	7	8	3749·633	3749·633	,,	,,	26661·8
Fe . . .	10r	10	M. III.	7	8	3748·410	3748·409	,,	,,	26670·5b
? } Fe }	? 3	} 7	II.	1	9	3747·082	3747·095	,,	,,	26679·8b
Fe . . .	7r	7	M.	6	5	3746·048	3746·054	,,	,,	26687·3a
Fe . . .	10	10	M.	8	6	3745·708	3745·701	,,	·,	26689·7a
Cr } Fe } † . Ti }	3 5 3	2 6 2	} M. III.	4	2	3743·506	3743·502	,,	,,	26705·4a
Fe . . .	25r	30	M. III.	7	8	3737·280	3737·282	1·03	7	26749·9b
Ca . . .	4r		M. IV.	2	3	3737·081	3737·075	,,	·,	26751·4b
Mn } Ni }	2 6	5 3	} IV.		2		3736·969	,,	,,	26752·2
Fe . . .	40r	50	M. III.	8	7	3735·012	3735·014	,,	,,	26766·1a
Fe . . .	6r	7	M. III.	5	3	3733·467	3733·467	·,	,,	26777·3
Fe . . .	5	5	I.	1	15	3732·549	3732·542	,,	,,	26783·9b
Fe . . .	6r	7	M.	5	3	3727·768	3727·763	,,	7·6	26818·1a
Fe-Ti } † . Ni }	8, 5 4	} 10	M. III.	7	5	3722·712	3722·691	,,	,,	26854·5a
Fe . . .	40r	50	M. III.	11	10	3720·082	3720·086	,,	,,	26873·5a
Fe . . .	4	7	I.	1	12	3716·601	3716·585	,,	,,	26898·8b
Yt . . .	10r	3	M. III.	1	1	3710·442	3710·438	,,	,,	26943·4b

* Central line of symmetrical group.   † Iron line measured.

Table of Standard Wave-lengths—continued.

Element.	Intensity and character.		Kind of standard.	Weight.		Wave-lengths.		Reduction to vacuo.		Oscillation frequency in vacuo.
	In arc.	In sun.		In arc.	In sun.	In arc (a).	In sun (b).	$\lambda +$	$\frac{1}{\lambda} -$	
Fe . . .	10r	10	M. IV.	6	4	3709·395	3709·397	1·03	7·6	26951·0a
Fe . . .	5	5	I.	1	11	3707·201	3707·186	,,	..	26967·0b
Fe * . .	7r	8	M. III.	7	5	3705·715	3705·711	,,	,,	26977·7a
Fe . . .	5	5	I.	1	11	3695·208	3695·194	1·02	,,	27054·6b
Yt . . .		3	M. III.	1	1	3694·351	3694·349	,,	,,	27060·8b
Fe . . .	10r	8	M. III.	8	6	3687·609	3687·607	,,	,,	27110·2a
Fe . . .	5	6	I.	1	14	3684·268	3684·259	,,	,,	27134·9b
Pb . . .	60r	1	M.	5		3683·622		,,	7·7	27139·5
Va }	4		} 6							
Fe } †	3		I.	1	13	3683·209	3683·202	,,	,,	27142·6b
Co }	9									
Fe . . .	8r	8	M. III.	8	7	3680·064	3680·064	,,	,,	27165·7
Fe . . .		3	I.		13		3667·397	,,	,,	27259·6
Fe }	2		} 2							
Mn }	2		I.		7		3658·688	,,	..	27324·5
Ti . . .	10r	4	M. II.	2	7	3653·639	3653·639	1·01	,,	27362·3
Co . . .	5	3	I.		5		3652·692	..	,,	27369·4
Fe . . .	10r	10	M. III.	10	11	3647·995	3647·995	,,	,,	27404·6
Fe } †	5		} 5	1	14	3640·545	3640·536	,,	,,	27460·8b
Cr }	2									
Pb ‡ . .	50r	1	M.	4		3639·728		,,	,,	27466·9
Fe . . .	5	5	M. IV.	1	1	3638·454	3638·435	,,	7·8	27476·6b
Ti . . .	10r	3	M. II.	3	1	3635·615	3635·616	,,	,,	27497·9a
Yt ‡ . .	5	3	M.	1	1	3633·277	3633·259	,,	,,	27515·7b
Fe . . .	20r	20	M. IV.	11	10	3631·616	3631·619	,,	,,	27528·2a
Yt . . .	3	2	M. III.	1	1	3628·853	3628·853	,,	..	27549·1
Fe . . .	2	3	I.		10		3623·603	,,	,,	27589·1
Fe . . .	4	4	M. I.	1	14	3623·338	3623·332	,,	,,	27591·1b
Fe . . .	4	4	M. IV.	2	3	3622·161	3622·147	,,	,,	27600·1b
Fe . . .	4	4	M. III.	2	2	3621·616	3621·606	,,	,,	27604·3b
Yt . . .	3	1	M.	1	1	3621·096	3621·122	..	,,	27608·0b
Fe . . .	20r	20	M. IV.	11	10	3618·922	3618·924	,,	,,	27624·7a
Fe } †	4	3	} M. IV.	1	1	3617·939	3617·920	1·00	,,	27632·4b
Ca }		2								
Fe . . .	4	4	IV.	1	15	3612·237	3612·217	,,	,,	27676·0b
Yt . . .	7	3	M. III.	1	1	3611·196	3611·193	,,	,,	27683·9b
Fe . . .	15r	15	M. III.	11	10	3609·015	3609·015	,,	,,	27700·6
Fe § . .	4	6	M.	2	2	3606·836	3606·831	,,	,,	27717·4b
Fe . . .	5	7	M. IV.	2	2	3605·621	3605·635	,,	,,	27726·6b
Cr . . .	10r	4	M. IV.	1	2	3605·497	3605·483	,,	,,	27727·7b
Yt . . .	6	2	M. III.	1	1	3602·065	3602·061	,,	,,	27754·1b
Yt (Fe) .	10 ?	4	M. I.	1	1	3600·884	3600·880	,,	,,	27763·2b
Fe . . .	5	4	I.		12		3597·192	,,	,,	27791·7
C ‖ . . .		3	M.	7		3590·523		,,	7·9	27843·2
C . . .		2	M.	2		3586·041		,,	..	27878·0
C ¶ . . .	2	1	M.	8		3585·992		,,	,,	27878·4
Yt . . .	6	2	M.	1	1	3584·662	3584·662	,,	,,	27888·7

* Violet component of double.   † Iron line measured.
‡ Red component of double.
§ The solar line is a group of four; the second from the red is the brightest, and due to Fe.
‖ First line in first head of cyanogen band.
¶ First line in second head of cyanogen band.

Catalogue of Spectra.

TABLE OF STANDARD WAVE-LENGTHS—continued.

Element.	Intensity and character. In arc.	Intensity and character. In sun.	Kind of standard.	Weight. In arc.	Weight. In sun.	Wave-lengths. In arc (a).	Wave-lengths. In sun (b).	Reduction to vacuo. $\lambda +$	Reduction to vacuo. $\frac{1}{\lambda}$	Oscillation frequency in vacuo.
Fe ?	2	4	I.		12		3583·483	1·00	7·9	27897·9
Fe .	30r	40	M. IV.	9	6	N 3581·344	3581·344	,,	,,	27914·6
Fe .	10	10	M.	1	1	3570·412	3570·402	0·99	,,	28000·2b
Fe *	20r	20	M.	8	4	3570·253	3570·225	,,	,,	28001·3a
Fe .	10r	12	M.	6	4	3565·530	3565·528	,,	,,	28038·4a
Fe } Ti }	1 / 2	} 4	I.		12		3564·680	,,	,,	28045·1
Fe .	9r	8	M. III.	3	4	3558·674	3558·670	,,	,,	28092·5b
Fe .	2	3	I.		7		3550·006	,,	8·0	28161·0
Yt .	6	2	M. I.	1	1	3549·147	3549·145	,,	,,	28167·8b
?		4	I.		6		3545·333	,,	,,	28198·1
Fe .	3	5	I.		10		3540·266	,,	,,	28238·5
Th .	20r		M.	1		3529·547		0·98	,,	28324·3
Fe .	5r	7	M.	6	5	3521·409	3521·404	,,	,,	28389·7a
Th .	40r		M.	1		3519·342		,,	,,	28406·4
Co .	6r	5	I.		10		3518·487	,,	,,	28413·3
Fe †	7r	6	M.	2	3	3513·981	3513·947	,,	,,	28450·0b
Ti .	5	4	II.		8		3510·987	,,	,,	28474·0
Ni .	7r	7	I.		4		3500·993	,,	8·1	28555·2
Fe .	2	3	I.		4		3500·721	,,	,,	28557·5
? } Fe } +	6r	3 / 7	} M.	5	4	3497·991	3497·991	0·97	,,	28579·7
Fe *	5	5	M.	1	1	3497·266	3497·264	,,	,,	28585·7b
? } Ca }	? 4r	} 4	I.		8		3491·464	,,	,,	28633·2
Fe .	10r	10	M.	7	3	3490·724	3490·721	,,	,,	28639·3a
Ni .	4r	5	II.		9		3486·036	,,	,,	28677·8
Ni } Fe } Co }	2 / 3 / 2	} 4	I.		10		3478·001	,,	,,	28744·1
Fe ‡	7r	8	M.	5	2	3476·848	3476·831	,,	,,	28753·6a
Fe ‡	10r	10	M.	7	3	3475·602	3475·594	,,	,,	28763·9a
Fe } Co } §	10r / 10r	6 / 4	} M.	7	3	3466·010	3465·991	,,	8·2	28843·4a
Sr ?	8	3	I.		8		3464·609	,,	,,	28855·1
Co .	6r	4	I.		10		3455·384	0·96	,,	28932·1
Fe .	8r	8	M. IV.	6	4	3444·024	3444·032	,,	,,	29027·6a
Fe .	10	10	M. IV.	6	4	3441·135	3441·135	,,	,,	29052·0
Fe .	15r	15	M. IV.	7	4	3440·756	3440·759	,,	,,	29055·2a
Fe *	6	5	M.	2	1	3427·279	3427·282	,,	8·3	29169·4a
?		2	I.		15		3425·721	,,	,,	29182·6
Fe .	5	4	II.	1	18	3406·955	3406·955	0·95	,,	29343·4b
Fe .	2	1	II.	1	18	3406·602	3406·581	,,	,,	29346·6b
Ti } Co }	1 / 10r	3 / 3	} II.	1	12	3405·255	3405·272	,,	,,	29357·9b
Fe .	2	2	I.	1	12	3389·913	3389·887	,,	8·4	29491·1b
Ti } Ti }	5 / 5	3 / 3	} I.		9	?	3377·667	0·94	,,	29597·8
Zr .	4	1	I.		8		3356·222	,,	8·5	29786·9
Fe .	2	2	II.		9		3351·877	,,	,,	29825·5
Fe } Cr }	3 / 3	3 / 3	} II.		9		3348·011	,,	,,	29860·0

* Red component of double. † Violet component of double.
‡ Strongest line of a group of six. § Iron line measured.

TABLE OF STANDARD WAVE-LENGTHS—continued.

Element.	Intensity and character.		Kind of standard.	Weight.		Wave-lengths.		Reduction to vacuo.		Oscillation frequency in vacuo.
	In arc.	In sun.		In arc.	In sun.	In arc (a).	In sun (b).	$\lambda +$	$\dfrac{1}{\lambda}$	
Fe	2	2	11.		8		3331·741	0·93	8·5	30005·8
Ti	5	5	1.		10		3318·163	,,	8·6	30128·6
Co-Ti }	3, 6	4	} 1.		10		3308·928	,,	,,	30212·7
Mn }	2	1								
Fe *	10	7	M. IV.	1	5	3306·481	3306·471	,,	,,	30235·1b
Fe †	10	7	M. IV.	1	5	3306·119	3306·117	,,	,,	30238·4b
Fe }		3	} 11.		10		3303·648	,,	,,	30261·0
? }		3								
Na }	10r	5	M. IV.	1	6	3303·119	3303·107	,,	,,	30265·9b
Na }	15r	6	M. 1.	1	6	3302·504	3302·501	,,	,,	30271·5b
Mn-Di.	3, 2	4	1.		9		3295·957	0·92	,,	30331·6
Co-Ti }	4, 7	} 5	} 1.		10		3292·174	,,	,,	30366·5
Fe }	5									
Ti	6	5	1.		9		3287·791	,,	8·7	30406·9
Cu	30r	6	M. 1.	15	5	3274·090	3274·092	,,	,,	30534·1a
Va	10	4	1.		10		3267·839	,,	,,	30592·6
Fe }	1									
Ti }	3	} 4	11.		10		3260·384	,,	,,	30662·5
Mn }	4									
Cu	40r	9	M. IV.	15	5	3247·671	3247·680	0·91	8·8	30782·5a
Fe }		6	1.		12		3246·124	,,	,,	30797·2
? }										
Ti	10r	8	M.	1	1	3236·696	3236·697	,,	,,	30886·9b
Ti	6	4	III.		12		3232·404	,,	,,	30927·9
? }	?	} 5	1.		1		3231·421	,,	,,	30937·3
Ti }	5									
Fe	8	8	M.	3	1	3225·907	3225·923	,,	,,	30990·2a
Ti	6	4	1.		3		3224·368	,,	,,	31005·2
? }	?	7	} M. III.	3	1	3222·197	3222·203	,,	,,	31025·9a
Fe? }	6	5								
Fe		6	11.		1		3219·909	0·90	,,	31048·0
Fe		6	11.		1		3219·697	,,	,,	31050·0
Ti	4	3	1.		6		3218·390	,,	,,	31062·6
Fe	5	5	M.	1		3214·152		,,	8·9	31103·5
Ti	10r	4	M. I.	1	5	3200·040	3200·032	,,	,,	31240·8b
Ni	3	3	M.	1	1	3195·729	3195·702	,,	,,	31283·1b
Cr?	4	4	11.		5		3188·164	,,	,,	31357·1
La?	1	1	11.		5	F	3176·104	0·89	9·0	31476·1
F ?		5	1.		1		3172·175	,,	,,	31515·1
Mn		1	11.		5		3167·290	,,	,,	31563·7
Ca		8	M.	1	1	3158·994	3158·988	,,	,,	31646·7b
Fe		2	11.		3		3153·870	,,	,,	31698·1
Fe		3	11.		5		3140·869	0·88	9·1	31829·2
Co	4	2	11.		3		3137·441	,,	,,	31864·0
Ni	10r	8	M.	1		3134·223		,,	,,	31896·7
Zr	3	1	11.		5		3129·882	,,	,,	31941·0
Va	7	5	1.		9		3121·275	,,	,,	32029·1
Fe		2	1.		3		3115·160	,,	,,	32092·0
Cr?		3	11.		1		3109·434	,,	9·2	32151·0
?		2	III.		1		3106·677	,,	,,	32180·5
Ni	10r	6	M.	3		3101·994		0·87	,,	32228·1

* Second line from violet side of a group of four.
† Second line from red side of a group of five.

Table of Standard Wave-Lengths—continued.

Element.	Intensity and character. In arc.	Intensity and character. In sun.	Kind of standard.	Weight. In arc.	Weight. In sun.	Wave-lengths. In arc (a).	Wave-lengths. In sun (b).	Reduction to vacuo. $\lambda +$	Reduction to vacuo. $\frac{1}{\lambda}$ -	Oscillation frequency in vacuo.
Ni	20r	8	M.	3		3101·673		0·87	9·2	32231·5
Fe	6	6	M.	3		3100·779		,,	,,	32240·8
Fe (Mn)	4?	4	M.	3		3100·415		,,	,,	32244·5
Fe	4	7	M.	3		3100·064		,,	,,	32248·2
Fe	1	3	II.		9		3095·003	,,	,,	32300·9
?		2	II.		9		3094·739	,,	,,	32303·7
Al	4	2	M.	8		3092·962		,,	,,	32322·3
Al	20r	10	M.	15		3092·824		,,	,,	32323·7
Ti	8r	8	M.	1		3088·137		,,	,,	32372·8
?		4	I.		1		3086·891	,,	,,	32385·9
Fe	6r	7	M.	5		3083·849		,,	9·3	32417·7
Al	20r	7	M.	17		3082·272		,,	,,	32434·3
?		5	I.		1		3080·863	,,	,,	32449·1
Mn	7	2	I.		1		3079·724	,,	,,	32461·1
Ti	4	6	M.	3		3078·759		,,	,,	32471·3
Fe ?		4	I.		6		3078·148	,,	,,	32477·8
?		4	III.		6			3077·303	,,	,,	32486·7
Fe		2	M.	1		3077·216		,,	,,	32487·6
Fe	10r	10	M.	4		3075·849		,,	,,	32502·0
Ti	6	8	M.	3		3075·339		,,	,,	32507·4
Fe	10r	10	M.	10		3067·363		,,	,,	32592·0
Co	8r	3	M. I.	1	5	3061·952	3061·930	0·86	,,	32649·8b
?		3	II.		1		3061·098	,,	,,	32658·7
Fe	10r	10	M.	15		3059·200		,,	,,	32679·0
Fe	10r	10	M.	8		3057·557		,,	,,	32696·6
?		5	I.		5		3055·821	,,	,,	32715·1
?		3 / 3	} II.		1		3053·527	,,	9·4	32739·6
Fe		3	II.		5		3053·173	,,	,,	32743·4
?		3 / 3	} I.		5		3050·212	,,	,,	32775·2
Fe	20r	20	M.	13		3047·720		,,	,,	32802·0
?			II.	1			3046·778	,,	,,	32812·2
Mn	10r	3	II.	5			3044·683	,,	,,	32834·7
Ca	15r	4	M. IV.	3	2	3044·114	3044·119	,,	,,	32840·9a
Fe	15r	15	M.	10	2	3037·505	3037·492	,,	,,	32912·4a
?		5	III.	7			3035·850	,,	,,	32930·3
Fe			M.	1		3027·245		,,	,,	33023·9
Fe		10r	10	M.	7	3025·958		,,	,,	33038·0
?		4	II.		7		3025·394	,,	,,	33044·1
?		5	II.		7		3024·475	,,	9·5	33054·1
Fe	7r	7	M.	7		3024·154		,,	,,	33057·6
Fe	15r		M.	18		3021·191		0·85	,,	33090·0
Fe	25r		M.	18		3020·759		,,	,,	33094·8
Fe	10r		M.	15		3020·611		,,	,,	33096·4
Fe			M.	1		3019·752		,,	,,	33105·8
Fe	5		M.	1		3019·109		,,	,,	33112·9
Fe	5		M.	1		3017·747		,,	,,	33127·8
Fe		3	M.	1		3016·296		,,	,,	33143·7
?		6	IV.	4			3014·274	,,	,,	33166·0
?		4	IV.	5			3012·557	,,	,,	33184·9
Fe	4r		M.	3		3009·696		,,	,,	33216·4
Ca	7r		M.	3		3009·327		,,	,,	33220·5
Fe	6r		M.	15		3008·255		,,	,,	33232·4

Table of Standard Wave-lengths—continued.

Element	Intensity and character.		Kind of standard.	Weight.		Wave-lengths.		Reduction to vacuo.		Oscillation frequency in vacuo.
	In arc.	In sun.		In arc.	In sun.	In arc (a).	In sun (b).	$\lambda +$	$\frac{1}{\lambda} -$	
Fe	1		M.	3		3007·408		0·85	9·5	33241·7
Fe	2		M.	1		3007·260		,,	,,	33243·4
Ca	15r		M.	3		3006·978		,,	,,	33246·5
?		4	III.	1			3005·404	,,	,,	33263·9
?		3	III.	1			3005·160	,,	,,	33266·6
Fe	8r		M.	15		3001·070		,,	,,	33312·0
Ca	8r		M.	3		3000·976		,,	,,	33313·0
Ca	6r		M.	3		2999·767		,,	,,	33326·4
Fe	4r		M.	5		2999·632		,,	,,	33327·9
Ca	10r		M.	3		2997·430		,,	9·6	33352·3
Ca	7r		M.	3		2995·074		,,	,,	33378·6
Fe	8r		M.	18		2994·547		,,	,,	33384·4
Si	4		M.	5		2987·766		,,	,,	33460·2
Fe			M.	1		2987·410		,,	,,	33464·2
Fe	10r		M.	15		2983·689		,,	,,	33506·0
Fe	2		M.	6		2981·570		0·84	,,	33529·8
Fe	12r		M.	15		2973·358		,,	,,	33622·4
Fe	6r		M.	7		2973·254		,,	,,	33623·6
Fe	4r		M.	7		2970·223		,,	9·7	33657·8
Fe	8r		M.	12		2967·016		,,	,,	33694·2
Fe			M.	1		2966·985		,,	,,	33694·6
Fe	5		M.	3		2965·381		,,	,,	33712·8
Fe	5		M.	3		2957·485		,,	,,	33802·8
Fe	7r		M.	1		2954·058		,,	,,	33842·0
Fe	8r		M.	4		2947·993		,,	,,	33911·7
Fe	10r		M.	4		2937·020		0·83	9·8	34038·3
Fe	8r		M.	3		2929·127		,,	,,	34130·1
Fe	7r		M.	3		2912·275		,,	9·9	34327·5
Si	15		M.	12		2881·695		0·82	10·0	34691·8
Mg	100r		M.	15		2852·239		0·81	10·1	35050·1
Fe	6		M.	5		2851·904		,,	,,	35054·2
Fe	5		M.	7		2844·085		,,	10·2	35150·5
Fe	3		M.	1		2843·744		,,	,,	35154·7
Fe	3		M.	1		2838·226		,,	,,	35223·1
Fe	4		M.	7		2832·545		,,	,,	35293·7
Fe	5		M.	1		2825·667		,,	,,	35379·7
Fe	3		M.	1		2823·3–9		0·80	10·3	35408·1
Fe	5		M.	3		2813·388		,,	,,	35534·0
Mg	20r		M.	10		2802·805		,,	,,	35668·2
Mn			M.	3		2801·183		,,	,,	35688·9
Mn			M.	3		2798·369		,,	10·4	35724·7
Mg	20r		M.	12		2795·632		,,	,,	35759·7
Mn			M.	3		2794·911		,,	,,	35768·9
Fe			M.	3		2788·201		,,	,,	35855·0
Mg *	5r		M.	5		2783·077		0·79	,,	35921·1
Fe			M.	1		2781·945		,,	,,	35935·7
Mg *	5r		M.	5		2781·521		,,	,,	35941·2
Mg *	8r		M.	5		2779·935		,,	,,	35961·7
Mg *	5r		M.	3		2778·381		,,	,,	35981·8
Fe			M.	2		2778·340		,,	,,	35982·3
Mg *	5r		M.	5		2776·798		,,	,,	36002·3
Fe			M.	2		2772·206		,,	10·5	36061·9

* A remarkable symmetrical group of five Mg lines.

Catalogue of Spectra.

TABLE OF STANDARD WAVE-LENGTHS—continued.

Element.	Intensity and character.		Kind of standard.	Weight.		Wave-lengths.		Reduction to vacuo.		Oscillation frequency in vacuo.
	In arc.	In sun.		In arc.	In sun.	In arc (a).	In sun (b).	$\lambda +$	$\dfrac{1}{\lambda} -$	
Fe			M.	2		2767·630		0·79	10·5	36121·5
Fe			M.	2		2762·110		,,	,,	36193·7
Fe			M.	2		2761·876		,,	,,	36196·8
Fe			M.	3		2756·427		,,	,,	36268·4
Fe			M.	2		2755·837		,,	,,	36276·1
Fe			M.	3		2750·237		,,	10·6	36349·9
Fe			M.	3		2742·485		,,	,,	36452·7
Fe?			M.	3		2737·405		0·78	,,	36520·3
Fe?			M.	3		2733·673		,,	,,	36570·2
Fe			M.	3		2723·668		,,	10·7	36704·5
Ca	5		M.	1		2721·762		,,	,,	36730·2
Fe			M.	3		2720·989		,,	,,	36740·6
Fe			M.	3		2719·119		,,	,,	36765·9
Fe			M.	2		2706·684		,,	,,	36934·9
Fe			M.	3		2679·148		0·77	10·9	37314·4
Si	5		M.	7		2631·392		0·76	11·1	37991·6
Fe			M.	3		2631·125		,,	,,	37995·5
Fe			M.	2		2611·965		,,	,,	38274·3
Fe			M.	3		2599·494		0·75	11·2	38457·8
Fe			M.	2		2598·460		,,	,,	38473·1
Mn			M.	2		2593·810		,,	,,	38542·1
Fe			M.	2		2585·963		,,	11·3	38659·0
Fe?			M.	2		2584·629		,,	,,	38679·0
Mn			M.	2		2576·195		,,	,,	38805·6
Al	10		M.	5		2575·198		,,	,,	38820·7
Al	10		M.	5		2568·085		,,	11·4	38928·1
Fe			M.	2		2549·704		0·74	,,	39208·8
Fe			M.	3		2546·068		,,	11·5	39264·8
Fe			M.	3		2541·058		,,	,,	39342·2
Hg	50r		M.	2		2536·648		,,	,,	39410·6
Fe			M.	3		2535·699		,,	,,	39425·4
Si	10		M.	5		2528·599		,,	11·6	39536·0
Fe			M.	3		2527·530		,,	,,	39552·7
Si	9		M.	10		2524·206		,,	,,	39604·8
Fe			M.	3		2522·948		,,	,,	39624·6
Si	8		M.	10		2519·297		,,	,,	39682·0
Fe			M.	3		2518·188		,,	,,	39699·5
Si	15		M.	7		2516·210		0·73	,,	39730·7
Si	7		M.	10		2514·417		,,	,,	39759·1
Fe			M.	3		2510·934		,,	11·7	39814·1
Si	10		M.	15		2506·994		,,	,,	39876·7
			M.	3		2501·223		,,	,,	39968·7
B	20		M.	20		2497·821		,,	,,	40023·2
B	15		M.	20		2496·867		,,	,,	40038·5
Fe			M.	3		2491·244		,,	11·8	40128·8
Fe			M.	3		2490·723		,,	,,	40137·2
Fe			M.	3		2489·838		,,	,,	40151·5
Fe			M.	3		2488·238		,,	,,	40176·3
Fe			M.	3		2484·283		,,	,,	40241·3
Fe			M.	3		2483·359		,,	,,	40256·2
Fe			M.	3		2479·871		,,	,,	40312·9
C	10		M.	15		2478·661		,,	,,	40332·6
Fe			M.	3		2472·974		,,	11·9	40425·2
Fe			M.	3		2462·743		0·72	,,	40593·2

Table of Standard Wave-lengths—continued.

Element.	Intensity and character.		Kind of standard.	Weight.		Wave-lengths.		Reduction to vacuo.		Oscillation frequency in vacuo.
	In arc.	In sun.		In arc.	In sun.	In arc (a).	In sun (b).	$\lambda +$	$\frac{1}{\lambda}$	
Fe			M.	3		2457·680		0·72	12·0	40676·8
Si	3		M.	10		2452·219		,,	,,	40767·4
Fe ?			M.	3		2447·785		,,	,,	40841·3
Si			M.	10		2443·460		,,	12·1	40913·5
Si	3		M.	10		2438·864		,,	,,	40990·6
Si	8		M.	15		2435·247		,,	,,	41051·5
Fe			M.	2		2410·604		0·71	12·3	41471·1
Fe			M.	2		2406·743		,,	,,	41537·6
Fe			M.	2		2404·971		,,	,,	41568·2
Fe			M.	2		2399·328		,,	,,	41666·0
Ca	25r		M.	5		2398·667		,,	,,	41677·5
Fe ?			M.	3		2395·715		,,	12·4	41728·8
Fe			M.	2		2388·710		,,	,,	41851·2
Fe ?			M.	3		2382·122		,,	12·5	41966·0
Fe			M.	2		2373·771		0·70	,,	42114·6
Al	7		M.	3		2373·213		,,	,,	42124·5
Al	6		M.	3		2367·144		,,	12·6	42232·4
Fe			M.	2		2364·897		,,	,,	42272·5
Fe			M.	2		2348·385		,,	12·7	42569·8
Fe			M.	2		2343·571		,,	,,	42656·4
Ba	20r		M.	1		2335·267		,,	12·8	42808·9
Ba	20r		M.	1		2304·364		0·69	13·0	43382·9
Fe ?			M.	2		2298·246		,,	13·1	43498·3
Ca	20r		M.	3		2275·602		0·68	13·3	43931·1
Sr	10r		M.	1		2275·376		,,	,,	43935·5
Al	4		M.	2		2269·161		,,	,,	44055·8
Al	3		M.	2		2263·507		,,	,,	44165·9
Si	2		M.	2		2218·146		0·67	13·7	45069·0
Si	4		M.	2		2216·760		,,	,,	45097·2
Si	2		M.	2		2211·759		,,	13·8	45199·1
Si	3		M.	2		2210·939		,,	,,	45215·8
Si	2		M.	2		2208·060		,,	,,	45274·8
Sr	3		M.	1		2165·990		0·66	14·2	46154·1
Sr	2		M.	1		2152·912		,,	14·3	46434·4

EXPLANATORY NOTE.—The first column gives the symbol of the element whose wave-length has been measured, e.g. O signifies oxygen, wv water-vapour, etc. If a letter stands at the left within brackets : thus, [A] [C], it is the "name" of the line in the solar spectrum. A mark of interrogation after the symbol means that it is doubtful if the line is really due to that element. Two symbols on the same line (e.g. Mn Di, 3295·957) signify that these two elements have apparently coincident lines as their wave-length. Two or more symbols bracketed (e.g. Si Mn Fe } 3260·384) mean that the first has a line coinciding with one side of the corresponding solar line, the second with the middle, etc. A mark of interrogation alone signifies that the chemical origin of the line is unknown. The fifth and sixth columns give the "weights" to be attached to the lines as standards in the arc and solar spectrum respectively. The fourth column gives the character of the standard. M. means a standard in the arc spectrum ; I. a remarkably good standard in the solar spectrum ; II. a good solar standard ; III. an ordinary solar standard ; and IV. a rather poor solar standard. Columns 7 and 8 give the wave-lengths in air at about 20° C. and 760 mm. Lines marked with two dashes are double : thus, 6″. r signifies reversed.

AIR.

Spark-spectrum or Elementary Line-spectrum.

Wave-length.	Intensity and character.		Wave-length.	Intensity and character.		Wave-length.	Intensity and character.	
6603·4	4s	N	⎰ 4710·1	5	O	(15)		
6563·0	7s	H	⎱ 4709·7	2	N	⎰ 4241·9	6b	N
6480·8	5s	N	⎰ 4705·6	6	O	⎨ 4236·7	6b	N
6171·9	5s	NO	⎱ 4705·0	2	N	⎱ 4228·5	6b	N
5950·2	4s	N	4699·4	6	O	(10)		
⎰ 5942·6	10n	N	(3)			⎰ 4190·1	7	O
⎱ 5933·6	10n	N	4676·4	6	O	⎱ 4185·7	7	O
5929·6	4s	N	(7)			(7)		
5768·5	3	N	⎰ 4649·2	8	O	⎰ 4153·6	6	O
5747·5	3	N	⎨ 4643·4	9	N	⎨ 4151·9	5	N
(1)			⎱ 4641·9	9	O	⎱ 4145·9″	7	NO
5712·3	6	N	(1)			(5)		
5686·3	5	N	4638·9	5	O	⎰ 4133·8	6	N
5679·8	12	N	4634·0	3	N	⎨ 4132·8	6	O
5676·0	5	N	4630·7	12	N	⎨ 4123·8	5	NO
5667·1	9	N	4621·6	9	N	⎨ 4121·6	4	O
(3)			4614·0	8	N	⎨ 4120·5	6	O
5535·2	6	N	4609·5	2	O	⎱ 4119·4	9	NO
(2)			4607·3	8	N	(6)		
5496·6	6	N	4601·6	9	N	4097·5″	8b	NO
5479·8″	5b	N	4596·3	6	O	(5)		
5462·8	5	N	4590·9 ⎱	7b	O	⎰ 4076·1	9	O
5453·8″	5	N	4590·0 ⎰			⎨ 4072·4	9	O
(21)			(10)			⎱ 4070·0	8	O
⎰ 5180·0	5	N	4507·7	6	N	(2)		
⎱ 5176·7″	1	NO	(10)			⎰ 4041·4	6b	N
(4)			⎰ 4447·2	12	N	⎱ 4035·3	5b	N
5045·7	7	N	⎱ 4447·1	4	O	(4)		
(3)			(4)			⎰ 3995·1	12	N
5011·1″	5	N	4426·0	5	N	⎱ 3983·0	4	O
5007·8	5	N	⎰ 4417·2	9	O	(3)		
⎰ 5005·7	10	N	⎱ 4415·1	9	O	⎰ 3956·2	7	N
⎱ 5002·7	10	N	(9)			⎱ 3954·8	5	O
4994·9	6	N	4367·9	7	O	(5)		
(19)			(2)			3919·2″	10	NO
4803·6	7	N	⎰ 4351·5	6	O	3912·3	5	O
4788·3	6	N	⎱ 4349·5	8	O	(30)		
4780·1	5	N	4347·6″	6	NO	3749·8	6	O
(10)			4345·7	6	O			

The following symbols are employed in these tables to indicate the character of the lines:—s denotes that the line is sharply defined; n, that the line is ill defined or nebulous; b denotes a band, the position of the brightest part being given; b″ denotes a band, sharply defined, on the least refracted side, and fading away towards the blue; b′ a band sharply defined on its more refracted side, and fading away towards the red; c denotes that the line is continuous, and d that it is discontinuous, or a "short" line; r denotes that the line is often "reversed."

The intensities of the lines are expressed upon an ascending scale from 1 to 10 (or sometimes more); 1 being the feeblest.

Lines marked with two dashes, thus, 4347·6″, are double.

ALUMINIUM.

Wave-length.	Intensity and character.		Wave-length.	Intensity and character.	
	Arc.	Spark.		Arc.	Spark.
7057·9		5s	1+ {2660·5	10r	5sd
7042·5		6s	{2652·6	10r	5sd
(3)			2575·5	4r	7sd
*6245·2		8nc	5* {2575·2	10r	7sd
*6235·2		8nc	{2568·1	10r	
5723·5		10sc	(2)		
5696·6		10sc	6*+ {2378·5	6r	1
(1)			{2373·4	4r	
5057·4		10nc	2373·2	8r	} 2n
4663·1		10nc	2372·2	4r	2n
4530·5		6nc	2367·1	10r	2n
4511·9		6sd	(6)		
4479·4		6sd	7* {2269·2	8	1n
(1)			{2263·8	2r	
3+ {3961·7	10r	9sc	6+ {2263·5	8r	
{3944·2	10r	9sc	{2258·3	2	
3587·0		10b	8* {2210·1	4r	
3093·0	6r		{2204·7	4r	
4* {3092·8	10r	9sc	(9)		
{3082·3	10r	9sc	{1990·6		
3066·3	6	8	{1989·9		
3061·4	6	8	{1935·9		
3060·0	6	1	{1935·3		
3057·3	6	8b″	{1862·8		
3054·8	6	8	{1862·2		
3050·2	6	8b″	{1854·8		
2816·4		10	{1854·1		

The oscillation frequencies $\left(\frac{1}{\lambda}\right)$ in air of the pairs marked * can be calculated from the formula $10^8 \frac{1}{\lambda} = a - bn^{-2} - cn^{-4}$, where $a = 48308\cdot2$ for the *first* line and $48420\cdot2$ for the *second* line of the pair, $b = 15666\cdot2$, $c = 250533\cdot1$; and for the pairs marked †, $a = 48244\cdot5$ for the *first* line and $48356\cdot5$ for the *second* line, $b = 12752\cdot7$, $c = 68781\cdot9$. The figure before the * or † gives the value of n.

ANTIMONY.

Wave-length.	Intensity and character.		Wave-length.	Intensity and character.	
	Arc.	Spark.		Arc.	Spark.
6302·8		8sd	3425·9		6nd
6245·7		4sd	(6)		
6210·1		4sd	3383·2	2	6sc
6194·4		4sd	(4)		
6156·2		4sd	3337·3		8nd
6129·6		10sc	(1)		
6079·1		10sc	3305		6sd
6052·2		4sd	(5)		
6004·7		10sc	3267·6	6r	10sc
5980·6		4sd	(3)		
5910·1		8nc	3241·3		8nd
5894·6		8nc	3232·6	6r	
5792·5		4nd	(9)		
5639·1		8nc	3029·9	6r	6sd
5568·7		8nc	(14)		
5464·5		6nc	2878·0	10r	7sc
5380·2		6nc	(4)		
5242·7		6nd	2851·2	2	8
5178·2		6nd	(8)		
(5)			2790·6		8
4949·7		8nc	(2)		
4878·6		6nd	2770·0	8r	8sc
(6)			(5)		
4592·4		6nc	2719·0		6sc
(11)			(1)		
4352·4		7sd	2670·7	6r	7n
4265·0		6sd	(6)		
(12)			2598·2	10r	10r
4033·7	4	8	2590·4		7nd
(15)			(9)		
3739·5		8sd	2528·6	10r	10r
3722·9	4	8	(11)		
(10)			2478·4		6sc
3637·9	4	8sc	(8)		
(1)			2445·7	4r	6sc
3630·0		5sd	(23)		
(1)			2311·6	10r	2n
3597·7		8nd	2306·6	8r	1n
3566·7		6nd	(7)		
3559·5		6nd	2262·6	6	
3534·0		5sd	(7)		
3519·7		5sd	2179·3	6r	6nc
3504·8		6nd	2176·0	10r	6nc
3498·6		6nd	(5)		
3474·0		6nd	2098·5	6	2nc
(2)			2068·5	10r	4nc

ARGON.

Wave-length.	Intensity and character.	Wave-length.	Intensity and character.	Wave-length.	Intensity and character.
(6)		5496·2	6	(7)	
7504·0	7	(5)		3868·7	7
(1)		5451·9	6	(4)	
7384·2	5	(49)		3850·7	8
(4)		4880·1	8	(4)	
7273·1	5	(1)		3834·8	8
(3)		4866·1	6	(12)	
7067·5	5	(1)		3781·1	7
(1)		4847·9	6	(15)	
6965·8	6	(2)		3729·5	9
(7)		4806·2	8	(21)	
6753·1	5	(5)		3678·4	6
(5)		4736·0	6	(7)	
6677·6	6	(6)		3634·6	6
(15)		4609·7	7	(12)	
6416·5	8	(1)		3588·6	9
(1)		4579·5	6	(3)	
6384·9	5	(5)		3582·5	7
(4)		4545·3	6	(9)	
6307·9	5	(3)		3576·8	8
(1)		4510·9	7	3567·9	7
6297·1	5	(4)		(1)	
(11)		4426·2	6	⎧ 3563·5	6
6216·1	6	(13)		⎨ 3561·5	7
6212·7	6	4348·1	9	⎩ 3559·7	8
(7)		4345·2	7	(5)	
6173·3	6	(3)		⎰ 3546·0	7
6172·7	5	4335·4	6	⎱ 3545·8	7
6170·4	5	4333·6	8	(9)	
(3)		(4)		3511·3	6
6155·5	5	4300·2	8	(14)	
6145·6	6	(3)		3491·7	9
(12)		4277·6	6	(6)	
6105·9	6	4272·3	8	3477·0	6
(2)		4266·4	8	(56)	
6099·0	6	(1)		3301·9	6
(8)		4259·5	9	(3)	
6059·6	7	(7)		3285·9	7
6053·0	6	4200·7	10	(53)	
6043·5	8	4198·4	10	3093·6	6
(2)		⎰ 4191·0	10	(17)	
6032·4	9	⎱ 4190·8	7	2979·3	6
(8)		4182·0	7	(2)	
5987·6	5	(2)		2943·0	7
(6)		4164·4	7	(20)	
5942·9	5	(1)		2806·3	8
(1)		4158·6	10	(7)	
5929·1	6	(8)		2769·7	8
(4)		4104·1	7	(3)	
5912·3	7	(5)		2753·9	8
(3)		4044·5	8	2744·9	8
5888·8	6	(5)		(1)	
(20)		4014·0	7	2732·7	6
5607·4	7	(5)		(2)	
(8)		3949·1	8	2708·4	8
5559·0	7	(5)		(12)	
(6)		3928·8	7	2647·6	8

Argon—continued.

Wave-length.	Intensity and character.	Wave-length.	Intensity and character.	Wave-length.	Intensity and character.
(19) 2562·3	6	2515·6 (12)	8	2454·5 (7)	6
(6) 2544·8	6	2491·0 (7)	6	2438·8 (14)	6
(6) 2516·8	8	2479·2 (11)	6	2415·7 (136)	6

ARSENIC.

Wave-length.	Intensity and character.		Wave-length.	Intensity and character.	
	Arc.	Spark.		Arc.	Spark.
6170·6		8sc	2898·8	4r	2
6110·2		8nc	2860·5	6r	10sc
6022·8		4sd	(1)		
5652·1		8nc	2831·0		8nc
5559·2		8nc	2780·3	8r	10nc
5499·1		6nc	2745·1	6r	10sc
5332·1		6nc	2493·0	1	8sc
5230·5		5nc	2456·6	4r	8sc
5104·5		5nc	2437·3	1	8sc
(1)			2381·3	4r	8sc
4495·5		8sd	⎰ 2370·9	4r	8nc
4466·6		8sd	⎱ 2369·7	4r	8nc
(7)			(1)		
4037·2		30sd	2349·9	10r	10nc
3948·8		6sd	2288·2	10r	10nc
3931·4		6sd	2271·5	4	6sc
3922·6		100sd	2266·8	4	3sd
(2)			2230·0		6nc
3119·7	4	8nc	(1)		
(1)			2165·6	4	8nc
3033·0	4	6sc	2156·3		8sd
2991·2			2134·4		8nd
2959·8		10nd			

BARIUM.

Wave-length.	Intensity and character.		Wave-length.	Intensity and character.	
	Arc.	Spark.		Arc.	Spark.
6527·6	4	6sd	4506·1	6r	6
6498·9	4		(4)		
6497·1	6r	10sc	4432·1	6r	8
6483·1	4	6sd	(2)		
6451·0	4	6sd	4402·7	8r	8
6341·9	4	6sd	(2)		
6141·9	10r	10sc	4350·5	8r	6
6111·0	6	6sc	(6)		
(1)			4283·3	8r	8
6063·3	6	6sd	(7)		
6019·7	6	6sd	4166·2	4	10r
5997·3	4	6sd	4130·9	8r	10b
(1)			(3)		
5971·9	8	6sd	3995·9	6	2
(1)			3993·6	10r	8
5907·9	6		(1)		
5853·9	10r	10sc	3938·1	6	2
5826·5	8r	6sd	3935·9	8r	4
(1)			(2)		
5805·9	6r		3910·1	8r	6r
5800·5	6r	6sc	(1)		
(1)			3892·0	6n	10b
5777·8	10r		(28)		
(3)			3544·9	6nr	2n
5680·3	6r		(3)		
(2)			3525·2	6nr	2b
5535·7	10r	10sc	3501·3	10r	8
5519·4	8r	4sc	(5)		
(2)			3368·3		8
5424·8	8r	6sc	3357·0	6b"r	1n
(18)			(16)		
4934·2	10r	10nc	3152·8		6
(1)			(1)		
4900·1	8		3119·3	1n	6
(1)			3104·0		6
4726·6	8r	2	(2)		
(1)			3071·7	6r	6
4700·6	6b"	1	(18)		
4691·7	6r		2771·5	6	8b
4673·7	6b"		(11)		
(8)			2634·9	8	8
4579·8	8r	6	(14)		
4574·1	6r	4	2347·7	6	4n
4554·2	10r	10b r	2335·3	8r	4r
4525·2	6	10b	(2)		
4523·5	6	2n	2304·3	8r	2r

Catalogue of Spectra.   213

BERYLLIUM.

Wave-length.	Intensity and character.		Wave-length.	Intensity and character.	
	Arc.	Spark.		Arc.	Spark.
4572·9		1	2650·7″		7
4489·6			2494·8 ⎫		3r
3321·5 ⎱		3	2494·7 ⎭		
3321·2 ⎰			2348·7		3
3131·2	10	15	(1)		
3130·6	10	20r			

BISMUTH.

Wave-length.	Intensity and character.		Wave-length.	Intensity and character.	
	Arc.	Spark.		Arc.	Spark.
6600·3		4sd	(3)		
6493·8		6sc	3397·3	4r	10r
6130·1		8uc	(8)		
6057·7		8nc	3067·8	10r	10b^{r}cr
(2)			(2)		
5862·6		8uc	3024·8	8r	8r
5817·1		6sd	2993·5	8r	8r
(1)			2989·1	8r	8r
5717·6		8nc	(2)		
(2)			2938·4	10r	10r
5552·4	8b^r	4sd	2898·1	10r	10r
5451·0		8nc	(4)		
(1)			2809·7	8r	2n
5271·1		8nc	(1)		
5209·1		8nc	2780·6	8r	4nr
(1)			2730·6	6r	4
5144·5		10nc	(4)		
5124·5		10nc	2696·8	6r	4
(2)			(1)		
4993·9		10sc	2628·0	8r	4n
(5)			(4)		
4722·7	10r	10sc	2524·6	8r	2b
(3)			2515·7	6r	1b
4561·4		7sd	(1)		
(6)			2489·5	6b	
4302·6		9b^{r}d	(4)		
(1)			2401·0	8r	2u
4259·9		9sd	(8)		
(4)			2276·6	8n	2b
4122·0 ⎰	6	8	2230·7	10r	1nr
4121·7 ⎱	6	8	2228·3	8r	1n
4079·4		10n	(2)		
(7)			2203·2	6u	
3793·0		8b	2189·7	8r	
(2)			2176·7	6r	
3695·6		10	(1)		
(1)			2157·0	10r	
3613·9		4b	(1)		
3596·3	4r	10scr	2153·0	8r	
(2)			2134·4	10r	
3511·0	4r	8sc	2133·7	8r	
(3)			2110·3	10r	
3451·1		8u	2061·8	10r	

214   *An Introduction to the Study of Spectrum Analysis.*

BORON.
Spark-spectrum.

Wave-length.	Intensity and character.	Wave-length.	Intensity and character.
3957·9	2	2496·8 *	10
3941·7	2	2388·5	1
3829·3	1	2267·0	2
3824·5	1	2266·4	2
3451·3	6	2088·8	2
3246·9	1	2088·4	2
2689·0	1	2066·2	2
2686·2	1	2064·6	2
2497·7	10		

* Also observed in the arc.

BROMINE.
Vacuum Tube Spectrum.

Wave-length.	Intensity and character.	Wave-length.	Intensity and character.	Wave-length.	Intensity and character.
6682·8	2	4849·0	6s	4525·8	8b″
6632·0	5	(3)		(1)	
(4)		4816·9	8s	4513·7	5s
6351·0	10	(4)		(1)	
(4)		4785·6	10s	4478·0	5b″
6149·9	10	4780·5	6s	4472·8	8
(10)		(1)		(7)	
5852·4	5	4776·6	7s	4441·9	8b″
(1)		(3)		(2)	
5831·0	7	4767·3	8s	4425·3	5s
(14)		4766·3	5b″	(5)	
5590·1	8	(4)		4396·5	5
(11)		4742·9	8s	(6)	
5507·0	8	4735·7	5b″	4365·8	8s
5495·2	7	(3)		(2)	
5489·0	6	4719·9	8	4291·5	6
(3)		(4)		4237·0	6s
5466·4	5	4705·0	10b	(1)	
(2)		(3)		4224·0	8
5135·3	5	4693·5	8s	(1)	
(1)		(2)		4193·6	6
5425·2	5	4678·9	8b	(1)	
5423·0	7	(2)		4179·8	8
5395·7	5	4672·7	6s	4175·9	5s
(5)		(1)		(6)	
5335·3	5	4652·2	6s	4140·4	6s
(1)		(4)		(1)	
5332·2	10	4623·0	8s	4135·8	5s
(1)		4614·9	6s	(12)	
5304·3	7	(1)		4024·2	5b″
(5)		4601·6	5n	(3)	
5238·5	8	(1)		4008·9	6b″
(6)		4575·9	6b″	4007·4	5s
5182·6	7	(1)		(6)	
(2)		4543·1	8s	3986·7	8s
5164·6	5	(1)		3980·6	10n
(14)		4538·9	5b	3980·2	5s
4930·8	5s	(1)		3968·8	5s
4929·0	5s	4530·0	5s	3955·5	8b″
(5)		(1)		3950·7	7b″

Catalogue of Spectra.

BROMINE—continued.

Wave-length.	Intensity and character.	Wave-length.	Intensity and character.	Wave-length.	Intensity and character.
3939·9	5b″	3919·8	6s	3857·4	6s
3938·8	5b″	(1)		(1)	
3935·3	6b″	3914·4	9	3834·9	6b″
3929·7	6b	(2)		(9)	
3924·2	8b″	3891·8	8s	3740·7	5b
3923·5	6	(1)		(6)	
3920·8	6b″	3871·4	6s		

CADMIUM.

| Wave-length. | Intensity and character. | | Wave-length. | Intensity and character. | |
	Arc.	Spark.		Arc.	Spark.
(1)			4† 3133·3	8b″	8s
6467·4		6n	(8)		
6439·3	10scr	10s	3085·4		5s
(9)			4† 3081·0	6b″	5s
5490·2		6s	(16)		
5472·5		6s	5* 2980·8	8r	10s
(1)			5* 2881·3	4r	
5379·3		10s	2880·9	8r	10b
5338·6		10s	(8)		
(4)			5† 2868·4	6b″	5b
5154·9	6b″	1s	(1)		
5086·1	10r	10s	5* 2837·0	8r	8b
3†{ 4800·1	10r	10s	(7)		
4678·4	10r	10s	5† 2775·1	6b″	6s
4662·7	8b″	3s	(2)		
4415·9	6sc	10s	6* 2764·0	6r	4s
4413·3	6	2	(1)		
4217·1		6s	2748·7	2b″	10s
4127·1		6s	5† 2734·0	6b″	3
4095·0		7s	(3)		
{ 3988·4		5s	6* 2677·6	8n	8
{ 3984·7		3s	(3)		
3977·8		6s	6* 2639·6	6r	3b
3976·8		6s	(6)		
3958·9		7s	2573·1	4	10s
(2)			(21)		
3940·4		8s	2329·3	8r	7s
(13)			2321·2	1	8s
4* 3613·0	8r	8s	2313·0	4	10b
3610·7	10r	10s	2306·7	4r	5s
(3)			2288·1	10br	10sr
4* 3467·8	8r	10s	2267·5	4r	3s
3466·3	10r	10s	2265·1	4r	10sr
4* 3403·7	10r	10s	(1)		
(5)			2239·9	6r	3
3261·2	10r	8s	(3)		
4† 3252·6	8b″	7s	2194·7	1	5s
3250·5	7s	7s	(3)		
(17)			2144·5	4r	5sr

* These lines form a series of triplets, the oscillation frequency of which can be calculated from the formula $10^8 \frac{1}{\lambda} = a - bn^{-2} - cn^{-4}$, in which $a = 40755\cdot21$ for the *first* line, 41914·60 for the *second*, and 42456·64 for the *third* line, $b = 128635$, $c = 1289619$.

† These lines form a series of triplets for which $a = 40797\cdot12$ for the *first* line, 41968·80 for the *second*, and 42510·58 for the *third*; $b = 126146$, $c = 555137$.

CÆSIUM.

Wave-length.	Intensity and character.		Wave-length.	Intensity and character.	
	Arc.	Spark.		Arc.	Spark.
8919·9	10		4604·0		7
8527·7	10		* 4593·3	6r	6r
* 6973·9	6n		* 4555·4	8r	10r
(2)			(2)		
* 6723·6	8n		4277·3		5n
(8)			* 3888·8	4r	
* 6010·6	4n		* 3876·7	6r	1n
(1)			(3)		
* 5845·1	4n		* 3611·8	4r	1n
(2)			(2)		
* 5664·0	6n		2332·5		3n
* 5635·1	4n		(4)		
(13)			2267·6		3n

The lines marked * occur in the flame-spectrum.

Catalogue of Spectra.

CALCIUM.

Wave-length.	Intensity and character.		Wave-length.	Intensity and character.	
	Arc.	Spark.		Arc.	Spark.
6499·9	4	8sc	(2)		
6494·0	4	10sc	4318·8	8r	8sc
6471·9	4	8sc	(2)		
6462·8	6r	10sc	4307·9	8r	6sd
6450·0	1	8	4302·7	10r	10sc
6439·4	10r	10sc	4299·1	6r	6sd
(6)			4289·5	8r	8sc
{ 6169·9	6	5sc	4283·2	8r	8sc
{ 6169·4	4	5sc	(7)		
6166·8	4	5	4226·9	10r	10nc
(1)			(9)		
3 † 6162·5	10r	10sc	4 † 3973·9	6b^v	4
(1)			H 3968·6	10r	80nc
3 † 6122·5	10r	10sc	4 † 3957·2	6b^v	2s
3 † 6103·0	8r	8sc	3949·1	4b^v	1n
5867·9	6b^v		K 3933·8	10r	100nc
5857·8	10n	6sc	(8)		
5603·1	8	4sd	3737·2	4	15
5601·5	8	6sd	(1)		
5598·7	8n	6sd	3706·2	4	10
5594·6	10n	8sc	(3)		
5590·3	8	4sd	5 * 3644·5	10r	2n
5589·0	10	10sc	5 * 3630·8	8r	1n
5582·2	8r	4sd	5 * 3624·2	8r	1n
5513·1	8		(6)		
5349·7	10	8sc	5 † 3487·8	6b^v	2b^v
5270·5	10	8sc	5 † 3475·0	4b^v	2b^v
5265·8	8	6sc	5 † 3468·7	4b^v	
5264·5	6	4sd	6 * 3361·9	8b^v	
5262·5	6	2sc	6 * 3350·2	8b^v	
5261·9	6	2sc	6 * 3344·5	6b^v	
(1)			6 † 3286·3	4b^v	
5189·0	6r	6sc	6 † 3274·9	2b^v	
5041·9	8b^v	8sc	6 † 3269·3	2b^v	
4878·3	10b^v	6sc	7 * 3225·7	4b^v	
(♦)			7 * 3215·2	4b^v	
4586·1	10r	4sd	7 * 3209·7	2b^v	
4581·7	8r	4sd	7 † 3181·4	4	7b^v
4578·8	8r	4sd	3179·4	6	10b^v
4527·2	6		7 † 3170·2	2	1n
(1)			7 † 3166·9	1n	
4 * 4456·1	8r	2sc	3159·1		10b^{v}r
(1)			8 * 3150·9	6	
4455·0	10r	10sc	8 * 3140·9	2n	
4 * 4435·9	8r	2sc	8 * 3136·1	2n	
4435·1	10r	10sc	(7)		
4 * 4425·6	10r	10sc	2398·7	8r	2n
(7)			2275·6	8r	2
4355·4	6b		2200·8	8r	1s

The lines marked * and † form a series of triplets, the oscillation frequencies of which are given by the formula $10^8 \frac{1}{\lambda} = a - bn^{-2} - cn^{-4}$, where $a = 33919\cdot51$ for the *first* line, $34022\cdot12$ for the *second*, and $34073\cdot82$ for the *third* line of the triplet, $b = 123547$, $c = 961696$ in the triplets marked *; for those marked †, $a = 34041\cdot17$ or $34146\cdot95$ or $34199\cdot09$, $b = 120398$, $c = 346097$. The figure preceding the sign * or † shows the value of n.

CARBON.

LINE-SPECTRUM.

Wave-length.	Intensity and character.	Wave-length.	Intensity and character.
⎰ 6584·2	4s	2993·2	4n
⎱ 6578·7	5s	2967·6	3s
5379·8	2s	⎰ 2837·4	8s
5151·2	3	⎱ 2836·2	8s
5144·9	3s	2747·3	6n
5132·9	3s	2641·4	4s
4267·5	7s	2511·8	7s
3920·8	2b	2508·0	6s
*3883·8	3	2478·7	10s
3877·0	3	(4)	
*3872·0	3	2296·8	6n
(6)			

* Due to cyanogen.

CARBON.

BAND-SPECTRUM.

Wave-length.	Intensity and character.	Wave-length.	Intensity and character.
⎧ 6188·1	3b^r	⎧ 4737·2	4b^r
⎪ 6120·0	4b^r	⎪ 4715·3	3b^r
α ⎨ 6052·0	3b^r	ε ⎨ 4697·6	2b^r
⎪ 5999·0	2b^r	⎪ 4684·0	1b^r
⎩ 5955·0	1b^r	⎩ 4677·0	1b^r
⎧ 5635·4	8b^r	⎧ 4381·9	
⎪ 5585·5	7b^r	⎪ to	2b
γ ⎨ 5540·9	3b^r	⎪ 4356·0	
⎪ 5500·0	2b^r	ζ ⎨ 4334·4	1s
⎩ 5470·0	2b^r	⎪ 4315·0	5b^r
⎧ 5165·2	10b^r	⎪ to	
δ ⎨ 5129·4	5b^r	⎩ 4234·0	
⎪ 5101·0	3b^r		
⎩ 5081·9	1b^r		

CARBON OXIDE.

Wave-length.	Intensity and character.	Wave-length.	Intensity and character.
6079·0	4b^r	4837·6	5b^r
5611·5	5b^r	4517·7	5b^r
5199·4	4b^r	4393·7	4b^r

Catalogue of Spectra.

CERIUM.

Wave-length.	Intensity and character.		Wave-length.	Intensity and character.	
	Arc.	Spark.		Arc.	Spark.
(4) 5472·8		6s	4300·5		4
(2) 5410·3		8s	(2) 4296·9		10
5393·5		8s	(4) 4290·1		6
5353·3		10s	(34) 4248·8		6
5331·1		6s	(4) 4246·1		5
5274·3		10s	(4) 4240·1		5
(3) 5187·8		6s	(12) 4227·9		4
(3) 5079·5		6s	(2) 4222·8		5b"
(4) 4714·1		8n	(15) 4203·1		5
4628·3		10s	4201·4		4
(3) 4594·1		4	4198·8		6
(5) 4572·5		10s	(4) 4196·5		4
(2) 4562·5		5	(4) 4193·4		4
(1) 4560·5		4	4193·2		4
(6) 4539·9		8n	(6) 4186·7		10
(3) 4528·6		8n	(12) 4170·0		5
4527·5		10n	(1) 4167·0		5
4523·2		8s	(2) 4165·7		10
(10) 4487·0		4	4163·7		4
(2) 4484·0		4	(5) 4159·2		4
(1) 4479·5		4	(5) 4152·1		9
(1) 4471·4		6	(1) 4150·1		10
(5) 4460·1		8	(2) 4146·4		4
(5) 4449·5		4	4145·2		7
(1) 4444·9		4	(2) 4142·6		5
(15) 4419·0		6	(6) 4137·8		9
(19) 4391·8		8s	(3) 4134·0		10
(5) 4382·3		8s	(3) 4131·3		4
(10) 4364·8		4	4130·8		4
(13) 4350·0		4	(4) 4127·5		4
(9) 4337·9		4	(4) 4124·9		4
(18) 4306·9		4	4124·0		5b"
(5)			(4) 4120·0		7

CERIUM—continued.

Wave-length	Intensity and character.		Wave-length	Intensity and character.	
	Arc.	Spark.		Arc.	Spark.
(1) 4118·3		6	(5) 4024·7		5
(3) 4115·5		5	(10) 4015·0		4
(9) 4107·6		4	4012·6		10
(2) 4105·1		4	(7) 4003·9		4b"
(2) 4101·9		5	(7) 3999·4		6
(20) 4083·4		5	(3) 3994·0		4
(1) 4081·4		4	(49) 3952·7		7b"
(13) 4073·6		4	(14) 3942·9		5
(14) 4062·4		4	(200) 3801·7		8
(11) 4053·7		4	(251) 3577·6		4
(9) 4046·5		4b"	(8) 3561·0		4b"
4045·4		4	(70) 3471·0		5
(1) 4042·7		5	(6) 3459·5		4
(2) 4040·9		7	(1) 3454·5		4
(6) 4031·5		4b"	(92) 3055·7		4
(3) 4028·6		4b"	(47)		

CHLORINE.
VACUUM TUBE SPECTRUM.

Wave-length	Intensity and character.	Wave-length	Intensity and character.	Wave-length	Intensity and character.
(13) 5423·4	10b"	*4253·6	10b"	(1) 3820·4	5
5392·3	6b	4241·5	8b"	(3) 3805·4	6
(1) {5221·5	6b	(11) *4132·7	9b"	(1) 3799·0	5b"
{5218·1	8b"	(20) 3861·0	10s	(1) 3781·4	5s
(21) *4819·6	9b	(6) 3851·5	8s } b"	(5) 3750·1	5s
*4810·2	9b	3851·2	10s }	(26) 3353·4	5s
*4794·6	10b	(2) 3845·8	8s }		
(39) *4373·1	8s	3845·6	5s } b"	(1) 3329·1	5b
(3) *4343·8	10sr	3843·4	5s }	(5)	
(4) *4307·6	8s	(2) 3833·5	6b"		
(8)		(2) 3827·8	5		

The lines marked * occur in the spark-spectrum.

CHROMIUM.

Wave-length.	Intensity and character.		Wave-length.	Intensity and character.	
	Arc.	Spark.		Arc.	Spark.
(2) 5791·2	6	2	(1) 4530·9	6	7
(36) 5410·0	10	8sc	(3) 4526·6	6	7
(10) {5348·5 / 5346·0	8 / 8		(12) 4497·0	5	6sd
(4) 5328·5	8n		(55) 4385·1	6	6b″
(4) 5298·1	8		(10) 4371·4	6	7
(2) 5296·9	8	2sd	(3) 4359·8	6	7
(3) 5276·2	6		(3) 4351·9	8	8sc
(1) 5275·3	6	4sd	4351·2	6	7b″
(2) 5265·9	6		(1) 4344·7	7	8sc
(1) 5264·3	8	4sd	(2) {4339·8 / 4339·6	6 / 6	8sc / 8sc
(3) 5247·7	6	4sd	(25) 4289·9	15nr	10scr
(15) {5208·6 / 5206·2 / 5204·7	10nr / 10nr / 10nr	10sc / 10sc / 10sc	(3) 4274·9	20nr	10scr
			(11) 4254·5	30nr	10scr
(35) 4922·4	5	4sd	(122) 3976·8	6	9
(56) 4718·6	6		(1) 3971·4	6	3
(1) 4708·2	6		(3) 3963·9	5	10
(30) {4652·3 / 4651·4	7 / 7 }	4sd	(25) 3928·8	6	6
(5) 4646·3	7	4sd	(4) 3919·3	7	8
(9) 4626·3	6	1	(132) 3605·5	10nr	10r
(6) 4616·3	6	7	(4) 3593·6	10nr	10r
(8) 4600·9	6	6	(2) 3578·8	10nr	10r
(4) 4591·6	6	5	(122) 3430·5		10
(7) 4588·4	1	10	(10) 3422·9		10
(14) 4558·9	2	10	(1) 3421·4		10
(3) 4546·1	6	7	(6) 3408·9		10
(7) {4540·9 / 4540·7	6 / 6	5 / 5	(3) 3403·5		10
(1) 4535·9	6	6	(31) 3368·2		10
			(4) 3360·5		10
			(15)		

CHROMIUM—continued.

Wave-length.	Intensity and character.		Wave-length.	Intensity and character.	
	Arc.	Spark.		Arc.	Spark.
3342·8		10	(5)		
(1)			3120·5		10
3340·0		10	3118·8		10
(28)			(253)		
3307·2		10	2843·3		10r
(76)			(8)		
3197·2		10	2835·7		10r
(10)			(76)		
3180·8		10	2766·6		10
(40)			(9)		
3132·2		10	3762·7		10
(4)			(543)		
3125·1		10			

COBALT.

Wave-length.	Intensity and character.		Wave-length.	Intensity and character.	
	Arc.	Spark.		Arc.	Spark.
6143·8		6sc	4749·9	9	4sd
6122·5		6sc	(25)		
(3)			4663·6	8	1
6004·7		8nc	(9)		
(9)			4629·5	9	1
5483·6	8	4sd	(11)		
(5)			4597·0	8	1
5453·6	2	6sc	4594·7	8	1
(1)			(2)		
5444·8	7	6sc	4581·8	10	4sd
(18)			(5)		
5369·8	6s	6sc	4565·7	9	2
(5)			(5)		
⎰ 5353·7	3	6sc	4549·8	8	1
⎱ 5352·2	5	6sc	(6)		
(3)			4531·1	10	4sd
⎰ 5343·6	6	2sd	(20)		
⎱ 5342·9	8	2sd	4469·7	8	1
(20)			(71)		
5280·8	6	6sc	4121·5	9	8
(2)			4118·9	9	8
5266·7	6	2sd	4110·7	8	2
(81)			(8)		
4868·0	10	10sc	4092·6	8	6
(5)			(18)		
4840·4	9	10sc	4045·5	8	2
(3)			(9)		
4813·7	9	10sc	⎰ 3998·0	8	6
(4)			⎱ 3995·5	9	8
4793·0	8	10sc	(23)		
(3)			3936·1	8	6
4780·1	8	10sc	(16)		
(7)			3894·2	10ur	10

Catalogue of Spectra.

COBALT—continued.

Wave-length.	Intensity and character.		Wave-length.	Intensity and character.	
	Arc.	Spark.		Arc.	Spark.
(11) 3873·2	9n	10	3367·3	10	5
(9) 3845·6	9n	10	(17) 3354·5	10	7
(77) 3621·3		8	(14) 3334·3	10	5
(11) 3587·3	10nr	10	(42) 3283·6	6	7
(12) 3569·5	10nr	10	(8) 3274·1		7
(17) 3529·9	9nr	10	(19) 3247·7		7
(1) 3527·0	9nr	8	3247·3	3	7
(12) 3523·6	6r	10	(74) 3154·8	6	7
(12) 3506·4	8nr	10	(6) 3140·1	8	5
(4) 3502·4	9nr	8	(1) 3137·5	8	5
(11) 3495·8	7	10	(9) 3121·7 } 3121·6 }	8	5
(4) 3489·5	8r	10	(35) 3086·9	8	6
(9) 3474·1	8n	10	(10) 3072·5	8	6
(6) 3465·9	10	8	(21) 3044·1	6	7
(1) 3462·9	8	8	(63) 2954·8		8
(9) 3453·6	4	8	(2) 2943·2	8	6n
(5) 3449·6 } 3449·3 }	10	{ 7 7 }	(58) 2871·3		7
(4) 3443·8	6	7	(31) 2825·3	8	6
(11) 3433·2 } (1) 3431·7 }	10	{ 7 7 }	(116) 2694·7	1	8
			(26) 2663·6	1	8
(13) 3417·3	8	7	(4) 2653·7		7
(3) 3412·8 3412·5	10 10	7 7	(3) 2648·7	10	7
(1) 3409·3	10	7	(9) 2632·3	1	8
(1) 3405·3	10	8	(16) 2618·8	8	4
(7) 3395·5	10	7	(1) 2614·4	1	7
(3) 3388·3 3387·8	10 10	7 5	(16) 2587·2	1	8
(5) 3378·9	10	4	(2) 2582·3	1	8n
(13)			(1) 2580·4	3	8n
			(9) 2564·2	1	8
			(1)		

224   *An Introduction to the Study of Spectrum Analysis.*

COBALT—*continued.*

Wave-length.	Intensity and character.		Wave-length.	Intensity and character.	
	Arc.	Spark.		Arc.	Spark.
2562·3	10	2	(9)		
(1)			2425·0	10	4
2560·1	1	7	(13)		
2559·5	1	8	2411·6	10	4
(14)			(3)		
2546·8		7	2407·7	10	4
(7)			(8)		
2542·0 }	8	{ 8n	2402·1 }	8	{ 2
2540·7 }		{ 6	2401·6 }		{ 2
(11)			(2)		
2531·9	10	2n	2397·4	10	6
(3)			(7)		
2528·7	8	7	2388·9	10	6
(2)			(1)		
2525·1	10	7	2386·4	8	4
(3)			(2)		
2521·0	10	2	2383·5	8	5
2519·9		8	(6)		
2517·9	8	2	2378·6	10	7
(7)			(17)		
2511·2	10	7	2363·8	6	7
(3)			(13)		
2506·5	10	8	2353·5	6	5
(6)			(46)		
2496·8	8	2	2307·7	8	4
(30)			(16)		
2472·9	8	2	2293·4	8	4
(10)			(6)		
2456·2	8	2	2286·3	8	5
(24)			(55)		
2432·6	10	5			

COPPER.

Wave-length.	Intensity and character.		Wave-length.	Intensity and character.	
	Arc.	Spark.		Arc.	Spark.
6381·1		6s	5105·8	8r	8s
6219·5		4s	(30)		
5782·3	8s	8s	4704·8	8s	5s
(3)			(2)		
5700·4	8s	6s	4675·0	6b	6s
(57)			4651·3	8s	8s
5292·8	6s	6s	(9)		
(8)			4587·2	10n	8s
5220·2	6s	6s	(1)		
4 * 5218·4	10b^{r}r	10sr	4539·6	8br	3b
(3)			4 † 4531·0	8b^{r}r	2s
4 * 5153·4	8nr	10sr	(1)		
(7)			4507·8	6n	1n

Catalogue of Spectra.

COPPER—continued.

Wave-length.	Intensity and character.		Wave-length.	Intensity and character.	
	Arc.	Spark.		Arc.	Spark.
(2)			(11)		
4 † 4480·5	8b"r	3b	2545·1		10s
4415·9	6b	1b	(5)		
4378·3	8r	1n	2529·6		8s
4275·3	8r	10s	(13)		
(5)			2506·5		10s
5 * 4062·9	10b"	7b"	(6)		
(1)			2492·2	6r	6s
5 * 4022·9	10b"	4s	2489·8		8s
(70)			(7)		
3602·1	6b	4n	2473·6		8s
3599·2	6b	1n	2468·7		8s
(12)			(17)		
3450·4	6b	3s	2441·7	6r	6s
(13)			(15)		
3308·1	8b	7s	2406·8	8b"	1s
(1)			(3)		
3290·6	6n	3b	2392·8	8b"r	4
(2)			(4)		
3274·1	10r	8s	2370·0	6	10s
(1)			(20)		
3247·6	10r	10s	2303·2	6	4s
(15)			(1)		
3126·2	6b	6s	2294·4	10r	6s
(1)			(9)		
3108·6	6b	5s	2263·2	6r	2b
(5)			(4)		
3063·5	6	3s	2247·1	4b	7s
(8)			(1)		
2961·2	6r	5s	2242·6	4	7s
(13)			(2)		
2766·5	6b"r	2s	2230·2	8r	3b
(11)			(1)		
2713·8		8s	2227·9	8r	2n
2703·5		9s	(1)		
2701·3		10s	2225·8	6r	2s
(2)			(2)		
2689·7		10s	2215·4	6r	3s
(9)			2214·6	8r	3s
2618·5	10r	8s	(3)		
2609·4		7s	2199·8	8r	3s
2600·5		10s	(5)		
2599·1		8s	2179·4	6r	5s
(12)			(41)		
2571·2		7n			

The lines marked 4 * 5 * form a series of pairs, the oscillation frequency of which can be calculated from the formula $10^8 \frac{1}{\lambda} = a - bn^{-2} - cn^{-4}$, where $a = 31591\cdot6$ for the *first* line and $31840\cdot1$ for the *second* line, $b = 131150$, $c = 1085060$. For the lines marked †, $a = 31591\cdot6$ or $31840\cdot1$, $b = 124809$, $c = 440582$.

CYANOGEN.

Wave-length.	Intensity and character.	Wave-length.	Intensity and character.
6819	8bʳ	4216·1	10bʳ
6582	7bᵛ	4197·2	10bʳ
6452	5bʳ	θ 4181·5	9bʳ
6328	5bʳ	4177·7	8bʳ
6203	4bʳ	4165·4	8bʳ
4600	10bʳ	4158·2	7bʳ
4574	10bʳ	3883·6	10bʳ
4550	9bʳ	3871·5	9bʳ
ς 4532	9bʳ	ι 3861·9	8bʳ
4515	8bʳ	3855·1	7bʳ
4505	7bʳ	3590·5	10bʳ
4500	6bʳ	3586·0	9bʳ
4381·9		3584·0	9bʳ
4371·3		3361·0	10bʳ
4365·0			

DIDYMIUM.

Wave-length.	Intensity and character.		Wave-length.	Intensity and character.	
	Arc.	Spark.		Arc.	Spark.
6741·2		4s	5173·9		4s
6386·0		4s	(3)		
(35)			5130·7		6s
5689·0		4s	5111·3		4s
5676·9		4s	(2)		
(3)			5102·8		4s
5620·5		3s	(6)		
(2)			4995·2		
5594·5		4s	(3)		
(4)			4959·0		4s
5485·9		6s	4955·0		4s
(14)			4944·0		4s
5372·0		6s	4924·4		6s
5361·5		6s	4901·9		4s
5357·5		4s	4897·4		5s
5322·9		4s	4890·9		5s
5319·9		8s	(1)		
(2)			4881·9		5s
5293·5		8s	(1)		
(2)			4859·5		4s
5273·5		6s	4825·0		4s
(2)			4812·0		4s
5359·5		4s	(8)		
5255·5		4s	4706·9		4s
(1)			(3)		
5249·5		8s	4683·4		4s
(7)			(3)		
5192·5		6s	4633·8		4s
5191·5		6s	4622·3		4s
5180·0		4s			

See also Neodidymium and Praseodidymium.

ERBIUM.

Wave-length.	Intensity and character.		Wave-length.	Intensity and character.	
	Arc.	Spark.		Arc.	Spark.
(7)			3729·7		5
5827·0		8	(24)		
5763·0		6	3707·7		5
(6)			(18)		
5344·4		6	3692·8		10
5257·0		8	(47)		
5218·0		6	3646·1		7
5189·0		6	(13)		
(4)			3633·7		5
4952·0		8	(22)		
4899·9		8	3617·9		5
4872·4		6	(1)		
(1)			3616·7		7
4820·0		6	(16)		
(5)			⎰ 3599·9		7
4675·8		6	⎱ 3599·6		5
(50)			(103)		
4500·9		6	3499·3		10
(37)			(101)		
4419·8		8	3392·2		5
(72)			(4)		
4252·1		5	3385·3		7
(34)			(13)		
4143·1		5	3372·9		10
(39)			(58)		
4055·6		5	3316·6		5
(50)			(5)		
3974·8		5	3312·6		5
(41)			(39)		
3906·5		10	3265·0		5
(4)			(28)		
3903·0		5	3230·7		5
(3)			(89)		
3896·5		8U^v	3122·8		5
(35)			(247)		
3830·7		6	2723·3		5
(43)			(15)		
3761·5		5	2698·5		
(35)			(238)		

EUROPIUM.

Wave-length.	Intensity and character.		Wave-length.	Intensity and character.	
	Arc.	Spark.		Arc.	Spark.
(5) 4662·1	50	5	(68) 3972·2	50	50
(7) 4627·4	100r	8	(26) 3930·7	50	50
(5) 4594·2	100r	10	(15) 3907·3	30	30
(13) 4522·8	20	15	(65) 3819·8	50	50
(15) 4435·7	50	30	(91) 3725·1	20	30
(78) 4205·2	100	50	(29) 3688·6	20	10
(47) 4129·9	100	100	(737)		

GALLIUM.

Wave-length.	Intensity and character.		Wave-length.	Intensity and character.	
	Arc.	Spark.		Arc.	Spark.
6412·4		6	4864·6		6b
6326·7		8	4255·8		
5994·9		4	4172·2	10	10r
5851·5		4	(3)		
5428·9			4033·2	10	6r
5369·5		4	(15)		

GERMANIUM.

Wave-length.	Intensity and character.		Wave-length.	Intensity and character.	
	Arc.	Spark.		Arc.	Spark.
6020		10	2754·7		20r
5892		10	(1)		
4686·1		10r	2709·7		20
(2)			2691·5		15
4261·0		10	{ 2651·6		15r
4226·8		50r	{ 2651·2		15r
4179·2		20	(2)		
(16)			2592·6		15r
3269·7		10	(11)		
(5)			2417·4		10
3039·2		20r	(15)		
(4)					

GOLD.

Wave-length.	Intensity and character.		Wave-length.	Intensity and character.	
	Arc.	Spark.		Arc.	Spark.
6278·4	4	8sc	(3)		
5957·2	4	6sc	2748·3		5s
(1)			(17)		
5837·6	6		2676·1	10r	12s
5656·0	4		(7)		
5064·7	2		2641·6		6s
4792·8	6	4r	(44)		
(8)			2503·3		7s
4488·4	4	4r	(26)		
(1)			2428·1	10r	15r
4437·4	4	2r	(35)		
(5)			2365·0	4	6r
4315·4		8r	(4)		
(11)			2352·7	4	5s
4065·2	6	15	(7)		
(2)			2340·3		7b
4053·0		7	(9)		
(4)			2322·4		7s
4016·3		5r	(4)		
(16)			2316·0		6s
3898·0	4b	10r	2314·8		6s
(33)			(2)		
3804·2		5	2309·5		6s
(57)			(1)		
3633·4		5s	2304·9		9b
(16)			(7)		
3586·7		5b″	2291·6		6b
(36)			(3)		
⎰ 3122·9	6r	6	2283·4	4	5s
⎱ 3122·6		5s	(23)		
(9)			2242·7		5s
3035·4	6n	1b	(5)		
3029·3	6	2	2229·1		6n
(5)			(9)		
2932·3	6b	2	2201·4		5s
(1)			(23)		
2915·6	4	9s	2110·8		6s
(12)			(5)		
2838·1		5s	2082·1		5s
(2)			(5)		
2825·6		6s	2044·7		5s
2822·8		5	(13)		
2820·1		9n	1921·4		8
(1)			1919·4		6
2802·3		10s	(6)		

HELIUM.

Wave-length.	Intensity and character.	Wave-length.	Intensity and character.	Wave-length.	Intensity and character.
20400	10	⎰ 4388·8	10	3705·2	3
11170	15	⎱ 4388·1	3	(2)	
7281·8	3	4143·9	2	3634·4	2
(1)		(1)		3613·8	3
7065·5	5	4121·0	3	3587·4	2
6678·4	5	4026·3	5	(17)	
⎰ 5876·1	1	(2)		3447·7	2
⎱ 5875·8	5	3964·9	4	(6)	
5047·8	2	(2)		3187·8	8
5015·7	6	3888·8	10	(1)	
4922·1	4	(2)		2945·2	6
(1)		3867·6	2	2829·2	4
4713·3	3	(2)		2763·9	2
4471·6	6	3819·8	4	(4)	
(1)		(6)			

HYDROGEN.

Wave-length.	Intensity.	Wave-length.	Intensity.	Wave-length.	Intensity.
C 6563·0	20	η 3835·6	1	ν 3712·0	
(6)		(2)		ξ 3704·1	
F 4861·5	20	θ 3798·0	1	ο 3697·4	
(12)		(3)		π 3691·5	
γ 4340·7	15	ι 3770·7	1	ρ 3686·9	
(5)		(1)		σ 3682·9	
δ 4101·8	10	κ 3752·0	1	τ 3679·4	
(9)		(1)		υ 3676·4	
ε 3970·2	8	λ 3734·1	1	φ 3673·9	
(5)		(1)		χ 3671·0	
ζ 3889·1	7	μ 3722·2	1		
(8)		(1)			

The wave-lengths of the (series) lines of hydrogen are given by Balmer's formula $\frac{1}{\lambda} = 27418\cdot3(1 - 4m^{-2})$, in which λ denotes the wave-ength and m has the values 3, 4, 5, 6, etc.

INDIUM.

Wave-length.	Intensity.		Wave-length.	Intensity.	
	Arc.	Spark.		Arc.	Spark.
6908		6s	2941·4		10
6194		10s	2932·7	6r	1
(1)			2890·3		4
6096		8n	2754·0	6r	1n
(3)			5 * 2714·0	6r	1n
5821		8n	2710·4	10r	2n
(1)			(1)		
5645		8a	5 † 2601·8	6r	1n
5252		10n	(2)		
⎰ 4682·4		8s	5 * 2560·2	8r	1n
⎨ 4656·1		8s	6 * 2523·1	4r	
⎱ 4637·8		8s	2521·4	8r	
3 † 4511·4	10r	50r	(1)		
(3)			6 † 2468·1	4r	
3 † 4101·9	8r	50r	5 † 2460·1	6r	
(8)			(3)		
4 * 3258·7	6r	3	6 * 2389·6	8r	
3256·2	10r	8	(2)		
(2)			6 † 2340·3	6r	
4 * 3039·5	10r	4nr	7 * 2306·8	1r	5
3008·3		10	(11)		
2983·5		8n			

The oscillation frequencies (in air) of the pairs marked * can be calculated from the formula $10^8 \frac{1}{\lambda} = a - bn^{-2} - cn^{-4}$, where $a = 44515·4$ for the *first* line and $46728·6$ for the *second* line of the pair, $b = 13930·8$, $c = 131103·2$; and for the pairs marked †, $a = 44535·0$ for the *first* line and $46748·2$ for the *second* line of the pair, $b = 12676·6$, $c = 64358·4$. The figure preceding the sign * or † shows the value of n.

IODINE.

SPARK-SPECTRUM.

Wave-length.	Intensity.	Wave-length.	Intensity.	Wave-length.	Intensity.
6131	8	5696	9	5371	6
6076	9	5686	10	5349	10
5961	10	5631	10	5339	10
5791	5	5497	9	5244	10
5781	10	5471	10	5159	10
5766	10	5448	10	5066	8
5741	10	5408	10	4635	6
5716	10				

232   *An Introduction to the Study of Spectrum Analysis.*

IRIDIUM.

Wave-length.	Intensity and character.		Wave-length.	Intensity and character.	
	Arc.	Spark.		Arc.	Spark.
(54)			(91)		
4616·5	6		3266·6	6	4
(17)			(34)		
4426·5	6		3232·1	5r	4
(5)			3230·9	5	
4399·6	6	8	3229·4	5r	4
(10)			(10)		
4311·7	5	6	3220·9	6r	6
(6)			(8)		
4268·3	4	6	3212·2	3	8
(30)			(11)		
4070·1	4	6	3199·1	5	4
(9)			(23)		
4020·2	5	8n	3169·0	5	4
(3)			(17)		
3992·3	6	6	3159·3	5	
(4)			(15)		
3976·5	5	6	3137·8		6
(13)			(2)		
3915·5	1	6	3133·4	5r	8
(3)			(7)		
3902·6	3	8	3120·9	5	4
3895·7		6	(16)		
(2)			3100·6	2	6
3865·8		6	(11)		
(3)			3088·2	4	6
3800·2	2	8	(17)		
(1)			3069·2	2	6
3747·4	4	6	3069·0	4	6
(3)			(5)		
3731·5	4	6n	3064·9	3	8
(9)			(25)		
3692·4		6	3042·8	2	8
3689·5		6	(4)		
(1)			3039·4	5	4
3675·2	4	8	(99)		
(1)			2924·9	7	8
3661·9	5		(67)		
(2)			2849·8	6	6
3653·4	1	10	(8)		
(6)			2839·3	6	4
3628·8	5	4	(6)		
(6)			2833·3	4	8
3606·0	2	10	(9)		
(5)			2824·6	6	4
3573·9	3	8	(2)		
(6)			2823·3	5	
3513·8	4	6	(16)		
(22)			2800·9	4	}6
3449·1	6	4	2800·8	1	
(6)			(24)		
3437·2	6	6	2775·1	2	6
(50)			(65)		
3368·6	6	4	2694·3	6	
(5)			(23)		
3360·9	7		2664·9	5	
3360·0	6		(2)		

IRIDIUM—continued.

Wave-length.	Intensity and character.		Wave-length.	Intensity and character.	
	Arc.	Spark.		Arc.	Spark.
2662·1	6		(90)		
(61)			2398·8	0	6
2586·1	0	8	(6)		
(5)			2384·9		6
2579·6	2	6	(2)		
(26)			2381·7	2	6
2544·1	5r		(4)		
(23)			2368·1	4	8
2512·7	2	6	(37)		

IRON.

Wave-length.	Arc.	Spark.	Wave-length.	Arc.	Spark.
7515·1	6		(5)		
7500·0	6		6518·5	6	
7449·8	6		(7)		
7414·8	6		6495·1	10	
7392·3	6		(18)		
(12)			6431·0	8	
7206·6	4		(1)		
7187·2	8		6421·5	8	
7181·8	3		6420·2	6n	
(20)			(2)		
6972·8	5		6411·8	8	
(3)			(1)		
6944·8	6		6408·3	6	
(1)			(2)		
6916·8	6		6400·1	10	
(7)			(4)		
6854·9	6		6393·6	8	
6843·6	6		(8)		
6841·4	6		6380·9	6	
(2)			(20)		
6827·8	6		6337·0	10	
(11)			6335·4	8	
6678·1	8		(6)		
(2)			6222·8	6	
6663·6	6		(2)		
(4)			6318·2	10	
6633·9	6n		(6)		
(3)			6302·7	6	
6609·3	6		6301·6	10	
(3)			(2)		
6594·0	6		6297·9	6	
6593·1	10		(3)		
(5)			6291·1	6n	
6575·2	6		(8)		
(2)			6270·4	6	
6569·4	8n		(2)		
(1)			6265·3	8	
6546·4	10		(4)		

234 An Introduction to the Study of Spectrum Analysis.

IRON—continued.

Wave-length.	Arc.	Spark.	Wave-length.	Arc.	Spark.
6256·5	6		5956·9	6	
6254·4	6		(2)		
6252·7	10		5952·9	8	
(4)			(6)		
6246·5	8		5934·8	8	
(10)			(1)		
6232·8	6		5930·2	10	
(1)			(10)		
6230·9	10		5916·4	6	
(9)			(1)		
6219·4	8		5914·3	10n	
(3)			(3)		
6215·3	6		5905·8	6	
6213·6	8		(26)		
(5)			5862·5	10	
6200·5	6		5859·8	8	
(3)			(18)		
6191·7	10		5816·5	6	
(7)			(19)		
6180·3	6		5782·3	8	
(3)			(2)		
6170·6	6n		5775·2	6	
(9)			(4)		
6157·9	6		5763·2	10	
(12)			(9)		
6141·9	6		5753·3	8	
(3)			(9)		
6137·8	10		5731·9	6	
(1)			(6)		
6136·8	10		5718·0	6	
(7)			(6)		
6128·0	6		5709·6	8	
(16)			(7)		
6103·4	8n		5701·7	6	
6102·3	8n		(10)		
(15)			5686·6	6	
6078·6	6n		(10)		
(5)			5662·7	8	
6065·6	10		(2)		
(6)			5658·9	10	
6056·2	6n		(18)		
(3)			5638·5	6	
6042·2	6		(13)		
(7)			5624·7	8	
6027·2	6		(8)		
(1)			5615·8	10	
6024·2	10n		(7)		
(1)			5603·1	8	
6020·3	6n		(9)		
(5)			5586·9	10	
6008·8	8		(4)		
(3)			5576·2	8	
6003·2	6		(1)		
(9)			5578·0	10	
5987·2	6n		(1)		
5985·0	8n		5569·8	10	
5983·9	6n		(2)		
(1)			5565·8	6n	
5976·9	8		(4)		
5975·5	6		5555·0	6n	
(12)			(33)		

Catalogue of Spectra.

IRON—continued.

Wave-length.	Arc.	Spark.	Wave-length.	Arc.	Spark.
5506·9	8		5281·9	8	6s
(3)			(5)		
5501·6	8		5273·6	6	1s
(4)			(3)		
5497·5	6		5270·4	10	10s
(13)			5269·6	10n	10s
5476·8	8		(1)		
(1)			5266·7	10	8s
5474·1	6		(1)		
(9)			5263·4	6	4s
5463·4	8n		(5)		
(4)			5250·8	6	1s
5455·8	10		(5)		
(7)			5242·6	6	1s
5447·1	10		(4)		
5445·2	8n		5233·1	10	10s
(8)			(2)		
5434·7	8		5230·0	6	
(2)			(2)		
5429·7	10		5227·3	10	⎫ 10s
(4)			5227·0		⎬
5424·2	10n		(12)		⎭
(4)			5216·4	6	
5415·4	10n		(3)		
(1)			5208·7	6	6s
5411·1	8n		(5)		
(3)			5202·4	8	6s
5405·9	10		(8)		
5404·3	8n		5195·0	8	6s
(2)			(2)		
5400·6	6n		5192·5	10	8s
(2)			(1)		
5397·3	10		5191·6	10	4s
(2)			(10)		
5393·3	8		5171·7	8	4s
(5)			(3)		
5383·5	10n		5169·1	6	6s
(7)			5167·5	10	8s
5371·6	10		(3)		
5370·1	8n		5162·5	6n	4s
5367·6	8n		(6)		
(1)			5153·3	6	
5365·0	6n		(1)		
(5)			5151·0	6	
5353·5	6		(1)		
(8)			5148·4	6n	1s
5341·1	8		(7)		
5340·1	8		5139·6	10	⎫ 8s
(3)			5139·3	10	⎬
5333·0	6		(1)		⎭
(2)			5137·5	6n	
5328·5	8		(1)		
5328·2	10		5133·6	8	2s
(1)			(6)		
5324·3	10		5125·3	8n	
(10)			(1)		
5307·5	6		5123·8	6	
(2)			(7)		
5302·5	10	6s	5110·5	6	
(13)			(1)		
5283·8	10	6s	5107·8	6	6s

IRON—continued.

Wave-length.	Arc.	Spark.	Wave-length.	Arc.	Spark.
(2) 5105·7	8		4679·0	8	1
(7) 5098·8	6	2n	(5) 4668·4	6	1
(5) 5083·5	6		4667·6	6	1
(3) 5079·9	6		(8) 4654·7	10	6s
5079·4	6n		(3) 4647·6	8	1
(5) 5068·9	8		(5) 4638·1	6	1
(1) 5065·1	6n	4s	4637·7	6	1
(8) 5051·7	6	8s	(3) 4633·0	4	6s
(2) 5049·9	8	8s	(6) 4625·2	6	1
(3) 5041·9	8	6s	4619·4	6	1
5041·2	4	6s	(4) 4611·5	8	6s
(22) 5015·1	6		4607·8	6	1
(5) 5012·2	6		(4) 4603·0	8	4s
(2) 5006·2	8	} 4s	(3) 4598·3	6	1
5005·8	6		(6) 4592·8	8	1
(3) 5002·0	8	2s	(29) 4556·2	8	1
(14) 4982·7	6		(7) 4548·0	8	2
(14) 4966·2	6		(19) 4531·3	8	2
(5) 4957·8	8	} 10s	(2) 4528·8	10	6
4957·4	6		(4) 4525·3	6	2
(14) 4938·9	6		(19) 4494·8	8	5
(13) 4924·0	1	6s	(6) 4489·9	4	1
4920·6	10	10s	(3) 4484·4	6	2
4919·4	8	8s	(2) 4482·4	8	4
(16) 4891·6	10		(8) 4476·2	10	5
4890·9	8	10s	(7) 4469·6	8	2
(8) 4878·3	6	6s	(3) 4466·7	8	5
(4) 4872·3	8	8s	(6) 4461·8	6	3
4871·4	8	8s	(3) 4459·3	8	4
(8) 4859·9	8	4s	(6) 4454·5	6	2
(44) 4789·7	6	2s	(6) 4447·9	8	3
(36) 4736·9	10	1	(8) 4443·3	8	3
(18) 4707·5	8	2s	(1) 4442·5	8	4
(6) 4691·6	6	6s			
(10)					

Catalogue of Spectra.

IRON—*continued*.

Wave-length.	Arc.	Spark.	Wave-length.	Arc.	Spark.
(11) 4433·4	6	2	(4) 4247·6	8	4n
(3) 4430·8	8	2	(2) 4245·4	6	3
(4) 4427·5	8	3	(9) 4239·9	6	3
(6) 4422·7	8	3	4239·0	8	4
(7) 4415·3	10	8	(3) 4236·1	10	8
(6) 4408·6	6	2	(3) 4233·8	10	6
4407·8	6	2	(9) 4227·6	10	7
(2) 4404·9	10	10	(3) 4225·6	6	3
(2) 4401·5	6	1	(1) 4224·3	6	3
(8) 4391·1	6	1	(1) 4222·4	8	4
(3) 4388·6	6	2	(3) 4219·5	8	6
(5) 4383·7	10r	10	(1) 4217·7	6	2
(6) 4376·1	8	4	4216·3	6	2
(7) 4369·9	8	3	(5) 4210·5	8	5
(3) 4367·8	6	2	(6) 4204·1	6	4
(7) 4352·9	8	3	(3) 4202·2	10	9
(19) 4337·2	10	5	(3) 4199·3	10	8
(8) 4325·9	10	10	(1) 4198·5	10	6
(11) 4315·3	10	5	(2) 4196·4	6	2
(5) 4309·5	6	3	(1) 4195·5	6	3
(1) G 4308·0	10	10	(6) 4191·6	10	4
(2) 4305·6	6	2	(6) 4187·9	10	7
(9) 4299·4	10	7r	4187·2	10	7
(7) 4294·3	10r	6	(2) 4185·0	8	4
(15) 4285·6	6	2	(3) 4182·5	6	2
(7) 4282·6	10	6	4181·9	8	7
(16) 4271·9	10r	10	(7) 4177·7	6	1
4271·3	10r	7	(1) 4176·6	6	2
(5) 4267·9	6	2	4175·8	8	4
(7) 4260·7	10	10	4175·0	6	1
(18) 4250·9	10	8	(4) 4172·8	6	2
4250·3	10	7	(1) 4172·2	8	3
			(2) 4171·1	8	3
			(17)		

IRON—*continued*.

Wave-length.	Arc.	Spark.	Wave-length.	Arc.	Spark.
4158·9	6	2	4067·4	6	2
4157·9	6	2	4067·0	6	3
(1)			(5)		
4156·9	8	4	4063·8	10r	10
(1)			(2)		
4154·9	6	3	4062·6	8	3
4154·7	6	4	(7)		
4154·0	6	3n	4057·9	6	
(6)			(19)		
4149·4	6	2	4046·0	10r	10
4147·7	8	2	(7)		
(4)			4034·6	6	1
4144·0	10	7	4033·2	6	1
4143·6	10	5	(4)		
(10)			4030·7	6	2n
4137·2	8	4	(10)		
(3)			4022·0	6	3
4134·8	10	5	(10)		
(3)			4014·6	6	4
4133·0	8	4	(6)		
4132·2	10	8	4009·8	6	3
(7)			(4)		
4127·7	6	3	4005·3	8	8
(9)			(8)		
4122·6	6	2	3998·2	6	3
4121·9	6	2	3997·5	6	4
(2)			(8)		
4120·3	6	2	3986·3	6	1
(3)			(1)		
4118·7	10	5	3984·1	6	3
(8)			(1)		
4114·6	6	3	3981·9	6	2
(7)			(4)		
4109·9	8	4	3977·9	8	4
(2)			(11)		
4107·6	8	4	3971·4	6	2
(5)			(3)		
4104·2	6	1	3969·4	8	8
(4)			(17)		
4100·9	6	1	3956·8	6	4
(3)			(6)		
4098·3	8	2	3952·7	6	2
(2)			3951·3	6	3
4096·1	8	2	3950·1	6	3
(17)			(1)		
4085·4	6	3	3948·9	6	4
4085·1	6	3	(8)		
4084·7	8	3	3942·6	6	2
(9)			(1)		
4080·0	6	2	3941·0	6	2
(3)			(4)		
4078·4	6	2	3936·0	6	2
(2)			(6)		
4076·7	8	3	3928·1	8	7
(2)			(3)		
4074·9	6	3	3923·1	8	6
(4)			(2)		
4071·9	8r	10	3920·4	6	5
4070·9	6	2	(3)		
(1)			3917·3	6	3
4068·1	8	3	3916·9	6	3

Catalogue of Spectra. 239

IRON—*continued.*

Wave-length.	Arc.	Spark.	Wave-length.	Arc.	Spark.
(9)			3805·5	6	5
3906·6	6	5	(6)		
(1)			3799·7	6r	7
3904·0	6	2	3798·6	6r	6
3903·1	8	7	(1)		
(2)			3797·6	6	4
3899·9	6	6	(4)		
(2)			3795·1	8r	6
3898·1	6	4	(11)		
(1)			3790·2	6	5
3895·8	6	5	(1)		
(10)			3788·0	6	5
3888·6	6	6	(10)		
3887·2	6	5	3779·6	6	1
3886·4	6	8	(14)		
(5)			3767·3	8r	7
3278·7	8	8	(2)		
(1)			3765·7	8	5
3278·2	8	7	3763·9	8r	7
(5)			(5)		
3873·9	6	4	3758·4	8r	8
(2)			(8)		
3872·6	8	8	3749·6	8r	10
(6)			(1)		
3867·3	6	3	3748·4	7r	7
3865·7	8	6	(2)		
(5)			3746·0	6	7
3860·1	10r	9	3745·7	8r	7
3859·4	6	4	(2)		
3856·5	8r	8	3743·5	6r	7
(4)			(6)		
3852·7	6	2	3738·4	6	3
3851·0	6	3	3737·3	8r	8
3850·1	8r	6	3735·4	6	3
(1)			3735·0	9r	10
3846·9	6	3	(1)		
(6)			3732·5	6	4
3843·4	6	4	(4)		
(1)			3727·8	6	?
3841·2	8r	8	(2)		
3840·6	8r	8	3724·5	6	3
(1)			3722·7	6r	6
3839·4	6	4	(4)		
(2)			3720·1	10r	8
3836·5	6	2	(1)		
3834·4	8r	8	3716·6	6	3
(9)			(5)		
3828·0	7r	9	3709·4	6r	6
(2)			(1)		
3826·0	8r	9	3708·0	6	5
(1)			(4)		
3824·6	6r	7	3704·6	6	3
(6)			(5)		
3820·6	9r	9	3701·2	6	4
(6)			(6)		
3816·0	8r	9	3694·1	6	4
(4)			(10)		
3813·2	5	5	3687·7	6	3
(9)			3687·6	6r	6
3806·8	6	4	(3)		
(4)			3686·1	6	3

240 *An Introduction to the Study of Spectrum Analysis.*

IRON—*continued.*

Wave-length.	Arc.	Spark.	Wave-length.	Arc.	Spark.
(3)			(9)		
3682·3	6	4	3527·9	6	2
(22)			(1)		
3669·7	6	3	3526·5	6	3
(19)			3526·2	6	3
3659·7	6	2	(9)		
(11)			3521·4	8r	6
3651·6	6	4	(10)		
(5)			3514·0	8	5
3648·0	8r	9	(21)		
(7)			3498·0	6	5
3640·5	6	5	3497·2	6	3
(13)			(9)		
3631·6	6r	10	3490·7	8	6
(13)			3489·7	6	1
3623·3	6	2	(16)		
3622·2	6	5	3476·8	8r	5
(1)			(4)		
3621·6	6	4	3475·6	8r	7
(5)			(8)		
3618·9	8r	10	3471·5	8	2
(1)			(8)		
3617·9	6	4	3466·0	10	7
(15)			(8)		
3610·3	6	4	3460·1	6	1
3609·0	8	9	(11)		
(2)			3452·3	6	2
3606·8	6	4	3452·0	6	1n
(1)			(1)		
3605·6	6	5	3450·5	6	2
(20)			3447·4	6	2
3594·8	6	2	(4)		
(18)			3445·3	8	4
3587·1	8	5	3444·0	10	5
(1)			(5)		
3586·2	6	4	3441·1	10r	6
(4)			3440·8	10r	7
3584·8	6	4	(12)		
(6)			3428·3	6	2
3581·3	10r	10r	3427·3	8	5
(8)			3426·7	6	2
3574·0	6	2	3426·4	6	2
(2)			3425·1	6	1
3572·1	6	2	3424·4	10r	3
(2)			(1)		
3570·3	10r	8	3422·7	10	1
(9)			(3)		
3565·5	8r	8r	3418·6	8	3
(6)			(1)		
3558·7	8r	6	3417·9	8	3
3557·0	8	*3	(3)		
3555·0	10	5	3415·6	6	1
(14)			(1)		
3545·8	6	2	3413·3	10	5
(4)			(4)		
3542·2	6	5	3410·3	6	1
3541·2	6	4	(2)		
(8)			3407·6	10	6
3536·7	6	4	3406·9	6	2
(2)			(6)		
3533·3	6	3	3404·4	10	3

Catalogue of Spectra.

IRON—continued.

Wave-length.	Arc.	Spark.	Wave-length.	Arc.	Spark.
(1)			(5)		
3402·4	6	2	3254·5	8	2
3401·6	6	1	(4)		
(1)			3251·3	6	1
3399·5	10	5	(5)		
(4)			3248·3	6	1
3394·7	6	1	(8)		
(4)			3244·3	8	2
3392·8	8	3	(6)		
(10)			3239·6	8	3
3384·1	8	2	(9)		
(4)			3234·1	6	1
3380·2	8	3	(4)		
3379·1	6	2	3231·1	6	2
3378·8	6r	2	(9)		
(7)			3227·9	6	6
3370·9	10	4	(2)		
3369·6	8	3	3225·9	10r	5
(1)			(4)		
3367·0	6	2	3222·2	10r	4
(11)			3219·9	8	2
3355·4	6	2	3219·7	8	2
(6)			(1)		
3348·1	6	1	3217·5	8	2
(4)			3216·1	8	2
3342·3	6	1	(2)		
(2)			3214·2	8	3
3340·6	6	1	(1)		
(3)			3212·1	6	3
3337·8	6	1	(7)		
(6)			3205·5	8	2
3329·0	8	2	(5)		
(3)			3200·6	8	2
3323·8	6	1	3199·6	8	1
(7)			(2)		
3314·9	8	2	3197·0	8	3
(6)			(5)		
3310·5	6	1	3193·4	6	2
(2)			3192·9	6	2
3307·4	6		(1)		
(1)			3192·9	6	2
3306·5	10	7	(20)		
3306·1	10	7	3180·3	10	2
(10)			(3)		
3298·3	8	1	3178·1	6	1
(5)			(4)		
3292·7	8	2	3175·5	8	1
3292·1	8	2	(5)		
3291·1	6	1	3171·5	6	1
(7)			(4)		
3286·9	10	5	3166·6	6	1
(9)			3166·0	6	1n
3280·4	8	2	(4)		
(6)			3162·1	6	1
3274·1	8	3	(1)		
(4)			3160·8	8	1
3271·1	8	3	(4)		
(3)			3158·0	6	1n
3265·7	8	3	3157·2	8	1
(12)			(6)		
3257·7	6	1	3153·3	6	1n

242 *An Introduction to the Study of Spectrum Analysis.*

IRON—*continued.*

Wave-length.	Arc.	Spark.	Wave-length.	Arc.	Spark.
(1) 3151·5	8	1	3020·8	10r	2
(10) 3144·1	6	1	(1) 3019·1	8	1
(2) 3142·6	6	1n	(1) 3017·7	8	1
			3016·3	6	1
(9) 3134·2	8	1	(5) 3011·6	6	1
3132·6	6r		(1) 3009·7	10r	2
(4) 3126·2	6		(1) 3008·3	10r	2
3125·8	8	1	3007·4	10	1
(8) 3119·6	6	1	(4) 3003·1	6	1
(1) 3116·7	8	1	(4) 3001·1	8r	2
(22) 3100·8	8	2	3000·6	6	1
3100·4	6	2	2999·6	10r	2
3100·1	10	2	(2) 2996·5	6	
(1) 3098·3	6	1	(2) 2994·6	10r	3
(7) 3091·7	8	2	(2) 2990·5	6	1
(8) 3075·8	10r	2	(4) 2987·4	8	1
(11) 3067·4	10r	3	(2) 2985·7	6	4
(12) 3059·2	10r	3	2984·9	8	6
3057·6	10r	3	2983·7	10r	2
(2) 3055·4	6	1	(3) 2981·6	8	1
(3) 3053·2	6	1	2980·6	6	
(4) 3047·7	10r	3	(5) 2976·3	6	1
(3) 3045·2	6	1b	(1) 2973·4	8r	2
			2973·3	8r	2
(2) 3042·8	8	1	(3) 2970·2	10r	2
3042·1	6	1	2969·5	10	1
3041·8	8	1	(2) 2967·0	10r	2
(1) 3040·6	8	1	(2) 2965·4	8r	1
(5) 3037·5	6r	3	(11) 2960·1	8	1
3037·4	6		(4) 2957·5	6	1
(5) 3031·8	6	1	(3) 2954·1	9r	2
3031·3	6	1	(1) 2953·9	6	3
(1) 3030·2	8	1	(2) 2950·3	8n	1n
(1) 3026·6	8	1	(1) 2949·3	6	2
(1) 3025·7	6	1	(2) 2948·6	6	1
(1) 3024·2	8	1	(1) 2948·0	8r	2
(1) 3021·2	8r	2			

Catalogue of Spectra.

IRON—*continued*.

Wave-length.	Arc.	Spark.	Wave-length.	Arc.	Spark.
2947·8	8	3	(2)		
(5)			2864·0	8	1
2944·5	6	4	2863·5	10	1
(3)			2862·6	6	
2941·5	8r	1	(5)		
(3)			2859·0	6	1n
2937·9	8n		(7)		
2937·0	10r	2	2853·8	10	1n
(11)			(1)		
2929·1	8r	2	2852·2	6	1
(6)			2851·9	10r	2
2926·7	8	3	(1)		
2926·0	6		2850·7	6	
2925·4	6	1	(2)		
(1)			2848·8	8	
2923·9	6	1	(2)		
2923·4	8n	1	2846·9	6	
(4)			(1)		
2920·8	6	1	2845·6	8	
(5)			2844·1	10r	2
2918·1	8	1	2843·6	8	1
(2)			(8)		
2914·3	6		2840·5	6	2
(1)			2840·1	10	
2912·3	10	1	(2)		
(2)			2838·2	8	1
2909·6	6		(3)		
(1)			2835·6	6	1
2909·0	6		(6)		
(1)			2832·5	10r	2
2907·6	6	1	(4)		
(9)			2828·9	6	3
2902·0	8n	1	(8)		
2901·5	6	1	2825·8	6r	1
2899·5	8	1	2825·7	8r	2
(2)			(1)		
2898·5	6n		2824·4	6	
(4)			2823·4	8r	3
2895·1	8	1	(7)		
2894·6	8	1	2819·4	6	1
(5)			(2)		
2892·6	6		2817·6	8	1n
(9)			(1)		
2887·9	6	1	2815·6	6	
(2)			(2)		
2886·4	6	1	2813·4	10r	2
(2)			(7)		
2883·8	6	3	2808·4	6	
(1)			(2)		
2881·6	10		2807·1	10r	2
2880·9	6	2	(4)		
(6)			2804·6	10r	2
2877·4	8	1	(1)		
(5)			2803·7	6	1n
2874·3	8r	1	(2)		
(4)			2801·2	8	1n
2872·4	8	3	(6)		
(5)			2798·4	8	1
2869·4	8	1	2797·9	8	1
(7)			(3)		
2866·7	8	1	2795·6	8	3

IRON—*continued.*

Wave-length.	Arc.	Spark.	Wave-length.	Arc.	Spark.
2795·0	10	1u	(2)		
2794·8	6		2747·6	6	
(3)			2747·1	5r	7
2792·4	6	1	2746·6	10r	7
2792·0	6	1	(2)		
2791·5	6	1	2745·2	6r	1
(1)			2744·6	8r	1
2789·9	8	1	2744·2	8r	1
(1)			2743·6	6	
2788·2	10r	3n	2743·2	10	8
2788·0	10		2742·5	10r	2
(7)			(5)		
2783·8	8	7	2739·6	10r	10
(1)			(5)		
2781·9	8	1	2737·4	8r	2
(5)			2737·0	8	5
2779·3	6	5	(2)		
2778·9	6	1	2735·7	6	
(1)			2735·6	6r	2
2778·3	8r	2	2735·5	6	
2778·1	6	2	(2)		
(4)			2734·4	8	1
2774·8	8	3	(1)		
(3)			2733·6	10	2
2773·3	8	1	(5)		
(3)			2730·8	8	4
2772·2	8r	2	(3)		
(6)			2728·9	6	2
2769·4	6	4	(1)		
(3)			2728·1	6	1
2767·6	10	7r	2727·6	8	8
2767·0	6	1	(2)		
(7)			2726·2	10	1
2764·4	8	1	(3)		
2763·2	6	1	2725·0	8r	4
2762·8	6	1	(2)		
(1)			2723·7	10r	2
2762·1	8r	2	(2)		
2761·9	8r	3	2721·0	10r	3
(2)			2720·3	6	1
2761·0	6	1	2719·5	6	2
(3)			2719·1	10r	2
2759·9	8	1	2718·5	8r	1
(3)			(7)		
2757·9	6	1u	2714·5	10	7
2757·4	8r	2	(4)		
(2)			2711·7	6	
2756·4	8r	2	(1)		
2755·8	10r	10	2710·6	6	1
(3)			(4)		
2754·5	6	1	2708·7	10	1
2754·1	6	1	(3)		
2753·7	6	1	2706·7	8r	3
2753·4	6	7	2706·1	6	
(5)			(3)		
2750·9	8		2704·1	6	5
(1)			(5)		
2750·2	10r	1	2699·2	8	1
2749·6	6		(3)		
2749·4	6	10	2697·1	8	
2749·2	6		2696·4	8u	1

Catalogue of Spectra.

IRON—continued.

Wave-length.	Arc.	Spark.	Wave-length.	Arc.	Spark.
2696·1 (10)	6n	1n	2613·9 (2)	8r	9
2692·7	4	6	2612·0 (5)	10r	9
2690·2	6	1	2607·2 (2)	8r	9b″
2689·9 (1)	6	1	2605·8	8	5
2689·3 (10)	8	3	2604·9 (2)	6	1n
2684·8	4	6	2599·5 (1)	10r	10r
2680·5 (2)	6	1n	2598·5 (2)	10r	9
2679·1 (8)	10r	2	2594·2	6	1n
2673·3 (5)	6		2593·8 (1)	6	4
2669·6 (3)	8	1	2592·9	4	6
2668·0 (2)	6		2591·6 (3)	8	6
2667·0	6		2588·1 (1)	10r	5b″
2666·9	8		2586·0	10	8b″
2666·7	4	7	2584·6	8	3
2666·4 (2)	8		2582·4 (4)	10	7
2664·7 (3)	8	7	2579·9	6	2n
2662·1 (1)	8	1n	2578·0 (1)	10	5
2661·3	8		2576·8	8	5
2660·5 (2)	6	1b	2576·2	6	1
2656·8	6		2575·8 (1)	10	1
2656·2 (4)	8	1n	2574·5 (2)	6	5
2651·8 (3)	6	1	2572·8 (2)	6	
2647·6 (1)	8	1n	2570·6	8	
2645·5	6	2	2569·7 (3)	6	3
2644·1	10	2	2567·0 (3)	8	4
2641·7 (5)	8	1n	2563·5	10	5
2635·9 (6)	8	2	2562·6 (3)	10	6
2631·4	10	4	2560·6 (5)	6	
2631·1 (3)	10	4	2557·0	6	1
2628·4 (2)	10r	8	2556·4 (4)	6	1
2625·8 (2)	10	7	2553·3 (1)	8	2
2623·6 (1)	10	2	2551·2 (2)	8	4
2621·7 (1)	8	6	2549·7	8r	4
2620·5 (4)	6	3	2548·7 (1)	6	3
2617·7 (3)	6r	7	2547·1	8	
2615·5 (2)	6	1	2546·3 (1)	8	
			2546·1	10r	2
			2544·8	8n	1

246 *An Introduction to the Study of Spectrum Analysis.*

IRON—*continued.*

Wave-length.	Arc.	Spark.	Wave-length.	Arc.	Spark.
2544·0	6r	3	(1)		
(2)			2497·9	6	5
2542·2	8r	3	2497·1	6	1
2541·1	8r	5	2496·6	6r	2
(3)			2496·0	8	
2539·0	10	5	(3)		
2537·3	10r	3b	2493·3	10r	8
2536·9	8	5	(2)		
2535·7	6r	5	2491·5	6	4
(1)			2491·2	10r	2
2534·5	4	6	(2)		
2533·9	10	7	2490·7	10r	3
(2)			2489·8	8r	5
2532·4	6	1b	2488·2	10r	2n
(1)			(7)		
2530·8	8	2	2484·3	8r	3
2529·9	6r	4	2483·4	10r	4n
2529·6	4	6	(2)		
2529·4	8n	2n	2480·2	6	5
2529·2	8r	2n	2480·0	6	
2528·6	6	1	2479·9	10r	3
(1)			(4)		
2527·7	8	3	2476·8	8	2
2527·5	10r	3	(1)		
2526·3	8	6	2474·9	8r	3
2525·5	6	7	(1)		
2525·1	6	3n	2473·0	10r	2n
(1)			2472·8	6	
2524·4	6r	3	2472·4	6r	3
2523·8	6r	3	(4)		
2522·9	10r	6	2469·0	8r	2
(1)			(1)		
2522·7	6	3	2467·8	6n	1
2522·0	6	4	2466·8	6n	4
2521·1	6	5	(1)		
(3)			2465·2	8r	4
2518·2	10r	4	(4)		
2517·8	6	1	2462·7	10r	2
2517·2	6	5	(3)		
(1)			2461·3	8	5
2516·2	8	2	(1)		
(1)			2460·4	6	5n
2514·4	6	6	(1)		
(2)			2458·8	8	6
2512·4	6	3	(1)		
(2)			2457·7	8r	2b*e*
2511·8	4	7	(4)		
2510·9	8r	3	2453·6	8	2
(1)			(9)		
2508·8	6	1	2447·8	8r	4
2508·0	6r	2	(5)		
(1)			2444·6	6	6
2507·0	6	1	2443·9	6	2
(2)			2442·7	10r	3
2505·6	8		(1)		
(2)			2440·2	8r	1
2503·5	8	4	2439·8	8r	2
2502·5	8	4	2439·4	6	6
2501·9	8	1	2438·3	6	1
2501·2	8r	2	(1)		
2499·0	10	7b*e*	2436·4	8	2

Catalogue of Spectra.

IRON—continued.

Wave-length.	Arc.	Spark.	Wave-length.	Arc.	Spark.
(1)			2362·1	8	4
2435·0	6	5	2360·4	8	5
(4)			2360·1	8	5
2432·9	2	6	2359·2	6	7
2432·3	4	6	(2)		
2431·1	8	1	2355·0	6	5
2430·2	6	7	2351·3	2	6
2429·5	8	3	(5)		
(2)			2348·4	10	7
2428·4	4	6	2348·2	10	7
(5)			2345·4	2	6
2424·2	8	7	2344·4	6	
(2)			2344·1	6	3
2421·8	8	1n	2343·6	6	9
(11)			(4)		
2413·4	10r	8	2338·1	8	8
(2)			(4)		
2411·2	10	7	2332·9	10	8
2410·6	10r	8	2331·4	8	7
(5)			(1)		
2406·7	10r	6	2327·5	8	6
2405·0	10r	7	(1)		
2404·5	8	4	2320·4	6	2
(5)			(6)		
2399·3	10r	8	2313·2	6	1
(1)			(5)		
2395·7	10r	7	2309·0	6	2
(4)			(4)		
2391·5	6	4	2303·5	6	2
(1)			(7)		
2388·7	8	7	2298·2	6	2
(4)			2297·8	6	1
2384·5	6	5	(3)		
2383·2	8	2	2293·9	6	2
2382·1	10	9	(2)		
2380·8	6	5	2291·2	6	1
2379·4	8	7	(3)		
(4)			2289·0	8	
2375·3	8	6	2287·7	6	1n
(1)			2287·4	6	1
2373·8	10r	8	2284·1	6	3
(2)			(6)		
2370·6	6	3	2280·0	6	4
(1)			(12)		
2368·7	8	8	2267·5	6	3
2366·7	6	3	(50)		
(1)			2230·1	6	2
2364·9	10	7	2227·8	6	2
(1)			(50)		

248   *An Introduction to the Study of Spectrum Analysis.*

LANTHANUM.

Wave-length.	Intensity and character.		Wave-length.	Intensity and character.	
	Arc.	Spark.		Arc.	Spark.
(2)			4655·7	8	8
6393·5		8	(4)		
(7)			4575·1	8	6
6250·0		8	(2)		
(8)			4558·7	7	6
5973·9		6	(2)		
5930·3	1	8	4549·7	7	
(16)			4526·3	8	5
5795·8	4	6	4525·5	7	4
5791·5	4	6	4522·5	10	8
5789·4	6	6	(6)		
5769·5	5	8	4430·1	10	8
(9)			4427·7	8	5
5588·6	3	6	(6)		
(10)			4383·6	7	5
5501·6	8	8	4378·3	8	3
(7)			(2)		
5455·4	8	8	4354·6	8	7
(1)			4335·1	7	5
5382·0	1n	8	4333·9	15	15
5381·2	2	8	(1)		
5377·3	2	8	4316·1	8	1
(1)			(1)		
5340·8	1	8	4296·2	10	8r
(1)			4287·1	10	20
5302·8	2	8	(2)		
5302·1	3	8	4269·7		10
(6)			4263·7	7	8
5188·4	11	8	(2)		
5183·7	0	10	4238·5	10	10
5177·5	3	6	(1)		
(5)			4226·9	6	
5128·1	4	6	4217·7	6	10
5114·7	4	6	4196·7		10
(7)			4192·5	8	8
5002·0	11		(5)		
4999·6	0	6	4152·1	8	10
(6)			(1)		
4922·0	6	10	4141·9	10	10
4921·1	6	10	(2)		
4900·1	6	10	4123·4	3	30r
4861·1	4	8	(2)		
(4)			4099·7	8	10
4824·2	5	10	(1)		
4809·7	5	} 8	4090·9	6	
4809·2	5		(3)		
4804·2	4	8	4086·8	10	20
(2)			(2)		
4748·9	4	8	4077·5	10	15
4743·3	7	8	(8)		
(6)			4050·2	6	10
4692·7	6	8	4046·0	10	
(2)			4043·1	8	20r
4672·0	4	6	(3)		
4669·1	5	6	4031·8	7	20
(2)			4026·0	7	4

Catalogue of Spectra.

LANTHANUM—continued.

Wave-length.	Intensity and character.		Wave-length.	Intensity and character.	
	Arc.	Spark.		Arc.	Spark.
(6)			3759·2	7	20
3988·7	5	30	(17)		
3949·3	6	50	3645·5	5	8
3936·4	7	3	(16)		
3929·4		15	3517·3		50r
3921·7		10	(5)		
3916·1	4	10	3381·0	8	10
3886·5	7	15	(2)		
3871·9		20	3337·6	6	15
(2)			(6)		
3849·2		10	3171·8		20
(5)			(15)		
3795·0		50	2651·8		8
3793·9	7		(7)		
3791·0	6	50	2379·5		10
(10)			(6)		

LEAD.

Wave-length.	Intensity and character.		Wave-length.	Intensity and character.	
	Arc.	Spark.		Arc.	Spark.
6657·3		10s	4019·7	4r	8s
6453·3		6s	(10)		
6041·2		6n	3854·0		10s
6002·1	2b″	6n	(2)		
(1)			3833·0		8n
5875·0		6n	(1)		
(2)			3786·4		10n
5608·2		10n	(2)		
5547·2		8n	3740·1	8r	10n
5373·6		10n	(7)		
(1)			3683·6	10r	10r
5201·6	4b″	6	(1)		
(2)			3671·7	4r	8n
5045·9		8n	(2)		
5005·6	6b″	6s	3639·7	10r	10n
(6)			(7)		
4387·3		9n	3572·9	8r	10n
(3)			(38)		
4245·2		10r	3262·5	6	1
(1)			(4)		
4168·2	4r	6	3243·0		6
(3)			3240·3	6	2
4062·3	4r	6	(3)		
4058·0	10r	10nr	3220·7	6	2
(1)			(1)		

250 *An Introduction to the Study of Spectrum Analysis.*

LEAD—*continued.*

Wave-length.	Intensity and character.		Wave-length.	Intensity and character.	
	Arc.	Spark.		Arc.	Spark.
3176·6		10	2562·3		8
(1)			(5)		
3137·8		10	2476·5	6r	8
(4)			(1)		
3089·2		6	2446·3	6r	6
(8)			2443·9	6r	6
3044·0		8	(2)		
(12)			2428·7	6r	2
2873·4	6r	10	(2)		
(2)			2411·8	6r	2
2833·2	10r	10r	(1)		
2823·3	6r	10r	2402·0	6r	2
(2)			2393·9	8r	4r
2802·1	8r	10r	(3)		
(6)			2332·5	6r	1
2697·7	6rn	2n	2247·0	10r	1n
2663·3	6r	10	2237·5	8r	1n
(1)			2175·9	6r	
2650·8	8n	4n	2170·1	10r	
(3)			2115·1	8r	
2614·3	8r	10r	2112·0	6	
2577·3	6r	8	2088·5	8r	
(2)					

LITHIUM.

Wave-length.	Intensity and character.			Wave-length.	Intensity and character.		
	Flame.	Arc.	Spark.		Flame.	Arc.	Spark.
6708·2	10	10sr	10s	(1)			
6103·8	3	10sr	10	3794·9		4n	
4972·1		6b	4	(2)			
4602·4	2	10sr	10nr	3232·8	4	8sr	5n
4273·4		4n	4n	2741·4		6sr	2
4132·4		8nr	6n	2562·6		4sr	
(1)				2475·1		4sr	
3915·2		6nr					

MAGNESIUM.

Wave-length.	Intensity and character.		Wave-length.	Intensity and character.	
	Arc.	Spark.		Arc.	Spark.
5711·6	2	8s	5 * ⎧ 3097·1	10sr	2n
5528·7	6	6s	⎨ 3093·1	8sr	2n
⎧ 5183·8	10sr	10sr	⎩ 3091·2	8sr	2n
3 † ⎨ 5172·9	10sr	9sr	⎧ 2942·2	8n	1n
⎩ 5167·6	8sr	8sr	5 † ⎨ 2938·7	6n	
(1)			⎩ 2937·0	4n	10n
4703·3	8n	1n	2928·7	4	10n
(7)			(1)		
4481·3		10b	2915·6	4	10n
(3)			(1)		
4352·2	8n	2n	⎧ 2852·2	10nr	8r
(22)			6 * ⎨ 2848·5	4n	
3895·8		6n	⎩ 2846·9	4n	
(5)			2802·8	10r	10r
⎧ 3838·4	10sr	10r	2798·2	4	8r
4 * ⎨ 3832·5	10sr	10r	2795·6	10r	10r
⎩ 3829·5	10sr	10n	2790·9	4	10n
(25)			2783·1	8r	4
⎧ 3336·8	10n	8n	6 † 2781·5	8sr	4
4 † ⎨ 3332·3	8n	8n	2779·9	10sr	6
⎩ 3330·1	8n	6n	6 † 2778·4	8sr	4
(12)			6 † 2776·8	8sr	4
			(25)		

The lines marked * and † form a series of triplets of which the oscillation frequency in air can be calculated (very nearly) from the formula $10^8 \frac{1}{\lambda} = a - bn^{-2} - cn^{-4}$, when for the triplets marked *, $a = 39796\cdot10$ for the *first* line, $39836\cdot79$ for the *second*, and $39857\cdot00$ for the third line of the triplet, $b = 130398$, $c = 1432050$; and in the triplets marked †, $a = 39836\cdot74$ for the *first* line, $39877\cdot95$ for the *second*, and $39897\cdot91$ for the *third* line of the triplet, $b = 125471$, $c = 518781$. The figure preceding the sign * or † shows the value of n.

MANGANESE.

Wave-length.	Intensity and character.		Wave-length.	Intensity and character.	
	Arc.	Spark.		Arc.	Spark.
6021·8	10s	10s	4436·5	6	4
6016·6	10s	10s	(2)		
6013·6	10s	10s	4415·1	6	4
(9)			(16)		
5538·1	7		4281·3	6	4
(1)			(1)		
5517·0	7	2	4266·1	6	3
(5)			(2)		
5481·7	6		4257·8	6	4
5470·9	7		4239·9	6	
(3)			4235·5	6	
5420·6	4	6	4235·3	6	6
5413·9	5	6	(27)		
5407·6	7	2	4111·0	6	
(1)			(10)		
5399·7	6	4	4083·8	9	6
5394·9	6	4	4083·1	9	6
(1)			4079·6	9	4
5377·8	6	6	4079·4	9	4
(4)			(1)		
5341·2	9	6	4070·4	6	
(34)			(3)		
4823·7	10nr	8	4063·4	7	
4783·6	10nr	6	4061·9	6	
4766·6	7	4	4059·5	6	
4766·0	7	4	4059·1	7	4
4762·6	8	4	(1)		
4761·7	7		4055·7	9	6
4754·2	10nr	6	(4)		
4739·3	6s	5	4048·9	8	6
4727·6	7	4	4045·3	6	
4709·9	7	4	4041·5	10n	6
(6)			(1)		
4605·6	5n	4	4035·9	6	6
(9)			4034·6	20nr	6
4502·4	7	4	4033·2	20nr	6
4499·1	7	4	4030·9	20nr	8
(2)			4026·6	6	
4490·3	7	4	(1)		
(1)			4018·3	7	
4472·9	6	4	(55)		
4470·3	6	4	3844·1	7	4
4464·9	7	4	3841·2	8	4
4462·2	8n	6	3839·9	7	4
4461·2	7	4	(1)		
(1)			3834·5	9	4
4458·4	7	4	3834·0	7	4
4457·7	6	4	(2)		
4457·2	6	4	3824·0	7	4
4456·0	6		3823·6	8	6
4455·5	6		(2)		
4455·2	6	4	3809·7	6	4
4453·2	6		3806·9	9	10
(1)			(3)		
4451·8	7	6	3790·4	6	4
(1)			(13)		

Catalogue of Spectra.

MANGANESE—continued.

Wave-length.	Intensity and character.		Wave-length.	Intensity and character.	
	Arc.	Spark.		Arc.	Spark.
3732·1	5	2	(4)		
(2)			3031·2		6
3719·1	5	4	3020·0		6
3706·2	5	4	2949·3		10
(4)			2939·4		8
3693·8	5	4	2933·1		8
(13)			(4)		
3623·9	5	4	2889·5		6
3619·4	6	4	(1)		
3610·4	6	6	2879·5		6
3608·6	6	6	(13)		
3607·7	6	6	2705·7		6
(2)			2701·7		6
3595·2	5	6	(1)		
3586·7	6	6	2688·3		6
3578·0	7	6	(3)		
3570·2	5n	8nr	2672·8		6
(1)			(5)		
3569·7	8n	6	2639·9		6
(1)			(1)		
3548·2	5n	10r	2632·5		6
3548·1	5n	10n	2625·7		6
3532·1	5n	10	2618·2		6
3532·0	5n	10	(1)		
3497·7	3	8	2605·8		6n
3474·2		10	2576·2		10n
3496·0	4	8	(6)		
3488·8	4	10	2452·6		6
3483·0	4	10	(9)		
3474·2		10	2438·2		8n
3460·5	5	10	(10)		
3442·1		10	2128·0		6n
(5)			(61)		
3228·2		6			

MERCURY.

Wave-length.	Intensity and character.			Wave-length.	Intensity and character.		
	Vacuum tube.	Arc.	Spark.		Vacuum tube.	Arc.	Spark.
6152·3	9		9	(3)			
5889·1	8		8	5596·0	8		8
(1)				(2)			
5872·1	8		8	5571·2	8		
(5)				(7)			
5804·3	10	2b″	10	3+5461·0	10	10r	10
5790·5	2	10r	10	(3)			
(1)				5426·5	10		10
5769·6	10	10r	10	(66)			
(6)				4916·4	4	6b″	4
5679·1	10		10	(12)			

254 An Introduction to the Study of Spectrum Analysis.

MERCURY—*continued.*

Wave-length.	Vacuum tube.	Arc.	Spark.	Wave-length.	Vacuum tube.	Arc.	Spark.
4826·0 (1)	8		8	3942·3 (5)	8		
4797·4 (57)	8			3925·5 (74)	8b		
4486·8 (13)	8			3774·3 (43)	8b		
4425·9 (7)	8b			4 * 3663·3 (3)	10	6r	10b
4401·5	10b			3654·9 (1)	8	6r	10b
4391·9	10b			3650·3 (39)	10	10r	10b
4385·7	8			3390·5 (3)	5n	6a	8n
4382·9	8			4 † 3341·7 (9)	6	6b″	10n
4378·7	8			4 * 3131·9	5	8r	10b
4376·1 (2)	10			3131·7	5	8r	10b
3 † 4358·6	10	10r	10b	3125·8 (6)	5	8b″	10b
4347·7 (2)	10	6b″	2	5 * 3023·7 (7)	2	2n	10b
4336·9 (4)	8			4 * 2967·4 (7)	8	10r	10
4320·4 (19)	8			5 † 2925·5 (2)	7	8b″	2n
4264·2	8b			4 † 2893·7 (6)	7	6b″	10
4261·6 (11)	8b			2847·9 (15)	8	4n	10
4227·4 (4)	8			6 † 2759·8	2	6	2
4216·8 (9)	10b		2	4 † 2752·9 (13)	6	8b″	2n
4178·5 (5)	8			2655·3	2	6r	2
4162·0 (11)	8			5 * 2653·9	2	6r	2
4120·9 (1)	8		8	2652·2 (1)	3	8r	2
4115·3 (2)	8		8	2642·7 (9)	2n	6b″	2n
4104·1 (9)	8			5 † 2576·3 (5)	3	8b″	3
3 † 4078·1 (11)	10	8r	10	2536·7	6	10br	6r
4046·8 (6)	10	6r	10b	5 * 2534·9 (14)	3	8r	3
4024·4 (7)	8b		2n	5 † 2464·2 (1)	4	6b″	2
4006·0 (10)	8b			6 † 2447·0 (7)	2	6b″	2
3984·1 (4)	10b	4	10b	6 * 2378·4 (28)	3	6b″	2
3967·9 (8)	8b						

The lines marked * form a series of triplets for which in the formula $10^8 \frac{1}{\lambda} = a - bn^{-2} - cn^{-4}$, $a = 40159\cdot60$ for the *first* line, $44792\cdot87$ for the *second*, and $46560\cdot78$ for the *third*, $b = 127484$, $c = 1252695$.

For the triplets marked †, $a = 40217\cdot98$ or $44851\cdot01$ or $46618\cdot44$, $b = 126361$, $c = 613268$.

MOLYBDENUM.

Wave-length.	Intensity and character.		Wave-length.	Intensity and character.	
	Arc.	Spark.		Arc.	Spark.
6030·2		10s	(19)		
(2)			4672·1	6	2
5888·6	8	10n	(3)		
(6)			4662·9	6	2
5858·5	8	8s	(14)		
(16)			4627·7	5	1
5792·1	8	6s	4626·7	7	2
(13)			(9)		
5751·7	9	6s	4610·1	6	4
(11)			(6)		
5723·0	7		4595·3	6	2
(4)			(13)		
5706·0	6		4576·7	6s	2
(7)			(14)		
5689·4	9	6s	4553·5	3	6
(11)			(6)		
5650·4	8	4s	4537·0	6	4
(3)			(7)		
5632·7	8	4s	4524·5	6	2
(4)			(3)		
5611·2	6		4517·3	6	2
(8)			(4)		
5570·7	12	10s	4506·2	6	2
(12)			4506·1		
5533·3	12	10s	(5)		
(7)			4491·5	6	4
5506·7	12	10s	(5)		
(11)			4474·8	8	6
5473·6	6		(3)		
(22)			4468·5	6	2
5364·5	7		(1)		
5360·8	9	4n	4465·0	6	1
(20)			(2)		
5241·1	6		4457·5	7	4
5238·4	6		(1)		
(8)			4449·9	6	2
5174·4	6		(19)		
5173·1	6		4435·1		4
5171·3	6		(1)		
(45)			4433·6	3s	4
4957·8	6	1n	(10)		
(21)			4411·9	6	6
4868·2	6	4n	(20)		
(12)			ν 4381·8	8	4
4830·7	6s	4s	(4)		
(4)			4377·9		6
4819·5	6	4s	(9)		
(19)			4363·8	3	8
4776·5	6		(2)		
(5)			4350·5	6	6
4760·4	8	6	(18)		
(13)			4326·3	6	4
4731·6	7	4	(10)		
4729·4	6		4311·8 }		4
(8)			4311·1 }		
4708·4	6		(4)		
4707·4	7	4	4294·1	6	2

256   An Introduction to the Study of Spectrum Analysis.

MOLYBDENUM—continued.

Wave-length.	Intensity and character.		Wave-length.	Intensity and character.	
	Arc.	Spark.		Arc.	Spark.
4293·4	6	4	(22)		
4292·3	6	2	3798·4	20nr	10r
(2)			(18)		
4288·8	6	4	3786·4	2	4
(1)			(2)		
4284·8	6n	1	3783·3		4
(4)			3782·2	3	4
4279·2	2	6	(42)		
4277·4	6	6	3755·6	2	4
4277·1	6	6	(10)		
(4)			3748·3		4
4269·4	5	6	(8)		
(12)			3744·6	4	4
4250·9	3	6	(3)		
(2)			3742·5	5	6
4244·9	3n	4	(7)		
(8)			3732·8	6	2
4232·8	6	4	(3)		
(12)			3727·9	6	2
4209·8	2	6	(9)		
(14)			3717·1	2	4n
4188·5	8	4	(20)		
(1)			3702·7	4	8
4186·0	6	4	(5)		
(28)			3695·1	7	2
4143·7	8	6	(2)		
(15)			3692·8	4	6
4122·5	2	1	(5)		
4120·3	6	4	3688·4	4	10
4119·7		4	(1)		
(8)			3684·3		4
4107·6	6	1	(3)		
(10)			3680·8 }	7	4
4084·5	6	4	3680·7 }		
(1)			(7)		
4081·6	6	4	3673·0	6	
(6)			3670·9		4
4070·0	6	4	(3)		
(5)			3665·0	6	
4062·2	5	4	(6)		
(50)			3659·5	7	2
3986·4	4	4	3658·5	2	4
(20)			(10)		
3961·7		10	3652·6		6
(14)			3651·3		6
3943·2	6	2	(12)		
(1)			3635·3	4	10
3941·6		6	(5)		
(35)			3624·6	6	2
3903·4	20nr	10	(5)		
(20)			3614·4	6	4
3864·2	20nr	10r	(3)		
(12)			3612·2	4	4
3833·9	6	1	(27)		
(1)			3596·5	2	4
3832·5		6	(12)		
(7)			3585·7	2	4
3829·0	6	1	(1)		

Catalogue of Spectra.

MOLYBDENUM—continued.

Wave-length.	Arc.	Spark.	Wave-length.	Arc.	Spark.
3583·3	8	1	3240·8		4
3582·0	7	1	(15)		
(3)			3229·8		6
3575·9	8	1	(22)		
(15)			3216·2		4
3558·2	6	2	(22)		
(13)			3201·6		4
3537·4	6	4	3200·4		
(7)			(6)		
3524·7	4	6	3196·0		4
(103)			(5)		
3446·3		4	3192·3		4
(20)			(4)		
3435·5		4	3187·8		4
(22)			(7)		
3422·8		4	3183·1		4
(26)			(11)		
3402·9		2	3176·4		4
(12)			(1)		
3392·4		4	3175·2		4
(3)			(2)		
3380·4		4	3173·0		4
3379·9		4	(26)		
(14)			3155·8		4
3368·0		4	(19)		
(26)			3141·9 }		4
3346·5		4	3141·6 }		4
(19)			(5)		
3329·4		4	3139·0		4
(8)			(3)		
3321·3 }		6	3136·6		4
3321·0 }			(5)		
(6)			3132·9 }		4
3313·8 }		4	3132·7 }		
3313·1 }			(2)		
(27)			3130·2		4
3292·5		6n	(10)		
3290·9		4	3122·1		6
(3)			(8)		
3287·4		2	3116·2		4
(5)			(7)		
3284·8		2	3111·0		4
(1)			(30)		
3283·0		4	3092·2		4
(5)			(8)		
3279·1		4	3087·7		6
(2)			(8)		
3276·4		4	3082·8		4
(4)			(6)		
3271·8		4	3077·7		6
3267·8 }		4	(21)		
3267·0 }		4	3067·7		4
(19)			(13)		
3254·8 }		4	3060·9		4
3253·9 }		4	(3)		
(5)			3058·0		4
3250·9		4	(7)		
(14)			3053·6		4

MOLYBDENUM—*continued*.

Wave-length.	Intensity and character.		Wave-length.	Intensity and character.	
	Arc.	Spark.		Arc.	Spark.
3052·4 (29)		4	2891·1 (2)		4
3033·4 (13)		4	2888·3 (12)		4
3023·4 (1)		4	2879·1 (5)		6
3021·7 (3)		4	2873·0		4
3018·6 (6)		4	2871·6 (13)		6
3014·2 (10)		2	2863·9 (12)		4
3008·3 (6)		4	2853·3 (4)		6
3004·5 (8)		4	2848·4 (27)		8
3000·4 (53)		4	2827·9 (15)		4
2972·7		4	2817·6		4
2972·0 (12)		4	2816·3 (10)		8
2963·9 (9)		4	2807·8 (25)		6
2957·0 (18)		4	2785·1 (4)		4
2946·0		4	2780·1 (4)		6
2944·9 (6)		4	2775·5		6
2941·3 (3)		4	2774·5 (3)		4
2938·4 (1)		4n	2769·9 (18)		4
2936·9 (2)		4	2756·2 (5)		4
2934·4 (3)		4	2750·0 (15)		4
2930·6 (3)		4	2738·0 (7)		4
2927·6 (2)		4	2732·9 (5)		4
2925·5		4	2727·1 (11)		4
2924·5		4	2717·4 (20)		4
2923·5 (6)		4	2701·4 (17)		4
2919·0 (6)		4	2688·1 (3)		4
2913·9 (2)		4	2684·2 (2)		4
2912·0 (2)		4	2681·5 (6)		4
2909·2 (9)		4	2676·6 (2)		
2903·1 (12)		6	2673·4		4
2894·5 (1)		4	2672·9		4
2893·0 (2)		4	2671·9 (14)		4
			2660·6		4

Catalogue of Spectra.

MOLYBDENUM—continued.

Wave-length.	Intensity and character.		Wave-length.	Intensity and character.	
	Arc.	Spark.		Arc.	Spark.
(10)			2457·9		4
2653·4		4	(3)		
(10)			2455·5		4
2646·6		4	(21)		
2644·4		1	2437·8		4
(6)			2436·0		4
2638·9		4	(11)		
(3)			2424·1		4
2636·8		4	2422·2		4
(4)			(13)		
2633·7		4	2412·8		4
(70)			(4)		
2595·5		4	2410·2		4
(53)			(5)		
2555·6		4	2403·7		6
(13)			(3)		
2547·5		4	2399·3		4
(5)			(17)		
2542·9		4	2387·0		4
(5)			(10)		
2538·6		6	2377·3		4
(16)			(13)		
2527·3		4n	2366·4		4
(3)			(4)		
2524·8		4	2359·9		4
(66)			(16)		
2487·8		4	2341·7		4
(11)			2340·5		4
2481·3		6	(12)		
(6)			2331·0		4
2477·7		4	(5)		
(1)			2325·6		4
2474·3		4	(20)		
(8)			2295·0		4
2466·8		4	(35)		
(9)					

NEODIDYMIUM.

Wave-length.	Intensity and character.		Wave-length.	Intensity and character.	
	Arc.	Spark.		Arc.	Spark.
(48)			4446·5		8
4542·8		5	(32)		
(68)			4411·2		7
4463·2		9	(2)		
(9)			4408·9		5
4456·6		5	(5)		
(6)			4401·0		5
4451·7		10	(8)		
(2)			4390·9		6

260 *An Introduction to the Study of Spectrum Analysis.*

NEODIDYMIUM—*continued.*

Wave-length.	Intensity and character.		Wave-length.	Intensity and character.	
	Arc.	Spark.		Arc.	Spark.
(4) 4385·9		7	4135·5 (1)		7
(7) 4375·2		6	4133·5 (34)		5
(22) 4358·3		8	⎧ 4109·6 ⎨ ⎩ 4109·3		8 6
(2) 4356·1		5	(11) 4100·9		5
(8) 4351·4		8	(61) 4061·3		10
(8) 4338·8		8	(14) 4051·3		6
(7) 4328·1		6	(16) 4040·9		7
(2) 4325·9		7	(16) 4031·9		10
(16) 4314·6		8	(12) 4023·2		5
(11) 4304·6		5	(22) 4012·4		10
4303·8		10	(34) 3994·8	5	5
(7) 4298·0		5	(7) 3991·9		5
(11) 4284·7		7	(1) 3990·3		6
(2) 4282·7		7	(31) 3973·4	6	6
(8) 4275·3		5	(14) 3963·3	6	6
(16) 4262·1		5	(5) 3958·2		5
(12) 4252·1		7	(9) 3953·6		5
(5) 4247·6		8	(4) 3951·3	8	8r
(4) 4241·4		5	(14) 3941·7	8	8
4240·0		6	(2) 3939·0		5
(8) 4232·5		6	(40) 3911·3	7	7
(10) 4223·2		6	(18) 3902·0	5	5
(15) 4211·4		5	(1) 3900·4		6
(51) 4177·5		10	(46) 3863·5		8
4175·8		5	(18) 3851·8		5
(17) 4165·2		5	(251) 3735·8		5
(9) 4156·3		10	(776)		
(14) 4143·3		8			
(8)					

Catalogue of Spectra.

NICKEL.

Wave-length.	Intensity and character.		Wave-length.	Intensity and character.	
	Arc.	Spark.		Arc.	Spark.
6176·9	6u	6n	3995·4	7	
(7)			(3)		
5893·1	5	10	3973·7	8	4
(9)			(3)		
5709·8	7		3944·2	7n	1u
(1)			(8)		
5682·4	7		3858·4	9r	8
(12)			(7)		
5592·4	7		3807·3	8	8
(7)			(2)		
5477·1	10	6	3783·7	8	6
(18)			(1)		
5155·9	7u	2	3775·7	9	6
(2)			(7)		
5146·6	8n	2	3736·9	7s	8
5143·0	7n	2	(3)		
5137·2	8s	2	3722·6	6	6
(5)			(7)		
5115·6	8s	2s	3674·3	7s	3
(1)			(11)		
5100·1	7n	2s	3619·5	10nr	10
(5)			3612·9	7	6
5084·3	8n		(1)		
(1)			3610·6	4r	8
5081·3	10n	2s	(3)		
5080·7	10	2s	3597·8	7n	10
(6)			(2)		
5035·6	10	6s	3572·0	7nr	8
(1)			3566·5	9nr	10
5017·7	7	6s	(10)		
(7)			3524·6	10nr	10
4984·3	7	2s	(4)		
4980·4	7	2s	3515·2	9nr	10
(12)			(1)		
4904·6	7	6s	3510·5	8nr	10
(4)			(2)		
4873·6	4	10	3501·0	6	8
(1)			(1)		
4866·4	7	10	3493·1	9nr	10
(3)			(4)		
4855·6	6	10	3472·7	7nr	8
(27)			(3)		
4714·6	9	10	3461·8	8nr	10
(14)			3458·6	8nr	10
4605·1	8	2	3458·5	3	8
(3)			(2)		
4592·7	7	2	3453·0	4	7
(12)			(4)		
4470·6	8	2	3446·3	10	8
(2)			(6)		
4462·6	8	2	3433·7	10	7
4459·2	9	4	(2)		
(8)			3423·8	8	7
4401·7	9	4	(4)		
(21)			3414·9	8	8
4288·2	7	2	(12)		
(35)			3393·1	8	7

NICKEL—*continued.*

Wave-length.	Intensity and character.		Wave-length.	Intensity and character.	
	Arc.	Spark.		Arc.	Spark.
(3) 3380·7	10	7	3002·6 2992·7	8 8	6 7
(5) 3369·7	6	8	(15) 2944·1	10	6
(54) 3247·7	1	7	(7) 2913·7	8	6
(1) 3243·2	6	7	(41) 2821·3	10	4
(6) 3233·1	10	8	(10) 2802·8		7
(10) 3217·9		7	(7) 2795·6		7
(47) 3134·3	10	8	(111) 2546·0	6	7
(10) 3102·0	8	8	(23) 2510·9	8	8
3101·6	6	8	(29) 2141·8	10	2
(6) 3080·8	6	7	(3) 2437·9	6	7
(1) 3064·7	6	7	(17) 2416·2	8	7
(1) 3057·7		8	(20) 2394·5	8	7
3054·4	6	7	(104) 2270·2	10	1
3050·9	8	8	(1) 2264·6	10	4
(2) 3038·0	8	7	(22) 2216·5	10	1
(9) 3012·1	10	8	(16)		
(1) 3003·7	8	8			

NIOBIUM.

Wave-length.	Intensity and character.		Wave-length.	Intensity and character.	
	Arc.	Spark.		Arc.	Spark.
(217) 4168·3		6	(1) 4119·3		7
(1) 4164·9		7	(11) 4101·1		9
4163·8		7	(13) 4079·9		10
(5) 4152·8		5	(18) 4059·1		15
(8) 4139·9		6	(62) 3976·7		6
(3) 4137·2		5	(71) 3879·5		5n
(11) 4124·0		7	(35)		

Catalogue of Spectra.

NIOBIUM—continued.

Wave-length.	Intensity and character.		Wave-length.	Intensity and character.	
	Arc.	Spark.		Arc.	Spark.
3832·0 (5)		6	3094·3 (37)		10
3819·0 (11)		10	3032·9 (1)		5
3801·3 (6)		7	3028·5 (16)		5
3791·3 (9)		5	2994·9 (12)		5
3781·5 (40)		6u	2974·2		5
3740·9 (16)		8	2972·7 (6)		5
3717·2 (23)		10	2951·0 (3)		10
3696·0 (7)		5	2941·6 (9)		9
3688·1 (36)		5n	2927·9 (7)		10
3659·7 (9)		8	2810·7 (18)		6
3651·4 (111)		5	2883·3 (6)		7
3517·8 (6)		5	2877·1		6
3510·5 (48)		8	2875·5 (1)		6
3432·9 (4)		8	2868·6 (84)		5
3426·7		8	2753·2 (44)		6
3425·6 (9)		7	2697·2 (17)		6
3408·8 (120)		5	2676·0 (1)		5
3263·5 (2)		5	2673·7 (33)		5
3260·7 (18)		5	2642·3 (17)		5
3236·6 (4)		5	2618·5 (16)		5
3225·6 (2)		7	2599·0 (8)		10
3215·7 (5)		5	2591·1 (4)		7
3206·5 (4)		6	2584·1 (74)		8
3195·1 (9)		8	2501·5 (1)		5
3180·4 (6)		6	2499·8 (46)		7
3163·5 (10)		8	2457·1 (44)		8
3145·5 (12)		6	2422·0 (10)		5
3127·6 (14)		7	2414·0 (175)		5

NITROGEN.

Spark-spectrum or Elementary Line Spectrum.

Wave-length.	Intensity and character.	Wave-length.	Intensity and character.	Wave-length.	Intensity and character.
6603·4	4s	5045·7	7s	(10)	
6480·8	5s	5026·7	8s	4447·2	12
6171·9	5s	5017·7	6s	(3)	
5950·2	4s	5011·1″	5s	4426·1	5
5942·6 ⎱	10n ⎱	5007·8	5s	(5)	
5933·0 ⎰	10n ⎰	5005·7 ⎱ n	10 ⎱ n	4346·7	6n
5929·6	4s	5002·7 ⎰	10 ⎰	(3)	
5768·5	3	4994·9	6s	4241·9	6b
5747·5	3	(7)		4236·7	6b
(1)		4803·6	7s	4228·5	6b
5712·3	6s	4788·3	6s	(8)	
5686·3	5s	4780·1	10s	4151·9	5
5679·8	12n	(10)		4146·0	4n
5676·0	5s	4709·9	2	4133·8	6
5667·1	9n	4705·2	2	(3)	
(3)		4643·4	9	4097·5	2b
5535·2	6n	(1)		(3)	
(2)		4634·0	3	4041·4	6b
5496·6	6n	4630·8	12	4035·3	5b
5479·8″	5b	4621·7	9	(4)	
5462·8	5s	4614·1	8	3995·3	15
5453·8″	5s	4607·3	8	3956·2	7
(3)		4601·5	9	(1)	
5180·0	5s	(4)		3919·2	10
(4)		4507·7	6	(24)	

Lines marked with two dashes are double.

NITROGEN.
Vacuum Tube.

Wave-length.	Wave-length.	Wave-length.
(32)	4094·0	3446·2
4975·0	4059·0	3371·2
4917·1	3998·0	3338·6
4813·9	3942·55	3309·4
4722·6	3894·25	3281·8
4666·35	3856·9	3267·5
4648·4	3804·85	3158·9
4573·7	3755·15	3135·7
4489·6	3710·15	3116·4
4415·7	3671·35	3103·8
4356·3	3642·0	2976·7
4344·4	3576·85	2961·9
4269·15	3536·5	2953·0
4200·85	3500·15	2819·7
4141·2	3469·05	2814·15

This "positive band" spectrum of nitrogen consists of some seventy or eighty "bands," each most intense at the least refracted edge, which generally consists of three "lines" forming a "head" to the band. The measurements are of the *central* line of the head.

OSMIUM.

Wave-length.	Intensity and character.		Wave-length.	Intensity and character.	
	Arc.	Spark.		Arc.	Spark.
(12)			3370·7	4	6
4794·2	5		(8)		
(6)			3358·1	4	2
4664·0	4	1	(6)		
4617·0	4	1	3336·3	4	2
(3)			(3)		
4550·6	4	8	3327·6	4	2
(23)			(3)		
4420·6	5	10	3324·5	4	2
(6)			(10)		
4395·0	4	8	3311·0	4	2
(14)			(4)		
4328·8	3	6	3301·7	7	2
(3)			(9)		
4311·6	4	8	3278·1	4	
(4)			(1)		
4294·1	2	10	3275·3	4	1
(9)			(7)		
4261·0	4	10	3269·3	4	4
(6)			3268·1	6	8
4212·0	3	10	3267·4		8
(2)			3263·0	4	4
4175·8	1	8	3262·5	6	8
4173·4	2	8	(3)		
(5)			3257·1	4	2
4135·9	4	10	(12)		
(2)			3238·8	4	10
4112·2	2	8	(5)		
(9)			3232·2	4	10
4066·9	3	10	3213·5		10
(21)			(1)		
3977·4	4	4	3174·0		8
(3)			(1)		
3963·8	4	6	3165·8		8
(16)			3156·3		10
3782·3		8	(2)		
3752·7		10	3058·8		10
3689·2	4	2	3042·8		8
(7)			3041·0		8
3640·5	1	4	3030·8		8
3639·7		8	3018·1		8
(6)			(2)		
3561·1		8	2949·6		6
3560·0		6	(2)		
3528·8	3	6	2919·9		8
(3)			2912·4		8
3504·8	4	4	2909·0		10
(16)			(3)		
3449·4	4	2	2844·4		6
(6)			2838·7		8
3434·0	4	1n	(3)		
3427·8	5	1	2658·7		6
(12)			(1)		
3402·0	4	1	2637·1		6
(8)			(6)		
3388·0	4	2	2367·4		6
(11)					

OXYGEN.

Spark-spectrum or Elementary Line Spectrum.

Wave-length.	Intensity and character.	Wave-length.	Intensity and character.	Wave-length.	Intensity and character.
6171·9	5s	4367·0	6	4105·1	5u
5206·4	6s	(2)		(4)	
5190·6	4s	4351·5	6	4076·1	9
5176·3	3s	4349·6	8	4072·4	9
4710·1	5s	4347·6	5s	4070·0	9
4705·6	6s	4345·7	6	(1)	
4699·4	8s	(5)		3982·9	4
4676·4	3s	4319·8	3	3973·4	8
(2)		4317·3	3	3954·5	5
4649·2	8s	(2)		(1)	
4641·9	9s	4190·1	7	3945·2	3
4638·9	5	4185·7	7	3919·2	10
4609·7	2n	(3)		3912·2	5
4596·3	6s	4153·6	6	(10)	
4591·1	5s	(2)		3749·7	6
(4)		4133·0	2n	(1)	
4447·1	4	(1)		3727·5	4
(1)		4124·3	5	3712·9	2
4417·1 }	9 }	(2)		(22)	
4415·1 }	9 }	4119·5	5s		
(9)		(3)			

Oxygen, sulphur, and selenium have also a "compound line spectrum" consisting of a series of triplets, which can be represented by a formula—

$$\frac{1}{\lambda} = a - bn^{-2} - cn^{-4}$$

PALLADIUM.

Wave-length.	Intensity and character.		Wave-length.	Intensity and character.	
	Arc.	Spark.		Arc.	Spark.
6130·4		2s	(1)		
(3)			3517·1	8r	10
5736·8	5	5s	3489·9	4r	8
(2)			(1)		
5695·3	9	6s	3481·3	7r	10
(4)			(1)		
5670·3	10	6s	3460·9	7r	10
(2)			(1)		
5655·6	5n		3441·5	6r	10
5642·9	5		3433·6	5r	10
(1)			3421·4	8r	10
5619·7	9	6s	(2)		
5608·2	5n		3404·7	10r	10
(3)			(5)		
5547·2	9	6s	3380·8	5n	
5543·0	10	6s	3373·1	6r	10
5529·7	6	6s	(6)		
(3)			3302·3	6r	10
5395·5	8b"	8s	(2)		
(8)			3287·4	5	4
5295·7	10	10s	(2)		
(2)			3267·5		6
5235·0	7	8s	3258·9	6r	8
(1)			3251·8	5r	8
5164·0	10	10s	3242·9	10r	10
(2)			(4)		
5117·2	7	8s	3114·2	5r	8
(1)			(23)		
5110·9	6	8s	3032·3	1	6
(6)			(2)		
4875·6	7	6s	3028·0	4r	6
(2)			(9)		
4817·7	9	6s	2999·7		6
(2)			2980·8		8
4788·3	8	6s	(10)		
(8)			2922·6	7r	4
4541·3	5n		(11)		
4516·4	5n		2763·2	8r	4
(2)			(4)		
4473·8	7	6	2658·8	2	6
(4)			(3)		
4406·8	5		2636·0		8
(10)			2628·4		6
4213·1	6r	10	(3)		
4170·0	5	4	2565·6	0	8
(3)			(1)		
4087·5	6	8	2552·0	0	8
(5)			(9)		
3958·8	5r	10	2505·8	2	6
3894·3	6r	8	2498·8	3	6
3799·3	5r	8	2489·0	4	8
3719·1	4r	10	2486·6	1	6
3690·5	6r	10n	(1)		
(2)			2476·5	10r	
3634·8	10r	10	(6)		
3609·7	9r	10	2448·0	10r	4
(2)			(1)		
3571·3	5r	10	2441·5	6nr	
(1)			(19)		
3553·2	7r	10			

PLATINUM.

Wave-length.	Intensity and character.		Wave-length.	Intensity and character.	
	Arc.	Spark.		Arc.	Spark.
6523·3 (3)		6s	3247·4 (29)	2	6
5964·7 (12)		6s	3204·2 (41)	6	6
5478·7	6	4s	3139·5 (58)	7	4
5476·0	6	4s			
5390·6 (8)	4	6s	3064·8 (22)	6r	8
5369·2	4	8s	3036·6 (30)	6	4
5301·2 (6)	6	10s	3001·3 (2)	2	6
5227·8 (6)	6	8s	2998·1 (60)	7r	2
5044·6 (25)	6		2929·9 (38)	8r	6
4552·6 (9)	5u	8n	2894·0 (13)	6	4
4498·9 (13)	6	4	2877·6 (33)		6n
4442·7 (51)	6	4	2830·4 (31)	8r	4
4118·9 (29)	5	6	2794·3 (15)	5r	6
3966·5 (10)	3	6	2774·9 (42)	2	6
3923·4 (35)	5	8	2734·1 (9)	8r	4n
3818·8 (47)	5	6	2719·1 (10)	6r	4
3687·6 (7)	4	8	2702·5 (2)	6r	6
3674·2	4	6	2698·5 (22)	6	4
3672·2 (12)	4	6	2659·5 (7)	10r	6
3643·3	6	6n	2647·0 (6)	6r	4
3639·0 (3)	6	6			
3629·0	3	6	2628·1 (1)	7r	6
3628·3 (64)	5	8	2625·4 (71)	2	6
3485·4 (30)	6	6	2514·0 (18)	1	6
3408·3 (27)	7	6	2487·2 (13)	4r	6
3323·9 (18)	6	2	2467·5 (19)	6r	6
3302·0 (8)	8n	8	2428·2 (1)	8r	1u
3290·4 (3)	6	4	2425·0 (31)	2	6
3274·0 (18)		6	2377·3 (93)		6
3256·0 (9)	6	4			

POTASSIUM.

Wave-length.	Intensity and character.		Wave-length.	Intensity and character.	
	Arc.	Spark.		Arc.	Spark.
* ⎰ 7699·3	10nr	8s	* ⎰ 4047·4	6r	10s
⎱ 7665·6	10nr	8s	⎱ 4044·3	8r	10s
* ⎰ 6938·8	8	8s	(4)		
⎱ 6911·2	8	7s	4001·2		6s
(2)			(8)		
* ⎰ 5802·0	6n	4s	3898·1		8s
⎱ 5782·7	6n	3s	(22)		
* 5359·9	4n	8s	* ⎰ 3447·5	6r	10
(2)			⎱ 3446·5		
* 5340·1	4n	8s	3440·5		6
(18)			(3)		
4609·5		6s	3385·4		6s
(7)			3381·4		6s
4263·2		6s	(2)		
4225·7		6s	3345·5		8s
4223·1		6s	(6)		
(1)			* 3217·3	6r	2
4186·3		8s	(11)		
4149·1		6s	3062·4		6s
4134·7		6s	(31)		
(1)					

The lines marked * occur in the flame-spectrum.

PRASEODIDYMIUM.

Wave-length.	Intensity and character.		Wave-length.	Intensity and character.	
	Arc.	Spark.		Arc.	Spark.
(53)			(16)		
4534·4		6	4371·8		5
(7)			(2)		
4510·4		10	4368·6		10
(6)			(11)		
4496·7		10	4352·1		7
(14)			4350·6		5
4468·9		7	(1)		
(7)			4347·7		6
4450·1		5	(3)		
(7)			4344·6		8
4429·4		12	(7)		
(9)			4334·2		10
4409·0		10	(26)		
(3)			4306·0		10
4406·0		8	(1)		
(8)			4303·8		5
4396·3		5	(3)		
(1)			4299·2		5
4395·2		5	4298·0		8

PRASEODIDYMIUM—continued.

Wave-length.	Intensity and character.		Wave-length.	Intensity and character.	
	Arc.	Spark.		Arc.	Spark.
(16)			4079·9		8
4282·7		7	(19)		
4280·3		7	4063·0		10n
(8)			4062·4		6n
4272·5		7	(5)		
(16)			4056·7		10n
4254·6		6	(2)		
(5)			4055·0		10n
4247·8		8	(4)		
(5)			4051·3		6
4241·3		15	(5)		
(16)			4045·0		8
4225·5		20	(14)		
(1)			4034·0		6
4223·2		20	(5)		
(14)			4029·8		5
4208·5		5	(5)		
(1)			4025·7		5
4206·9		20	(3)		
(17)			4022·9		7
4191·8		6	(1)		
(1)			4021·1		6
4189·7		20n	(5)		
(11)			4015·5		6
4179·6		20n	(7)		
(4)			4010·7		5n
4175·8		5	(3)		
(3)			4008·9		15
4172·5		8n	(2)		
4172·0		8	4004·8		7
(6)			(10)		
4164·4		15	3997·1		5
(19)			(1)		
4148·5		7	3995·9		5
(3)			3994·9		8
4146·7		7	(5)		
(3)			3989·7		9
4143·2		20	(9)		
(1)			3982·2		10
4141·3		10	(15)		
(5)			3972·3		6
4133·7		5	3971·8		5
(2)			3971·3		7
4130·9		6	(6)		
4129·2		6	3966·7		7
(13)			(2)		
4118·6		15	3965·4	6	6
(19)			3965·0		8
4100·9		20	3964·4	5	5
(3)			(5)		
4098·5			3960·7		5n
4097·0		7	(4)		
		7	3956·9	6	6
(12)			(1)		
4087·3		5	3953·6		8
(5)			(6)		
4083·5		5	3949·6	8	8
(1)			(2)		
4082·1		10			
4081·2		6			

Catalogue of Spectra.

PRASEODIDYMIUM —continued.

Wave-length.	Intensity and character.		Wave-length.	Intensity and character.	
	Arc.	Spark.		Arc.	Spark.
3947·8 (33)		8	3846·8 (20)		5
3925·6 (8)	8	8	3830·9 (12)		6
3919·0 (8)	10	10	3821·9 (5)		5
3913·1 (7)		5	3818·4 (3)		7
3908·5	10	10	3816·7 (9)		10
3908·2 (18)		6n	3805·0 (5)		8
3889·5 (8)		5	3800·5 (74)		5
3880·6 (1)		5	3762·0 (148)		5
3879·3 (2)		5	3645·8 (245)		7
3877·8		10	3367·7 (5)		5
3876·3 (7)		6	3359·6 (1)		5
3865·6 (17)		10	3357·8 (8)		5
3852·9 (1)		6	3341·6 (240)		5
3851·7		5			
3851·0 (2)		6			

RADIUM.

Wave-length.	Intensity and character.			Wave-length.	Intensity and character.		
	Flame.	Arc.	Spark.		Flame.	Arc.	Spark.
6653	strong			5400·3 (11)			8
{ 6700 to 6530	strong band			4856·2	{ strong sharp		8
				4826·1 (2)			10
6349	strong			4682·4 (2)	weak		50
{ 6329 6330 to 6130	{ strong band			4533·3			10
				4436·5			20
5813·8			10	4340·8 (2)			50
5660·8			10	3814·6			100
5616·7 (3)			8	3649·8 (2)			50
5502·1 (2)			8	2813·8			10
5406·8			8	2709·0			8

RHODIUM.

Wave-length.	Intensity and character.		Wave-length.	Intensity and character.	
	Arc.	Spark.		Arc.	Spark.
5983·8	4		5184·3	4	
(7)			(2)		
5831·7	4		5176·1	6	
(1)			(3)		
5807·1	4		5157·8	5	
(3)			(1)		
5792·8	4		5155·7	5	
(8)			(4)		
5700·6	4		5090·8	5	
(1)			(1)		
5686·5	4		5088·9	4	
(1)			(1)		
5659·8	4		5085·7	4	
(4)			(1)		
5608·5	4		5064·5	4	
(2)			(8)		
5599·6	6n		4077·9	4	
(5)			(1)		
5544·8	6br		4963·8	4	
(1)			(10)		
5535·2	5n		4865·9	4	
(1)			(3)		
5504·8	4n		4851·8	6	
(3)			4844·1	6	
5484·4	4n		4842·6	4	
(3)			(3)		
5471·0	5n		4810·6	6	
(2)			(11)		
5445·4	4n		4745·3	6	
(1)			(2)		
5441·5	4n		4721·1	6	
5439·8	4		(2)		
(2)			4704·2	5	
5425·6	4n		(4)		
5424·9	4		4675·2	7	
(2)			(1)		
5404·9	4n		4643·3	6	
5390·6	5		(3)		
(2)			4620·1	5	
5379·3	5		(6)		
(4)			4569·2	6	
5354·6	7		(2)		
(4)			4561·1	5	
5329·9	4		(2)		
(2)			4551·8	6	
5292·3	4		(2)		
(7)			4528·9	5	4
5237·3	5		(12)		
5230·8	4		4380·1	5n	1n
(1)			(1)		
5228·8	4		4375·0	7r	10
(2)			4373·2	5	
5212·9	4		(9)		
5211·6	4		4296·9	4	4
(3)			4288·9	7	8
5193·3	7		(10)		
(2)			4211·3	5r	10

Catalogue of Spectra.

RHODIUM—continued.

Wave-length.	Intensity and character.		Wave-length.	Intensity and character.	
	Arc.	Spark.		Arc.	Spark.
(1)			(1)		
4196·7	3	6	3748·3	4	4
(2)			3744·3	4	4
4154·5	2	6	3737·4	4	6
(1)			3735·4	4	8
4135·4	4r	8	(2)		
4129·1	6r	8	3713·2	4r	8
(1)			3701·1	8r	8
4121·9	4r	6	3692·5	10r	10
4119·9	4	4	3690·9	4r	8
(1)			3681·2	6	8
4097·7	5	6	3674·9	5	4
(3)			3667·1	4	4
4083·0	5	8	3666·4	7	8
(8)			3662·0	3	4
4023·3	5	6	(1)		
3996·3	5	8	3658·1	8r	10
3995·8	4	6	3655·0	5	4
3984·6	5	6	(3)		
(1)			3639·7	6	4
3975·5	5	6	(1)		
(2)			3626·8	7	10
3959·0	5r	10	3620·6	5	4
3958·3	4	4	3614·9	4	8
(1)			(2)		
3942·9	5	6	3612·9	5r	8
3936·0	4	4	(1)		
(1)			3606·0	5	6
3934·4	4r	8	(2)		
3922·3	4	4	3597·3	6r	8
(6)			3596·3	4r	10
3877·5	2	4	3583·2	10r	6
(1)			3570·3	10	8
3870·2		6	(2)		
(1)			3549·7	5	10
3856·7	4r	10	3544·1	5	8
(2)			3542·1	4	4
3834·0	5r	8	3538·3	3	8
(1)			3528·2	7r	10
3828·6	2	8	(2)		
(1)			3513·3	4	4
3822·4	4r	8	(4)		
3818·3	5	8	3507·5	4r	8
(2)			(1)		
3816·6	1	6	3502·7	8r	8
(3)			3498·9	7	8
3806·9	4	4	3494·6	5	
3806·1	4	6	(5)		
3799·5	4r	10	3484·2	4	4
3793·4	4r	8	(1)		
3792·4		4	3479·1	4r	4
3788·6	5	6	3478·0		8
3778·3	4	4	(2)		
(2)			3474·9	5r	8
3770·1	4	4	(1)		
3765·2	5r	8	3472·4	5	4
(3)			3470·8	4r	8
3754·4	3	6	(1)		

T

RHODIUM—continued.

Wave-length.	Intensity and character.		Wave-length.	Intensity and character.	
	Arc.	Spark.		Arc.	Spark.
3469·8	5		3305·3	4	
(1)			(4)		
3462·2	5r	8	3300·6	4	4
(2)			(5)		
3458·1	6	4	3296·8	4	1
3457·2	5	4	(1)		
(2)			3294·4	5	4
3455·4	4	4	(3)		
(2)			3289·7	5	
3450·4	5		3289·3	5	4
3448·7	5		(1)		
3447·9	6		3286·5	4	
(4)			(2)		
3440·7	4	6	3283·7	4r	6
3435·0	10r	10	(1)		
(2)			3281·8	4	4
3424·5	4	4	3280·7	4r	8
(3)			(1)		
3421·3		8	3276·1	4	
3420·3	4	8	3274·9	4	
(2)			3271·7	8	4
3412·4	6	8	(1)		
(5)			3268·6	5	
3406·7	5	4	(4)		
(3)			3263·3	8	6
3399·8	7	4	(3)		
3397·0	8r	10	3255·1	4	
(8)			(7)		
3385·9	6	4	3237·8	4	
3381·6	4		(3)		
(1)			3232·6	4	
3380·8	4		(5)		
3377·8	4		3218·4	4	
(1)			3218·0	4	
3377·3	5	4	3215·0	4	
(5)			(1)		
3372·4	7	8	3214·4	4	
3369·8	5		(3)		
(1)			3207·4	2	6
3368·5	6	6	3206·2	4	
(4)			(1)		
3362·3	5		3197·3	4	
3361·0	8	6	3194·7	4	
3360·0	6	4	(4)		
(4)			3191·3	6	4
3354·9	4		(1)		
(4)			3189·2	5	
3345·2	10		3188·8		6
3344·3	5		3188·0	1	6
(1)			(2)		
3343·0	5		3185·7	5	
(1)			(5)		
3338·7	7	4	3179·8	5	
(3)			3178·5	4	
3331·4	4		3177·2	4	
3331·2	4		(2)		
3323·2	6r	8	3172·4		
(6)			(9)		

Catalogue of Spectra.

RHODIUM—continued.

Wave-length.	Intensity and character.		Wave-length.	Intensity and character.	
	Arc.	Spark.		Arc.	Spark.
3159·4		8	(1)		
3155·5	6	8	2958·9	4	
(1)			(18)		
3152·7	6		2932·4	4	
3150·4	4		2929·3	4	
(3)			(2)		
3147·7	4		2926·9	0	6
(9)			(2)		
3137·8	5		2924·1	4	8
3137·4	4		2923·2	4	
(3)			(3)		
3130·9	4		2915·5	4	
(3)			(1)		
3123·8	6	4	2914·1	4	
3122·9	6		(3)		
(3)			2912·7	4	
3115·0	5		2910·3	4	10
(2)			(8)		
3105·1	4		2900·1	4	
3102·6	4		(6)		
(1)			2892·3	4	
3093·6	0	6	2890·0	4	
(5)			(1)		
3087·5	4		2889·2	4	
(2)			(2)		
3084·1	4	4	2886·1	4	
(10)			(2)		
3067·4	6		2882·5	4	
(9)			(1)		
3058·0	4		2878·8	4	1n
(1)			(5)		
3055·8	0	6	2873·7	4	1n
(9)			(1)		
3049·0	0	6	2871·5	5r	
(1)			(6)		
3047·4	0	6	2864·5	4	
3046·8	4		2863·1	6	1
(8)			(2)		
3028·5	4		2860·9	4	
(7)			(4)		
3020·0	0	6	2855·3	1	
(9)			(7)		
3009·1	4	6	2845·9	2	8
(1)			(1)		
3004·6	5		2844·5	1r	
(6)			2842·3	4r	
2989·0	0	6	2841·9	4	
(2)			(2)		
2987·1	5		2836·8	4	
2986·3	7	4	(2)		
(2)			2834·2	4	
2983·2	4		(6)		
(2)			2827·4	4	
2977·8	5		2826·8	4	1
(4)			2826·5	4	
2968·8	6	4	2819·3		8
(2)			(28)		
2963·7	2	10	2791·3	4	
(3)			(4)		
2959·8	4		2783·4	5	

RHODIUM—continued.

Wave-length.	Intensity and character.		Wave-length.	Intensity and character.	
	Arc.	Spark.		Arc.	Spark.
2781·8 (4)		6	2606·5 (1)	4	1
2778·2	4	6	2603·5 (6)	4	1
2775·9 (2)	2	6	2597·0 (1)	3	8
2771·6 (1)	4		2592·2 (17)	0	6
2768·3	4		2567·4 (6)	4	
2767·8 (12)	4		2558·7 (1)	4	
2740·0 (3)	1	8	2557·3		6
2737·5 (5)	2	8	2555·5 (5)	4	1
2729·0 (12)	6	6	2545·8	4	
2715·4 (2)	2	8	2545·4 (3)		8
2714·5 (4)	4		2539·9 (2)	4r	
2705·7 (1)	3	10	2536·8 (13)	4	
2703·8 (6)	6	1	2520·6 (5)	2	8
2694·4 (7)	4		2510·7 (5)	2	8
2687·0	4		2504·4 (8)	4r	
2686·6 (1)	4		2494·6 (2)	4r	1
2684·3	2	8	2491·9		6
2683·7 (1)	0	8	2490·9 (2)	3	8
2680·7 (2)	4		2487·6 (7)	4	
2676·2 (1)	4	1	2475·7	0	8
2674·6 (3)		8	2475·1 (8)	4	
2671·1 (11)	4		2463·7	4r	
2663·8		6	2461·1 (1)	2	8
2659·2		8	2459·0 (1)	2	8
2652·7	5		2455·8 (2)	2	8
2652·0 (6)	0	10	2450·7 (4)	4	
2643·1 (7)	4	4	2444·3 (18)	4r	
2635·4	4	6	2421·1	2	6
2635·1 (5)	4		2415·9 (16)		6
2628·2 (3)	0	8	2396·6	0	8
2625·5 (4)	1	8	2392·4 (1)		6
2622·7 (4)	4		2386·2 (7)	4	
2613·7 (3)	4r		2384·8 (4)	1	6
2609·3 (2)	0	8	2290·1		8

RUBIDIUM.

Wave-length.	Intensity and character.		Wave-length.	Intensity and character.	
	Arc.	Spark.		Arc.	Spark.
{ 7950·5	10br		5431·8	2n	
{ 7806·0	10br		5363·0	2n	
6298·7	4n	10s	{ 4215·7	6r	10
6206·7	4n	8s	{ 4202·0	8r	20r
6159·8	1u	6s	3591·7	4r	1n
6071·2	2n	6s	3587·2	6r	1n
5724·4	6n		3351·0	2r	
5654·2	2n		3348·9	4r	
5648·2	1n				

All these lines occur in the flame-spectrum.

RUTHENIUM.

Wave-length.	Intensity and character.		Wave-length.	Intensity and character.	
	Arc.	Spark.		Arc.	Spark.
(7) 5815·2	5		(14) 4758·0	6	
(12) 5747·6	5		(13) 4709·7	6	6
(11) 5699·2	9		(13) 4647·8	5	4
(17) 5636·4	7		(15) 4599·3	6	4
(14) 5560·0	6		(8) 4584·6	4	8
(6) 5510·9	6		(5) 4554·7	6r	10
(5) 5484·5	6		(35) 4460·2	6	8
(6) 5455·0	6		(5) 4439·9	5	4
(6) 5401·2	5		(6) 4410·2	6	8
(5) 5362·0	5		(7) 4390·6	6	8
(33) 5171·2	6		(3) 4385·8 } 4385·6 }	5	4
(9) 5136·7	5		(6) 4372·4	5	8
(42) 4903·2	5		(6) 4361·4	5	6
(12) 4869·3	6		(2) 4354·3	6	4
(11) 4815·7	5		(1)		

278 *An Introduction to the Study of Spectrum Analysis.*

RUTHENIUM—*continued.*

Wave-length.	Intensity and character.		Wave-length.	Intensity and character.	
	Arc.	Spark.		Arc.	Spark.
4349·9	5	4	3909·2	5	4
(2)			(31)		
4342·2	6	4	3868·0	1	6
(16)			(2)		
4320·0	5	4	3862·8	4	6
(6)			(5)		
4307·7	4	6	3857·7	1	6
(4)			(55)		
4297·9	8	8	3799·5	4r	8
(1)			3799·0	4	8
4296·1	5	4	(4)		
4295·0	5	4	3790·6	5	8
(4)			(3)		
4284·5	6	4	3786·2	5	8
(11)			(24)		
4259·2	5	4	3756·1	4	6
(8)			(11)		
4243·2	6	6	3743·0	4	6
4241·2	6	6	3712·4	5	6
(7)			(10)		
4230·5	6	4	3730·6	7	10
(5)			3728·2	5	10
4217·4	7	6	3727·1	4	10
4214·6	4	6	(51)		
(1)			3669·6	4	6
4212·2	5	10	(5)		
(2)			3661·5	7	10
4206·2	4	10	(20)		
(2)			3635·1	7	8
4200·4	7	10	(7)		
(15)			3626·9	5	4
4167·7	5	6	3625·3	5	4
(9)			(19)		
4145·9	4	6	3589·9	4	8
4144·3	4	8	(2)		
(15)			3596·3	5r	8
4112·9	4	6	(1)		
(6)			3593·2	4r	8
4098·0	4	6	(3)		
(4)			3589·4	4	8
4085·6	5	4	(15)		
(3)			3570·7	2	6
4080·8	7	8	(30)		
(2)			3539·4	2	6
4076·9	5	4	(31)		
(13)			3499·1	10r	10
4051·6	4	6	(20)		
(15)			3473·9	5	4
4022·3	5	6	(23)		
(19)			3436·9	5r	10
3985·0	5	6	(7)		
(4)			3428·5	4r	10
3978·6	5	4	(6)		
(6)			3417·5	7	8
3952·9	5	2	(8)		
(17)			3409·4	5	4
3926·1	6	4	(10)		
(8)			3359·2	6	6

Catalogue of Spectra.

RUTHENIUM—continued.

Wave-length.	Intensity and character.		Wave-length.	Intensity and character.	
	Arc.	Spark.		Arc.	Spark.
(6)			2976·7	4	10
3350·4	0	6	(12)		
(11)			2965·7	3	8
3339·7	6	4	(20)		
(13)			2945·8	4	10
3319·0	6	2	(16)		
(4)			2927·9	0	6
3315·4	3	6	(13)		
(12)			2916·4	6	6
3301·7	5	2	(47)		
(8)			2882·2	2	6
3294·3	6	10	(14)		
(16)			2875·1	5m	2
3274·8	5	2	(13)		
(6)			2866·7	5	2
3268·3	5	2	(42)		
(8)			2841·8	2	6
3260·5	5	4	(52)		
(23)			2810·8	0	6
3238·7	5	2	(35)		
(7)			2787·9	3	6
3228·6	4	8	(13)		
(3)			2778·5	3	6
3226·5	5	2	(19)		
(46)			2769·0	4	6
3188·5	5	4	(54)		
(9)			2744·1	2	6
3177·2	4	10	(18)		
(6)			2734·4	3	8
3168·6	5	2	(14)		
(33)			2725·5	4	8
3099·4	5	4	2724·9	3	6
(2)			(13)		
3096·7	6	4	2717·5	2	6
(2)			(8)		
3094·0		6	2712·5	4	8
(34)			(36)		
3056·9	0	6	2692·1	4	10
(20)			(19)		
3036·6	4	8	2678·8	4	10
(22)			(270)		
3017·4	5	4	2543·4	2	8
(21)			(95)		
2999·0	1	6	2479·0	2	6
(7)			(40)		
2995·1	5	2	2455·6	5	4
(5)			(85)		
2991·7	3	8	2402·8	4	8
(2)			(54)		
2989·1	6	4	2358·0	2	6
(13)			(50)		

SCANDIUM.

Wave-length.	Intensity and character.		Wave-length.	Intensity and character.	
	Arc.	Spark.		Arc.	Spark.
6305·1		10	4247·0		100
(4)			(22)		
6210·9		8	3652·0		20
(6)			3645·5		15
* 6080·0		10b″	3642·9		50
6072·6		8b″	3630·9		100
6065·1		8b″	(2)		
6038·0		10b″	3614·0		100
(14)			(1)		
5700·5		8	3590·7		10
5687·0		8	3589·8		10
* (1)			3581·1		20
5672·0		8	3576·5		30
(2)			3572·7		50
5657·5		8	3567·9		20
(3)			3558·7		20
5527·0		12	3535·9		15
(16)			(8)		
5240·0		8	3372·3		10
(14)			3369·1		10
5031·3		10	3362·1		8
(20)			3361·4		8
4315·8		15	3359·8		8
4300·6		20	3353·9		20
(1)			(46)		
4374·7		20	2734·1		7
(2)			2699·1		10
4325·2		20	(8)		
4321·0		20	2552·5		8
4314·3		30	(8)		
(3)					

* Lines due to the oxide.

SELENIUM.

Wave-length.	Intensity and character.		Wave-length.	Intensity and character.	
	Arc.	Spark.		Arc.	Spark.
6500		9	5142		9
6479		9	(3)		
6432		8	5094		10
(9)			(1)		
5697		8	5067		6
(3)			(5)		
5596		8	{ 4993		10
(6)			{ 4972		10
5305		10	(1)		
{ 5270		10	{ 4842		10
{ 5251		9	{ 4840		10
(2)			(8)		
5225		10	4606		10
5176		10	(14)		
(1)					

See note under "Oxygen."

SILICON.

Wave-length.	Intensity and character.		Wave-length.	Intensity and character.	
	Arc.	Spark.		Arc.	Spark.
5948·8			(3)		
5772·4			2631·4		8
5708·6			(1)		
5645·8			2541·9		8
(4)			(2)		
4131·0		4b	2528·6	8	8
4128·2		4b	2524·2	6	6
(5)			2519·3	8	8
3905·8		5r	2516·2	10	10
(2)			2514·4	7	7
3862·8		4n	2507·0	8	8
3856·2		5n	(6)		
(12)			2435·2	8	8
2881·7	10	10	(11)		

SILVER.

Wave-length.	Intensity and character.		Wave-length.	Intensity and character.	
	Arc.	Spark.		Arc.	Spark.
(28)			2580·7		8s
4 * 5471·7	6	5s	2575·7	6b	1u
5465·7	10r	10s	(9)		
(6)			2535·5		6s
4 * 5209·2	10r	8s	(9)		
(7)			2506·7		9s
4 † 4668·7	8b″	2s	(4)		
(8)			2477·4		6s
4 † 4476·3	6b′	5s	2473·9		8s
(9)			(7)		
5 * 4212·1	8r		2453·4		7s
4210·9		8s	2447·9	2	8s
(1)			(4)		
5 * 4055·5	6r	6s	2437·8	4	10s
(3)			(5)		
5 † 3981·9	5b″		2429·6		7s
(7)			(3)		
5 † 3841·3	2b″		2420·1		8s
6 * 3810·6	2n	3s	(1)		
6 † 3710·1	1n		2413·3	4	10s
6 * 3681·8	2b″		2411·1		8s
7 * 3624·0	1n		(16)		
(5)			2375·3	10	2b
7 * 3505·4	1b		(7)		
(18)			2358·9		6s
3383·0	10r	10s	2357·9		8s
(43)			(10)		
3280·8	10r	10s	2331·3	4	8s
(56)			(2)		
3130·1	6b	2n	2324·7	4	8s
(31)			(1)		
2938·5	6b	3b	2320·3	4	8s
(10)			(2)		
2824·5	8b		2317·1	4	8s
(6)			(1)		
2767·6		8s	2312·5	8n	
(14)			2309·7	10r	4b
2711·9		8s	(7)		
(6)			2280·0		8s
2660·5		8s	(7)		
(6)			2248·8	6	6s
2614·6		6s	2246·5		5s
(7)			(47)		

For the lines marked 4* 5* 6* 7* in the formula $10^8 \frac{1}{\lambda} = a - bn^{-2} - cn^{-4}$, $a = 30712 \cdot 4$ or $31633 \cdot 2$, $b = 13062 \cdot 1$, $c = 109382 \cdot 3$. For those marked 4† 5† 6†, $a = 30696 \cdot 2$ or $31617 \cdot 0$, $b = 12378 \cdot 8$, $c = 39430 \cdot 3$.

SODIUM.

Wave-length.	Intensity and character.			Wave-length.	Intensity and character.		
	Flame.	Arc.	Spark.		Flame.	Arc.	Spark.
8200·0 ⎫ 8188·0 ⎭				4752·2 ⎫ 4748·4 ⎭		4n 4n	2s 2s
6161·1 ⎫ 6154·6 ⎭	6 6	8n 8n	8s 8s	4669·4 ⎫ 4665·2 ⎭	4n 4n	4n 4n	3n 3s
5896·2 ⎫ 5890·2 ⎭	10s 10s	10sr 10sr	10s 10s	(13) 3303·1 ⎫ 3302·5 ⎭	8s 8s	8r 8r	10s 10s
5688·3 ⎫ 5682·9 ⎭	8n 8n	8n 8n	6n 6s	(18) 2852·9	2	6r	10s
(2) 5153·7 ⎫ 5149·2 ⎭	6 6	6n 6n	5s 5s	(2) 2680·5		4r	8s
4983·5 4979·3	6n 6n	6n 6n	6s 6s	(9)			

STRONTIUM.

Wave-length.	Intensity and character.		Wave-length.	Intensity and character.	
	Arc.	Spark.		Arc.	Spark.
6550·?	6	4s	4872·7	10r	6s
(1)			(1)		
6504·2	4	8s	4868·9	6n	2
6408·6	6	10s	4855·3	6n	2
6386·7	6	6s	4*4832·2	10r	6s
6380·9	4	4s	4812·0	10r	6s
(5)			4784·4	6	6s
5543·5	6b	4s	(1)		
5540·3	6	6s	4742·1	6	6s
5535·0	6	8s	(1)		
5522·0	8r	8s	4722·4	8	6s
5504·5	10r	8s	4678·4	6n	
(1)			4607·5	10r	10r
5486·4	8	6s	4531·5	6	1
5481·1	10r	10s	(1)		
5451·1	8	5s	4438·2	6n	3
(2)			(1)		
5257·1	8r	8s	4361·9	6n	3
5238·8	10r	10s	4338·0	6b″	1b
5229·5	8r	6s	(3)		
5225·4	8	6s	4305·6	6	30b″
5222·4	8	6s	4215·7	10r	100b″
(1)			4162·0	6	20b
5156·4	10r	2s	4077·9	10r	100b″
4*4971·8	4		5*4032·5	4b″	1
4968·1	8	4s	4030·5	6b″	7n
4962·4	10r	8s	5*3969·4	4	1
4892·2	8r	1s	5*3940·9	4b″	
4*4876·3	8r	6s	6*3705·9	6n	3n

284 *An Introduction to the Study of Spectrum Analysis.*

STRONTIUM—*continued*.

Wave-length.	Intensity and character.		Wave-length.	Intensity and character.	
	Arc.	Spark.		Arc.	Spark.
6 * 3653·3	4n	1n	3366·4	8	4
6 * 3629·1	4		3351·3	10r	3n
7 * 3547·9	6n		3330·2	8	4
(1)			3322·3	8	3
7 * 3499·4	6n		3307·6	10r	1n
7 * 3477·3	2n		3301·8	8	3
3475·0	6	20n	(6)		
3464·6	8	100br	2932·0	8	
(4)			(5)		
3380·9	8	80nr			

* These lines form a series of triplets for which, in the formula $10^8 \cdot \frac{1}{\lambda} = a - bn^{-2} - cn^{-4}$, $a = 31030\cdot64$ for the *first* line, $31424\cdot67$ for the *second*, and $31610\cdot58$ for the *third*, $b = 122328$, and $c = 837473$.

SULPHUR.

Wave-length.	Intensity and character.		Wave-length.	Intensity and character.	
	Arc.	Spark.		Arc.	Spark.
(4)			5104		7
6389		7	(2)		
6319		8	5033		10
6308		9	5021		10
6290		10	5014		8
(4)			4995		6
5672		7	(3)		
5661		8	4926		8
5651		8	(3)		
5640		10	4817		8
5605		10	(5)		
5562		8	4716		8
(5)			(5)		
5508		8	4552		10
5471		8	4525		10
5452		9	4486		10
5439		8	4465		10
5430		6	(6)		
5343		10	4295		8
5320		10	4283		8
5215		10	(1)		
5201		10	4269		7
(1)			(1)		
5143		7	4251		7
(2)			(7)		

See note under "Oxygen."

Catalogue of Spectra.

TANTALUM.

Wave-length.	Intensity and character.		Wave-length.	Intensity and character.	
	Arc.	Spark.		Arc.	Spark.
(11)			3798·3		6
4607·0		5	(6)		
(117)			3791·4		6
4205·5		5	(1)		
(6)			3787·2		5
4191·5		6	(25)		
(11)			3759·7		5
4168·3		8	(10)		
(1)			3742·6		5r
⎰ 4164·8		8	(5)		
⎱ 4163·8		8	3739·9		5
(3)			(4)		
4152·7		8	3726·4		5
(9)			(5)		
4139·9		8	3717·2		8
(2)			(1)		
4137·3		7	3713·2		6r
(13)			(15)		
4124·0		10	3688·1		5n
(10)			3683·7		8
4101·1		10	(17)		
(13)			3659·7		6
4079·9		12	(3)		
(15)			3651·3		6
4059·1		15	(51)		
(21)			3580·4		6
4032·7		5	(4)		
(42)			3576·0		6
3966·4		5	(31)		
(44)			3535·5		6
3905·8		10r	(17)		
(51)			3510·5		5
3832·0		6	(51)		
(6)			3432·9		5
3819·0		5	(137)		
(6)			3225·6		5
3803·1		5	(532)		
(3)					

286   *An Introduction to the Study of Spectrum Analysis.*

TELLURIUM.

Wave-length.	Intensity and character.		Wave-length.	Intensity and character.	
	Arc.	Spark.		Arc.	Spark.
6438·2	10s		(2)		
(8)			3521·0		8s
5974·1	10s		(1)		
5936·2	8s		3496·6		8s
(6)			(8)		
5756·1	10s		3407·0		6
(1)			(7)		
5707·6	10s		3362·7		8s
5648·1	10s		(24)		
(1)			3175·4		6
5575·2	8s		(13)		
(2)			3047·0		10n
5448·5	8s		(2)		
(1)			3017·9		6b
5218·2	8,1		(11)		
(23)			2967·2		4b
4302·1	5s		(7)		
(3)			2942·3		4b
4275·3	6s		(5)		
4260·5	6s		2895·6		10n
(1)			2868·9		8n
4221·7	6s		(1)		
(4)			2858·3		10n
4062·3	6s		(6)		
4055·1	6s		2793·1		6b
(3)			(1)		
4006·7	8s		2769·8		8
3984·5	6s		(4)		
(3)			2711·7		4b
3969·3	6s		(28)		
(3)			2530·9		8
3842·0	8s		(15)		
(8)			2428·1		4
3736·5	8s		(8)		
(7)			2385·9		8r
3650·0	6s		2383·1		8r
(1)			(6)		
3617·6	6s		2259·1		6r
(3)			(13)		
3552·2	8s				

THALLIUM.

Wave-length.	Intensity and character.			Wave-length.	Intensity and character.		
	Flame.	Arc.	Spark.		Flame.	Arc.	Spark.
5948·0			6n	7 * 2609·9		4r	
3 † 5350·6	10s	10r	10ur	2609·1		6r	2r
3 † 3775·9		10r	20sr	(1)			
4 * 3529·6		8r	10s	4 † 2580·2		8r	3nr
3519·4		10r	20sr	2552·6		6r	4s
4 † 3229·9		10r	6n	(3)			
3091·9			8s	5 * 2379·7		8r	10r
5 * 2921·6		6r	8n	(3)			
2918·4		10r	10n	4 † 2316·0		6r	4
5 † 2826·3		8r	2s	2298·2			7s
4 * 2768·0		10r	6ur	(2)			
(4)				6 * 2237·9		6r	3r
6 * 2710·8		4r		(4)			
2709·3		8r	3nr	6 † 2207·1		4r	2n
(3)				7 † 2168·7		4r	
6 † 2665·7		6r	3n	(16)			

The lines marked * form a series of pairs for which in the formula $10^8 \frac{1}{\lambda} = a - bn^{-2} - cn^{-4}$, $a = 41542·7$ for the *first* line, 49337·6 for the *second*, $b = 13229·3$, $c = 126522·3$. For the pairs marked †, $a = 41506·4$ or 49301·3, $b = 12261·7$, $c = 79068·3$.

THORIUM.

Wave-length.	Intensity and character.		Wave-length.	Intensity and character.	
	Arc.	Spark.		Arc.	Spark.
5538·1		6s	(46)		
5447·0		6s	4310·2		4
5375·5		6s	(73)		
4920·0		6s	4209·0		5
4864·6		6s	(51)		
(52)			4140·4		4
4589·3		4	(14)		
(17)			4116·9		5
4563·5		5	(23)		
(1)			4085·2		4
4555·8		8	(13)		
(38)			4069·4		4
4510·7		5	(51)		
(16)			4019·3		10
4465·5		4	(201)		
(53)			3813·2		4
4391·3		8	(88)		
(1)			3763·0		4
4387·9		5	(13)		
(3)			3752·7		6
4382·1		8	(12)		

THORIUM—*continued*.

Wave-length.	Intensity and character.		Wave-length.	Intensity and character.	
	Arc.	Spark.		Arc.	Spark.
3741·4 (3)		6	3392·2 (9)		5
3739·0 (7)		4	3377·6 (37)		8
3731·0 (34)		4	3351·4 (11)		4
3704·2 (14)		4	3339·7 (7)		6
3692·6 (3)		6r	3334·7 (10)		4
3688·9 (11)		4	3325·3 (12)		4r
3679·9 (1)		5	3313·9 (8)		10
3678·2 (2)		4	3300·6 (14)		12
3675·7 (13)		4	3290·7 (16)		10
3663·9 (3)		4	3272·5 (48)		16
3661·7 (1)		6n	3232·2 (12)		7
3659·7 (8)		6n	3221·4 (5)		12
3652·3 (1)		4	3216·7 (27)		8
3621·3 (6)		4	3188·4 (10)		5
3617·2 (9)		5	3180·4 (39)		4
3609·6 (13)		4	3148·1 (25)		5
3601·2 (24)		7	3112·5 (12)		4
3575·4 (2)		4	3098·0 (15)		6
3572·5 (39)		4	3079·0 (68)		4
3558·9 (9)		10	2978·8 (32)		8
3529·1 (20)		5	2932·6 (28)		5
3511·8 (3)		6r	2899·0 (41)		6
3507·7 (51)		10	2837·4 (3)		5
3470·1 (5)		5r	2832·5 (49)		4
3465·9 (3)		4r	2769·0 (42)		4
3463·0 (32)		4r	2708·4 (14)		4
3439·8 (5)		4	2687·0 (50)		6
3434·1 (38)		4	2583·5 (5)		4
3402·8 (17)		4	2571·7 (3)		5

Catalogue of Spectra.

THORIUM—continued.

Wave-length.	Intensity and character.		Wave-length.	Intensity and character.	
	Arc.	Spark.		Arc.	Spark.
2564·5		6	2463·3		7
(3)			(8)		
2555·3 } 2554·8 }		4	2441·4		9
(3)			(3)		
2549·7		4	2431·8		7
(4)			(2)		
2545·2		4	2428·1		8
(16)			(3)		
2514·4		4	2413·6		6
2512·8		8	(13)		
(6)			2371·5		4
2501·2		5	(3)		
(7)			2363·2		4
2475·4		4	(11)		
2474·1		5	2319·6		4
(4)			(21)		

THULIUM.

Wave-length.	Intensity and character.		Wave-length.	Intensity and character.	
	Arc.	Spark.		Arc.	Spark.
4616·1		2	3453·8		3
4522·7		2	(1)		
(3)			3441·6		4
4242·3		4	(4)		
4203·9		4	3425·2		5
(1)			(7)		
4187·8		3	3362·8		4
(1)			(5)		
4106·0		3	3291·1		3
4094·3		3	(3)		
3996·7		3	3269·1		3
(10)			(10)		
3848·2		7	3241·7		3
3795·9		5	(15)		
(4)			3173·0		3
3762·1		4	(4)		
3761·5		5	3151·2		3
(3)			3134·0		3
3734·3		3	3131·4		6
(1)			(11)		
3718·0		3	3073·2		3
(1)			(6)		
3701·5		5	3020·7		5
3700·4		5	(19)		
(23)			2869·4		3
3462·4		5	(62)		

290 *An Introduction to the Study of Spectrum Analysis.*

TIN.

Wave-length	Intensity and character.		Wave-length	Intensity and character.	
	Arc.	Spark.		Arc.	Spark.
6453·5		10n	2661·3	6r	2
5799·2		10n	2658·9		10
5631·9	8	8s	(1)		
5588·7		10n	2643·8		10
5563·7		10n	2632·1		8
(2)			(1)		
5333·1		8n	2594·5	6r	4
(2)			(1)		
5101·4		6s	2571·7	8r	8n
(2)			2558·1	6b″	
4859·1		6	2546·6	8r	6
4585·4		8s	2531·3	6b″	
4524·9	8	10n	(3)		
(9)			2495·8	8r	6
3907·4		8b	(1)		
(3)			2483·5	8r	6
3801·2	6r	10n	(4)		
(3)			2429·6	10r	8r
3655·9	4	8	2421·8	10r	8r
(3)			2408·3	6r	1
3573·8		6n	(5)		
(10)			2354·9	10r	4r
3352·5		10b	2334·9	8r	2
3330·7	6r	10	2317·3	10r	2r
(2)			2286·8	6r	1n
5283·6		10b	(1)		
3262·4	8r	10br	2269·0	10r	1n
(9)			2267·3	6r	1n
3175·1	8r	10br	(3)		
3141·9	4	8	2251·9	6r	1n
3034·2	10r	10r	2246·1	10r	1n
3032·9	4r	10	2231·8	6r	4s
(1)			2209·8	10r	6s
3009·2	10r	10r	2199·5	10r	1n
(2)			2194·6	8r	1n
2913·6	6r	8	2171·5	6r	
2896·2		8	2151·2	6r	2s
2887·8		6	2148·7	8r	
(2)			2141·1	10r	
2863·4	10r	10br	2121·5	6r	
2850·7	6r	8	2113·9	6r	4s
(1)			2100·9	6r	
2840·1	10r	10br	2096·4	10r	
(5)			2091·7	6r	
2813·7	4r	6	2080·2	6r	4s
(4)			2073·0	8r	
2788·1	6br	1n	2068·7	6	
(1)			2063·8	6	
2779·9	6r	8	2058·3	6	
2706·6	10r	10r	2053·8	6	
(3)					

TITANIUM.

Wave-length.	Intensity and character.		Wave-length.	Intensity and character.	
	Arc.	Spark.		Arc.	Spark.
6557·0		4s	5369·8	5	8s
(1)			(7)		
6261·4	8r	8s	5297·4	5	10s
6258·6	10r	10n	(3)		
6222·0		6s	5283·6	5	10s
6215·2	6	6s	(1)		
6125·4		8s	5266·2	5	4s
6098·6	6	6s	(10)		
6091·6	8	8s	5225·1	5	6s
6084·4	6	6s	(1)		
6065·8	8	8s	5221·5	5	10n
5999·3	8	8s	(4)		
5979·1	10	10s	5210·6	6	10n
5966·5	10	10s	(4)		
5952·7	10	10s	5193·1	6	10s
5922·2	6r	6s	(2)		
5919·6	6r	6s	5173·9	6	8s
5899·6	6	10s	5152·4	5	8s
(1)			5117·6	5	6s
5866·7	7	10s	5145·6	5	6s
(1)			(2)		
5804·5	6n		5129·3	3	10s
5786·2	6n		5120·6	5	10s
(1)			5113·6	5	8s
5774·3	6		(3)		
5766·6	5n		5087·2	6	8n
5762·5	5n		(5)		
(2)			5064·8	7	10s
5739·7	5	6s	(7)		
(2)			5040·1	7	8s
5715·3	5	4s	5038·6	7	8s
(3)			⎰ 5036·7	7	10s
5702·9	5	2n	⎱ 5036·1	7	10s
5689·7	6	8s	5025·7	6	6s
(1)			5025·0	6	6s
5675·6	7	10s	5023·0	7	6s
(1)			5020·2	7	8s
5662·4	6	10s	5016·3	7	8s
5648·8	5	4s	5014·4	8	10s
5644·4	6	10s	5013·4	6	4s
5565·7	6	6s	(1)		
5514·8	6	10s	5007·4	8	10s
1 5514·6	6		5001·2	5	4s
5512·7	6	10s	4999·7	8	10s
(1)			4997·3	5	
5504·1	5	8s	4991·2	8	10s
5490·4	6	8s	4989·3	5	6s
5488·4	5	6s	4981·9	8	10s
5482·1	5		(2)		
5481·6	5	8s	4975·5	5	4s
5477·9	5	6s	(7)		
(9)			4928·5	5	8s
5429·4	5	8s	(2)		
(2)			4921·9	5	6s
5409·8	5	8s	4920·0	5	6s
(6)			(1)		

TITANIUM—*continued*.

Wave-length.	Intensity and character.		Wave-length.	Intensity and character.	
	Arc.	Spark.		Arc.	Spark.
4913·8	6	6s	(3)		
(1)			4623·2	6	9
4900·1	6	8s	(2)		
(3)			4617·4	7	10
4885·2	7	10s	(13)		
(2)			4590·1	4	7
4870·3	6	8s	(7)		
4868·4	6	8s	4572·2	6	20
(1)			(6)		
4856·2	6	8s	4563·9	5	15
(2)			(5)		
4841·0	7	8s	4555·6	6	8
(3)			(3)		
4820·6	6	8n	4552·6	7	9
(4)			4549·8	6	15r
4805·6	5	10s	4548·9	7	8
(1)			(4)		
4799·9	5	4s	4544·8	7	7r
(2)			4536·2	6	
4792·6	5	8s	4536·1	6	} 6
(1)			4535·8	6	6
4778·4	5	6s	4535·0	7	7
(2)			4534·2	5	8
4759·4	6	10s	4533·4	7	8n
(1)			(1)		
4758·3	6	10s	4527·5	6	9
(1)			(3)		
4742·9	6	8s	4523·0	6	10
(3)			(1)		
4731·3	5	3	4518·2	7	8
4723·3	5	3	(2)		
4722·8	5	3	4512·9	6	10
(3)			(5)		
4710·3	6	5	4501·4	6	15
(5)			(1)		
4698·9	6	6	4496·3	6	7
(2)			4495·2	6	2n
4693·8	5	2	(3)		
(1)			4489·2	5	5
4691·5	6	6	4488·5	3	7
(5)			(2)		
4682·1	7	8	4481·4	5	7
(3)			(2)		
4675·3	5	1	4475·0	5	3
(2)			4471·4	5	5
4667·8	8	7	(2)		
(5)			4468·7	6	15
4656·6	6	6	4466·0	5	5
(5)			(5)		
4650·2	5	5	4457·6	7	10
(1)			(1)		
4645·4	5	6	4455·5	6	8
(2)			(1)		
4640·1	5	5	{ 4453·9	5	7
{ 4639·8	5	4	{ 4453·5	6	7
{ 4639·5	5	5	(1)		
(7)			4451·1	6	8
4629·5	5	7	4450·7	4	6

Catalogue of Spectra.

TITANIUM—continued.

Wave-length.	Intensity and character.		Wave-length.	Intensity and character.	
	Arc.	Spark.		Arc.	Spark.
4449·3	6	10	4291·1	6	4
(1)			4290·4	5	9
4444·0	6	15	(1)		
(3)			4289·2	7	8
4440·5	5	4	(1)		
(3)			4287·6	7	6
4434·2	6	5	4286·2	7	7
(3)			4285·2	5	4
4430·6	5	4	4282·9	6	6
(3)			4281·5	5	4
4434·2	6	5	(5)		
(3)			4274·7	6	8
4430·6	5	3	(7)		
(1)			4263·3	6	8
4427·3	8	8	4261·8	5	3nr
4426·2	5	5	(2)		
(2)			4256·2	5	4nr
4423·0	5	3	(7)		
(2)			4238·0	5	5
{ 4417·9	5	6	(12)		
{ 4417·5	6	5	4186·3	7	6
(9)			(12)		
4404·4	6	7	{ 4172·0	4	10
(1)			{ 4171·1	5	
4399·9	5	10	(5)		
(2)			4163·8	5	20
4395·2	7	15	(3)		
(1)			4158·8	5	2n
4394·0	6	3	4151·1	5	5
(13)			(9)		
4369·8	5	3a	4137·4	5n	4n
(13)			(2)		
4338·1	6	10	4127·7	5	7r
(4)			4123·7	5n	5n
4326·5	6	4	(5)		
4325·3	6	6	4112·9	5s	5
(1)			4111·9	5s	1n
4321·8	6	5r	(6)		
(1)			4082·6	5s	7
4318·8	7	7	(2)		
(1)			4078·6	6	9
{ 4315·2	4	7	(10)		
{ 4315·0	7	7	4060·4	5	6
4314·5	5	2	(4)		
4313·0	6	8	4055·2	5	6
(5)			4054·0	3	8
4306·1	8	15	(9)		
(1)			4030·6	5n	5n
4302·2	5	6	4028·5	3	10
4301·2	7	6	(1)		
4300·7	7	4	4026·6	5n	4n
4300·2	6	8	(1)		
4299·8	6	2	4024·7	6	5
4299·4	6	3	(1)		
4298·8	7	7	4022·0	5n	4n
4295·9	7	8	(4)		
4294·3	6	10	4013·7	5n	3n
(2)			4012·6	3s	7

294 *An Introduction to the Study of Spectrum Analysis.*

TITANIUM—*continued.*

Wave-length.	Intensity and character.		Wave-length.	Intensity and character.	
	Arc.	Spark.		Arc.	Spark.
(1) 4009·1	6	8	3761·5	7	50r
(6) 3998·8	8	15	3759·4	7	50r
(3) 3989·9	8	20r	3757·8	4s	10
(3) 3982·6	5	5	(1) 3753·8	5	4
3981·9	7	15	3753·0	7	7
(1) 3964·4	5s	7	(1) 3748·3	4	9
3963·0	5s	7	3741·8	4s	30r
3958·3	7	10	3741·2	6	8
3956·5	7	9	(9) 3729·9	7	8
3948·8	7	10	(2) 3725·3	5	6
3947·9	6	9	3724·7	5	7
(4) 3930·0	5	6	(2) 3722·7	5	3
3926·5	5	3	3721·8	4	8
3924·7	5	7	(12) 3706·4	3	9
(5) 3914·4	5	3	(13) 3694·6	5	3
3913·6	5	30	(1) 3690·0	6	4
(2) 3905·0	7	10	(5) 3685·3	8n	50r
3901·1	5	10	(10) 3671·8	6	6
3900·7	5	50r	(3) 3669·1	5	5
(2) 3895·1	7	4n	(6) 3662·4	5	15
(4) 3883·0	7n	8n	(1) 3660·8	6	4
3882·5	5n	} 8n	3659·9	5s	15
3882·3	6n		3658·2	7	6
(2) 3875·1	6n	5n	(2) 3654·7	6	5
(1) 3873·4	5n	3n	3653·6	10n	15
(5) 3869·5	5n	2	(1) 3616·3	5s	4
3868·6	5n	2n	(2) 3642·8	10n	10
(1) 3866·6	6n	5n	3641·5	5s	20
(2) 3863·0	5n	2n	(1) 3635·6	9n	8
(3) 3858·3	5n	3n	(8) 3625·0	4s	15
(5) 3853·9	5n	4n	(26) 3599·2	5	
3855·2	5n	3n	3598·9	5	5
(40) 3822·2	5s	3n	(1) 3596·2	5	10
(32) 3786·2	5	6	(33) 3547·2	5	4
(3) 3776·2	2	8	(4) 3535·6	5	20
(2) 3771·8	5	7	(2)		
(1)					

Catalogue of Spectra.

TITANIUM—continued.

Wave-length.	Intensity and character.		Wave-length.	Intensity and character.	
	Arc.	Spark.		Arc.	Spark.
3530·5	6s		3382·5		10
(3)			(1)		
3520·4	4s	20	3379·1		10
(6)			3378·4		10
3511·0	6s	50	(14)		
(5)			3261·7		30
3505·0	6	50	(4)		
(11)			3253·0		10
3491·2	6s	10	(2)		
(9)			3248·8		20
3480·7	5	3	(3)		
(2)			3242·1		20r
3477·4	5	15	(2)		
(8)			3239·2		10r
3461·7		15	3236·7		15r
(4)			(1)		
3456·6		15	3234·6		20r
(8)			(10)		
3444·5		15b^n	3223·0		10
(31)			(3)		
3394·7		30	3218·4		10
(6)			3217·2		10
3388·0		15	(16)		
(2)			3202·7		15n
3383·9		50r	(11)		
(1)			3191·0		20n
3380·4		15r	(12)		
(5)			3168·7		15n
3372·9		30r	(46)		
(9)			3088·1		15r
3361·3		50b	(133)		
(8)			2828·3		10n
{ 3349·7		10r	(5)		
{ 3349·2		20	2818·0		10n
(2)			(6)		
3342·0		20r	2810·4		10n
3340·5		15	(5)		
(3)			2805·0		10
3335·4		20	(178)		
3332·2		15	2563·5		10
3329·6		20	(14)		
3326·9		10	2540·1		10
(3)			(5)		
3823·0		30r	3527·9		10
3321·9		10	(8)		
(1)			2516·1		20
3318·2		10	(54)		
(22)			2414·1		15
3287·8		15	(164)		

296 *An Introduction to the Study of Spectrum Analysis.*

TUNGSTEN.

Wave-length.	Intensity and character.		Wave-length.	Intensity and character.	
	Arc.	Spark.		Arc.	Spark.
5806·0		4s	(6)		
5734·1		6s	4269·5		6
5649·1		4s	(5)		
(1)			4263·5		4
5514·1		10s	(1)		
5492·6		8s	4260·4		4
5224·2		10s	(1)		
5071·4		6s	4259·5		4
5053·9		10s	(17)		
5014·9		6s	4244·4		4
5007·9		6s	(2)		
4982·0		4s	4241·5		4
4888·5		8s	(29)		
4843·1		10s	4219·5		4
(7)			(3)		
4680·8	6		4215·6		6
(18)			(9)		
4660·0	6		4207·1		4
(1)			(2)		
4657·6	4		4204·5		4
(40)			(30)		
4592·6	4		4175·7		4
4588·9	4		(5)		
(12)			4171·2		4
4570·8	4		4170·6		4
(12)			4168·8		4
4554·2	8		(25)		
(54)			4137·6		4
4484·3	6		4137·5		4
(72)			(15)		
4408·4	4		4118·2		4
(14)			(6)		
4385·0	4		4109·9		4
4383·6	4		(4)		
(3)			4102·9		6
4378·7	4		(21)		
(7)			4081·1		4
4366·2	4		(6)		
4364·9	4		4074·5		6
(9)			(3)		
4348·2	6		4070·0		6
(11)			(19)		
4335·7	4		4045·8		4
4332·0	4		(29)		
(20)			4015·3		4
4307·0	4		(10)		
(4)			4008·9		8
4303·4	4		(26)		
(1)			3983·4	4	4
4302·3	6		(2)		
(5)			3979·3	4	4
4294·8	8		(6)		
(22)			3970·7		4
4275·6	4		(1)		
(1)			3965·1	6	6
4274·7	4		(70)		

Catalogue of Spectra.

TUNGSTEN—continued.

Wave-length.	Intensity and character.		Wave-length.	Intensity and character.	
	Arc.	Spark.		Arc.	Spark.
3897·1		4	3545·4		4
(15)			(13)		
3881·5		4	3536·5		4
(17)			(9)		
3868·0		4	3529·7		4
(22)			(29)		
3851·7		4	3508·9		6
(3)			(17)		
3846·3		4	3495·4		4
(14)			(9)		
3835·1		4	3486·3		4
(24)			(11)		
3817·6		4	{ 3475·6		4
(42)			{ 3475·5		4
3780·9		4	(15)		
(4)			3463·7		6
3773·8		4	(19)		
(4)			3450·0		4
3768·6		4	(42)		
(30)			3416·8		4
3741·9		4	(19)		
(4)			3402·0		6
3736·4		6	(4)		
(22)			3399·1		6
3716·2		4	(35)		
(10)			3376·2		8
{ 3708·7		4	(24)		
{ 3708·1		4	3361·2		4
(18)			(2)		
3694·7		4	3358·7		6
(2)			(25)		
{ 3692·8		4	{ 3343·6		4
{ 3692·0		4	{ 3343·3		4
(16)			{ 3342·6		6
3682·2		4	(73)		
(25)			3286·7		4
{ 3658·0		4	(27)		
{ 3657·7		6	3262·4		4
{ 3657·5		6	(56)		
(10)			3215·7		4
{ 3646·7		6	(24)		
{ 3645·8		6	3203·4		4
(6)			(35)		
3641·6		8	3179·6		4n
(31)			(4)		
3617·7		6	3176·1		4
(6)			(23)		
3614·0		8	3160·2		4
3612·0		4	3159·0		4b
(24)			(21)		
3592·6		8	3142·0		4
(23)			(96)		
3572·6		8	3077·6		6
(24)			(35)		
3555·3		4	3051·4		4
(9)			(42)		
3549·2		6	3024·5		4
(2)			(115)		

298 *An Introduction to the Study of Spectrum Analysis.*

TUNGSTEN—*continued.*

Wave-length.	Intensity and character.		Wave-length.	Intensity and character.	
	Arc.	Spark.		Arc.	Spark.
2952·3 (246)	4		2581·2 (2)	4	
2799·2 (42)	4		{ 2579·6		4
2764·4 (74)	1		{ 2579·3 (15)		4
2702·2 (6)	4		{ 2572·3		4
2697·8 (20)	4		{ 2571·5 (12)		4
2679·8 (18)	4		2563·2 (13)		4
2664·4 (24)	4		2555·1 (59)		4
2647·8 (36)	4		2522·1 (20)		1
2620·2 (4)	4		2510·5 (31)		1
2615·5 (13)	1		{ 2489·4		1
2603·1	1		{ 2488·9 (17)		4
2602·6 (13)	4		2477·9 (48)		4
2589·2 (12)	1		2446·5 (70)		4
			2397·1 (186)		4

Catalogue of Spectra.

URANIUM.

Wave-length.	Intensity and character.		Wave-length.	Intensity and character.	
	Arc.	Spark.		Arc.	Spark.
5914·1		8s	4282·7 }		3
5620·1		6s	4282·2 }		
5580·2		6s	(14)		
5563·6		6s	4274·2		3
5528·1		10s	(8)		
5510·1		6s	4269·8		4
5494·6		10s	(62)		
5482·5		10s	4241·9		4
5480·5		10s	(7)		
5478·0		10s	4236·2		3
5385·1		6s	(133)		
5027·9		6s	4171·8		3
4732·0		6s	(28)		
4627·3		5	4155·6		3
(7)			(26)		
4620·4		3r	4141·4		3
(16)			(27)		
4605·4		3	4124·9		3
4603·9		4	(15)		
(44)			4116·3		3
4573·9		3	(52)		
(7)			4090·3		4
4570·1		3	(16)		
(2)			4080·8		3
4567·9		3	(59)		
(16)			4050·2		3
4555·3		4	(271)		
(19)			3932·2		3
4543·8		7	(51)		
(7)			3914·4		3
4538·4		4	(52)		
(21)			3890·5		3
4515·5		4	(61)		
(10)			3859·7		3
4510·5		3	(65)		
(24)			3831·6		3
4491·0		3	(387)		
(31)			3670·3		3
4472·6		6	(93)		
(12)			3630·8		3
4465·3		3	(122)		
(3)			3585·0		3
4463·2		3	(731)		
(58)			3306·1		3
4434·1		3	(35)		
(152)			3291·5		3
4355·9		4	(143)		
(16)			3229·6		3
4347·4		3	(679)		
(8)			2908·3		3
4341·9		4	(529)		
(29)			2698·1		3
4326·1		3	(253)		
(64)			2478·7		3
4297·3		3	(264)		
(17)			2418·5 }		3
4288·0		3	2418·2 }		
4287·1		3	(133)		
(11)					

VANADIUM.

Wave-length.	Intensity and character.		Wave-length.	Intensity and character.	
	Arc.	Spark.		Arc.	Spark.
5727·3	8		4407·9	9	12
(6)			4406·9	9	12
5698·8	8		(5)		
(141)			4400·8	8	18
4875·7	8		(5)		
(3)			4395·4	9	20
4864·9	8		(6)		
(6)			4390·1	9r	30
4851·7	8		(2)		
(100)			4384·9	9	40r
4670·7	8		(6)		
(27)			4379·4	9	40r
4619·9	5	10	(27)		
(16)			4353·0	7	12
4600·3	3	10b″	(8)		
4594·3	9	12	4341·2	6	14b″
(4)			(6)		
4586·6	9	12	4333·0	6	12
(3)			(2)		
4580·6	8	10b″	4330·2	3	12b″
(2)			(38)		
4577·4	8	10	4296·3	5	10
4572·0	6	10b″	4292·0	6	10b″
(3)			(10)		
4564·8		12	4284·2	6	12
(2)			(1)		
4560·9	6	12	4279·1	3	10
(6)			4277·1	6	12
4549·8	6	12	(7)		
(1)			4268·8	6	14
4545·6	7	14	(59)		
(50)			4210·0	5	12
4489·1	7	16b″	4205·2	2	16
(8)			(17)		
4474·9	7	10	4183·6	2	16
4474·3	6	10	(46)		
(6)			4131·6	7	14
4469·9	7	12b″	(1)		
(8)			4132·1	7	16
4462·6	7	14	(3)		
(1)			4128·2	7	16
4460·5	9	12b″	(9)		
4460·0	8	11	4118·3	5	10
(12)			4116·7	6	14
4452·2	8	14	4115·3	7	16
(3)			(6)		
4441·4	7	10	4109·9	7	14
(2)			(6)		
4441·9	7	14	4102·3	6	10
(2)			4099·9	7	16
4438·0	7	12b″	(3)		
(2)			4095·6	6	12
4436·3	7	10	(5)		
(25)			4090·7	6	16
4408·7	9	14b″r	(3)		
4408·4	8	10	4080·6		20

Catalogue of Spectra.

VANADIUM—continued.

Wave-length.	Intensity and character.		Wave-length.	Intensity and character.	
	Arc.	Spark.		Arc.	Spark.
(7) 4065·2		12	3715·6 (10)	4s	20
(10) 4051·5	5	10	3703·7 (1)	7	12b^r
4051·1 (11)	5	10	3700·5 (5)		12
4035·8 (13)	1	16	3692·4 (22)	6	10
4023·5 (18)	1	20	3669·6 (4)	3	16
4005·9 (1)	4	16	3661·5 (33)		12
4003·1 (5)	3	10	3619·1 (15)	2s	12
3997·3	3	10	3593·5 (1)	4	16
3992·9 (3)	6	12	3592·2	4	18
3990·7 (12)	6	12	3589·9 (23)	4	18
3977·9 (1)		10	5566·3 (6)	3	12
3973·8 (10)	4	16	3557·0 (10)	5s	20
3952·1 (32)	4s	18	3545·3 (2)	4	20r
3916·6 (2)	3	14	3541·5 (7)		16
3914·4 (79)	2	11	3530·9 (6)	1	20
3847·5 (44)	5s	10	3524·9 (4)	3	16
3815·6 (23)	4	10	3522·0 (1)		12
3795·1 (7)	7	10	3520·2 (1)		14
3787·6 (10)	2	16	3517·4 (11)		20r
3778·8	5s	10	3504·6 (6)	3	16
3778·5 (9)	2	12	3497·1	2	14
3773·1 (3)		10	3493·3 (3)	2	12
3771·1 (11)	4	20	3486·1 (16)	2	12
3760·4 (13)	2	10	3457·3 (83)		14
3750·1 (2)		12n	3338·0 (14)		12
3746·0 (7)	4s	14	3321·7 (33)		10
3736·2 (2)		10	3282·7 (2)	2	10
3732·9 (6)	4s	14	3280·0 (4)	2	16
3728·5		10	3276·3 (4)	16	20r
3723·5 (13)	4	16b^r	3271·2	16	20r
3718·3		10	3270·2		10

VANADIUM—continued.

Wave-length.	Intensity and character.		Wave-length.	Intensity and character.	
	Arc.	Spark.		Arc.	Spark.
(1)			(20)		
3267·8	16	20r	2976·6		10r
3266·0	2	10	(3)		
(11)			2972·3		10
3254·8	4	10	(3)		
(1)			2968·4		12r
3251·9	2	10	(8)		
3250·9	2	10	2957·7		10
(10)			(5)		
3238·0	4	12	2952·1		10r
(19)			(7)		
3217·2	2	12	2944·7		10r
(24)			(3)		
3190·8	10	16r	2941·5		10r
(1)			(12)		
3188·6	2	10r	2926·5		10
(1)			(1)		
3187·8	8	10r	2924·8		10r
(1)			2924·1		10r
3185·5	20	4r	(2)		
3184·1	20	4r	2920·5		10
3183·5	18	4r	(31)		
(11)			2893·5		10r
3167·6		10	2892·8		10r
(26)			(1)		
3139·9	2	10	2891·8		10r
(2)			(2)		
3136·6		12	2889·7		10r
3135·1	2	12	2888·4		10
3133·5	10	10	(2)		
(2)			2884·9		12r
3130·4	10	12	(1)		
(2)			2882·6		10
3126·3	10	8	(1)		
(1)			2880·1		10
3125·4	10		(12)		
(2)			2869·2		12
3123·0	2	10	(11)		
(4)			2854·4		12
3118·5	16	12r	(1)		
(3)			2850·3		10
3110·8	2	12r	(1)		
(9)			2817·6		10
3102·4	20	12r	(35)		
3101·0	2	10	2810·4		12
(1)			(10)		
3094·3		12	2803·6		10
3093·2		16r	(3)		
(19)			2799·6		10
3067·2		10	(21)		
(2)			2781·7		12n
3063·8		10	(3)		
(8)			2777·9		10
3053·5		10	(6)		
(4)			2772·2		10b?
3048·8		10	(3)		
(36)			2768·7		10
3001·3		10r	(2)		

Catalogue of Spectra.

VANADIUM—continued.

Wave-length.	Intensity and character.		Wave-length.	Intensity and character.	
	Arc.	Spark.		Arc.	Spark.
2766·6		10	(57)		
2765·8		14b″	2595·2		16
(4)			(2)		
2760·6		10r	2593·2		16
(7)			(9)		
2753·5		16b″	2585·0		10
(4)			(4)		
2747·6		10	2577·8		10
(20)			(3)		
2729·8		10	2574·6		10
(14)			(4)		
2715·8		16	2571·1		10
(5)			(21)		
2711·9		10	2554·3		14
(3)			(1)		
2708·0		10	2553·1		12
2706·9		10	(5)		
(4)			2549·4		14
2702·3		14	2548·8		12
(1)			2548·3		14
2701·2		10	(7)		
(11)			2542·6		10b
2690·9		12	(13)		
2690·4		10	2529·0		14
2690·0		10	2528·6		14
2688·8		10	2528·0		18
2688·1		10	2526·8		16
(7)			(2)		
2683·2		10	2525·1		10
2683·0		10	(5)		
(2)			2521·6		12
2679·4		14	2521·3		10
2678·7		12	(8)		
2677·9		12	2516·2		14
(4)			(2)		
2672·1		14	2514·7		12
2670·4		10	(14)		
(7)			2506·3		10
2663·4		18	(6)		
(1)			2503·1		10
2661·7		10	(21)		
(4)			2483·1		10
2655·8		16	2482·4		10
(2)			(1)		
2652·9		10	2479·6		12
(4)			2479·1		12
2649·5		16	(10)		
2648·0		12	2465·3		10
(3)			(11)		
2645·9		14	2453·4		10
(1)			(7)		
2644·5		16	2447·7		10
(3)			(3)		
2642·3		14	2445·0		10b″
2641·0		16	(3)		
(12)			2445·0		10b″
2630·7		12	(13)		
2629·9		10n	2430·1		10

VANADIUM—continued.

Wave-length.	Intensity and character.		Wave-length.	Intensity and character.	
	Arc.	Spark.		Arc.	Spark.
(7) 2447·7		10	2371·2 (3)		18
(3) 2445·0		10b"	2366·4 (3)		16
(13) 2430·1		10	2358·8 (5)		14
(13) 2417·6		10br	2352·2 (8)		10
(3) 2414·0		11	2346·4 (1)		10
(5) 2407·2		12	2343·2		10
(1) 2405·3		16	2342·3 (9)		10
(3) 2399·8		12	2334·3 (1)		10
(6) 2393·7		18	2331·9 (1)		10
(14) 2382·6		16	2330·5 (4)		12
2381·0		10	2325·2		10
(1) 2379·2		10	2323·9 (2)		12
(4) 2373·1		10	2318·1 (72)		10
(2)			2233·0 (59)		10

YTTERBIUM.

Wave-length.	Intensity and character.		Wave-length.	Intensity and character.	
	Arc.	Spark.		Arc.	Spark.
(2) 5720·2	5		(36) 4184·1		10
(7) 5556·7	5		(13) 4135·2		10
(5) 5476·9	6		(42) 3988·1	10r	15
(4) 5402·8	5		(108) 3694·3	10r	200
(16) 5135·3	5		(5) 3675·2		10
(44) 4658·2	5	1	(23) 3620·0		10
(10) 4576·4	5	2	(21) 3560·9		10
(15) 4439·4	5	2	(1) 3554·6		10

Catalogue of Spectra.

YTTERBIUM—continued.

Wave-length.	Intensity and character.		Wave-length.	Intensity and character.	
	Arc.	Spark.		Arc.	Spark.
(28)			(14)		
3478·9		20	2891·5	5	8
(2)			(6)		
3462·7		10	2818·9		10
(3)			(6)		
3464·6	5n }	3	2803·6		10
3464·3	3n }		(32)		
(6)			2750·6	4	10
3454·2		15	(45)		
(22)			2667·1		15
3397·2		10	2666·2		15
(14)			(7)		
3359·7	5		2653·8	3	10
(7)			(10)		
3343·1	5		2642·7		10
(10)			(16)		
3315·2	5		2615·5		15
3312·3	6	1	(6)		
(9)			2603·4		10!
3289·5	15r	100	(19)		
(121)			2567·7		10
3005·9	3	10	(47)		
(55)			2464·6	6r	1
2911·5	5	10	(81)		

YTTRIUM.

Wave-length.	Intensity and character.		Wave-length.	Intensity and character.	
	Arc.	Spark.		Arc.	Spark.
(12)			(1)		
6435·2	5		5521·8	6r	
(64)			(1)		
5706·9	5		5510·1	5	
(4)			5503·7	5	
5663·1	6		5497·6	5	
(2)			(5)		
5648·7	5		5466·7	6	
(5)			(3)		
5630·3	5		5403·0	4	
(5)			(4)		
5582·1	5		5269·7	5	
(6)			(1)		
5544·8	5		5205·9	6	
(1)			5200·6	5	
5527·8	6		(2)		

X

YTTRIUM—continued.

Wave-length.	Intensity and character.		Wave-length.	Intensity and character.	
	Arc.	Spark.		Arc.	Spark.
5123·4	4		(6)		
(2)			3950·5	5	20n
5087·6	5		(49)		
(13)			3833·0		20
4900·3	6		(4)		
(4)			3818·5		10
4883·9	6		(9)		
(6)			3788·8	5	30
4855·1	6		(9)		
(3)			3774·5	5	100
4840·1	5		(27)		
(15)			3710·4	6r	100
4761·2	5		(7)		
(12)			3664·7	8	20
4682·5	6		(15)		
(1)			3533·28		
4675·0	6		(3)		
(7)			3628·9	7	10
4643·9	6		3621·1	5	4
(22)			3611·2	6	30
4527·4	5	3	3602·1	6	20
(3)			3600·9	7	50
4506·1	6	2	3593·1	5	2
(20)			(12)		
4422·8	6	10	3584·7		10
(4)			(15)		
4398·2	5	15	3549·2	7	20
(8)			(3)		
4375·1	8	100r	3496·2	6	10
(3)			(6)		
4358·9	5	8	3449·0	5	4
(3)			(22)		
4349·0	7	1	3328·0	6	20
(11)			(9)		
4309·8	6	20	3242·4	7	20
(2)			3246·8	6	10
4302·4	5	2	(1)		
(7)			3203·4	5	8
4251·3	5	1	3200·4	5	8
(14)			3195·7	7	8
4177·7	5	50	(2)		
(3)			3179·5	5	
4143·0	6r	7	(32)		
4128·5	6r	7	2946·1		20
(3)			(19)		
4102·5	7r	6	2817·1		30
(1)			(21)		
4083·9	5	3	2414·8		15
(2)			(3)		
4077·5	6r	4	2367·3		20
(8)			(6)		
3982·7	6	20n			

ZINC.

Wave-length.	Intensity and character.		Wave-length.	Intensity and character.	
	Arc.	Spark.		Arc.	Spark.
6364·0		10	⎧ 5 * 2801·0	10r	8
6103·1		10n	⎪ 2781·3	4b^r	
6023·5		8n	⎪ (1)		
5894·6		8s	⎨ 2771·0	6r	8
(18)			⎪ 5 * 2770·9	8r	
5182·2	8b″		⎪ (1)		
4924·8		10n	⎩ 5 * 2756·5	6r	6
4912·3		10n	(13)		
⎧ 4810·7	10r		⎧ 5 † 2712·6	8b″	2
3 † ⎨ 4722·3	10r	10	⎪ 2706·6	6	1n
⎪ (1)			⎪ (3)		
⎩ 4680·4	10r	10	⎨ 5 † 2684·3	8b″	2n
(1)			⎪ (1)		
4630·1	8b″	2n	⎩ 5 † 2670·7	6b″	1n
(16)			2663·2	8	
4058·0	8	2	(1)		
(31)			⎧ 6 * 2608·6	8r	2n
3671·6	6		⎨ (3)		
(38)			⎩ 6 * 2582·6	8r	2n
3345·5	8r	10r	(1)		
⎧ 4 * 3345·1	10r	10r	⎧ 6 * 2570·0	6r	2
⎨ 4 * 3303·0	8r	10r	⎪ 6 † 2568·0	6b″	
3302·7	8r	10r	⎨ (1)		
⎩ 4 * 3282·4	8r		⎪ 2558·0	4	10
(30)			⎪ (5)		
3076·0	8r	8	⎩ 6 † 2542·5	6b″	1n
⎧ 3072·2	10r	10b″	(6)		
4 † ⎨ 3035·9	10b	8b″	⎧ 6 † 2530·3	2b″	1
⎪ (1)			⎪ 7 * 2516·0	6n	
⎩ 3018·5	8b″	4b″	⎨ (3)		
(9)			⎪ 2502·1	4	10
2873·4	6		⎪ (3)		
(2)			⎨ 7 * 2491·7	6n	2n
2863·4	6		⎪ (3)		
(1)			⎩ 7 * 2479·9	4b″	1n
2833·1	8r	1	(22)		
(1)			2393·9	8	
2823·3	6		(9)		
			2246·9	6	
			2138·3	6	
			(1)		

The lines marked * and † form a series of triplets of which the oscillation freqnencies in air can be calculated (very nearly) from the formula $10^8 \frac{1}{\lambda} = a - bn^{-2} - cn^{-4}$, when $a = 42945\cdot32$ for the *first* line, $43331\cdot71$ for the *second*, and $43521\cdot48$ for the *third* line of the triplet, $b = 131641$, $c = 1236125$ in the triplets marked *. In the triplets marked †, $a = 42954\cdot59$ or $43343\cdot65$ or $43533\cdot32$, $b = 126919$, $c = 632850$. The figure preceding the sign * or † shows the value of n.

ZIRCONIUM.

Wave-length.	Intensity and character.		Wave-length.	Intensity and character.	
	Arc.	Spark.		Arc.	Spark.
6344·8	`	6s	(5)		
6311·3		6s	4227·9	8	4
6141·8		10s	(7)		
6133·8		6s	4182·7	5	8
6128·1		10s	(5)		
5385·6		4s	4161·4	7	10
5350·5		6s	4156·4	8	10
5191·7		6s	(4)		
4816·1		10s	4149·4	10	20
4772·1		10s	(16)		
(2)			4121·6	5	5
4739·6	1	10s	(13)		
(4)			{ 4090·9	3	3
4710·3	3	10s	{ 4090·7	6	6
(1)			(6)		
4688·0	3	10s	4081·4	10	6
(20)			(7)		
4542·4	4	3	4072·8	10	6
(3)			(5)		
4535·9	5	5	4064·3	8	6
(19)			(11)		
4497·1	7	10	4055·2	5	5
(1)			(3)		
4494·6	3	10	4049·7	5	
(15)			4048·8	7	10
4454·9	5	5	(2)		
(6)			4045·8	6	8
4443·3		10	4043·7	5	3
(43)			(13)		
4380·0	7	12	4029·8	5	4
(3)			(1)		
4371·1	7	10	4027·4	5	3
(7)			4025·1	5	3
4359·9	8	10	(24)		
(6)			3999·2		15
4348·0	8	3	(2)		
(8)			3991·3	8	15
4341·3	7	3	(13)		
(20)			3981·7	10	3
4317·4	5	6	(20)		
(14)			3958·3	8	15
4303·0	5	5	(29)		
(3)			3929·7	6	5
4294·9	7	5r	3921·9	5	3
(9)			(5)		
4282·3	5	8	3916·1	5	8
(10)			(7)		
4268·1	5	5	3900·7	5	3
(7)			(9)		
4258·2	7	5	3891·5	8	3
(11)			(17)		
4241·8	8	6	3837·0		12
4241·3	8	5	(37)		
4240·5	8	3	3767·0		10
4239·4	8	4	(11)		
(2)			3751·8		12
4236·2	5	5	(2)		

Catalogue of Spectra.

ZIRCONIUM—continued.

Wave-length	Intensity and character.		Wave-length	Intensity and character.	
	Arc.	Spark.		Arc.	Spark.
3746·2 (14)		10	3396·5 (1)	7	3
3731·5 (20)		10	3393·3	7	4
3709·5 (10)		10	3392·4 (1)	10	15
3698·4 (12)		10	3388·4	7	5
3691·5	8		3388·0 (4)	7	5
3680·7 (3)	5		3377·6	5	3
3675·0 (10)		10	3376·4 (21)	5	3
3663·8 (28)	8	4	3344·9 (2)	7	4
3624·0 (7)	8	4	3340·6	7	6
3614·9 (3)	5	10	3338·6 (1)	7	4
3612·1 (9)	1	10	3334·7	7	4
3601·3 (21)	10	4	3334·4 (7)	7	4
3577·1 (3)		10	3323·1 (2)	7	4
3572·6 (15)	10	12	3319·2 (2)	7	3
3556·7 (5)	5	15	3314·6	7	4
3552·1 (6)	3	10	3313·8 (3)	5	3
3542·9 (20)		12	3306·4 (4)	7	6
3519·7 (22)	10	3	3288·9 (4)	5	3
3496·3 (9)	7	20	3284·8 (3)	10	4
3481·3 (1)	5	10	3279·4 (4)	10	5
3479·6 (8)		10	3273·2 (2)	7	8
3471·3 (5)	6	4	3269·8 (9)	7	1
3463·2 (16)		12	3250·6 (3)	7	1
3438·4 (5)	5	15	3241·2 (3)	7	4
3430·7 (11)	3	10	3234·2 (2)	7	2
3410·4 (1)	7	8	3228·9 (4)	7	4
3408·2	7	5	3214·3 (1)	7	4
3405·0 (1)	5	6	3212·1 (10)	5	2
3403·0 (2)	5	4	3192·0	7	3
3399·0 (2)	7		3191·3 (1)	7	1
			3182·9	10	5
			3182·0 (2)	7	3
			3178·2 (5)	7	3

ZIRCONIUM—*continued.*

Wave-length.	Intensity and character.		Wave-length.	Intensity and character.	
	Arc.	Spark.		Arc.	Spark.
3166·4	6	2	2700·3		4
3166·1	7	3	(7)		
3165·6	7	2	2690·6		4
3164·4	10	3	(1)		
(2)			2686·4		4
3157·9	7	1	(1)		
3157·1	7	2	2682·3		5
3155·8	7	3	(1)		
(3)			2678·8		5
3138·8	10	4	(5)		
(2)			2664·4		5
3133·6	8	4	(2)		
3132·2	7	1	2656·6		1
(2)			(2)		
3129·9	10	1	2643·9		5
3129·3	10	1	(6)		
(1)			2631·0		4
3126·0	10	3	2628·3		4
(1)			(4)		
3120·8	8	1	2620·7		8
(3)			(14)		
3111·0	10	1	2593·8		5
(1)			(3)		
3106·7	10	4	2571·5		8
3099·3	10	3	2569·0		7
(1)			(3)		
3095·2	8	3	2550·9		4
(8)			2542·2		4
3060·2	5	1	(20)		
(1)			2457·5		6
3054·9	10	4	2449·9		5
(43)			2448·9		6
2927·1		4	(1)		
(43)			2444·2		4
2844·7		4	(5)		
(65)			2420·8		4
2726·6		4	(25)		
(1)			2357·5		4
2722·7		4	(29)		
(12)					

APPENDIX.

On the Relative Behaviour of the H and K Lines of the Spectrum of Calcium.

By Sir William Huggins and Lady Huggins.

THE remarkable relative behaviour of the lines in the spectra of certain substances as they appear at and near the Sun's limb, and in the atmospheres of stars of different classes, has long been before our minds as a problem of great interest, which there is reason to believe is capable of solution by the methods of the laboratory, and on which we have worked from time to time for many years. Without waiting for the results of other researches which are in progress, we think it is desirable to put on record some definite results on the behaviour of calcium, which appear to us to be conclusive and of great importance in forming a correct interpretation of many solar and stellar phenomena.

As early as 1872 Professor Young, from a few weeks' work at Sherman on the spectra of the chromosphere and of the prominences, was able to point out that "the selection of lines seems most capricious; one is taken and another left, though belonging to the same element, of equal intensity, and close beside the first." Especially he noticed that while the H and K lines of calcium are almost always observable, the strong blue line as well as other lines of this metal are very seldom seen. In his table of the chromospheric lines, Professor Young gives for the frequency of this strong blue line the small number 3; while for the frequency of H and K he gives respectively the high numbers 75 and 50.

From 1863, when I mapped the spectrum of calcium with a strong spark from metallic calcium (*Phil. Trans.*, 1864, p. 139), I have constantly used the lines of calcium as a comparison spectrum in solar work. The experience was familiar to me that as the quantity of calcium salt on the electrodes became very small, H and K continued strong, even when the other calcium lines had almost disappeared. The suggestion then occurred to me that this behaviour of the lines might furnish a clue to the phenomena which take place near the Sun's limb.

We were encouraged to use this experience as a guiding thought in the experiments about to be described, by the consideration that in the higher solar regions, where H and K appeared alone of the calcium lines, the density must be much less than at the lower level of the reversing layer. It seemed very probable that in the simple fact of difference of density lay the true explanation of the modifications of the calcium spectrum as they are presented to us in solar and stellar phenomena.

The problem before us was, therefore, to find by experiments in the laboratory, under what conditions the lines of calcium other than the lines H and K, and in particular the strong blue line at 4226·9, were so greatly enfeebled relatively to H and K that they became quite insignificant, and, if possible, disappeared altogether from the spectrum, leaving the very simple spectrum of the two lines H and K, or nearly so.

Professor Lockyer states that "Some of the substances which have been investigated, including iron, calcium, and magnesium, have probably a definite spectrum, consisting of a few lines, which can only be produced at a temperature higher than any which is at present available in laboratory experiments" (*Proc. R. S.*, lxi. p. 205).

In the case of calcium :—

"(4) A spectrum consisting of the two lines at 3706·18 and 3737·08 and the H and K lines, corresponding to a temperature higher than the average temperature of the spark, as before explained" (*Ibid.*, p. 161).

Such a spectrum was not actually obtained, but experiments with a large intensity coil suggested that by a still greater increase of intensity of the spark such a simple spectrum might appear. The intensity of the strong blue line was reduced to one-half of H and K (*Ibid.*, Table, p. 162).

Kayser and Runge found 106 lines of the calcium spectrum to belong to the system of triplets. Among the remaining lines they pointed out pairs with constant differences of wave frequencies; notably H and K, with a difference of wave frequency of 222·9, and the more refrangible pair at 3637·08 and 3706·18, with a difference of 223·1.

Messrs. Humphreys and Mohler, in their experiments on the effect of pressure on the wave-lengths of metallic lines, found that in the case of calcium the H and K lines were shifted only one-half as much as the blue line at 4226·9. We know far too little to justify us in forming any theoretical conclusions from this peculiarity of behaviour. Indeed, there are no certain reasons why the lines of any substance should be equally shifted.

It is well known that calcium, in common with nearly all substances, gives a more complex spectrum under the conditions of the arc and spark than under those of a flame. Now, in the Fraunhofer lines we have, as first shown by Kirchhoff and Bunsen, absorption spectra of the elements which correspond, speaking broadly, with those of the bright-lined spectra of the same substances as they are produced by the spark. In order, therefore, to study the modifications which the calcium undergoes in the higher regions of the chromosphere, in the prominences, and possibly in lower parts of the corona, as well as in the atmospheres of stars of different orders, it was clearly desirable that we should start with an ordinary spark spectrum. It was suggested to us strongly by the known rarer state of the gases in the regions above the photosphere, as well as by my long experience with the behaviour of calcium in comparison spectra, that the modifications of the calcium spectrum which we were seeking would be likely to show themselves under conditions of greatly reduced density of the calcium vapour.

Experiments.

For reasons which will be obvious later on, we elected to use throughout the experiments a spark of very small intensity.

1. The break of a 6-inch Apps coil was fixed at the position of smallest acting force of the spring. So much battery power only was employed as would be just sufficient to move the break. Under these conditions, when a jar was not in connection, the feeble spark would not pass when the distance between the points exceeded 1¼ inch.

2. In all the experiments a jar was intercalated.

3. The same length of exposure, a very short one of a second and a half, sufficient to bring out only the strongest lines of the spectrum, was used in each experiment.

4. Two sets of similar experiments were made ; in one case with electrodes of platinum, and in the other with electrodes of iron. In the latter case the chief lines of iron were present with those of calcium.

Methods adopted for reducing the density of the calcium vapour :—

(*a*) The spark was taken between electrodes of metallic calcium. It was assumed, as was confirmed by the appearance of the spark, that with metallic calcium for electrodes the largest amount of calcium vapour would be present.

(*b*) The tips of the electrodes, iron or platinum, were slightly moistened with a strong solution of calcic chloride.

(*c*) The tips were slightly washed with pure water.

(*d*) The tips were again washed with pure water.

(*e*) The tips were then slightly moistened with a very weak solution made by adding a drop of the strong solution to two ounces of water.

Our expectations were completely confirmed. Under the conditions (*a*) of greatest density of the calcium vapour, when metallic calcium was employed, the blue line was as strong and possessed the same diffuse character as H and K:

As the density of the calcium was reduced, the lines were not found to be equally enfeebled, but, on the contrary, the blue line and the greater number of the lines were increasingly reduced in intensity relatively to H and K, until at last with the twice-washed electrodes (*d*) the spectrum was simplified to the condition usually existing in the prominences, in which H and K only are present.

We now proceed to a more precise statement of the changes of relative intensity as they are presented in the photographs which accompany this paper.

A. Photograph of the spark when both electrodes consist of metallic calcium. Here we have present doubtless the largest amount and the greatest density of calcium vapour. The winged character of H and K, of the blue line, and of the pair more refrangible than H and K, is well seen, showing that this appearance comes out when the gas is dense. If the greater extension of the wings of H is allowed for, and the line H carefully distinguished from the fine lines close to it, it will be seen to possess very nearly the same strength, both as regards width and length, as the blue line at 4226·9. The strength of this blue line under this condition of density is about the same as that of the line at 3737, and rather greater than the line beyond at 3706.

B. Spark taken with one electrode only of metallic calcium, the other electrode being of platinum. In this case the effect of a smaller density of the calcium vapour is clearly shown in the greatly reduced wingedness of the lines. It will be remarked that the diminished density has had the greatest influence on the pair at 3737 and 3706 ; these lines are now much less strong than the blue line, which still holds its own, and remains about as strong as H and K. The lines of the more refrangible pair are no longer diffuse at the edges.

C. Spark taken between platinum electrodes moistened with a strong solution of calcium chloride. Here the effect of a smaller quantity of vapour begins to tell strongly upon the intensity of the blue line relatively to H and K. It may now be estimated at less than one-fourth of the intensity of H. At the same time H and K have almost completely lost their diffuse character, and have become thinner and more defined.

314   *Appendix.*

D. The electrodes as left in the former experiment were slightly washed with pure water, leaving a trace only of calcium chloride. There is, as might be expected, an advance in the enfeeblement of the blue line and of the more refrangible pair, relatively to H and K.

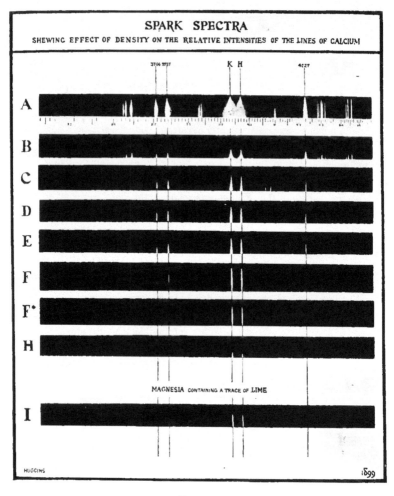

FIG. 134.

E. The electrodes were again slightly washed with pure water, so that a still smaller trace of calcium chloride must have remained upon them.

The enfeeblement of the blue line and of the pair has now become very great, while H and K, though thinner, remain strong.

F. The electrodes were once more washed with pure water, reducing still further the trace of calcium chloride which remained upon the platinum wires. The blue line has now practically disappeared, and the refrangible pair become very thin. The H and K lines have become thin and defined as they usually present themselves in the prominences.

F*. The conditions are similar to those of F, but the reduction of density has been carried still further.

H. Once more the electrodes were washed with the expectation of having removed completely the last remaining trace of calcium. To our surprise, when the photograph was developed, the lines H and K came out alone. The more refrangible pair had now faded out as well as the blue line. H and K were now thin, and extended but a short distance in the spectrum.

It must be remembered that the only condition which was varied during this set of experiments was the amount or density of the calcium vapour. The changes of relative intensity, and the modifications of the calcium spectrum produced thereby, as shown in the succession of photographs on the plate, correspond closely to the behaviour of calcium at different levels near the sun's limb, and in the atmospheres of stars of different orders. There can remain no doubt that the true interpretation of the changes in appearance of the calcium lines in the celestial bodies is to be found in the different states of density of the celestial gases from which the lines are emitted, or by which they are absorbed.

A similar set of experiments was made with iron electrodes. Precisely similar results as to the relative enfeeblement of the lines as with calcium chloride on platinum electrodes were obtained. Of course the iron lines were also present. As might be anticipated, in consequence of the simultaneous presence of the iron vapour, the lines of calcium were thinner than when platinum was used.

Outside the range of wave-lengths which could be conveniently given on the plate, far on in the ultra-violet, there is a pair of strong lines which behave very much as H and K. It remains visible in photograph H when the pair at 3737 and 3706 have disappeared. This pair is situated at 3158·98 and 3179·45.

It is desirable to point out again that all the photographs on the plate, and the far ultra-violet lines, were obtained with a spark of quite unusually small intensity, which was purposely made as little hot as possible, in order to emphasize the important fact that the determining condition of the spectral changes under discussion is not one of increase of temperature.

In the modifications of the calcium spectrum arising from variations in the relative intensities of the lines which have been discussed in this paper, and which correspond to those observed in the celestial bodies, there does not appear to be any reason for assuming, much less any direct evidence in favour of, a true dissociation of calcium, that is, of its resolution into chemically different kinds of matter.

It would be remarkable if, by decomposition through increase of temperature, a large number of lines of a spectrum should become relatively enfeebled, and that as the result of decomposition a spectrum should become simpler, and not, as analogy would suggest, more complex.

It is of importance to keep in mind that the recent chemical use of the word *dissociation* is not equivalent to true decomposition, *i.e.* to a resolution of the original substance into two or more chemically different kinds of matter. It may, and does often, mean not more than a different arrangement of the parts of the molecule, while those parts are all chemically matter of the same kind as the original molecule ; as in the case of the resolution of a compound molecule of peroxide of nitrogen into two identical half molecules, or in the separation of a molecule of elementary iodine into two half molecules or atoms of identical chemical characters. Such dissociations are well known, and are not of infrequent occurrence, and may, indeed, take place in connection with some of the spectral changes of a substance observed under different conditions. On the other hand, a true decomposition of a chemical element, that is, a breaking up of the molecule into simpler and quite other kinds of matter, though a notion familiar to chemists since Prout's time, and regarded as theoretically possible, is as yet unknown as a matter of fact.

Conclusions.

These experiments seem to us to furnish an adequate and consistent explanation of the behaviour of the calcium lines at and near the sun's limb. Near the photosphere, where the absorption mainly takes place by which the dark lines of the solar spectrum are formed, there would be, we should expect, a much greater density of calcium vapour than at a higher level, and we find the Fraunhofer line at 4226·9 strong, but much less broad than H and K. The recent photograph of the reversing layer shows that the broad shading of H and K is not reproduced there, but probably, as Mr. Jewell concludes from his measures, lower down, where the gas is still denser, which is in agreement with photograph A on the plate.

Higher up in the chromosphere, in the prominences, and possibly in the lower coronal regions, the decrease of the density of the gases composing them must be rapid, and the temperature gradient as determined by expansion must be rapid. We have clearly to do, in these regions, with calcium vapour in a rarer state, and, except so far as the molecules may have carried up within themselves to some extent the higher heat of a lower level, or through imperfect transparency the gases may have received heat from the sun's radiation, it must be at a much lower temperature than near the photosphere. Now, the changes of the calcium spectrum which take place in these regions are those which correspond in our experiments to a very small amount of calcium vapour, and a spark of small intensity.

On account of the violent commotion which must exist through the strong convection currents at the sun's limb, we should not be surprised to find some calcium vapour, notwithstanding its greater density, carried high up, together with the lighter substances such as hydrogen and helium. Our experiments show how strongly the H and K lines may come out when only a trace of calcium vapour is present, and so, it seems to us, offer a possible explanation of the great height at which these lines may be sometimes recognized. At no very great distance from the surface of the sun the gases must become too tenuous to give a visible spectrum, and it may well be that the brilliant radiations of even very rare calcium gas at H and K may show in our instruments for some distance after the hydrogen and the other light matter associated with it have become too subtle to furnish a spectrum that we can detect.

The relative behaviour of the lines of the calcium spectrum as they present themselves in the different orders of stellar spectra, when interpreted by the terrestrial experiments described in this paper, will throw important light on many of the important questions which are still pending in celestial physics. In forming conclusions as to the state of the stellar atmospheres from the different densities which may be indicated by the modifications of the calcium spectrum, it must be borne in mind that, as I have said elsewhere—

"The conditions of the radiating photosphere and those of the gases above it, on which the character of the spectrum of the star depends, will be determined, not alone by temperature, but also by the force of gravity in these regions; this force will be fixed by the star's mass and its stage of condensation, and will become greater as the star continues to condense."*

It may be, though on this point we have no sufficient data, that though the stars are built up of matter essentially similar to that of the sun, the proportion of the different elements is not the same in stars which have condensed in parts of the heavens widely different from each other, or at epochs greatly separated in time. It does not seem desirable to discuss any of these questions at the present time, as we hope before long to offer some explanation of the, to some extent analogous, relative behaviour of the lines of some other substances as observed in the sun and stars.

Addendum.—The following letter from our friend, Professor Liveing, which he has given us permission to publish, contains an account of early experiments on the spectrum of calcium, which not only support, by a different method of working, the conclusions of our paper, but also seem to show the possible occurrence of the line H without the line K. In our experiments, as will be seen in the spectra on the plate, both lines are always present, while the K line is stronger and longer than the line H; which agrees with the photographs of the prominences taken by Hale, and by Deslandres:—

"I have been looking up some observations of Dewar's and mine on the H and K lines of calcium made in 1879. We found that when we used, for the arc, carbon poles which had been heated for two days in chlorine to remove metals, the calcium lines were not visible at first in the arc, but after a time H was seen alone and not strong; after a further time K was seen, and then other calcium lines came out. No doubt the calcium had been pretty well removed from the carbon rods to some depth, but not entirely from the interior, so that as the carbon burnt away in the arc the calcium in the interior became manifest.

"Again, we found that when we used a perforated pole, and passed a stream of hydrogen into the arc through it, H and K could be both entirely obliterated; but by then reducing the current of gas they gradually reappeared; and H always came out first, and afterwards K, and H remained stronger than K until they had both become strong and had resumed their ordinary appearance. This was seen many times.

"Both observations seem to me to confirm your conclusions. In the latter case the stream of hydrogen diluted the calcium vapour, and the degree of dilution was controlled by the rate at which the gas was introduced. The mass of gas passing was too small to reduce the temperature by any considerable amount, or even, I should think, by any sensible amount.

"We found also that metallic lithium introduced into the arc produced effects similiar to those produced by hydrogen, that is, it reduced very much the strength of the H and K lines. If more than a very minute piece of lithium were introduced, the arc was invariably broken, so that we did not notice the complete obliteration of H and K with the lithium. The reduction of the strength of H and K in this case I attribute to the dilution of the calcium vapour by that of the lithium."

* Address, *Report Brit. Assoc. Science*, 1891, p. 15.

Preliminary Note on Some Modifications of the Magnesium Line at λ4481 under Different Laboratory Conditions of the Spark-Discharge.

By Sir William Huggins and Lady Huggins.

In his "Note on the wave-length of the magnesium line at λ4481,"[*] Profesor Crew points out that an interesting problem still remains, namely, to discover the laboratory conditions under which the line becomes sharp, as in some stellar spectra.

For some years, at intervals, experiments have been made here in the laboratory on the spectrum of magnesium, with the hope of throwing light on the physical conditions of the stellar atmospheres, which we may assume to be indicated by the character of this line when present; a line which in the laboratory is subject to a very wide range of modifications, both of character and of intensity.

As it may be some time before these experiments are sufficiently complete for publication, it seems desirable to reproduce at once, with this preliminary note, out of the very large number of spectra which have been taken, a few representing the most typical forms of the modifications of this line.

The teaching of these experiments suggests that the condition of the spark-discharge which is most potent in bringing about modifications of this line, both in intensity and in character, is the greater or less suddenness of the blow of the discharge. To a small extent only does the character of the line appear to be affected by the quantity and the electromotive force of the electricity which is in action; indeed, such changes as may appear are probably brought about indirectly by the larger mass of material acted upon as the discharge is made more powerful.

The appearance of the line at λ4481 in the spectrum at the top of the plate may be taken as representing its normal condition with capacity in the secondary of the coil. When the jar is taken out of circuit, and the discharge of the secondary takes place directly between the magnesium electrodes, the line becomes thin, defined, and of small intensity, as in spectrum No. 2. In this case the electric blows are less sudden through the incoming of the full self-induction of the coil itself.

The researches of Schuster, Hemsalech, Schenck, Huff, and others have shown that a similar effect follows when the jar-discharge is slowed down by the introduction into the circuit of an independent self-induction. The condition of the line in spectrum No. 3 shows the effect of the introduction of a self-induction, the conditions of the discharge remaining otherwise the same as in photograph No. 1.

In spectrum No. 5 a stronger alternating current and a capacity four times as great as in No. 1 were employed, but the photograph is feeble from over-exposure. On the contrary, in No. 4 the coil was excited by a feeble continuous current, and the capacity in the circuit was reduced to a small jar.

The two spectra placed below were taken some years ago with another spectroscope. They are of interest in showing the great variation of intensity which the line at 4481 may undergo, without assuming its normal

[*] *Astrophysical Journal*, xvi. 246 (1902).

Appendix. 319

diffused character as in No. 1. The line in spectrum No. 4 appears to be

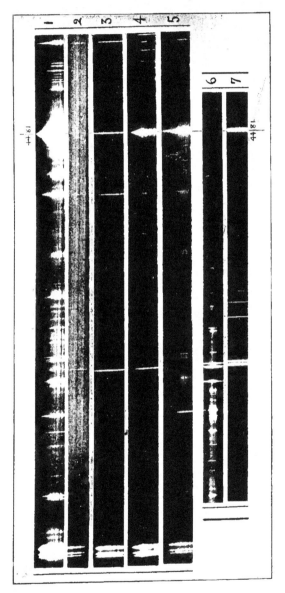

FIG. 135.—Spark-spectra of Magnesium.

intermediate in character between that of the line in No. 7 and that in No. 1.

We have still before us the task of the interpretation of the differences in the mode of production of the electric spark, especially as to greater or less suddenness, so as to enable us to connect them with definite conditions of temperature and density of those stellar atmospheres in which the magnesium present absorbs radiations similar in character to those photographed in the laboratory.

LONDON,
January 1, 1903.

INDEX

Aberration, chromatic, 7
—— of light, 41
——, spherical, 6
Abnormal solar spectrum, 166
Absorption spectra, 2, 34, 130
Achromatic lens, 8
Air-lines, 20
Aldebaran (α Tauri), 75
Algol (β Persei), 112
Alizarin spectrum, 136
Altair (α Aquilæ), 75
Aluminium oxide spectrum, 22, 160
—— series spectrum, 148
Andromeda, nebula in, 88
——, new star in, 107
Ångström and Thalén, 162
Ångström's "spectre normal," 47
Antimony spectrum, 24
Aquila, new star in, 107
α Aquilæ, 81
Arc-spectra, 39, 130, 155
Arcturus, 75, 78
Argon, 32
Argyrodite, 28
Arsenic spectrum, 32
"Atlas of Representative Stellar Spectra," 80
Atomic weights, calculation of, from spectra, 151
—— ——, international table of, 150
Attfield, carbon spectrum, 161
Auriga, new star in, 107

Balmer's formula, 139
Band-spectra, 160
Barium bromide flame-spectrum, 14, 150
—— chloride flame-spectrum, 14, 150
—— flame-spectrum, 13
—— iodide flame-spectrum, 15, 150
Beckley's spectograph, 54
Bellatrix, spectrum of, 81
Beryllium, spectrum of, 26, 154
Berzelianite, 28
Betelgeux (α Orionis), 32, 75
Biela's comet, 115

Bismuth flame-spectrum, 17
—— spark-spectrum, 24
Blood, absorption spectrum of, 133
Bolometer, 74
Boracic acid, spectrum of, 17
Bromine, absorption spectrum of, 36
——, emission spectrum of, 33
Bunsen, absorption spectrum of didymium compounds, 35
——, delicacy of spectral reactions, 10
——, discovery of rubidium and cæsium, 10
——, map of the spectra of the alkalies, etc., 9
Bunsen-flame spectrum, 15, 20, 160

Cadmium spectrum, 24, 128, 146, 151
Cæsium spectrum, 13, 145
Calcium spectrum, 10, 13, 21, 146, 156, 311
Carbon disulphide refractive index and dispersion, 7
—— in comets, 118
—— oxide spectrum, 164
—— spectrum, 28, 39, 161
Carbonic oxide poisoning, 133
Capella (α Aurigæ), 75, 81, 113
Cassiopeia, new star in, 107
Castor, 81
Cauchy's dispersion formula, 55
Centre of a lens, 6
Chlorine spectrum, 33
Chlorophyll, absorption spectrum of, 132, 135
Chromatic aberration, 7
Chromium salts, absorption spectrum of, 35
—— spectrum, 28
Chromosphere, 95, 105
Chromospheric lines, 106
Clerk Maxwell, electromagnetic theory of light, 167
Cobalt spectrum, 26, 129
Cochineal, absorption spectrum of, 137
Cœrulein, 127
Collimator, 8

Y

Comets, 113
——, spectra of, 119
Compounds, spectra of, 14, 160
Concave grating, 120
—— ——, astigmatism of, 159
Continuous spectra of solids, 11
Copper chloride spectrum, 17
—— oxide spectrum, 17
—— spectrum, 17, 129, 148
Corallin absorption spectrum, 137
Cornu, determination of velocity of light, 42
——, map of solar spectrum, 61
Corona, 99, 106
—— Borealis, new star in, 107
Coronium, 106
Crossley reflector of the Lick Observatory, 81
Crown glass refractive index and dispersion, 7
Cyanogen band in solar spectrum, 64
—— spectrum, 164
Cygni β a double star, 76, 113
Cygnus, new star in, 106

DENSITY, influence of, on the spectrum, 155, 311
Deslandres' formula for band-spectra, 161
Dibbits' carbon spectrum, 161
Didymium absorption spectrum, 35
Diffraction grating, 45, 120, 174
—— spectrum, 41, 47
Discontinuous spectra of gases, 11
Dispersion of light, 3
Dividing engine for ruling gratings, 120
Donati's comet, 114
Doppler's principle, 92
Dragon's blood, absorption spectrum of, 137

ECHELON diffraction grating, 174
Eclipse of the Sun, 96, 97, 99
Eder and Valenta, "Beiträge zur Photochemie und Spectralanalyse," 127
Electric arc, spectrum of, 37, 38
—— lamp, 27
Electricity used to produce spectra, 18
Electro-magnetic theory of light, 167
Elements present in the sun, 59
Eosin absorption spectrum, 137
Erbium salts, absorption spectra of, 36
Erythrosine, 127
Evolution of the stars, 75, 76

FABRY and Perot, measurements of wave-lengths, 157
Faculæ, 102

Fievez, map of the solar spectrum, 61
Fizeau's method of measuring the velocity of light, 41
Flame-spectra, 12
Flint-glass refractive index and dispersion, 7
Fluoresceine, absorption spectrum of, 137
Focus of a lens, 5
Foucault's electric lamp, 37
—— method of determining the velocity of light, 41
Fraunhofer lines, 49, 59

GEISSLER tube, 31
Gemini, new star in, 112
μ Geminorum, 77
Germanium spectrum, 26
Gold chloride flame-spectrum, 17
—— spark-spectrum, 25
Graphite electrodes, 125
Grating, diffraction, 45
——, Rowland's concave, 45, 121

HÆMOGLOBIN, absorption spectrum of, 132
Hale's spectroheliograph, 165
Halley's comet, 113
Hartley method of photographing spectra, 125
Hartmann's interpolation formula, 55
Helium, discovery of, 32, 86
—— spectrum, 31
—— stars, 75, 81
Helium-silicium stars, 81
Higgs's photograph of the solar spectrum, 61, 64, 68, 69
Huggins, "Atlas of Stellar Spectra," 79
—— on modifications of the magnesium line 4481..318
——, on stellar evolution, 80
——, on the behaviour of the calcium lines, 91, 311
——, on the nature of the nebulæ, 82
——, on the spectra of comets, 117
Hydrogen spectrum, 31, 89
—— ——, series in, 138
——, compound spectrum of, 139

IMPURITY lines in the arc-spectrum, 21, 39
Indium spectrum, 24, 154
Induction coil, 18
Infra-red spectrum, 74
Interference of light, 44
Interpolation by the graphical method, 51, 56

Interpolation curve, 49–51
—— formulæ, Cauchy, 55; Hartmann, 55
Iodine absorption spectrum, 36
—— spectrum, 33
Iron spectrum, 26, 131

JANSSEN, atmospheric absorption lines, 68

KAYSER and Runge, series formulæ, 141
King, new cyanogen bands, 161
Kirchhoff, law of absorption, 59
——, map of the solar spectrum, 59
Krypton discovery, 32
—— spectrum, 33

LANGLEY'S infra-red spectrum, 74
Lead chloride spectrum, 17
—— spark-spectrum, 24, 128
Lecoq de Boisbaudran, "Spectres Lumineux," 14
Lens between flame and slit, 20
——, centre of a, 6
——, image produced by, 7
——, refraction through a, 5
Leyden-jar and spark-discharger, 18, 20
Light, electro-magnetic theory of, 167
——, interference of, 44
——, velocity of, 41, 42
Lithium flame-spectrum, 12
——, series in the spectrum of, 142
Liveing and Dewar, carbon spectrum, 162
Lockyer, carbon spectrum, 162
——, dissociation of the elements, 91
Long and short lines, 20, 158
Lorentz, explanation of the "Zeeman effect," 173
α Lyræ, 75
β Lyræ, 81

MCCLEAN, photograph of the group "A," 70
Madder colours, absorption spectra of, 136
Mapping a spectrum, 9
Magenta, absorption spectrum of, 137
Magnesium oxide spectrum, 17, 22
—— spectrum, 24, 145
Manganese spectrum, 22
Mercury in magnetic field, 172
—— light, Cooper-Hewitt, 24
—— spectrum, 24, 146

Michelson echelon grating, 174
——, resolution of lines in the magnetic field, 171
——, wave-lengths of cadmium lines, 157
Micrometer, bifilar, 53
——, bright-line, 53
——, divided-lens, 53
——, tangent-screw, 52
Microspectroscope, 134
Mills spectrograph of the Lick Observatory, 93
Minimum deviation, 4
Mira (o Ceti), 75
Molybdenum spectrum, 26
Monochromatic light, 2
Morren, carbon spectrum, 161

NEBULÆ, 82
——, spectra of, 76, 81, 89
Nebular hypothesis, 84
Neon, 32
Nickel spectrum, 26, 131
Nitrogen peroxide absorption spectrum, 36
Nitrogen spectrum, 32
Novæ, or new stars, 107

ORION, great nebula of, 82
α Orionis, 75
Olzewski's spectrum of liquid oxygen, 68
Oscillation frequencies, 48, 57
Oxygen, absorption lines of atmospheric, 68
——, spectra of, 32

PALLADIUM spectrum, 26
Periodic law, 89, 149
Permanganates, absorption spectrum of, 35, 130
Perseus, new star in, 108
Phosphorus spectrum, 17
Photographic spectrum-plates, 126
Photography of the spectrum, 124
Photosphere, 95
Phyllocyanin and phylloxanthin absorption spectra, 135
Platinum spectrum, 26
Plücker tubes, 34
Plücker and Hittorf, carbon spectrum, 161
Pole-star a spectroscopic binary, 113
Pollux, 75
Potassium flame-spectrum, 13
——, series in the spectrum of, 144
Potsdam spectrograph, 105
Pressure, influence of, on the spectrum, 155

Prism, 1
——, direct-vision, 8
——, refraction through, 4
Procyon, 75, 81
Prominences, 96, 101
Protyle, 89
ζ Puppis, 89
Purpurin absorption spectrum, 136

QUARTZ lenses and prisms, their use in photographing the spectrum, 71, 123

RAIN-BAND, 68
Ramage, relationships in spectra, 151
Red stars, 75
Regulus, 75
Relationships in spectra, 138
Reflection, law of, 43
Refraction, law of, 3, 43
Refractive index, 3
Resolving power of a spectroscope, 121, 174, 178
Rigel, 75, 81
Roberts, photographs of nebulæ, 85
Rowland, accuracy of wave-length measurements, 157
——, concave grating, 45, 120
——, map of the solar spectrum, 61
——, table of solar wave-lengths, 65, 185
Rubidium flame-spectrum, 13, 145
Runge and Paschen, resolution of mercury lines in the magnetic field, 171
—— and Precht, calculation of atomic weights from spectra, 154
Rydberg and Schuster's rule, 153
Rydberg's formula, 144

SAFRANINE, absorption spectrum of, 137
Sagittarius, new star in, 106
Schumann's photographs of the extreme ultra-violet spectrum, 74
Schuster and Hemsalech, 90
—— and Rydberg's rule, 153
Secchi types of stellar spectra, 75
Selenium, spectrum of, 28
Self-induction, 159
Sensitiveness of photographic plates for different parts of the spectrum, 74
Silicates, treatment of, 13, 26
Silicon spectrum, 26
Silver spectrum, 24, 148
Sirius spectrum, 75
——, motion of, 94
Slit of spectroscope, 8

Smithells' carbon spectrum, 162
—— spectra of copper compounds, 17
Sodium flame-spectrum, 12
—— spark-spectrum, 22, 47, 144
Solar spectrum, 60, 65
Spark- and arc-spectra, 39, 128, 129, 131, 158
Spark, phenomena of the, 159
Spectra, relationships between, 141
Spectrograph, 105
Spectroheliograph, 165
Spectrometer, 122
Spectroscope, 8, 12, 59
Spectroscopic binaries, 112
Spherical aberration, 6
Standard wave-lengths, 185
Stars and Sun, temperature of the, 92
Stellar spectra, 72, 75, 78
Strontium spectrum, 14, 146
Sulphur spectra, 28
Sun, elements present in, 59
——, its photosphere, chromosphere, corona, and prominences, 95
Sun-spot spectrum, 102, 103
Sun-spots, 101, 102
Swan spectrum, 20, 160, 161
Swift's comet, 116

TELLURIC lines of the solar spectrum, 67, 68
Tellurium spectrum, 28
Thallium spectrum, 2, 24, 128, 148
Thiele's formula for band-spectra, 161
Thomson on "corpuscles," 90
Tin spectrum, 24, 128
Titanium-silicium stars, 81
Titanium spectrum, 26
Triplets in spectra, 145
Turmeric, absorption spectrum of, 137
Types of stellar spectra, 75

ULTRA-VIOLET spectra, 128
Undulatory theory of light, 43

VACUUM tubes, 31
Vanadium spectrum, 28
Vega (α Lyræ), 75, 76
Velocity of light, 41
—— of stars in the line of sight, 94
Vibrations of molecules and atoms, 158

WATER, refractive index and dispersion, 7
Water-vapour in the atmosphere, 68
Wave-length, determination of, 47
White stars, spectrum of, 76

Wine, adulteration of, 137
Wolf-Rayet stars, 78
Wollaston, carbon spectrum, 161

XENON, 32

YELLOW stars, 74

"ZEEMAN effect," 168
Zinc spectrum, 24, 128, 145
Zirconium spectrum, 28

THE END.

BY THE SAME AUTHOR

INDEX OF SPECTRA

With a Preface by Sir H. E. ROSCOE, F.R.S., D.C.L., etc., and an Introduction on the Methods of Measuring and Mapping Spectra. Revised Edition, greatly Enlarged. Abel Heywood & Son, Manchester. May be obtained from the Author at the following prices, post free:—First Edition (1872), with plates, 6s.; Enlarged Edition (1889), bound volume, including Appendix A, £1 1s. The two Editions, bound together, £1 7s.

And the following Appendices, in paper covers :—

Appendix B (Table of corrections to reduce to Rowland's standard, ultra-violet Spectra of Co and Ni, etc.), 3s.

Appendix C (Spectrum of Iron, telluric lines of solar spectrum, spectrum of Hydrogen), 5s.

Appendix D (Arc-spectra of Ga, Li, Na, K, Rb, Cs, Mg, Ca, Zn, Sr, Cd, Ba, Hg, absorption spectrum of Bromine, arc-spectrum of Alumina), 4s.

Appendix E (Spectra of Air, Cu, Ag, Au, Al, In, Tl, C, CN, N, Si, ammonia, and the Table of reductions to vacuum), 3s. 6d.

Appendix F (the arc-spectra of Cr, Sn, Pb, Sb, Bi, flame-spectra of K, Na, Li, Ca, Sr, Ba, etc.), 2s. 6d.

Appendix G (Rowland's Standard Wave-lengths, spectra of Mercury, Helium, Cd, etc., and oxy-hydrogen spectra), 4s.

Appendix H (the three spectra of Argon, the arc-spectrum of Titanium, the spark-spectra of Copper, Silver, and Gold), 4s.

Appendix I (the arc- and spark-spectra of Cobalt and Nickel, and Index), 4s.

Appendix J (the spark-spectra of Iron and Tungsten, and the arc- and spark-spectra of Platinum), 5s.

Appendix K (Spectrum of Chlorine, and the spark-spectrum of Molybdenum), 4s.

Appendix L (Spectra of Bromine, Gallium, and Radium, and the spark-spectrum of Uranium), 5s.

Appendix M (the arc-spectrum of Manganese and Vanadium, the spark-spectrum of Gold and Silicon, and the spectrum of Argon), 5s.

Appendix N (Flame-spectrum of Radium, infra-red spectra of the Alkalies, ultra-violet spectrum of Thorium), 3s.

Appendix O (Arc-spectrum of Molybdenum, spark-spectra of Calcium, Scandium, Indium, Beryllium, Lithium, Thallium, Potassium, Rubidium, Cæsium, Antimony, and Arsenic), 3s.

NOTE.—Appendices B to I inclusive are also supplied bound in one volume, price £1 11s. 6d.

"SHIRLEY," 166, VENNER ROAD, SYDENHAM.

A SELECT LIST OF BOOKS
IN
NATURAL AND PHYSICAL SCIENCE
MATHEMATICS AND TECHNOLOGY

PUBLISHED BY

Messrs. LONGMANS, GREEN, & CO.

LONDON: 39 PATERNOSTER ROW, E.C.
NEW YORK: 91 & 93 FIFTH AVENUE.
BOMBAY: 32 HORNBY ROAD.

	PAGE		PAGE
ADVANCED SCIENCE MANUALS	38	MEDICINE AND SURGERY	26
ALGEBRA	9	MENSURATION	8
AGRICULTURE	35	METALLURGY	19
ARCHITECTURE	14	MINERALOGY	19
ASTRONOMY	20	MINING	19
BACTERIOLOGY	33	NATURAL HISTORY AND GENERAL	
BIOLOGY	32	SCIENCE	23
BOTANY	34	NAVAL ARCHITECTURE	18
BUILDING CONSTRUCTION	14	NAVIGATION	20
CALCULUS	10	OPTICS	12
CHEMISTRY	2	PHOTOGRAPHY	12
CONIC SECTIONS	10	PHYSICS	5
DYNAMICS	6	PHYSIOGRAPHY	22
ELECTRICITY	16	PHYSIOLOGY	32
ELEMENTARY SCIENCE MANUALS	38	PRACTICAL ELEMENTARY SCIENCE	
ENGINEERING	17	SERIES	40
EUCLID	11	PROCTOR'S (R. A.) WORKS	21
GARDENING	35	SOUND	13
GEOLOGY	22	STATICS	6
GEOMETRY	11	STEAM, OIL, AND GAS ENGINES	15
HEALTH AND HYGIENE	25	STRENGTH OF MATERIALS	17
HEAT	13	SURVEYING	8
HYDROSTATICS	6	TECHNOLOGY	24
LIGHT	13	TELEGRAPHY	17
LOGARITHMS	10	TELEPHONE	17
LONDON SCIENCE CLASS-BOOKS	40	TEXT-BOOKS OF SCIENCE	37
LONGMANS' CIVIL ENGINEERING		THERMODYNAMICS	13
SERIES	18	TRIGONOMETRY	13
MACHINE DRAWING AND DESIGN	19	TYNDALL'S (JOHN) WORKS	36
MAGNETISM	16	VETERINARY MEDICINE, ETC.	31
MANUFACTURES	24	WORKSHOP APPLIANCES	18
MECHANICS	6	ZOOLOGY	32

CHEMISTRY.

ADDYMAN.—AGRICULTURAL ANALYSIS. A Manual of Quantitative Analysis for Students of Agriculture. By FRANK T. ADDYMAN, B.Sc. Lond., F.I.C. With 49 Illustrations. Crown 8vo., 5s. net.

ARRHENIUS.—A TEXT-BOOK OF ELECTROCHEMISTRY. By SVANTE ARRHENIUS, Professor at the University of Stockholm. Translated from the German Edition by JOHN MCCRAE, Ph.D. With 58 Illustrations. 8vo., 9s. 6d. net.

COLEMAN AND ADDYMAN.—PRACTICAL AGRICULTURAL CHEMISTRY. By J. BERNARD COLEMAN, A.R.C.Sc., F.I.C., and FRANK T. ADDYMAN, B.Sc. Lond., F.I.C. With 24 Illustrations. Crown 8vo., 1s. 6d. net.

CROOKES.—SELECT METHODS IN CHEMICAL ANALYSIS, chiefly Inorganic. By Sir WILLIAM CROOKES, F.R.S., etc. Third Edition, Rewritten and Enlarged. With 67 Woodcuts. 8vo., 21s. net.

FURNEAUX.—ELEMENTARY CHEMISTRY, Inorganic and Organic. By W. FURNEAUX, F.R.G.S., Lecturer on Chemistry, London School Board. With 65 Illustrations and 155 Experiments. Crown 8vo., 2s. 6d.

GARRETT AND HARDEN.—AN ELEMENTARY COURSE OF PRACTICAL ORGANIC CHEMISTRY. By F. C. GARRETT, M.Sc. (Vict. et Dunelm.), Assistant Lecturer and Demonstrator in Chemistry, the Durham College of Science, Newcastle-on-Tyne; and ARTHUR HARDEN, M.Sc. (Vict.), Ph.D., Assistant Lecturer and Demonstrator in Chemistry, Manchester University. With 19 Illustrations. Crown 8vo., 3s.

JAGO.—Works by W. JAGO, F.C.S., F.I.C.
  INORGANIC CHEMISTRY, THEORETICAL AND PRACTICAL. With an Introduction to the Principles of Chemical Analysis, Inorganic and Organic. With 63 Woodcuts and numerous Questions and Exercises. Fcp. 8vo., 2s. 6d.
  AN INTRODUCTION TO PRACTICAL INORGANIC CHEMISTRY. Crown 8vo., 1s. 6d.
  INORGANIC CHEMISTRY, THEORETICAL AND PRACTICAL. A Manual for Students in Advanced Classes of the Science and Art Department. With Plate of Spectra and 78 Woodcuts. Crown 8vo., 4s. 6d.

KLÖCKER. — FERMENTATION ORGANISMS : a Laboratory Handbook. By ALB. KLÖCKER. Translated by G. E. ALLAN, B.Sc., and J. H. MILLAR, F.I.C. With 146 Illustrations in the text. 8vo., 12s. net.

MELLOR.—HIGHER MATHEMATICS FOR STUDENTS OF CHEMISTRY AND PHYSICS. With Special Reference to Practical Work. By J. W. MELLOR, D.Sc., late Senior Scholar, and 1851 Exhibition Scholar, New Zealand University; Research Fellow, the Owens College, Manchester. With 142 Diagrams. 8vo., 12s. 6d. net.

MENDELÉEFF.—Works by D. MENDELÉEFF, Professor of Chemistry in the University of St. Petersburg.
  THE PRINCIPLES OF CHEMISTRY. Translated from the Russian (Sixth Edition) by GEORGE KAMENSKY, A.R.S.M., of the Imperial Mint, St. Petersburg; and Edited by T. A. LAWSON, B.Sc., Ph.D., Fellow of the Institute of Chemistry. With 96 Diagrams and Illustrations. 2 vols. 8vo., 36s.
  AN ATTEMPT TOWARDS A CHEMICAL CONCEPTION OF THE ETHER. Translated from the Russian by GEORGE KAMENSKY, A.R.S.M. 8vo., 2s. net.

CHEMISTRY—*Continued.*

MEYER.—OUTLINES OF THEORETICAL CHEMISTRY. By Lothar Meyer, Professor of Chemistry in the University of Tübingen. Translated by Professors P. Phillips Bedson, D.Sc., and W. Carleton Williams, B.Sc. 8vo., 9s.

MILLER.—INTRODUCTION TO THE STUDY OF INORGANIC CHEMISTRY. By W. Allen Miller, M.D., LL.D. With 71 Illustrations. Fcp. 8vo., 3s. 6d.

MUIR.—A COURSE OF PRACTICAL CHEMISTRY. By M. M. P. Muir, M.A., Fellow and Prælector in Chemistry of Gonville and Caius College, Cambridge. (3 Parts.)

    Part I. Elementary. Crown 8vo., 4s. 6d.

    Part II. Intermediate. Crown 8vo., 4s. 6d.

    Part III. [*In preparation.*

NEWTH.—Works by G. S. NEWTH, F.I.C., F.C.S., Demonstrator in the Royal College of Science, London.

    CHEMICAL LECTURE EXPERIMENTS. With 230 Illustrations. Crown 8vo., 6s.

    CHEMICAL ANALYSIS, QUANTITATIVE AND QUALITATIVE. With 100 Illustrations. Crown 8vo., 6s. 6d.

    A TEXT-BOOK OF INORGANIC CHEMISTRY. With 155 Illustrations. Crown 8vo., 6s. 6d.

    ELEMENTARY PRACTICAL CHEMISTRY. With 108 Illustrations and 254 Experiments. Crown 8vo., 2s. 6d.

PERKIN.—QUALITATIVE CHEMICAL ANALYSIS (ORGANIC AND INORGANIC). By F. Mollwo Perkin, Ph.D., Head of the Chemistry Department, Borough Polytechnic Institute, London. With 9 Illustrations and Spectrum Plate. 8vo., 3s. 6d.

PLIMMER. — THE CHEMICAL CHANGES AND PRODUCTS RESULTING FROM FERMENTATIONS. By R. H. Aders Plimmer. 8vo., 6s. net.

REYNOLDS.—EXPERIMENTAL CHEMISTRY FOR JUNIOR STUDENTS. By J. Emerson Reynolds, M.D., F.R.S., Professor of Chemistry, University of Dublin. Fcp. 8vo., with numerous Woodcuts.

    Part I. Introductory. Fcp. 8vo., 1s. 6d.

    Part II. Non-Metals, with an Appendix on Systematic Testing for Acids. Fcp. 8vo., 2s. 6d.

    Part III. Metals, and Allied Bodies. Fcp. 8vo., 3s. 6d.

    Part IV. Carbon Compounds. Fcp. 8vo., 4s.

SHENSTONE.—Works by W. A. SHENSTONE, F.R.S., Lecturer on Chemistry in Clifton College.

    THE METHODS OF GLASS-BLOWING AND OF WORKING SILICA IN THE OXY-GAS FLAME. For the Use of Physical and Chemical Students. With 43 Illustrations. Crown 8vo., 2s. 6d.

    A PRACTICAL INTRODUCTION TO CHEMISTRY. Intended to give a Practical acquaintance with the Elementary Facts and Principles of Chemistry. With 25 Illustrations. Crown 8vo., 2s.

CHEMISTRY—*Continued.*

SMITH AND HALL.—**THE TEACHING OF CHEMISTRY AND PHYSICS IN THE SECONDARY SCHOOL.** By ALEXANDER SMITH, B.Sc., Ph.D., Associate Professor of Chemistry in the University of Chicago, and EDWIN H. HALL, Ph.D., Professor of Physics in Harvard University. With 21 Woodcuts, Bibliographies, and Index. Crown 8vo., 6s. net.

TEXT-BOOKS OF PHYSICAL CHEMISTRY.
Edited by Sir WILLIAM RAMSAY, K.C.B., F.R.S

THE PHASE RULE AND ITS APPLICATIONS. By ALEX. FINDLAY, M.A., Ph.D., D.Sc., Lecturer and Demonstrator in Chemistry, University of Birmingham. With 118 Figures in the Text, and an INTRODUCTION TO PHYSICAL CHEMISTRY by Sir WM. RAMSAY, K.C.B., F.R.S. Cr. 8vo., 5s.

AN INTRODUCTION TO PHYSICAL CHEMISTRY. Being a General Introduction to the Series. By Sir WILLIAM RAMSAY, K.C.B., F.R.S. Crown 8vo., 1s. net.

ELECTRO-CHEMISTRY. Part I. General Theory. By R. A. LEHFELDT, D.Sc., Professor of Physics at the East London Technical College. Including a Chapter on the Relation of Chemical Constitution to Conductivity. By T. S. MOORE, F.A., B.Sc., Lecturer in the University of Birmingham. Crown 8vo., 5s.

Part II. Applications to Electrolysis, Primary and Secondary Batteries, etc. [*In preparation.*]

The following Volumes are also in preparation:—

STOICHIOMETRY. By SYDNEY YOUNG, D.Sc., F.R.S.

SPECTROSCOPY. By E. C. C. BALY, F.I.C.

RELATIONS BETWEEN CHEMICAL CONSTITUTION AND PHYSICAL PROPERTIES. By SAMUEL SMILES, D.Sc.

THERMODYNAMICS. By F. G. DONNAN, M.A., Ph.D.

CHEMICAL DYNAMICS AND REACTIONS. By J. W. MELLOR, D.Sc.

THORNTON AND PEARSON.—**NOTES ON VOLUMETRIC ANALYSIS.** By ARTHUR THORNTON, M.A., and MARCHANT PEARSON, B.A., Assistant Science Master, Bradford Grammar School. Medium 8vo., 2s.

THORPE.—Works by T. E. THORPE, C.B., D.Sc. (Vict.), Ph.D., F.R.S., Principal of the Government Laboratory, London. Assisted by Eminent Contributors.

A DICTIONARY OF APPLIED CHEMISTRY. 3 vols. 8vo. Vols. I. and II., 42s. each. Vol. III., 63s.

QUANTITATIVE CHEMICAL ANALYSIS. With 88 Woodcuts. Fcp. 8vo., 4s. 6d.

THORPE AND MUIR.—**QUALITATIVE CHEMICAL ANALYSIS AND LABORATORY PRACTICE.** By T. E. THORPE, C.B., Ph.D., D.Sc., F.R.S., and M. M. PATTISON MUIR, M.A. With Plate of Spectra and 57 Illustrations. Fcp. 8vo., 3s. 6d.

TILDEN.—Works by WILLIAM A. TILDEN, D.Sc. London, F.R.S., Professor of Chemistry in the Royal College of Science, South Kensington.

A SHORT HISTORY OF THE PROGRESS OF SCIENTIFIC CHEMISTRY IN OUR OWN TIMES. Crown 8vo., 5s. net.

INTRODUCTION TO THE STUDY OF CHEMICAL PHILOSOPHY. The Principles of Theoretical and Systematic Chemistry. With 5 Illustrations. Fcp. 8vo., 5s. With ANSWERS to Problems. Fcp. 8vo., 5s. 6d.

PRACTICAL CHEMISTRY. The principles of Qualitative Analysis. Fcp. 8vo., 1s. 6d.

CHEMISTRY—*Continued*.

WATTS DICTIONARY OF CHEMISTRY. Revised and entirely Rewritten by H. FORSTER MORLEY, M.A., D.Sc., Fellow of, and lately Assistant Professor of Chemistry in, University College, London; and M. M. PATTISON MUIR, M.A., F.R.S.E., Fellow, and Prælector in Chemistry, of Gonville and Caius College, Cambridge. Assisted by Eminent Contributors. 4 vols. 8vo., £5 net.

WHITELEY.—Works by R. LLOYD WHITELEY, F.I.C., Principal of the Municipal Science School, West Bromwich.

CHEMICAL CALCULATIONS. With Explanatory Notes, Problems and Answers, specially adapted for use in Colleges and Science Schools. With a Preface by Professor F. CLOWES, D.Sc. (Lond.), F.I.C. Crown 8vo., 2s.

ORGANIC CHEMISTRY: the Fatty Compounds. With 45 Illustrations. Crown 8vo., 3s. 6d.

PHYSICS, ETC.

BIDGOOD.—ELEMENTARY PHYSICS AND CHEMISTRY FOR THE USE OF SCHOOLS. (In Three Books.) By JOHN BIDGOOD, B.Sc., Headmaster of the Gateshead Secondary Day School.

Book I. Elementary Physics. With 120 Illustrations. Crown 8vo., 1s. 6d.

Book II. Physics and Chemistry. With 122 Illustrations. Crown 8vo., 1s. 6d.

Book III. Chemistry. With 108 Illustrations. Crown 8vo., 2s.

BOSE.—RESPONSE IN THE LIVING AND NON-LIVING. By JAGADIS CHUNDER BOSE, M.A. (Cantab.), D.Sc. (Lond.), Professor, Presidency College, Calcutta. With 117 Illustrations. 8vo., 10s. 6d.

GANOT.—Works by PROFESSOR GANOT. Translated and Edited by E. ATKINSON, Ph.D., F.C.S., and A. W. REINOLD M.A., F.R.S.

ELEMENTARY TREATISE ON PHYSICS, Experimental and Applied. With 9 Coloured Plates and Maps, and 1048 Woodcuts, and Appendix of Problems and Examples with Answers. Crown 8vo., 15s.

NATURAL PHILOSOPHY FOR GENERAL READERS AND YOUNG PEOPLE. With 7 Plates, 632 Woodcuts, and an Appendix of Questions. Crown 8vo., 7s. 6d.

GLAZEBROOK AND SHAW.—PRACTICAL PHYSICS. By R. T. GLAZEBROOK, M.A., F.R.S., and W. N. SHAW, M.A. With 134 Illustrations. Fcp. 8vo., 7s. 6d.

GUTHRIE.—MOLECULAR PHYSICS AND SOUND. By F. GUTHRIE, Ph.D. With 91 Diagrams. Fcp. 8vo., 1s. 6d.

HELMHOLTZ.—POPULAR LECTURES ON SCIENTIFIC SUBJECTS. By HERMANN VON HELMHOLTZ. Translated by E. ATKINSON, Ph.D., F.C.S., formerly Professor of Experimental Science, Staff College. With 68 Illustrations. 2 vols., crown 8vo., 3s. 6d. each.

HENDERSON.—ELEMENTARY PHYSICS. By JOHN HENDERSON, D.Sc. (Edin.), A.I.E.E., Physics Department, Borough Road Polytechnic. Crown 8vo., 2s. 6d.

PHYSICS, ETC.—*Continued.*

MACLEAN.—EXERCISES IN NATURAL PHILOSOPHY. By MAGNUS MACLEAN, D.Sc., Professor of Electrical Engineering at the Glasgow and West of Scotland Technical College. Crown 8vo., 4s. 6d.

MEYER.—THE KINETIC THEORY OF GASES. Elementary Treatise, with Mathematical Appendices. By Dr. OSKAR EMIL MEYER. 8vo., 15s. net.

VAN 'THOFF.—THE ARRANGEMENT OF ATOMS IN SPACE. By J. H. VAN T'HOFF. With a Preface by JOHANNES WISLICENUS, Professor of Chemistry at the University of Leipzig; and an Appendix 'Stereochemistry among Inorganic Substances,' by ALFRED WERNER, Professor of Chemistry at the University of Zürich. Crown 8vo., 6s. 6d.

WATSON.—Works by W. WATSON, A.R.C.S., F.R.S., D.Sc., Assistant Professor of Physics at the Royal College of Science, London.

ELEMENTARY PRACTICAL PHYSICS: a Laboratory Manual for Use in Organised Science Schools. With 120 Illustrations and 193 Exercises. Crown 8vo., 2s. 6d.

A TEXT-BOOK OF PHYSICS. With 568 Diagrams and Illustrations, and a Collection of Examples and Questions with Answers. Large crown 8vo., 10s. 6d.

WATTS.—AN INTRODUCTION TO THE STUDY OF SPECTRUM ANALYSIS. By W. MARSHALL WATTS, D.Sc. (Lond.), B.Sc. (Vict.), F.I.C., Senior Physical Science Master in the Giggleswick School. With 135 Illustrations and Coloured Plate. 8vo., 10s. 6d. net.

WORTHINGTON.—A FIRST COURSE OF PHYSICAL LABORATORY PRACTICE. Containing 264 Experiments. By A. M. WORTHINGTON, C.B., F.R.S. With Illustrations. Crown 8vo., 4s. 6d.

WRIGHT.—ELEMENTARY PHYSICS. By MARK R. WRIGHT, M.A., Professor of Normal Education, Durham College of Science. With 242 Illustrations. Crown 8vo., 2s. 6d.

MECHANICS, DYNAMICS, STATICS, HYDROSTATICS, ETC.

BALL.—A CLASS-BOOK OF MECHANICS. By Sir R. S. BALL, LL.D. 89 Diagrams. Fcp. 8vo., 1s. 6d.

GOODEVE.—Works by T. M. GOODEVE, M.A., formerly Professor of Mechanics at the Normal School of Science, and the Royal School of Mines.

THE ELEMENTS OF MECHANISM. With 357 Illustrations. Crown 8vo., 6s.

PRINCIPLES OF MECHANICS. With 253 Illustrations and numerous Examples. Crown 8vo., 6s.

A MANUAL OF MECHANICS: an Elementary Text-Book for Students of Applied Mechanics. With 138 Illustrations and Diagrams, and 188 Examples taken from the Science Department Examination Papers, with Answers. Fcp. 8vo., 2s. 6d.

GOODMAN.—MECHANICS APPLIED TO ENGINEERING. By JOHN GOODMAN, Wh.Sch., M.I.C.E., M.I.M.E., Professor of Engineering in the University of Leeds. With 714 Illustrations and numerous Examples. Crown 8vo., 9s. net.

MECHANICS, DYNAMICS, STATICS, HYDROSTATICS, ETC.—
Continued.

GRIEVE.—LESSONS IN ELEMENTARY MECHANICS.
By W. H. GRIEVE, late Engineer, R.N., Science Demonstrator for the London School Board, etc.
Stage 1. With 165 Illustrations and a large number of Examples. Fcp. 8vo., 1s. 6d.
Stage 2. With 122 Illustrations. Fcp. 8vo., 1s. 6d.
Stage 3. With 103 Illustrations. Fcp. 8vo., 1s. 6d.

MAGNUS.—Works by SIR PHILIP MAGNUS, B.Sc., B.A.

LESSONS IN ELEMENTARY MECHANICS. Introductory to the study of Physical Science. Designed for the Use of Schools, and of Candidates for the London Matriculation and other Examinations. With numerous Exercises, Examples, Examination Questions and Solutions, etc., from 1870-1895. With Answers, and 131 Woodcuts. Fcp. 8vo., 3s. 6d.

Key for the use of Teachers only, price 5s. 3½d.

HYDROSTATICS AND PNEUMATICS. Fcp. 8vo., 1s. 6d.; or, with Answers, 2s. The Worked Solutions of the Problems, 2s.

PULLEN.—MECHANICS: Theoretical, Applied, and Experimental. By W. W. F. PULLEN, Wh.Sch., M.I.M.E., A.M.I.C.E. With 318 Diagrams and numerous Examples. Crown 8vo., 4s. 6d.

ROBINSON.—ELEMENTS OF DYNAMICS (Kinetics and Statics). With numerous Exercises. A Text-book for Junior Students. By the Rev. J. L. ROBINSON, M.A. Crown 8vo., 6s.

SMITH.—Works by J. HAMBLIN SMITH, M.A.

ELEMENTARY STATICS. Crown 8vo., 3s.

ELEMENTARY HYDROSTATICS. Crown 8vo., 3s.

KEY TO STATICS AND HYDROSTATICS. Crown 8vo., 6s.

TARLETON.—AN INTRODUCTION TO THE MATHEMATICAL THEORY OF ATTRACTION. By FRANCIS A. TARLETON, LL.D., Sc.D., Fellow of Trinity College, and Professor of Natural Philosophy in the University of Dublin. Crown 8vo., 10s. 6d.

TAYLOR.—Works by J. E. TAYLOR, M.A., B.Sc. (Lond.).

THEORETICAL MECHANICS, including Hydrostatics and Pneumatics. With 175 Diagrams and Illustrations, and 522 Examination Questions and Answers. Crown 8vo., 2s. 6d.

THEORETICAL MECHANICS—SOLIDS. With 163 Illustrations, 120 Worked Examples and over 500 Examples from Examination Papers, etc. Crown 8vo., 2s. 6d.

THEORETICAL MECHANICS.—FLUIDS. With 122 Illustrations, numerous Worked Examples, and about 500 Examples from Examination Papers, etc. Crown 8vo., 2s. 6d.

THORNTON.—THEORETICAL MECHANICS—SOLIDS. Including Kinematics, Statics and Kinetics. By ARTHUR THORNTON, M.A., F.R.A.S. With 200 Illustrations, 130 Worked Examples, and over 900 Examples from Examination Papers, etc. Crown 8vo., 4s. 6d.

MECHANICS, DYNAMICS, STATICS, HYDROSTATICS, ETC.—
Continued.

TWISDEN.—Works by the Rev. JOHN F. TWISDEN, M.A.

PRACTICAL MECHANICS; an Elementary Introduction to their Study. With 855 Exercises, and 184 Figures and Diagrams. Crown 8vo., 10s. 6d.

THEORETICAL MECHANICS. With 172 Examples, numerous Exercises, and 154 Diagrams. Crown 8vo., 8s. 6d.

WILLIAMSON.—INTRODUCTION TO THE MATHEMATICAL THEORY OF THE STRESS AND STRAIN OF ELASTIC SOLIDS. By BENJAMIN WILLIAMSON, D.Sc., F.R.S. Crown 8vo., 5s.

WILLIAMSON AND TARLETON.—AN ELEMENTARY TREATISE ON DYNAMICS. Containing Applications to Thermodynamics, with numerous Examples. By BENJAMIN WILLIAMSON, D.Sc., F.R.S., and FRANCIS A. TARLETON, LL.D. Crown 8vo., 10s. 6d.

WORTHINGTON.—DYNAMICS OF ROTATION: an Elementary Introduction to Rigid Dynamics. By A. M. WORTHINGTON, C.B., F.R.S. Crown 8vo., 4s. 6d.

MENSURATION, SURVEYING, ETC.

BRABANT.—THE ELEMENTS OF PLANE AND SOLID MENSURATION. With Copious Examples and Answers. By F. G. BRABANT, M.A. Crown 8vo., 3s. 6d.

CHIVERS.—ELEMENTARY MENSURATION. By G. T. CHIVERS, Head Master of H.M. Dockyard School, Pembroke. With Answers to the Examples. Crown 8vo, 5s.

GRIBBLE.—PRELIMINARY SURVEY AND ESTIMATES. By THEODORE GRAHAM GRIBBLE, Civil Engineer. Including Elementary Astronomy, Route Surveying, Tacheometry, Curve Ranging, Graphic Mensuration, Estimates, Hydrography and Instruments. With 133 Illustrations, Quantity Diagrams, and a Manual of the Slide-Rule. Fcp. 8vo., 7s. 6d.

HILEY.—EXPLANATORY MENSURATION. By the Rev. ALFRED HILEY, M.A. With a Chapter on Land Surveying by the Rev. JOHN HUNTER, M.A. Containing numerous Examples, and embodying many of the Questions set in the Local Examination Papers. With Answers. 12mo., 2s. 6d.

HUNTER.—MENSURATION AND LAND SURVEYING. By the Rev. JOHN HUNTER, M.A. 18mo., 1s. KEY, 1s.

LODGE.—MENSURATION FOR SENIOR STUDENTS. By ALFRED LODGE, M.A., late Fereday Fellow of St. John's College, Oxford; Professor of Pure Mathematics at the Royal Indian Engineering College, Cooper's Hill. With Answers. Crown 8vo., 4s. 6d.

LONGMANS' SCHOOL MENSURATION. By ALFRED J. PEARCE, B.A. (Inter.), Hons. Matric. (London). With numerous Diagrams. Crown 8vo. With or without Answers. 2s. 6d.

MENSURATION, SURVEYING, ETC.—*Continued.*

LONGMANS' JUNIOR SCHOOL MENSURATION. To meet the Requirements of the Oxford and Cambridge Junior Local Examinations, the College of Preceptors, etc. By W. S. BEARD, F.R.G.S., Head Master of Fareham Modern School. With Answers to Exercises and Examination Papers. Crown 8vo., 1s.

LUPTON.—A PRACTICAL TREATISE ON MINE SURVEYING. By ARNOLD LUPTON, Mining Engineer, Certificated Colliery Manager, Surveyor, Member of the Institution of Civil Engineers, etc. With 216 Illustrations. Medium 8vo., 12s. net.

NESBIT.—PRACTICAL MENSURATION. By A. NESBIT. Illustrated by 700 Practical Examples and 700 Woodcuts. 12mo., 3s. 6d. KEY, 5s.

SMITH.—CIRCULAR SLIDE RULE. By G. L. SMITH. Fcp. 8vo., 1s. net.

ALGEBRA, ETC.

*** *For other Books, see Longmans & Co.'s Catalogue of Educational and School Books.*

ANNALS OF MATHEMATICS. (PUBLISHED UNDER THE AUSPICES OF HARVARD UNIVERSITY.) Issued Quarterly. 4to., 2s. net.

CONSTABLE AND MILLS.—ELEMENTARY ALGEBRA UP TO AND INCLUDING QUADRATIC EQUATIONS. By W. G. CONSTABLE, B.Sc., B.A., and J. MILLS, B.A. Crown 8vo., 2s. With Answers, 2s. 6d.
Also in Three Parts. Crown 8vo., cloth, limp, 9d. each. ANSWERS. Three Parts. Crown 8vo., paper covers, 6d. each.

CRACKNELL.—PRACTICAL MATHEMATICS. By A. G. CRACKNELL, M.A., B.Sc., Sixth Wrangler, etc. With Answers to the Examples. Crown 8vo., 3s. 6d.

LONGMANS' JUNIOR SCHOOL ALGEBRA. By WILLIAM S. BEARD, F.R.G.S., Head Master of the Modern School, Fareham. Crown 8vo., 1s. 6d. With Answers, 2s.

MELLOR.—HIGHER MATHEMATICS FOR STUDENTS OF CHEMISTRY AND PHYSICS. With special reference to Practical Work. By J. W. MELLOR, D.Sc., Research Fellow, The Owens College, Manchester. With 142 Diagrams. 8vo., 12s. 6d. net.

SMITH.—Works by J. HAMBLIN SMITH, M.A.

ELEMENTARY ALGEBRA. New Edition, with a large number of Additional Exercises. With or without Answers. Crown 8vo., 3s. 6d. Answers separately, 6d. KEY, Crown 8vo., 9s.
*** *The Original Edition of this Book is still on Sale, price 2s. 6d.*

EXERCISES IN ALGEBRA. With Answers. Fcap. 8vo., 2s. 6d. Copies may be had without the Answers.

WELSFORD AND MAYO.—ELEMENTARY ALGEBRA. By J. W. WELSFORD, M.A., formerly Fellow of Gonville and Caius College, Cambridge, and C. H. P. MAYO, M.A., formerly Scholar of St. Peter's College, Cambridge; Assistant Masters at Harrow School. Crown 8vo., 3s. 6d., or with Answers, 4s. 6d.

CONIC SECTIONS, ETC.

CASEY.—A TREATISE ON THE ANALYTICAL GEOMETRY OF THE POINT, LINE, CIRCLE, AND CONIC SECTIONS. By JOHN CASEY, LL.D., F.R.S. Crown 8vo., 12s.

SALMON.—A TREATISE ON CONIC SECTIONS, containing an Account of some of the most Important Modern Algebraic and Geometric Methods. By G. SALMON, D.D., F.R.S. 8vo., 12s.

SMITH.—GEOMETRICAL CONIC SECTIONS. By J. HAMBLIN SMITH, M.A. Crown 8vo., 3s. 6d.

THE CALCULUS, LOGARITHMS, ETC.

BARKER.—GRAPHICAL CALCULUS. By ARTHUR H. BARKER, B.A., B.Sc. With an Introduction by JOHN GOODMAN, A.M.I.C.E. With 61 Diagrams. Crown 8vo., 4s. 6d.

MURRAY.—Works by DANIEL ALEXANDER MURRAY, Ph.D.

AN INTRODUCTORY COURSE IN DIFFERENTIAL EQUATIONS. Crown 8vo., 4s. 6d.

A FIRST COURSE IN THE INFINITESIMAL CALCULUS. Crown 8vo., 7s. 6d.

O'DEA.—AN ELEMENTARY TREATISE ON LOGARITHMS, EXPONENTIAL AND LOGARITHMIC SERIES, UNDETERMINED CO-EFFICIENTS, AND THE THEORY OF DETERMINANTS. By JAMES J. O'DEA, M.A. Crown 8vo., 2s.

TATE.—PRINCIPLES OF THE DIFFERENTIAL AND INTEGRAL CALCULUS. By THOMAS TATE. 12mo., 4s. 6d.

TAYLOR.—Works by F. GLANVILLE TAYLOR.

AN INTRODUCTION TO THE DIFFERENTIAL AND INTEGRAL CALCULUS AND DIFFERENTIAL EQUATIONS. Cr. 8vo., 9s.

AN INTRODUCTION TO THE PRACTICAL USE OF LOGARITHMS, WITH EXAMPLES IN MENSURATION. With Answers to Exercises. Crown 8vo., 1s. 6d.

WILLIAMSON.—Works by BENJAMIN WILLIAMSON, D.Sc.

AN ELEMENTARY TREATISE ON THE DIFFERENTIAL CALCULUS; containing the Theory of Plane Curves with numerous Examples. Crown 8vo., 10s. 6d.

AN ELEMENTARY TREATISE ON THE INTEGRAL CALCULUS; containing Applications to Plane Curves and Surfaces, and also a Chapter on the Calculus of Variations, with numerous Examples. Crown 8vo., 10s. 6d.

GEOMETRY AND EUCLID.

*** For other Works, see Longmans & Co.'s Catalogue of Educational and School Books.

ALLMAN.—GREEK GEOMETRY FROM THALES TO EUCLID. By G. J. ALLMAN. 8vo., 10s 6d.

BARRELL.—ELEMENTARY GEOMETRY. By FRANK R. BARRELL, M.A., B.Sc., Professor of Mathematics, University College, Bristol.

    Section I. Part I., being the subject-matter of Euclid, Book I. Crown 8vo., 1s.
    Section I. Part II., containing the subject-matter of Euclid, Book III. 1-34, and Book IV. 4-9. Crown 8vo., 1s.
    Section I. complete. Crown 8vo., 2s.
    Section II., containing the remainder of Euclid, Books III. and IV., together with the subject-matter of Books II. and VI. With explanation of Ratio and Proportion, Trigonometric Ratios and Measurement of Circles. Crown 8vo., 1s. 6d.
    Sections I. and II. in one volume. Crown 8vo., 3s. 6d.
    Section III., containing the subject-matter of Euclid, Book XI., together with a full treatment of volume and surface of the cylinder, cone, sphere, etc. Crown 8vo., 1s. 6d.
    Sections I., II. and III. complete in one volume. Crown 8vo., 4s. 6d.

CASEY.—Works by JOHN CASEY, LL.D., F.R.S.

THE ELEMENTS OF EUCLID, BOOKS I.-VI. and Propositions, I.-XXI. of Book XI., and an Appendix of the Cylinder, Sphere, Cone, etc. With Copious Annotations and numerous Exercises. Fcp. 8vo., 4s. 6d. KEY to Exercises. Fcp. 8vo., 6s.

A SEQUEL TO THE ELEMENTS OF EUCLID. Part I. Books I.-VI. With numerous Examples. Fcp. 8vo., 3s. 6d.

A TREATISE ON THE ANALYTICAL GEOMETRY OF THE POINT, LINE, CIRCLE AND CONIC SECTIONS. Containing an Account of its most recent Extension. Crown 8vo., 12s.

HAMILTON.—ELEMENTS OF QUATERNIONS. By the late Sir WILLIAM ROWAN HAMILTON, LL.D., M.R.I.A. Edited by CHARLES JASPER JOLY, M.A., Fellow of Trinity College, Dublin. 2 vols. 4to. 21s. net each.

LONGMANS' LIST OF APPARATUS FOR USE IN GEOMETRY, ETC.

1. LONGMANS' ENGLISH AND METRIC RULER. Marked on one edge in Inches, Eighths, Tenths and Five-fifths. Marked on the other edge in Centimetres. Price 1d. net.

2. LOW'S IMPROVED SET SQUARES. Designs A & B. 45° to 60°.

  A 1 45° 4″   ⎱   ⎰ B 1 45° 4″ each 1/- net. | A 1 60° 4″   ⎱   ⎰ B 1 60° 4″ each 1/- net.
  A 2 45° 6″   ⎬-or-⎨ B 2 45° 6″   ,, 1/3 ,, | A 2 60° 6″   ⎬-or-⎨ B 2 60° 6″   ,, 1/3 ,,
  A 3 45° 6½″⎭   ⎩ B 3 45° 8½″ ,, 2/- ,, | A 3 60° 8½″⎭   ⎩ B 3 60° 8½″ ,, 2/- ,,

3. LOW'S IMPROVED PROTRACTORS (Celluloid). Protractor No. 2. 3″ radius, marked in degrees, 6d. net. Protractor No. 3. 4″ radius, marked in ½-degrees, 9d. net.

4. LOW'S ADJUSTABLE PROTRACTOR SET SQUARE. 2s. 6d. net.

5. LONGMANS' BLACKBOARD ENGLISH AND METRIC RULE. One Metre; marked in decimetres, centimetres, inches, half-inches and quarter-inches. 2s. 6d.

GEOMETRY AND EUCLID—*Continued.*

LOW.—TEXT-BOOK ON PRACTICAL, SOLID, AND DE-SCRIPTIVE GEOMETRY. By DAVID ALLAN LOW, Professor of Engineering, East London Technical College. Crown 8vo.
Part I. With 114 Figures, 2s.   Part II. With 64 Figures, 3s.

THE DIAGRAM MEASURER. An Instrument for measuring the Areas of Irregular Figures and specially useful for determining the Mean Effective Pressure from Indicator Diagrams from Steam, Gas and other Engines. Designed by D. A. Low. With Full Instructions for Use. 1s. net.

MORRIS AND HUSBAND.—PRACTICAL PLANE AND SOLID GEOMETRY. By I. HAMMOND MORRIS and JOSEPH HUSBAND. Fully Illustrated with Drawings. Crown 8vo., 2s. 6d.

MORRIS.—GEOMETRICAL DRAWING FOR ART STUDENTS. Embracing Plane Geometry and its Applications, the Use of Scales, and the Plans and Elevations of Solids as required in Section I. of Science Subjects. By I. HAMMOND MORRIS. Crown 8vo., 2s.

SMITH.—ELEMENTS OF GEOMETRY. By J. HAMBLIN SMITH, M.A. Containing Books 1 to 6, and portions of Books 11 and 12, of Euclid, with Exercises and Notes. Cr. 8vo., 3s. 6d.   KEY, crown 8vo., 8s. 6d.
Books 1 and 2, limp cloth, 1s. 6d., may be had separately.

SPOONER.—THE ELEMENTS OF GEOMETRICAL DRAWING: an Elementary Text-book on Practical Plane Geometry, including an Introduction to Solid Geometry. Written to include the requirements of the Syllabus of the Board of Education in Geometrical Drawing and for the use of Students preparing for the Military Entrance Examinations. By HENRY J. SPOONER, C.E., M.Inst.M.E. Crown 8vo., 3s. 6d.

WILSON.—GEOMETRICAL DRAWING. For the use of Candidates for Army Examinations, and as an Introduction to Mechanical Drawing. By W. N. WILSON, M.A. Parts I. and II. Crown 8vo., 4s. 6d. each

WINTER.—ELEMENTARY GEOMETRICAL DRAWING. By S. H. WINTER. Part I. Including Practical Plane Geometry, the Construction of Scales, the Use of the Sector, the Marquois Scales, and the Protractor. With 3 Plates and 1000 Exercises and Examination Papers. Post 8vo., 5s.

OPTICS, PHOTOGRAPHY, ETC.

ABNEY.—A TREATISE ON PHOTOGRAPHY. By Sir WILLIAM DE WIVELESLIE ABNEY, K.C.B., F.R.S., Principal Assistant Secretary of the Secondary Department of the Board of Education. With 134 Illustrations. Fcp. 8vo., 5s.

DRUDE.—THE THEORY OF OPTICS. By PAUL DRUDE, Professor of Physics at the University of Giessen. Translated from the German by C. RIBORG MANN and ROBERT A. MILLIKAN, Assistant Professors of Physics at the University of Chicago. With 110 Diagrams. 8vo., 15s. net.

GLAZEBROOK.—PHYSICAL OPTICS. By R. T. GLAZEBROOK, M.A., F.R.S., Principal of University College, Liverpool. With 183 Woodcuts of Apparatus, etc. Fcp. 8vo., 6s.

VANDERPOEL.—COLOR PROBLEMS: a Practical Manual for the Lay Student of Color. By EMILY NOYES VANDERPOEL. With 117 Plates in Color. Square 8vo., 21s. net.

WRIGHT.—OPTICAL PROJECTION: a Treatise on the Use of the Lantern in Exhibition and Scientific Demonstration. By LEWIS WRIGHT, Author of 'Light: a Course of Experimental Optics'. With 232 Illustrations. Crown 8vo., 6s.

TRIGONOMETRY.

CASEY.—A TREATISE ON ELEMENTARY TRIGONO-
METRY. By JOHN CASEY, LL.D., F.R.S., late Fellow of the Royal University of Ireland. With numerous Examples and Questions for Examination. 12mo., 3*s.*

GOODWIN.—PLANE AND SPHERICAL TRIGONOMETRY. By H. B. GOODWIN, M.A. In Three Parts, comprising those portions of the subjects, theoretical and practical, which are required in the Final Examination for Rank of Lieutenant at Greenwich. 8vo., 8*s.* 6*d.*

JONES.—THE BEGINNINGS OF TRIGONOMETRY. By A. CLEMENT JONES, M.A., Ph.D., late Open Scholar and Senior Hulme Exhibitioner of Brasenose College, Oxford; Senior Mathematical Master of Bradford Grammar School. Crown 8vo., 2*s.*

SMITH.—ELEMENTARY TRIGONOMETRY. By J. HAMBLIN SMITH, M.A. Crown 8vo., 4*s.* 6*d.* Key, 7*s.* 6*d.*

SOUND, LIGHT, HEAT, AND THERMODYNAMICS.

DEXTER.—ELEMENTARY PRACTICAL SOUND, LIGHT AND HEAT. By JOSEPH S. DEXTER, B.Sc. (Lond.), Physics Master, Technical Day School, The Polytechnic Institute, Regent Street. With 152 Illustrations. Crown 8vo., 2*s.* 6*d.*

EMTAGE.—LIGHT. By W. T. A. EMTAGE, M.A., Director of Public Instruction, Mauritius. With 232 Illustrations. Crown 8vo., 6*s.*

HELMHOLTZ.—ON THE SENSATIONS OF TONE AS A PHYSIOLOGICAL BASIS FOR THE THEORY OF MUSIC. By HERMANN VON HELMHOLTZ. Royal 8vo., 28*s.*

MAXWELL.—THEORY OF HEAT. By J. CLERK MAXWELL, M.A., F.R.SS., L. and E. With Corrections and Additions by Lord RAYLEIGH. With 38 Illustrations. Fcp. 8vo., 4*s.* 6*d.*

PLANCK.—TREATISE ON THERMODYNAMICS. By Dr. MAX PLANCK, Professor of Theoretical Physics in the University of Berlin. Translated, with the Author's sanction, by ALEXANDER OGG, M.A., B.Sc., Ph.D., late 1851 Exhibition Scholar, Aberdeen University; Assistant Master, Royal Naval Engineering College, Devonport. 8vo., 7*s.* 6*d.* net.

SMITH.—THE STUDY OF HEAT. By J. HAMBLIN SMITH, M.A., of Gonville and Caius College, Cambridge. Crown 8vo., 3*s.*

TYNDALL.—Works by JOHN TYNDALL, D.C.L., F.R.S. See p. 36.

WORMELL.—A CLASS-BOOK OF THERMODYNAMICS. By RICHARD WORMELL, B.Sc., M.A. Fcp. 8vo., 1*s.* 6*d.*

WRIGHT.—Works by MARK R. WRIGHT, M.A.

SOUND, LIGHT, AND HEAT. With 160 Diagrams and Illustrations. Crown 8vo., 2*s.* 6*d.*

ADVANCED HEAT. With 136 Diagrams and numerous Examples and Examination Papers. Crown 8vo., 4*s.* 6*d.*

ARCHITECTURE, BUILDING CONSTRUCTION, ETC.

ADVANCED BUILDING CONSTRUCTION. By the Author of 'Rivingtons' Notes on Building Construction'. With 385 Illustrations. Crown 8vo., 4s. 6d.

BENN.—STYLE IN FURNITURE. By R. Davis Benn. With 102 Plates by W. C. Baldock. 8vo., 21s. net.

BOOKER.—ELEMENTARY PRACTICAL BUILDING CONSTRUCTION. By F. W. Booker. With Illustrations. Crown 8vo., 2s. 6d.

BURRELL.—BUILDING CONSTRUCTION. By Edward J. Burrell, Second Master of the People's Palace Technical School, London. With 303 Working Drawings. Crown 8vo., 2s. 6d.

GWILT.—AN ENCYCLOPÆDIA OF ARCHITECTURE. By Joseph Gwilt, F.S.A. Revised (1888), with Alterations and Considerable Additions by Wyatt Papworth. With 1700 Engravings. 8vo., 21s. net.

HAMLIN.—A TEXT-BOOK OF THE HISTORY OF ARCHITECTURE. By A. D. F. Hamlin, A.M. With 229 Illustrations. Crown 8vo., 7s. 6d.

PARKER and UNWIN.—THE ART OF BUILDING A HOME: A Collection of Lectures and Illustrations. By Barry Parker and Raymond Unwin. With 68 Full-page Plates. 8vo., 10s. 6d. net.

RICHARDS.—BRICKLAYING AND BRICKCUTTING. By H. W. Richards, Examiner in Brickwork and Masonry to the City and Guilds of London Institute, Head of Building Trades Department, Northern Polytechnic Institute, London, N. With over 200 Illustrations. 8vo., 3s. 6d.

ROWE.—THE LIGHTING OF SCHOOLROOMS: a Manual for School Boards, Architects, Superintendents and Teachers. By Stuart H. Rowe, Ph.D. With 32 Illustrations. Crown 8vo., 3s. 6d. net.

SEDDON.—BUILDER'S WORK AND THE BUILDING TRADES. By Col. H. C. Seddon, R.E. With numerous Illustrations. Medium 8vo., 16s.

THOMAS.—THE VENTILATION, HEATING AND MANAGEMENT OF CHURCHES AND PUBLIC BUILDINGS. By J. W. Thomas, F.I.C., F.C.S. With 25 Illustrations. Crown 8vo., 2s. 6d.

VALDER.—BOOK OF TABLES, giving the Cubic Contents of from One to Thirty Pieces Deals, Battens and Scantlings of the Sizes usually imported or used in the Building Trades, together with an Appendix showing a large number of sizes, the Contents of which may be found by referring to the aforesaid Tables. By Thomas Valder. Oblong 4to., 6s. net.

RIVINGTONS' COURSE OF BUILDING CONSTRUCTION.

NOTES ON BUILDING CONSTRUCTION. Medium 8vo.
  Part I. With 695 Illustrations, 10s. 6d. net.
  Part II. With 496 Illustrations, 10s. 6d. net.
  Part III. Materials. With 188 Illustrations, 18s. net.
  Part IV. Calculations for Building Structures. With 551 Illustrations, 13s. net.

STEAM, OIL, AND GAS ENGINES.

BALE.—A HAND-BOOK FOR STEAM USERS; being Rules for Engine Drivers and Boiler Attendants, with Notes on Steam Engine and Boiler Management and Steam Boiler Explosions. By M. POWIS BALE, M.I.M.E., A.M.I.C.E. Fcp. 8vo., 2s. 6d.

CLERK.—THE GAS AND OIL ENGINE. By DUGALD CLERK, Member of the Institution of Civil Engineers, Fellow of the Chemical Society, Member of the Royal Institution, Fellow of the Institute of Patent Agents. With 228 Illustrations. 8vo., 15s.

DIPLOCK.—A NEW SYSTEM OF HEAVY GOODS TRANSPORT ON COMMON ROADS. By BRAMAH JOSEPH DIPLOCK. With 27 Illustrations and Diagrams. Medium 8vo., 6s. 6d. net.

FLETCHER. — ENGLISH AND AMERICAN STEAM CARRIAGES AND TRACTION ENGINES. By WILLIAM FLETCHER, M.Inst.Mech.E. With 250 Illustrations. 8vo., 15s. net.

HOLMES.—THE STEAM ENGINE. By GEORGE C. V. HOLMES, C.B., Chairman of the Board of Works, Dublin. With 212 Illustrations. Fcp. 8vo., 6s.

LOW.—THE DIAGRAM MEASURER. An Instrument for measuring the Areas of Irregular Figures and specially useful for determining the Mean Effective Pressure from Indicator Diagrams from Steam, Gas and other Engines. Designed by D. A. LOW, Professor of Engineering, East London Technical College, London. With Full Instructions for Use. 1s. net.

NEILSON.—THE STEAM TURBINE. By ROBERT M. NEILSON, Associate Member of the Institute of Mechanical Engineers, etc. With 28 Plates and 212 Illustrations in the Text. 8vo., 10s. 6d. net.

NORRIS.—A PRACTICAL TREATISE ON THE 'OTTO' CYCLE GAS ENGINE. By WILLIAM NORRIS, M.I.Mech.E. With 207 Illustrations. 8vo., 10s. 6d.

PARSONS.—STEAM BOILERS: THEIR THEORY AND DESIGN. By H. DE B. PARSONS, B.S., M.E., Consulting Engineer; Member of the American Society of Mechanical Engineers, American Society of Civil Engineers, etc.; Professor of Steam Engineering, Rensselaer Polytechnic Institute. With 170 Illustrations. 8vo., 10s. 6d. net.

RIPPER.—Works by WILLIAM RIPPER, Professor of Engineering in the Technical Department of University College, Sheffield.
  STEAM. With 185 Illustrations. Crown 8vo., 2s. 6d.
  STEAM ENGINE THEORY AND PRACTICE. With 441 Illustrations. 8vo., 9s.

SENNETT AND ORAM.—THE MARINE STEAM ENGINE: A Treatise for Engineering Students, Young Engineers and Officers of the Royal Navy and Mercantile Marine. By the late RICHARD SENNETT, Engineer-in-Chief of the Navy, etc.; and HENRY J. ORAM, Deputy Engineer-in-Chief at the Admiralty, Engineer Rear Admiral in H.M. Fleet, etc. With 414 Diagrams. 8vo., 21s.

STROMEYER.—MARINE BOILER MANAGEMENT AND CONSTRUCTION. Being a Treatise on Boiler Troubles and Repairs, Corrosion, Fuels, and Heat, on the properties of Iron and Steel, on Boiler Mechanics, Workshop Practices, and Boiler Design. By C. E. STROMEYER, Chief Engineer of the Manchester Steam Users' Association, Member of Council of the Institution of Naval Architects, etc. With 452 Diagrams, etc. 8vo., 12s. net.

ELECTRICITY AND MAGNETISM.

ARRHENIUS.—A TEXT-BOOK OF ELECTROCHEMIS-
TRY. By SVANTE ARRHENIUS, Professor at the University of Stockholm.
Translated from the German Edition by JOHN MCCRAE, Ph.D. With 58
Illustrations. 8vo., 9s. 6d. net.

CARUS-WILSON.—ELECTRO-DYNAMICS : the Direct-
Current Motor. By CHARLES ASHLEY CARUS-WILSON, M.A. Cantab. With
71 Diagrams, and a Series of Problems, with Answers. Crown 8vo., 7s. 6d.

CUMMING.—ELECTRICITY TREATED EXPERIMEN-
TALLY. By LINNÆUS CUMMING, M.A. With 242 Illustrations. Cr. 8vo., 4s. 6d.

GORE.—THE ART OF ELECTRO-METALLURGY, including
all known Processes of Electro-Deposition. By G. GORE, LL.D., F.R.S. With
56 Illustrations. Fcp. 8vo., 6s.

HENDERSON.—Works by JOHN HENDERSON, D.Sc., F.R.S.E.
PRACTICAL ELECTRICITY AND MAGNETISM. With
157 Illustrations and Diagrams. Crown 8vo., 7s. 6d.
PRELIMINARY PRACTICAL MAGNETISM AND ELEC-
TRICITY. Crown 8vo., 1s.

HIBBERT. — MAGNETISM AND ITS ELEMENTARY
MEASUREMENT. By W. HIBBERT, F.I.C., A.M.I.E.E. With 55
Diagrams. Crown 8vo., 2s.

JENKIN.—ELECTRICITY AND MAGNETISM. By FLEEMING
JENKIN, F.R.S., M.I.C.E. With 177 Illustrations. Fcp. 8vo., 3s. 6d.

JOUBERT.—ELEMENTARY TREATISE ON ELECTRICITY
AND MAGNETISM. By G. CAREY FOSTER, F.R.S. ; and ALFRED W.
PORTER, B.Sc. Founded on JOUBERT'S 'Traité Élémentaire d'Electricité'.
With 374 Illustrations and Diagrams. 8vo., 10s. 6d. net.

JOYCE.—EXAMPLES IN ELECTRICAL ENGINEERING.
By SAMUEL JOYCE, A.I.E.E. Crown 8vo., 5s.

MERRIFIELD.—MAGNETISM AND DEVIATION OF THE
COMPASS. By JOHN MERRIFIELD, LL.D., F.R.A.S., 18mo., 2s. 6d.

PARR.—PRACTICAL ELECTRICAL TESTING IN PHYSICS
AND ELECTRICAL ENGINEERING. By G. D. ASPINALL PARR, Assoc.
M.I.E.E. With 231 Illustrations. 8vo., 8s. 6d.

POYSER.—Works by A. W. POYSER, M.A.
MAGNETISM AND ELECTRICITY. With 235 Illustrations.
Crown 8vo., 2s. 6d.
ADVANCED ELECTRICITY AND MAGNETISM. With
317 Illustrations. Crown 8vo., 4s. 6d.

RHODES.—AN ELEMENTARY TREATISE ON ALTER-
NATING CURRENTS. By W. G. RHODES, M.Sc. (Vict.), Consulting
Engineer. With 80 Diagrams. 8vo., 7s. 6d. net.

SLINGO AND BROOKER.—Works by W. SLINGO and A.
BROOKER.
ELECTRICAL ENGINEERING FOR ELECTRIC LIGHT
ARTISANS AND STUDENTS. With 383 Illustrations. Crown 8vo., 12s.
PROBLEMS AND SOLUTIONS IN ELEMENTARY
ELECTRICITY AND MAGNETISM. With 98 Illustrations. Cr. 8vo., 2s.

TYNDALL.—Works by JOHN TYNDALL, D.C.L., F.R.S. See p. 36.

TELEGRAPHY AND THE TELEPHONE.

HOPKINS.—TELEPHONE LINES AND THEIR PRO-
PERTIES. By WILLIAM J. HOPKINS, Professor of Physics in the Drexel Institute, Philadelphia. Crown 8vo., 6s.

PREECE AND SIVEWRIGHT.—TELEGRAPHY. By Sir W. H. PREECE, K.C.B., F.R.S., V.P.Inst., C.E., etc., Consulting Engineer and Electrician, Post Office Telegraphs; and Sir J. SIVEWRIGHT, K.C.M.G., General Manager, South African Telegraphs. With 267 Illustrations. Fcp. 8vo., 6s.

ENGINEERING, STRENGTH OF MATERIALS, ETC.

ANDERSON.—THE STRENGTH OF MATERIALS AND STRUCTURES: the Strength of Materials as depending on their Quality and as ascertained by Testing Apparatus. By Sir J. ANDERSON, C.E., LL.D., F.R.S.E. With 66 Illustrations. Fcp. 8vo., 3s. 6d.

BARRY.—RAILWAY APPLIANCES: a Description of Details of Railway Construction subsequent to the completion of the Earthworks and Structures. By Sir JOHN WOLFE BARRY, K.C.B., F.R.S., M.I.C.E. With 218 Illustrations. Fcp. 8vo., 4s. 6d.

DIPLOCK.—A NEW SYSTEM OF HEAVY GOODS TRANS-PORT ON COMMON ROADS. By BRAHAM JOSEPH DIPLOCK. With 27 Illustrations. 8vo., 6s. 6d. net.

GOODMAN.—MECHANICS APPLIED TO ENGINEERING. By JOHN GOODMAN, Wh.Sch., M.I.C.E., M.I.M.E., Professor of Engineering in the University of Leeds. With 714 Illustrations and numerous Examples. Crown 8vo., 9s. net.

LOW.—A POCKET-BOOK FOR MECHANICAL EN-GINEERS. By DAVID ALLAN LOW (Whitworth Scholar), M.I.Mech.E., Professor of Engineering, East London Technical College (People's Palace), London. With over 1000 specially prepared Illustrations. Fcp. 8vo., gilt edges, rounded corners, 7s. 6d.

PARKINSON.—LIGHT RAILWAY CONSTRUCTION. By RICHARD MARION PARKINSON, Assoc.M.Inst.C.E. With 85 Diagrams. 8vo., 10s. 6d. net.

SMITH.—GRAPHICS, or the Art of Calculation by Drawing Lines, applied especially to Mechanical Engineering. By ROBERT H. SMITH, Professor of Engineering, Mason College, Birmingham. Part I. With separate Atlas of 29 Plates containing 97 Diagrams. 8vo., 15s.

STONEY.—THE THEORY OF STRESSES IN GIRDERS AND SIMILAR STRUCTURES; with Practical Observations on the Strength and other Properties of Materials. By BINDON B. STONEY, LL.D., F.R.S., M.I.C.E. With 5 Plates and 143 Illust. in the Text. Royal 8vo., 36s.

UNWIN.—THE TESTING OF MATERIALS OF CONSTRUC-TION. A Text-book for the Engineering Laboratory and a Collection of the Results of Experiment. By W. CAWTHORNE UNWIN, F.R.S., B.Sc. With 5 Plates and 188 Illustrations and Diagrams. 8vo., 16s. net.

WARREN.—ENGINEERING CONSTRUCTION IN IRON, STEEL, AND TIMBER. By WILLIAM HENRY WARREN, Challis Professor of Civil and Mechanical Engineering, University of Sydney. With 13 Folding Plates and 375 Diagrams. Royal 8vo., 16s. net.

WHEELER.—THE SEA COAST: Destruction, Littoral Drift, Protection. By W. H. WHEELER, M.Inst. C.E. With 38 Illustrations and Diagram. Medium 8vo., 10s. 6d. net.

LONGMANS' CIVIL ENGINEERING SERIES.

CIVIL ENGINEERING AS APPLIED TO CONSTRUCTION. By LEVESON FRANCIS VERNON-HARCOURT, M.A., M.Inst.C.E. With 368 Illustrations. Medium 8vo., 14s. net.

CONTENTS.—Materials, Preliminary Works, Foundations and Roads—Railway Bridge and Tunnel Engineering—River and Canal Engineering—Irrigation Works—Dock Works and Maritime Engineering—Sanitary Engineering.

NOTES ON DOCKS AND DOCK CONSTRUCTION. By C. COLSON, C.B., M.Inst.C.E. With 365 Illustrations. Medium 8vo., 21s. net.

CALCULATIONS IN HYDRAULIC ENGINEERING: a Practical Text-Book for the use of Students, Draughtsmen and Engineers. By T. CLAXTON FIDLER, M.Inst.C.E.

Part I. Fluid Pressure and the Calculation of its Effects in Engineering Structures. With numerous Illustns. and Examples. 8vo., 6s. 6d. net.

Part II. Calculations in Hydro-Kinetics. With numerous Illustrations and Examples. 8vo., 7s. 6d. net.

RAILWAY CONSTRUCTION. By W. H. MILLS, M.I.C.E., Engineer-in-Chief of the Great Northern Railway of Ireland. With 516 Illustrations and Diagrams. 8vo., 18s. net.

PRINCIPLES AND PRACTICE OF HARBOUR CONSTRUCTION. By WILLIAM SHIELD, F.R.S.E., M.Inst.C.E. With 97 Illustrations. Medium 8vo., 15s. net.

TIDAL RIVERS: their (1) Hydraulics, (2) Improvement, (3) Navigation. By W. H. WHEELER, M.Inst.C.E. With 75 Illustrations. Medium 8vo., 16s. net.

NAVAL ARCHITECTURE.

ATTWOOD.—Works by EDWARD L. ATTWOOD, M.Inst.N.A., Member of the Royal Corps of Naval Construction.

WAR SHIPS: A Text-book on the Construction, Protection, Stability, Turning, etc., of War Vessels. With numerous Diagrams. Medium 8vo., 10s. 6d. net.

TEXT-BOOK OF THEORETICAL NAVAL ARCHITECTURE: a Manual for Students of Science Classes and Draughtsmen Engaged in Shipbuilders' and Naval Architects' Drawing Offices. With 114 Diagrams. Crown 8vo., 7s. 6d.

HOLMS.—**PRACTICAL SHIPBUILDING:** a Treatise on the Structural Design and Building of Modern Steel Vessels, the work of construction, from the making of the raw material to the equipped vessel, including subsequent up-keep and repairs. By A. CAMPBELL HOLMS, Member of the Institution of Naval Architects, etc. In 2 vols. (Vol. I., Text, medium 8vo.; Vol. II., Diagrams and Illustrations, oblong 4to.) 48s. net.

WATSON.—**NAVAL ARCHITECTURE:** A Manual of Laying-off Iron, Steel and Composite Vessels. By THOMAS H. WATSON, Lecturer on Naval Architecture at the Durham College of Science, Newcastle-upon-Tyne. With numerous Illustrations. Royal 8vo., 15s. net.

WORKSHOP APPLIANCES, ETC.

NORTHCOTT.—**LATHES AND TURNING,** Simple, Mechanical and Ornamental. By W. H. NORTHCOTT. With 338 Illustrations. 8vo., 18s.

SHELLEY.—**WORKSHOP APPLIANCES,** including Descriptions of some of the Gauging and Measuring Instruments, Hand-cutting Tools, Lathes, Drilling, Planeing, and other Machine Tools used by Engineers. By C. P. B. SHELLEY, M.I.C.E. With an additional Chapter on Milling by R. R. LISTER. With 323 Illustrations. Fcp. 8vo., 5s.

Scientific Works published by Longmans, Green, & Co. 19

MACHINE DRAWING AND DESIGN.

LONGMANS' LIST OF APPARATUS FOR USE IN GEOMETRY, ETC.

1. LONGMANS' ENGLISH AND METRIC RULER. Marked on one edge in Inches, Eighths, Tenths and Five-fifths. Marked on the other edge in Centimetres. Price 1*d*. net.
2. LOW'S IMPROVED SET SQUARES. Designs A & B. 45° to 60°.

A 1 45° 4″   ⎧ B 1 45° 4″ each 1/- net.   A 1 60° 4″   ⎧ B 1 60° 4″ each 1/- net.
A 2 45° 6″ or ⎨ B 2 45° 6″ ,, 1/3 ,,   A 2 60° 6″ or ⎨ B 2 60° 6″ ,, 1/3 ,,
A 3 45° 6½″   ⎩ B 3 45° 8½″ ,, 2/- ,,   A 3 60° 8½″   ⎩ B 3 60° 8½″ ,, 2/- ,,

3. LOW'S IMPROVED PROTRACTORS (Celluloid). Protractor No. 2. 3″ radius, marked in degrees, 6*d*. net. Protractor No. 3. 4″ radius, marked in ½-degrees, 9*d*. net.
4. LOW'S ADJUSTABLE PROTRACTOR SET SQUARE. 2*s*. 6*d*. net.
5. LONGMANS' BLACKBOARD ENGLISH AND METRIC RULE. One Metre; marked in decimetres, centimetres, inches, half-inches and quarter-inches. 2*s*. 6*d*.

*** *A Detailed and Illustrated Prospectus will be sent on application.*

LOW.—Works by DAVID ALLAN LOW, Professor of Engineering, East London Technical College (People's Palace).

AN INTRODUCTION TO MACHINE DRAWING AND DESIGN. With 153 Illustrations and Diagrams. Crown 8vo., 2*s*. 6*d*.

THE DIAGRAM MEASURER. An Instrument for measuring the Areas of Irregular Figures and specially useful for determining the Mean Effective Pressure from Indicator Diagrams from Steam, Gas and other Engines. Designed by D. A. Low. With Full Instructions for Use. 1*s*. net.

LOW AND BEVIS.—**A MANUAL OF MACHINE DRAWING AND DESIGN.** By DAVID ALLAN LOW and ALFRED WILLIAM BEVIS M.I.Mech.E. With 700 Illustrations. 8vo., 7*s*. 6*d*.

UNWIN.—**THE ELEMENTS OF MACHINE DESIGN.** By W. CAWTHORNE UNWIN, F.R.S.
Part I. General Principles, Fastenings, and Transmissive Machinery. With 345 Diagrams, etc. Fcp. 8vo., 7*s*. 6*d*.
Part II. Chiefly on Engine Details. With 259 Illustrations. Fcp. 8vo., 6*s*.

MINERALOGY, MINING, METALLURGY, ETC.

BAUERMAN.—Works by HILARY BAUERMAN, F.G.S.

SYSTEMATIC MINERALOGY. With 373 Illustrations. Fcp. 8vo., 6*s*.

DESCRIPTIVE MINERALOGY. With 236 Illustrations. Fcp. 8vo., 6*s*.

BREARLEY AND IBBOTSON. — **THE ANALYSIS OF STEEL-WORKS MATERIALS.** By HARRY BREARLEY and FRED IBBOTSON, B.Sc. (Lond.), Demonstrator of Micrographic Analysis, University College, Sheffield. With 85 Illustrations. 8vo., 14*s*. net.

GORE.—**THE ART OF ELECTRO-METALLURGY.** By G. GORE, LL.D., F.R.S. With 56 Illustrations. Fcp. 8vo., 6*s*.

MINERALOGY, MINING, METALLURGY, ETC.—*Continued.*

HUNTINGTON AND M'MILLAN.—METALS: their Properties and Treatment. By A. K. HUNTINGTON, Professor of Metallurgy in King's College, London, and W. G. M'MILLAN, late Lecturer on Metallurgy in Mason's College, Birmingham. With 122 Illustrations. Fcp. 8vo., 7s. 6d.

LUPTON.—Works by ARNOLD LUPTON, M.I.C.E., F.G.S., etc.

MINING. An Elementary Treatise on the Getting of Minerals. With a Geological Map of the British Isles, and 596 Diagrams and Illustrations. Crown 8vo., 9s. net.

A PRACTICAL TREATISE ON MINE SURVEYING. With 209 Illustrations. 8vo., 12s. net.

RHEAD.—METALLURGY. By E. L. RHEAD, Lecturer on Metallurgy at the Municipal Technical School, Manchester. With 94 Illustrations. Fcp. 8vo., 3s. 6d.

RHEAD AND SEXTON.—ASSAYING AND METALLURGICAL ANALYSIS for the use of Students, Chemists and Assayers. By E. L. RHEAD, Lecturer on Metallurgy, Municipal School of Technology, Manchester; and A. HUMBOLDT SEXTON, F.I.C., F.C.S., Professor of Metallurgy, Glasgow and West of Scotland Technical College. 8vo., 10s. 6d. net.

RUTLEY.—THE STUDY OF ROCKS: an Elementary Text-book of Petrology. By F. RUTLEY, F.G.S. With 6 Plates and 88 other Illustrations. Fcp. 8vo., 4s. 6d.

ASTRONOMY, NAVIGATION, ETC.

ABBOTT.—ELEMENTARY THEORY OF THE TIDES: the Fundamental Theorems Demonstrated without Mathematics and the Influence on the Length of the Day Discussed. By T. K. ABBOTT, B.D., Fellow and Tutor, Trinity College, Dublin. Crown 8vo., 2s.

BALL.—Works by Sir ROBERT S. BALL, LL.D., F.R.S.

ELEMENTS OF ASTRONOMY. With 130 Figures and Diagrams. Fcp. 8vo., 6s. 6d.

A CLASS-BOOK OF ASTRONOMY. With 41 Diagrams. Fcp. 8vo., 1s. 6d.

GILL.—TEXT-BOOK ON NAVIGATION AND NAUTICAL ASTRONOMY. By J. GILL, F.R.A.S. New Edition Augmented and Re-arranged by W. V. MERRIFIELD, B.A. Medium 8vo., 10s. 6d. net.

HERSCHEL.—OUTLINES OF ASTRONOMY. By Sir JOHN F. W. HERSCHEL, Bart., K.H., etc. With 9 Plates and numerous Diagrams. 8vo., 12s.

LAUGHTON.—AN INTRODUCTION TO THE PRACTICAL AND THEORETICAL STUDY OF NAUTICAL SURVEYING. By JOHN KNOX LAUGHTON, M.A., F.R.A.S. With 35 Diagrams. Crown 8vo., 6s.

MARTIN.—NAVIGATION AND NAUTICAL ASTRONOMY. Compiled by Staff Commander W. R. MARTIN, R.N. Royal 8vo., 18s.

ASTRONOMY, NAVIGATION, ETC.—*Continued.*

MERRIFIELD.—A TREATISE ON NAVIGATION. For the Use of Students. By J. MERRIFIELD, LL.D., F.R.A.S., F.M.S. With Charts and Diagrams. Crown 8vo., 5s.

PARKER.—ELEMENTS OF ASTRONOMY. With Numerous Examples and Examination Papers. By GEORGE W. PARKER, M.A., of Trinity College, Dublin. With 84 Diagrams. 8vo., 5s. 6d. net.

WEBB.—CELESTIAL OBJECTS FOR COMMON TELESCOPES. By the Rev. T. W. WEBB, M.A., F.R.A.S. Fifth Edition, Revised and greatly Enlarged by the Rev. T. E. ESPIN, M.A., F.R.A.S. (Two Volumes.) Vol. I., with Portrait and a Reminiscence of the Author, 2 Plates, and numerous Illustrations. Crown 8vo., 6s. Vol. II., with numerous Illustrations. Crown 8vo., 6s. 6d.

WORKS BY RICHARD A. PROCTOR.

THE MOON: Her Motions, Aspect, Scenery, and Physical Condition. With many Plates and Charts, Wood Engravings, and 2 Lunar Photographs. Crown 8vo., 3s. 6d.

OTHER WORLDS THAN OURS: the Plurality of Worlds Studied Under the Light of Recent Scientific Researches. With 14 Illustrations; Map, Charts, etc. Crown 8vo., 3s. 6d.

OUR PLACE AMONG INFINITIES: a Series of Essays contrasting our Little Abode in Space and Time with the Infinities around us. Crown 8vo., 3s. 6d.

MYTHS AND MARVELS OF ASTRONOMY. Crown 8vo., 3s. 6d.

LIGHT SCIENCE FOR LEISURE HOURS: Familiar Essays on Scientific Subjects, Natural Phenomena, etc. Crown 8vo., 3s. 6d.

THE ORBS AROUND US; Essays on the Moon and Planets, Meteors and Comets, the Sun and Coloured Pairs of Suns. Crown 8vo., 3s. 6d.

THE EXPANSE OF HEAVEN: Essays on the Wonders of the Firmament. Crown 8vo., 3s. 6d.

OTHER SUNS THAN OURS: a Series of Essays on Suns—Old, Young, and Dead. With other Science Gleanings. Two Essays on Whist, and Correspondence with Sir John Herschel. With 9 Star-Maps and Diagrams Crown 8vo., 3s. 6d.

HALF-HOURS WITH THE TELESCOPE: a Popular Guide to the Use of the Telescope as a means of Amusement and Instruction. With 7 Plates. Fcp. 8vo., 2s. 6d.

NEW STAR ATLAS FOR THE LIBRARY, the School, and the Observatory, in Twelve Circular Maps (with Two Index-Plates). With an Introduction on the Study of the Stars. Illustrated by 9 Diagrams. Cr. 8vo., 5s.

OVER.

22   Scientific Works published by Longmans, Green, & Co.

WORKS BY RICHARD A. PROCTOR—*Continued.*

THE SOUTHERN SKIES: a Plain and Easy Guide to the Constellations of the Southern Hemisphere. Showing in 12 Maps the position of the principal Star-Groups night after night throughout the year. With an Introduction and a separate Explanation of each Map. True for every Year. 4to., 5s.

HALF-HOURS WITH THE STARS: a Plain and Easy Guide to the Knowledge of the Constellations. Showing in 12 Maps the position of the principal Star-Groups night after night throughout the year. With Introduction and a separate Explanation of each Map. True for every Year. 4to., 3s. net.

LARGER STAR ATLAS FOR OBSERVERS AND STUDENTS. In Twelve Circular Maps, showing 6000 Stars, 1500 Double Stars, Nebulæ, etc. With 2 Index-Plates. Folio, 15s.

THE STARS IN THEIR SEASONS: an Easy Guide to a Knowledge of the Star-Groups. In 12 Large Maps. Imperial 8vo., 5s.

ROUGH WAYS MADE SMOOTH. Familiar Essays on Scientific Subjects. Crown 8vo., 3s. 6d.

PLEASANT WAYS IN SCIENCE. Crown 8vo., 3s. 6d.

NATURE STUDIES. By R. A. PROCTOR, GRANT ALLEN, A. WILSON, T. FOSTER, and E. CLODD. Crown 8vo., 3s. 6d.

LEISURE READINGS. By R. A. PROCTOR, E. CLODD, A. WILSON, T. FOSTER, and A. C. RANYARD. Crown 8vo., 3s. 6d.

PHYSIOGRAPHY AND GEOLOGY.

BIRD.—Works by CHARLES BIRD, B.A.

ELEMENTARY GEOLOGY. With Geological Map of the British Isles, and 247 Illustrations. Crown 8vo., 2s. 6d.

ADVANCED GEOLOGY. A Manual for Students in Advanced Classes and for General Readers. With over 300 Illustrations, a Geological Map of the British Isles (coloured), and a set of Questions for Examination. Crown 8vo., 7s. 6d.

GREEN.—PHYSICAL GEOLOGY FOR STUDENTS AND GENERAL READERS. By A. H. GREEN, M.A., F.G.S. With 236 Illustrations. 8vo., 21s.

MORGAN.—Works by ALEX. MORGAN, M.A., D.Sc., F.R.S.E.

ELEMENTARY PHYSIOGRAPHY. Treated Experimentally. With 4 Maps and 243 Diagrams. Crown 8vo., 2s. 6d.

ADVANCED PHYSIOGRAPHY. With 215 Illustrations. Crown 8vo., 4s. 6d.

READE.—THE EVOLUTION OF EARTH STRUCTURE: with a Theory of Geomorphic Changes. By T. MELLARD READE, F.G.S., F.R.I.B.A., A.M.I.C.E., etc. With 41 Plates. 8vo., 21s. net.

PHYSIOGRAPHY AND GEOLOGY—*Continued.*

THORNTON.—Works by J. THORNTON, M.A.

ELEMENTARY PRACTICAL PHYSIOGRAPHY.
Part I. With 215 Illustrations. Crown 8vo., 2*s.* 6*d.*
Part II. With 98 Illustrations. Crown 8vo., 2*s.* 6*d.*

ELEMENTARY PHYSIOGRAPHY: an Introduction to the Study of Nature. With 13 Maps and 295 Illustrations. With Appendix on Astronomical Instruments and Measurements. Crown 8vo., 2*s.* 6*d.*

ADVANCED PHYSIOGRAPHY. With 11 Maps and 255 Illustrations. Crown 8vo., 4*s.* 6*d.*

NATURAL HISTORY AND GENERAL SCIENCE.

FURNEAUX.—Works by WILLIAM FURNEAUX, F.R.G.S.

THE OUTDOOR WORLD; or, The Young Collector's Handbook. With 18 Plates, 16 of which are coloured, and 549 Illustrations in the Text. Crown 8vo., 6*s.* net.

LIFE IN PONDS AND STREAMS. With 8 Coloured Plates and 331 Illustrations in the Text. Crown 8vo., 6*s.* net.

BUTTERFLIES AND MOTHS (British). With 12 Coloured Plates and 241 Illustrations in the Text. Crown 8vo., 6*s.* net.

THE SEA SHORE. With 8 Coloured Plates and 300 Illustrations in the Text. Crown 8vo., 6*s.* net.

HUDSON.—Works by W. H. HUDSON, C.M.Z.S.

BRITISH BIRDS. With 8 Coloured Plates from Original Drawings by A. THORBURN, and 8 Plates and 100 Figures by C. E. LODGE, and 3 Illustrations from Photographs. Crown 8vo., 6*s.* net.

BIRDS AND MAN. Large Crown 8vo., 6*s.* net.

MILLAIS.—Works by JOHN GUILLE MILLAIS, F.Z.S.

THE NATURAL HISTORY OF THE BRITISH SURFACE-FEEDING DUCKS. With 6 Photogravures and 66 Plates (41 in colours) from Drawings by the AUTHOR, ARCHIBALD THORBURN, and from Photographs. Royal 4to., £6 6*s.* net.

THE MAMMALS OF GREAT BRITAIN AND IRELAND. 3 vols. Quarto (13 in. by 12 in.), cloth, gilt edges.
Volume I. With 18 Photogravures by the AUTHOR; 31 Coloured Plates by the AUTHOR, ARCHIBALD THORBURN and G. E. LODGE; and 63 Uncoloured Plates by the AUTHOR and from Photographs. £6 6*s.* net.
_{*} *Only 1,025 copies printed for England and America.*

NANSEN.—THE NORWEGIAN NORTH POLAR EXPEDITION, 1893-1896: Scientific Results. Edited by FRIDTJOF NANSEN.
Volume I. With 44 Plates and numerous Illustrations in the Text. Demy 4to., 40*s.* net.
Volume II. With 2 Charts and 17 Plates. Demy 4to., 30*s.* net.
Volume III. With 33 Plates. Demy 4to., 32*s.* net.
Volume IV. With 33 Plates. Demy 4to., 21*s.* net.

STANLEY.—A FAMILIAR HISTORY OF BIRDS. By E. STANLEY, D.D., formerly Bishop of Norwich. With 160 Illustrations. Crown 8vo., 3*s.* 6*d.*

MANUFACTURES, TECHNOLOGY, ETC.

ASHLEY.—BRITISH INDUSTRIES: A Series of General Reviews for Business Men and Students. Edited by W. J. ASHLEY, M.A., Professor of Commerce in the University of Birmingham. Crown 8vo., 5*s*. 6*d*. net.

BELL.—JACQUARD WEAVING AND DESIGNING. By F. T. BELL. With 199 Diagrams. 8vo., 12*s*. net.

BROWN.—LABORATORY STUDIES FOR BREWING STUDENTS: a Systematic Course of Practical Work in the Scientific Principles underlying the Processes of Malting and Brewing. By ADRIAN J. BROWN, M.Sc., Director of the School of Brewing, and Professor of the Biology and Chemistry of Fermentation in the University of Birmingham, etc. With 36 Illustrations. 8vo., 7*s*. 6*d*. net.

CROSS AND BEVAN.—Works by C. F. CROSS and E. J. BEVAN.

CELLULOSE: an Outline of the Chemistry of the Structural Elements of Plants. With reference to their Natural History and Industrial Uses. (C. F. CROSS, E. J. BEVAN and C. BEADLE.) With 14 Plates. Crown 8vo., 12*s*. net.

RESEARCHES ON CELLULOSE, 1895-1900. Crown 8vo., 6*s*. net.

JACKSON.—A TEXT-BOOK ON CERAMIC CALCULATIONS: with Examples. By W. JACKSON, A.R.C.S., Lecturer in Pottery and Porcelain Manufacture for the Staffordshire Education Committee and the Hanley Education Committee. Crown 8vo., 3*s*. 6*d*. net.

MORRIS AND WILKINSON.—THE ELEMENTS OF COTTON SPINNING. By JOHN MORRIS and F. WILKINSON. With a Preface by Sir B. A. DOBSON, C.E., M.I.M.E. With 169 Diagrams and Illustrations. Crown 8vo., 7*s*. 6*d*. net.

RICHARDS.—BRICKLAYING AND BRICK-CUTTING. By H. W. RICHARDS, Examiner in Brickwork and Masonry to the City and Guilds of London Institute, Head of Building Trades Department, Northern Polytechnic Institute, London, N. With over 200 Illustrations. Med. 8vo., 3*s*. 6*d*.

TAYLOR.—COTTON WEAVING AND DESIGNING. By JOHN T. TAYLOR. With 373 Diagrams. Crown 8vo., 7*s*. 6*d*. net.

WATTS.—AN INTRODUCTORY MANUAL FOR SUGAR GROWERS. By FRANCIS WATTS, F.C.S., F.I.C, With 20 Illustrations. Crown 8vo., 6*s*.

HEALTH AND HYGIENE.

ASHBY.—HEALTH IN THE NURSERY. By HENRY ASHBY, M.D., F.R.C.P. With 25 Illustrations. Crown 8vo., 3s. net.

BUCKTON.—HEALTH IN THE HOUSE. By Mrs. C. M. BUCKTON. With 41 Woodcuts and Diagrams. Crown 8vo., 2s.

CORFIELD.—THE LAWS OF HEALTH. By W. H. CORFIELD, M.A., M.D. Fcp. 8vo., 1s. 6d.

FURNEAUX.—ELEMENTARY PRACTICAL HYGIENE.— Section I. By WILLIAM S. FURNEAUX. With 146 Illustrations. Cr. 8vo., 2s. 6d.

NOTTER AND FIRTH.—Works by J. L. NOTTER, M.A., M.D., and R. H. FIRTH, F.R.C.S.

 HYGIENE. With 95 Illustrations. Crown 8vo., 3s. 6d.

 PRACTICAL DOMESTIC HYGIENE. With 83 Illustrations. Crown 8vo., 2s. 6d.

POORE.—Works by GEORGE VIVIAN POORE, M.D.

 ESSAYS ON RURAL HYGIENE. With 12 Illustrations. Crown 8vo., 6s. 6d.

 THE DWELLING-HOUSE. With 36 Illustrations. Crown 8vo., 3s. 6d.

 COLONIAL AND CAMP SANITATION. With 11 Illustrations. Crown 8vo., 2s. net.

 THE EARTH IN RELATION TO THE PRESERVATION AND DESTRUCTION OF CONTAGIA: being the Milroy Lectures delivered at the Royal College of Physicians in 1899, together with other Papers on Sanitation. With 13 Illustrations. Crown 8vo., 5s.

WILSON.—A MANUAL OF HEALTH-SCIENCE. By ANDREW WILSON, F.R.S.E., F.L.S., etc. With 74 Illustrations. Crown 8vo., 2s. 6d.

MEDICINE AND SURGERY.

(And see *PHYSIOLOGY*, etc., page 32.)

ASHBY AND WRIGHT.—THE DISEASES OF CHILDREN, MEDICAL AND SURGICAL. By HENRY ASHBY, M.D., Lond., F.R.C.P., Physician to the General Hospital for Sick Children, Manchester; and G. A. WRIGHT, B.A., M.B. Oxon., F.R.C.S., Eng., Assistant-Surgeon to the Manchester Royal Infirmary, and Surgeon to the Children's Hospital. Enlarged and Improved Edition. With 192 Illustrations. 8vo., 25s.

BAIN.—A TEXT-BOOK OF MEDICAL PRACTICE. By Various Contributors. Edited by WILLIAM BAIN, M.D., M.R.C.P. With 68 Anatomical Illustrations. 8vo., 25s. net.

BENNETT.—Works by SIR WILLIAM BENNETT, K.C.V.O., F.R.C.S., Surgeon to St. George's Hospital; Member of the Board of Examiners, Royal College of Surgeons of England.

CLINICAL LECTURES ON VARICOSE VEINS OF THE LOWER EXTREMITIES. With 3 Plates. 8vo., 6s.

ON VARICOCELE; A PRACTICAL TREATISE. With 4 Tables and a Diagram. 8vo., 5s.

CLINICAL LECTURES ON ABDOMINAL HERNIA: chiefly in relation to Treatment, including the Radical Cure. With 12 Diagrams in the Text. 8vo., 8s. 6d.

ON VARIX, ITS CAUSES AND TREATMENT, WITH ESPECIAL REFERENCE TO THROMBOSIS. 8vo., 3s. 6d.

THE PRESENT POSITION OF THE TREATMENT OF SIMPLE FRACTURES OF THE LIMBS. 8vo., 2s. 6d.

LECTURES ON THE USE OF MASSAGE AND EARLY PASSIVE MOVEMENTS IN RECENT FRACTURES AND OTHER COMMON SURGICAL INJURIES: The Treatment of Internal Derangements of the Knee Joint and Management of Stiff Joints. With 17 Illustrations. 8vo., 6s.

CABOT.—A GUIDE TO THE CLINICAL EXAMINATION OF THE BLOOD FOR DIAGNOSTIC PURPOSES. By RICHARD C. CABOT, M.D., Physician to Out-patients, Massachusetts General Hospital. With 3 Coloured Plates and 28 Illustrations in the Text. 8vo., 16s.

CARR, PICK, DORAN, AND DUNCAN.—THE PRACTITIONER'S GUIDE. By J. WALTER CARR, M.D. (Lond.), F.R.C.P.; T. PICKERING PICK, F.R.C.S.; ALBAN H. G. DORAN, F.R.C.S.; ANDREW DUNCAN, M.D., B.Sc. (Lond.), F.R.C.S., M.R.C.P. 8vo., 21s. net.

COATS.—A MANUAL OF PATHOLOGY. By JOSEPH COATS, M.D., late Professor of Pathology in the University of Glasgow. Fifth Edition. Revised throughout and Edited by LEWIS R. SUTHERLAND, M.D., Professor of Pathology, University of St. Andrews. With 729 Illustrations and 2 Coloured Plates. 8vo., 28s. net.

Scientific Works *published by Longmans, Green, & Co.* 27

MEDICINE AND SURGERY—*Continued.*

CHEYNE AND BURGHARD.—A MANUAL OF SURGICAL TREATMENT. By W. WATSON CHEYNE, C.B., M.B., F.R.C.S., F.R.S., Professor of Clinical Surgery in King's College, London, Surgeon to King's College Hospital, etc.; and F. F. BURGHARD, M.D. and M.S. (Lond.), F.R.C.S., Teacher of Practical Surgery in King's College, London, Surgeon to King's College Hospital (Lond.), etc.

Part I. The Treatment of General Surgical Diseases, including Inflammation, Suppuration, Ulceration, Gangrene, Wounds and their Complications, Infective Diseases and Tumours; the Administration of Anæsthetics. With 66 Illustrations. Royal 8vo., 10s. 6d.

Part II. The Treatment of the Surgical Affections of the Tissues, including the Skin and Subcutaneous Tissues, the Nails, the Lymphatic Vessels and Glands, the Fasciæ, Bursæ, Muscles, Tendons and Tendonsheaths, Nerves, Arteries and Veins. Deformities. With 141 Illustrations. Royal 8vo., 14s.

Part III. The Treatment of the Surgical Affections of the Bones. Amputations. With 100 Illustrations. Royal 8vo., 12s.

Part IV. The Treatment of the Surgical Affections of the Joints (including Excisions) and the Spine. With 138 Illustrations. Royal 8vo., 14s.

Part V. The Treatment of the Surgical Affections of the Head, Face, Jaws, Lips, Larnyx and Trachea; and the Intrinsic Diseases of the Nose, Ear and Larynx, by H. LAMBERT LACK, M.D. (Lond.), F.R.C.S., Surgeon to the Hospital for Diseases of the Throat, Golden Square, and to the Throat and Ear Department, The Children's Hospital, Paddington Green. With 145 Illustrations. Royal 8vo., 18s.

Part VI. Section I. The Treatment of the Surgical Affections of the Tongue and Floor of the Mouth, the Pharynx, Neck, Œsophagus, Stomach and Intestines. With 124 Illustrations. Royal 8vo., 18s.

Section II. The Treatment of the Surgical Affections of the Rectum, Liver, Spleen, Pancreas, Throat, Breast and Genito-urinary Organs. With 113 Illustrations. Royal 8vo., 21s.

COOKE.—Works by THOMAS COOKE, F.R.C.S. Eng., B.A., B.Sc., M.D., Paris.

TABLETS OF ANATOMY. Being a Synopsis of Demonstrations given in the Westminster Hospital Medical School. Eleventh Edition in Three Parts, thoroughly brought up to date, and with over 700 Illustrations from all the best Sources, British and Foreign. Post 4to.

Part I. The Bones. 7s. 6d. net.

Part II. Limbs, Abdomen, Pelvis. 10s. 6d. net.

Part III. Head and Neck, Thorax, Brain. 10s. 6d. net.

APHORISMS IN APPLIED ANATOMY AND OPERATIVE SURGERY. Including 100 Typical *vivâ voce* Questions on Surface Marking, etc. Crown 8vo., 3s. 6d.

DAKIN.—A HANDBOOK OF MIDWIFERY. By WILLIAM RADFORD DAKIN, M.D., F.R.C.P., Obstetric Physician and Lecturer on Midwifery at St. George's Hospital, etc. With 394 Illustrations. Large crown 8vo., 18s.

MEDICINE AND SURGERY—*Continued.*

DICKINSON.—Works by W. HOWSHIP DICKINSON, M.D. Cantab., F.R.C.P.

ON RENAL AND URINARY AFFECTIONS. With 12 Plates and 122 Woodcuts. Three Parts. 8vo., £3 4s. 6d.

THE TONGUE AS AN INDICATION OF DISEASE: being the Lumleian Lectures delivered March, 1888. 8vo., 7s. 6d.

OCCASIONAL PAPERS ON MEDICAL SUBJECTS, 1855-1896. 8vo., 12s.

ERICHSEN.—THE SCIENCE AND ART OF SURGERY; a Treatise on Surgical Injuries, Diseases, and Operations. By Sir JOHN ERIC ERICHSEN, Bart., F.R.S., LL.D. Edin., Hon. M.Ch. and F.R.C.S. Ireland. Illustrated by nearly 1000 Engravings on Wood. 2 vols. Royal 8vo., 48s.

FOWLER AND GODLEE.—THE DISEASES OF THE LUNGS. By JAMES KINGSTON FOWLER, M.A., M.D., F.R.C.P., Physician to the Middlesex Hospital and to the Hospital for Consumption and Diseases of the Chest, Brompton, etc.; and RICKMAN JOHN GODLEE, Honorary Surgeon in Ordinary to His Majesty, M.S., F.R.C.S., Fellow and Professor of Clinical Surgery, University College, London, etc. With 160 Illustrations. 8vo., 25s.

GARROD.—Works by SIR ALFRED BARING GARROD, M.D., F.R.S., etc.

A TREATISE ON GOUT AND RHEUMATIC GOUT (RHEUMATOID ARTHRITIS). With 6 Plates, comprising 21 Figures (14 Coloured), and 27 Illustrations engraved on Wood. 8vo., 21s.

THE ESSENTIALS OF MATERIA MEDICA AND THERAPEUTICS. Crown 8vo., 12s. 6d.

GOADBY.—THE MYCOLOGY OF THE MOUTH : a Text-Book of Oral Bacteria. By KENNETH W. GOADBY, L.D.S. (Eng.), D.P.H. (Camb.), L.R.C.P., M.R.C.S., Bacteriologist and Lecturer on Bacteriology, National Dental Hospital, etc. With 82 Illustrations. 8vo., 8s. 6d. net.

GOODSALL AND MILES.—DISEASES OF THE ANUS AND RECTUM. By D. H. GOODSALL, F.R.C.S., Senior Surgeon, Metropolitan Hospital; Senior Surgeon, St. Mark's Hospital; and W. ERNEST MILES, F.R.C.S., Assistant Surgeon to the Cancer Hospital, Surgeon (out-patients), to the Gordon Hospital, etc. (In Two Parts.) Part I. With 91 Illustrations. 8vo., 7s. 6d. net.

GRAY.—ANATOMY, DESCRIPTIVE AND SURGICAL. By HENRY GRAY, F.R.S., late Lecturer on Anatomy at St. George's Hospital Medical School. The Fifteenth Edition Enlarged, edited by T. PICKERING PICK, F.R.C.S., Consulting Surgeon to St. George's Hospital, etc., and by ROBERT HOWDEN, M.A., M.B., C.M., Professor of Anatomy in the University of Durham, etc. With 772 Illustrations, a large proportion of which are Coloured, the Arteries being coloured red, the Veins blue, and the Nerves yellow. The attachments of the muscles to the bones, in the section on Osteology, are also shown in coloured outline. Royal 8vo., 32s. net.

MEDICINE AND SURGERY—*Continued.*

HALLIBURTON.—Works by W. D. HALLIBURTON, M.D., F.R.S., Professor of Physiology in King's College, London.

A TEXT-BOOK OF CHEMICAL PHYSIOLOGY AND PATHOLOGY. With 104 Illustrations. 8vo., 28s.

ESSENTIALS OF CHEMICAL PHYSIOLOGY. With 83 Illustrations. 8vo., 4s. 6d. net.

HILLIER.—THE PREVENTION OF CONSUMPTION. By ALFRED HILLIER, B.A., M.D., Secretary to the National Association for the Prevention of Consumption (England), Visiting Physician to the London Open-Air Sanatorium. Revised by Professor R. KOCH. With 14 Illustrations. Crown 8vo., 5s. net.

LANG.—THE METHODICAL EXAMINATION OF THE EYE. Being Part I. of a Guide to the Practice of Ophthalmology for Students and Practitioners. By WILLIAM LANG, F.R.C.S. Eng., Surgeon to the Royal London Ophthalmic Hospital, Moorfields, etc. With 15 Illustrations. Crown 8vo., 3s. 6d.

LUFF.—TEXT-BOOK OF FORENSIC MEDICINE AND TOXICOLOGY. By ARTHUR P. LUFF, M.D., B.Sc. (Lond.), Physician in Charge of Out-Patients and Lecturer on Medical Jurisprudence and Toxicology in St. Mary's Hospital. With 13 full-page Plates (1 in colours) and 33 Illustrations in the Text. 2 vols. Crown 8vo., 24s.

PAGET.—Edited by STEPHEN PAGET.

SELECTED ESSAYS AND ADDRESSES. By Sir JAMES PAGET. 8vo., 12s. 6d. net

MEMOIRS AND LETTERS OF SIR JAMES PAGET, BART., F.R.S., D.C.L., late Sergeant-Surgeon to Her Majesty Queen Victoria. With Portrait. 8vo., 6s. net.

PHILLIPS.—MATERIA MEDICA, PHARMACOLOGY AND THERAPEUTICS: Inorganic Substances. By CHARLES D. F. PHILLIPS, M.D., LL.D., F.R.S. Edin., late Lecturer on Materia Medica and Therapeutics at the Westminster Hospital Medical School; late Examiner in the University of Edinburgh. 8vo., 21s.

POOLE.—COOKERY FOR THE DIABETIC. By W. H. and Mrs. POOLE. With Preface by Dr. PAVY. Fcap. 8vo., 2s. 6d.

PROBYN-WILLIAMS.—A PRACTICAL GUIDE TO THE ADMINISTRATION OF ANÆSTHETICS. By R. J. PROBYN-WILLIAMS, M.D., Anæsthetist and Instructor in Anæsthetics at the London Hospital; Lecturer in Anæsthetics at the London Hospital Medical College, etc. With 34 Illustrations. Crown 8vo., 4s. 6d. net.

QUAIN.—QUAIN'S (SIR RICHARD) DICTIONARY OF MEDICINE. By Various Writers. Third Edition. Edited by H. MONTAGUE MURRAY, M.D., F.R.C.P., Joint Lecturer on Medicine, Charing Cross Medical School, and Physician, Charing Cross Hospital; assisted by JOHN HAROLD, M.B., B.Ch., B.A.O., Physician to St. John's and St. Elizabeth's Hospital; and W. CECIL BOSANQUET, M.A., M.D., M.R.C.P., Assistant Physician to Charing Cross Hospital, etc. With 21 Plates (14 in Colour) and numerous Illustrations in the Text. 8vo., 21s. net, buckram; or 30s. net, half-morocco.

MEDICINE AND SURGERY—*Continued.*

QUAIN.—QUAIN'S (JONES) ELEMENTS OF ANATOMY. The Tenth Edition. Edited by EDWARD ALBERT SCHÄFER, F.R.S., Professor of Physiology in the University of Edinburgh; and GEORGE DANCER THANE, Professor of Anatomy in University College, London.

VOL. I., PART I. EMBRYOLOGY. By E. A. SCHÄFER, F.R.S. With 200 Illustrations. Royal 8vo., 9s.

VOL. I., PART II. GENERAL ANATOMY OR HISTOLOGY. By E. A. SCHÄFER, F.R.S. With 491 Illustrations. Royal 8vo., 12s. 6d.

VOL. II., PART I. OSTEOLOGY—ARTHROLOGY. By G. D. THANE. With 224 Illus. Royal 8vo., 11s.

VOL. II., PART II. MYOLOGY—ANGEIOLOGY. By G. D. THANE. With 199 Illustrations. Royal 8vo., 16s.

VOL. III., PART I. THE SPINAL CORD AND BRAIN. By E. A. SCHÄFER, F.R.S. With 139 Illustrations. Royal 8vo., 12s. 6d.

VOL. III., PART II. THE NERVES. By G. D. THANE. With 102 Illustrations. Royal 8vo., 9s.

VOL. III., PART III. THE ORGANS OF THE SENSES. By E. A. SCHÄFER, F.R.S. With 178 Illustrations. Royal 8vo., 9s.

VOL. III., PART IV. SPLANCHNOLOGY. By E. A. SCHÄFER, F.R.S, and JOHNSON SYMINGTON, M.D. With 337 Illustrations. Royal 8vo., 16s.

APPENDIX. SUPERFICIAL AND SURGICAL ANATOMY. By Professor G. D. THANE and Professor R. J. GODLEE, M.S. With 29 Illustrations. Royal 8vo., 6s. 6d.

SCHÄFER.—Works by E. A. SCHÄFER, F.R.S., Professor of Physiology in the University of Edinburgh.

THE ESSENTIALS OF HISTOLOGY. Descriptive and Practical. For the Use of Students. With 463 Illustrations. 8vo., 9s. net.

DIRECTIONS FOR CLASS WORK IN PRACTICAL PHYSIOLOGY: Elementary Physiology of Muscle and Nerve and of the Vascular and Nervous Systems. With 48 Diagrams and 24 pages of plain paper at end for Notes. 8vo., 3s. net.

SMALE AND COLYER.—DISEASES AND INJURIES OF THE TEETH, including Pathology and Treatment. By MORTON SMALE, M.R.C.S., L.S.A., L.D.S., Dental Surgeon to St. Mary's Hospital, Dean of the School, Dental Hospital of London, etc.; and J. F. COLYER, L.R.C.P., M.R.C.S., L.D.S., Dental Surgeon to Charing Cross Hospital and to the Dental Hospital of London. Second Edition Revised and Enlarged by J. F. COLYER. With 640 Illustrations. Large crown 8vo., 21s. net.

SMITH (H. F.).—THE HANDBOOK FOR MIDWIVES. By HENRY FLY SMITH, B.A., M.B. Oxon., M.R.C.S. 41 Woodcuts. Cr. 8vo., 5s.

MEDICINE AND SURGERY—*Continued.*

STEVENSON.—WOUNDS IN WAR: the Mechanism of their Production and their Treatment. By Surgeon-General W. F. STEVENSON, C.B. (Army Medical Staff), B.A., M.B., M.Ch. Dublin University, Professor of Military Surgery, Royal Army Medical College, London. With 127 Illustrations. 8vo., 15s. net.

TAPPEINER. — INTRODUCTION TO CHEMICAL METHODS OF CLINICAL DIAGNOSIS. By Dr. H. TAPPEINER, Professor of Pharmacology and Principal of the Pharmacological Institute of the University of Munich. Translated by EDMOND J. McWEENEY, M.A., M.D. (Royal Univ. of Ireland), L.R.C.P.I., etc. Crown 8vo., 3s. 6d.

WALLER.—Works by AUGUSTUS D. WALLER, M.D., Lecturer on Physiology at St. Mary's Hospital Medical School, London; late External Examiner at the Victorian University.

AN INTRODUCTION TO HUMAN PHYSIOLOGY. Third Edition, Revised. With 314 Illustrations. 8vo., 18s.

LECTURES ON PHYSIOLOGY. First Series. On Animal Electricity. 8vo., 5s. net.

VETERINARY MEDICINE, ETC.

FITZWYGRAM.—HORSES AND STABLES. By Lieut.-General Sir F. FITZWYGRAM, Bart. With 56 pages of Illustrations. 8vo., 3s. net.

STEEL.—Works by JOHN HENRY STEEL, F.R.C.V.S., F.Z.S., A.V.D., late Professor of Veterinary Science and Principal of Bombay Veterinary College.

A TREATISE ON THE DISEASES OF THE DOG; being a Manual of Canine Pathology. Especially adapted for the use of Veterinary Practitioners and Students. With 88 Illustrations. 8vo., 10s. 6d.

A TREATISE ON THE DISEASES OF THE OX; being a Manual of Bovine Pathology. Especially adapted for the use of Veterinary Practitioners and Students. With 2 Plates and 117 Woodcuts. 8vo., 15s.

A TREATISE ON THE DISEASES OF THE SHEEP; being a Manual of Ovine Pathology for the use of Veterinary Practitioners and Students. With Coloured Plate and 99 Woodcuts. 8vo., 12s.

YOUATT.—Works by WILLIAM YOUATT.

THE HORSE. With 52 Wood Engravings. 8vo., 7s. 6d.

THE DOG. With 33 Wood Engravings. 8vo., 6s.

PHYSIOLOGY, BIOLOGY, ZOOLOGY, ETC.
(And see MEDICINE AND SURGERY, page 26.)

ASHBY.—NOTES ON PHYSIOLOGY FOR THE USE OF STUDENTS PREPARING FOR EXAMINATION. By HENRY ASHBY, M.D. Lond., F.R.C.P., Physician to the General Hospital for Sick Children, Manchester. With 148 Illustrations. 18mo., 5s.

BARNETT.—THE MAKING OF THE BODY: a Children's Book on Anatomy and Physiology. By Mrs. S. A. BARNETT. With 113 Illustrations. Crown 8vo., 1s. 9d.

BEDDARD.—ELEMENTARY PRACTICAL ZOOLOGY. By FRANK E. BEDDARD, M.A. Oxon. With 93 Illustrations. Crown 8vo., 2s. 6d.

BIDGOOD.—A COURSE OF PRACTICAL ELEMENTARY BIOLOGY. By JOHN BIDGOOD, B.Sc., F.L.S. With 226 Illustrations. Crown 8vo., 4s. 6d.

BOSE.—RESPONSE IN THE LIVING AND NON-LIVING. By JAGADIS CHUNDER BOSE, M.A. (Cantab.), D.Sc. (Lond.), Professor, Presidency College, Calcutta. With 117 Illustrations. 8vo., 10s. 6d.

BRODIE. — THE ESSENTIALS OF EXPERIMENTAL PHYSIOLOGY. For the Use of Students. By T. G. BRODIE, M.D., Lecturer on Physiology, St. Thomas's Hospital Medical School. With 2 Plates and 177 Illustrations in the Text. 8vo., 6s. 6d.

CHAPMAN.—THE FORAMINIFERA: An Introduction to the Study of the Protozoa. By FREDERICK CHAPMAN, A.L.S., F.R.M.S. With 14 Plates and 42 Illustrations in the Text. 8vo., 9s. net.

FURNEAUX.—HUMAN PHYSIOLOGY. By W. FURNEAUX, F.R.G.S. With 218 Illustrations. Crown 8vo., 2s. 6d.

HUDSON AND GOSSE.—THE ROTIFERA, or 'WHEEL-ANIMACULES'. By C. T. HUDSON, LL.D., and P. H. GOSSE, F.R.S. With 30 Coloured and 4 Uncoloured Plates. In 6 Parts. 4to., 10s. 6d. each. Supplement 12s. 6d. Complete in 2 vols., with Supplement, 4to., £4 4s.

MACALISTER.—Works by ALEXANDER MACALISTER, M.D.

AN INTRODUCTION TO THE SYSTEMATIC ZOOLOGY AND MORPHOLOGY OF VERTEBRATE ANIMALS. With 41 Diagrams. 8vo., 10s. 6d

ZOOLOGY OF THE INVERTEBRATE ANIMALS. With 77 Diagrams. Fcp. 8vo., 1s. 6d.

ZOOLOGY OF THE VERTEBRATE ANIMALS. With 59 Diagrams. Fcp. 8vo., 1s. 6d.

MACDOUGAL. — Works by DANIEL TREMBLY MACDOUGAL, Ph.D., Director of the Laboratories of the New York Botanical Garden.

PRACTICAL TEXT-BOOK OF PLANT PHYSIOLOGY. With 159 Illustrations. 8vo., 7s. 6d. net.

ELEMENTARY PLANT PHYSIOLOGY. With 108 Illustrations. Crown 8vo., 3s.

Scientific Works published by Longmans, Green, & Co. 33

PHYSIOLOGY, BIOLOGY, ZOOLOGY, ETC.—*Continued.*

MORGAN.—ANIMAL BIOLOGY : an Elementary Text-Book. By C. LLOYD MORGAN, F.R.S., Principal of University College, Bristol. With 103 Illustrations. Crown 8vo., 8s. 6d.

SCHÄFER.—DIRECTIONS FOR CLASS WORK IN PRACTICAL PHYSIOLOGY : Elementary Physiology of Muscle and Nerve and of the Vascular and Nervous Systems. By E. A. SCHÄFER, LL.D., F.R.S., Professor of Physiology in the University of Edinburgh. With 48 Diagrams. 8vo., 3s. net.

THORNTON.—Works by JOHN THORNTON, M.A.

HUMAN PHYSIOLOGY. With 284 Illustrations, some Coloured. Crown 8vo., 6s.

ELEMENTARY BIOLOGY, Descriptive and Experimental. With numerous Illustrations. Crown 8vo., 3s. 6d.

ELEMENTARY PRACTICAL PHYSIOLOGY. With 178 Illustrations (6 of which are Coloured). Crown 8vo., 3s. 6d.

BACTERIOLOGY.

CURTIS.—THE ESSENTIALS OF PRACTICAL BACTERIOLOGY : An Elementary Laboratory Book for Students and Practitioners. By H. J. CURTIS, B.S. and M.D. (Lond.), F.R.C.S. With 133 Illustrations. 8vo., 9s.

DHINGRA.—ELEMENTARY BACTERIOLOGY. By M. L. DHINGRA, M.D., C.M. Edin., Diplomate in State Medicine, University of Cambridge, etc. With Coloured Frontispiece and 26 Illustrations in the Text. Crown 8vo., 3s. net.

FRANKLAND.—MICRO-ORGANISMS IN WATER. Together with an Account of the Bacteriological Methods involved in their Investigation. Specially designed for the use of those connected with the Sanitary Aspects of Water-Supply. By PERCY FRANKLAND, Ph.D., B.Sc. (Lond.), F.R.S., and Mrs. PERCY FRANKLAND. With 2 Plates and Numerous Diagrams. 8vo., 16s. net.

FRANKLAND.—BACTERIA IN DAILY LIFE. By Mrs. PERCY FRANKLAND, F.R.M.S. Crown 8vo., 5s. net.

GOADBY.—THE MYCOLOGY OF THE MOUTH : A Text-Book of Oral Bacteria. By KENNETH W. GOADBY, L.D.S. Eng., etc. ; Bacteriologist and Lecturer on Bacteriology, National Dental Hospital, etc. With 82 Illustrations. 8vo., 8s. 6d. net.

KLÖCKER.—FERMENTATION ORGANISMS : a Laboratory Handbook. By ALB. KLÖCKER, Translated by G. E. ALLAN, B.Sc., Lecturer in the University of Birmingham, and J. H. MILLAR, F.I.C., formerly Lecturer in the British School of Malting and Brewing, and Revised by the Author. With 146 Illustrations. 8vo., 12s. net.

PLIMMER. — THE CHEMICAL CHANGES AND PRODUCTS RESULTING FROM FERMENTATION. By R. H. ADERS PLIMMER, D.Sc., Lond., Grocers' Research Student, Jenner Institute of Preventive Medicine. 8vo., 6s. net.

BOTANY.

AITKEN.—ELEMENTARY TEXT-BOOK OF BOTANY.
By EDITH AITKEN, late Scholar of Girton College. With 400 Diagrams. Crown 8vo., 4s. 6d.

BENNETT AND MURRAY.—HANDBOOK OF CRYPTO-
GAMIC BOTANY. By ALFRED W. BENNETT, M.A., B.Sc., F.L.S., Lecturer on Botany at St. Thomas's Hospital; and GEORGE MURRAY, F.L.S., Keeper of Botany, British Museum. With 378 Illustrations. 8vo., 16s.

CROSS AND BEVAN.—Works by C. F. CROSS, E. J. BEVAN and C. BEADLE.

CELLULOSE: an Outline of the Chemistry of the Structural Elements of Plants. With Reference to their Natural History and Industrial Uses. With 14 Plates. Crown 8vo., 12s. net.

RESEARCHES ON CELLULOSE, 1895-1900. Cr. 8vo., 6s. net.

EDMONDS.—Works by HENRY EDMONDS, B.Sc., London.

ELEMENTARY BOTANY With 341 Illustrations. Cr. 8vo., 2s. 6d.

BOTANY FOR BEGINNERS. With 85 Illustrations. Fcp. 8vo., 1s. 6d.

FARMER.—A PRACTICAL INTRODUCTION TO THE STUDY OF BOTANY: Flowering Plants. By J. BRETLAND FARMER, D.Sc., F.R.S., M.A., Professor of Botany in the Royal College of Science, London. With 121 Illustrations. Crown 8vo., 2s. 6d.

HENSLOW.—SOUTH AFRICAN FLOWERING PLANTS:
For the Use of Beginners, Students and Teachers. By the Rev. Professor G. HENSLOW, M.A., F.L.S., F.G.S., etc. With 112 Illustrations. Cr. 8vo., 5s.

HOFFMANN.—ALPINE FLORA: for Tourists and Amateur
Botanists. By Dr. JULIUS HOFFMANN. Translated by E. S. BARTON (Mrs. A. GEPP). With 40 Plates, containing 250 Coloured Figures, from Water-Colour Sketches by HERMANN FRIESE. With Text descriptive of the most widely distributed and attractive of Alpine Plants. 8vo., 7s. 6d. net.

KITCHENER.—A YEAR'S BOTANY. Adapted to Home and
School Use. By FRANCES A. KITCHENER. With 195 Illustrations. Cr. 8vo., 5s.

LINDLEY AND MOORE.—THE TREASURY OF BOTANY.
Edited by J. LINDLEY, M.D., F.R.S., and T. MOORE, F.L.S. With 20 Steel Plates and numerous Woodcuts. Two parts. Fcp. 8vo., 12s.

McNAB.—CLASS-BOOK OF BOTANY. By W. R. McNAB.

MORPHOLOGY AND PHYSI-
OLOGY. With 42 Diagrams. Fcp. 8vo., 1s. 6d.

CLASSIFICATION OF PLANTS.
With 118 Diagrams. Fcp. 8vo., 1s. 6d.

SORAUER.—A POPULAR TREATISE ON THE PHYSIO-
LOGY OF PLANTS. By Dr. PAUL SORAUER. Translated by F. E. WEISS, B.Sc., F.L.S. With 33 Illustrations. 8vo., 9s. net.

THOMÉ AND BENNETT.—STRUCTURAL AND PHYSIO-
LOGICAL BOTANY. By OTTO WILHELM THOMÉ and by ALFRED W. BENNETT, B.Sc., F.L.S. With Coloured Map and 600 Woodcuts. Fcp. 8vo., 6s.

Scientific Works published by Longmans, Green, & Co. 35

BOTANY—*Continued.*

TUBEUF.—DISEASES OF PLANTS INDUCED BY CRYPTOGAMIC PARASITES. Introduction to the Study of Pathogenic Fungi, Slime Fungi, Bacteria and Algæ. By Dr. KARL FREIHERR VON TUBEUF, Privatdocent in the University of Munich. English Edition by WILLIAM G. SMITH, B.Sc., Ph.D., Lecturer on Plant Physiology, University of Edinburgh. With 330 Illustrations. Royal 8vo., 18s. net.

WATTS.—A SCHOOL FLORA. For the use of Elementary Botanical Classes. By W. MARSHALL WATTS, D.Sc. Lond. Cr. 8vo., 2s. 6d.

AGRICULTURE AND GARDENING.

ADDYMAN.—AGRICULTURAL ANALYSIS. A Manual of Quantitative Analysis for Students of Agriculture. By FRANK T. ADDYMAN, B.Sc. (Lond.), F.I.C. With 49 Illustrations. Crown 8vo., 5s. net.

COLEMAN AND ADDYMAN.—PRACTICAL AGRICULTURAL CHEMISTRY. By J. BERNARD COLEMAN, A.R.C.Sc., F.I.C., and FRANK T. ADDYMAN, B.Sc. (Lond.), F.I.C. With 24 Illustrations. Crown 8vo., 1s. 6d. net.

HAGGARD.—Works by H. RIDER HAGGARD.

A FARMER'S YEAR: being his Commonplace Book for 1898. With 36 Illustrations by G. LEON LITTLE and three others. Crown 8vo., 7s. 6d. net.

RURAL ENGLAND: being an Account of Agricultural and Social Researches carried out in the years 1901 and 1902. With 23 Agricultural Maps and 75 Illustrations from Photographs. 2 vols. 8vo., 36s. net.

JEKYLL.—Works by GERTRUDE JEKYLL.

HOME AND GARDEN: Notes and Thoughts, Practical and Critical, of a Worker in both. With 53 Illustrations from Photographs. 8vo., 10s. 6d. net.

WOOD AND GARDEN: Notes and Thoughts, Practical and Critical, of a Working Amateur. With 71 Photographs. 8vo., 10s. 6d. net.

WEATHERS.—A PRACTICAL GUIDE TO GARDEN PLANTS. Containing Descriptions of the Hardiest and most Beautiful Annuals and Biennials, Hardy Herbaceous and Bulbous Perennials, Hardy Water and Bog Plants, Flowering and Ornamental Trees and Shrubs, Conifers, Hardy Ferns, Hardy Bamboos and other Ornamental Grasses; and also the best kinds of Fruit and Vegetables that may be grown in the Open Air in the British Islands, with Full and Practical Instructions as to Culture and Propagation. By JOHN WEATHERS, F.R.H.S., late Assistant Secretary to the Royal Horticultural Society, formerly of the Royal Gardens, Kew, etc. With 163 Diagrams. 8vo., 21s. net.

WEBB.—Works by HENRY J. WEBB, Ph.D., B.Sc. (Lond.).

ELEMENTARY AGRICULTURE. A Text-Book specially adapted to the requirements of the Board of Education, the Junior Examination of the Royal Agricultural Society, and other Elementary Examinations. With 34 Illustrations. Crown 8vo., 2s. 6d.

AGRICULTURE. A Manual for Advanced Science Students With 100 Illustrations. Crown 8vo., 7s. 6d. net.

WORKS BY JOHN TYNDALL, D.C.L., LL.D., F.R.S.

LECTURES ON SOUND. With Frontispiece of Fog-Syren, and 203 other Woodcuts and Diagrams in the Text. Crown 8vo., 10s. 6d.

HEAT, A MODE OF MOTION. With 125 Woodcuts and Diagrams. Crown 8vo., 12s.

LECTURES ON LIGHT DELIVERED IN THE UNITED STATES IN 1872 AND 1873. With Portrait, Lithographic Plate, and 59 Diagrams. Crown 8vo., 5s.

FRAGMENTS OF SCIENCE: a Series of Detached Essays, Addresses, and Reviews. 2 vols. Crown 8vo., 16s.
  Vol. I.—The Constitution of Nature—Radiation—On Radiant Heat in Relation to the Colour and Chemical Constitution of Bodies—New Chemical Reactions produced by Light—On Dust and Disease—Voyage to Algeria to observe the Eclipse—Niagara—The Parallel Roads of Glen Roy—Alpine Sculpture—Recent Experiments on Fog-Signals—On the Study of Physics—On Crystalline and Slaty Cleavage—On Paramagnetic and Diamagnetic Forces—Physical Basis of Solar Chemistry—Elementary Magnetism—On Force—Contributions to Molecular Physics—Life and Letters of FARADAY—The Copley Medallist of 1870—The Copley Medallist of 1871—Death by Lightning—Science and the Spirits.
  Vol. II.—Reflections on Prayer and Natural Law—Miracles and Special Providences—On Prayer as a Form of Physical Energy—Vitality—Matter and Force—Scientific Materialism—An Address to Students—Scientific Use of the Imagination—The Belfast Address—Apology for the Belfast Address—The Rev. JAMES MARTINEAU and the Belfast Address—Fermentation, and its Bearings on Surgery and Medicine—Spontaneous Generation—Science and Man—Professor VIRCHOW and Evolution—The Electric Light.

NEW FRAGMENTS. Crown 8vo., 10s. 6d.
  CONTENTS.—The Sabbath—Goethe's 'Farbenlehre'—Atoms, Molecules, and Ether Waves—Count Rumford—Louis Pasteur, his Life and Labours—The Rainbow and its Congeners—Address delivered at the Birkbeck Institution on October 22, 1884—Thomas Young—Life in the Alps—About Common Water—Personal Recollections of Thomas Carlyle—On Unveiling the Statue of Thomas Carlyle—On the Origin, Propagation, and Prevention of Phthisis—Old Alpine Jottings—A Morning on Alp Lusgen.

ESSAYS ON THE FLOATING MATTER OF THE AIR IN RELATION TO PUTREFACTION AND INFECTION. With 24 Woodcuts. Crown 8vo., 7s. 6d.

RESEARCHES ON DIAMAGNETISM AND MAGNECRYSTALLIC ACTION; including the Question of Diamagnetic Polarity. Crown 8vo., 12s.

NOTES OF A COURSE OF NINE LECTURES ON LIGHT, delivered at the Royal Institution of Great Britain, 1869. Crown 8vo., 1s. 6d.

NOTES OF A COURSE OF SEVEN LECTURES ON ELECTRICAL PHENOMENA AND THEORIES, delivered at the Royal Institution of Great Britain, 1870. Crown 8vo., 1s. 6d.

LESSONS IN ELECTRICITY AT THE ROYAL INSTITUTION 1875-1876. With 58 Woodcuts and Diagrams. Crown 8vo., 2s. 6d.

THE GLACIERS OF THE ALPS: being a Narrative of Excursions and Ascents. An Account of the Origin and Phenomena of Glaciers, and an Exposition of the Physical Principles to which they are related. With 7 Illustrations. Crown 8vo., 6s. 6d. net.

HOURS OF EXERCISE IN THE ALPS. With 7 Illustrations. Crown 8vo., 6s. 6d. net.

FARADAY AS A DISCOVERER. Crown 8vo., 3s. 6d.

Scientific Works published by Longmans, Green, & Co. 37

TEXT-BOOKS OF SCIENCE.

PHOTOGRAPHY. By Sir WILLIAM DE WIVELESLIE ABNEY, K.C.B., F.R.S. With 134 Illustrations. Fcp. 8vo., 5s.

THE STRENGTH OF MATERIALS AND STRUCTURES. By Sir J. ANDERSON, C.E. With 66 Illustrations. Fcp. 8vo., 3s. 6d.

RAILWAY APPLIANCES. By Sir JOHN WOLFE BARRY, K.C.B., F.R.S., M.I.C.E. With 218 Illustrations. Fcp. 8vo., 4s. 6d.

INTRODUCTION TO THE STUDY OF INORGANIC CHEMISTRY. By WILLIAM ALLEN MILLER, M.D., LL.D., F.R.S. With 72 Illustrations. 3s. 6d.

QUANTITATIVE CHEMICAL ANALYSIS. By T. E. THORPE, C.B., F.R.S., Ph.D. With 88 Illustrations. Fcp. 8vo., 4s. 6d.

QUALITATIVE ANALYSIS AND LABORATORY PRACTICE. By T. E. THORPE, C.B., Ph.D., F.R.S., and M. M. PATTISON MUIR, M.A. and F.R.S.E. With Plate of Spectra and 57 Illustrations. Fcp. 8vo., 3s. 6d.

INTRODUCTION TO THE STUDY OF CHEMICAL PHILOSOPHY. By WILLIAM A. TILDEN, D.Sc., London, F.R.S. With Illustrations. Fcp. 8vo., 5s. With Answers to Problems. Fcp. 8vo., 5s. 6d.

ELEMENTS OF ASTRONOMY. By Sir R. S. BALL, LL.D., F.R.S. With 130 Illustrations. Fcp. 8vo., 6s. 6d.

SYSTEMATIC MINERALOGY. By HILARY BAUERMAN, F.G.S. With 373 Illustrations. Fcp. 8vo., 6s.

DESCRIPTIVE MINERALOGY. By HILARY BAUERMAN, F.G.S., etc. With 236 Illustrations. Fcp. 8vo., 6s.

METALS: THEIR PROPERTIES AND TREATMENT. By A. K. HUNTINGTON and W. G. MCMILLAN. With 122 Illustrations. Fcp. 8vo., 7s. 6d.

THEORY OF HEAT. By J. CLERK MAXWELL, M.A., LL.D., Edin., F.R.SS., L. & E. With 38 Illustrations. Fcp. 8vo., 4s. 6d.

PRACTICAL PHYSICS. By R. T. GLAZEBROOK, M.A., F.R.S., and W. N. SHAW, M.A. With 134 Illustrations. Fcp. 8vo., 7s. 6d.

PRELIMINARY SURVEY AND ESTIMATES. By THEODORE GRAHAM GRIBBLE, Civil Engineer. Including Elementary Astronomy, Route Surveying, Tacheometry, Curve-ranging, Graphic Mensuration, Estimates, Hydrography and Instruments. With 133 Illustrations. Fcp. 8vo., 7s. 6d.

ALGEBRA AND TRIGONOMETRY. By WILLIAM NATHANIEL GRIFFIN, B.D. 3s. 6d.

THE STEAM ENGINE. By GEORGE C. V. HOLMES, C.B., Chairman of the Board of Works, Dublin. With 212 Illustrations. Fcp. 8vo., 6s.

ELECTRICITY AND MAGNETISM. By FLEEMING JENKIN, F.R.SS., L. & E. With 177 Illustrations. Fcp. 8vo., 3s. 6d.

THE ART OF ELECTRO-METALLURGY. By G. GORE, LL.D., F.R.S. With 56 Illus. Fcp. 8vo., 6s.

TELEGRAPHY. By Sir W. H. PREECE, K.C.B., F.R.S., M.I.C.E., and Sir J. SIVEWRIGHT, M.A., K.C.M.G. With 267 Illustrations. Fcp. 8vo., 6s.

PHYSICAL OPTICS. By R. T. GLAZEBROOK, M.A., F.R.S. With 183 Illustrations. Fcp. 8vo., 6s.

TECHNICAL ARITHMETIC AND MENSURATION. By CHARLES W. MERRIEFIELD, F.R.S. 3s. 6d. Key, by the Rev. JOHN HUNTER, M.A. Fcp. 8vo., 3s. 6d.

THE STUDY OF ROCKS. By FRANK RUTLEY, F.G.S. With 6 Plates and 88 Illustrations Fcp. 8vo., 4s. 6d.

WORKSHOP APPLIANCES, including Descriptions of some of the Machine Tools used by Engineers. By C. P. B. SHELLEY, M.I.C.E. With 323 Illustrations. Fcp. 8vo., 5s.

ELEMENTS OF MACHINE DESIGN. By W. CAWTHORNE UNWIN, F.R.S., B.Sc., M.I.C.E.
PART I. General Principles, Fastenings and Transmissive Machinery. With 345 Illustrations. Fcp. 8vo., 7s. 6d.
PART II. Chiefly on Engine Details. With 259 Illustrations. Fcp. 8vo., 6s.

STRUCTURAL AND PHYSIOLOGICAL BOTANY. By OTTO WILHELM THOMÉ, and A. W. BENNETT, M.A., B.Sc., F.L.S. With 600 Illustrations. Fcp. 8vo., 6s.

PLANE AND SOLID GEOMETRY. By H. W. WATSON, M.A. Fcp. 8vo., 3s. 6d.

ADVANCED SCIENCE MANUALS.

BUILDING CONSTRUCTION. By the Author of 'Rivington's Notes on Building Construction'. With 385 Illustrations and an Appendix of Examination Questions. Crown 8vo., 4s. 6d.

THEORETICAL MECHANICS. Solids, including Kinematics, Statics, and Kinetics. By A. THORNTON, M.A., F.R.A.S. With 220 Illustrations, 130 Worked Examples, and over 900 Examples from Examination Papers, etc. Crown 8vo., 4s. 6d.

HEAT. By MARK R. WRIGHT, Hon. Inter. B.Sc. (Lond.). With 136 Illustrations and numerous Examples and Examination Papers. Crown 8vo., 4s. 6d.

LIGHT. By W. J. A. EMTAGE, M.A. With 232 Illustrations. Cr. 8vo., 6s.

MAGNETISM AND ELECTRICITY. By ARTHUR WILLIAM POYSER, M.A. With 317 Illustrations. Crown 8vo., 4s. 6d.

INORGANIC CHEMISTRY, THEORETICAL AND PRACTICAL. By WILLIAM JAGO, F.C.S., F.I.C. With Plate of Spectra and 78 Woodcuts. Crown 8vo., 4s. 6d.

GEOLOGY: a Manual for Students in Advanced Classes and for General Readers. By CHARLES BIRD, B.A. (Lond.), F.G.S. With over 300 Illustrations, a Geological Map of the British Isles (coloured), and a set of Questions for Examination. Crown 8vo., 7s. 6d.

HUMAN PHYSIOLOGY: a Manual for Students in advanced Classes of the Science and Art Department. By JOHN THORNTON, M.A. With 284 Illustrations, some of which are Coloured, and a set of Questions for Examination. Crown 8vo., 6s.

PHYSIOGRAPHY. By JOHN THORNTON, M.A. With 11 Maps, 255 Illustrations, and Coloured Map of Ocean Deposits. Crown 8vo., 4s. 6d.

AGRICULTURE. By HENRY J. WEBB, Ph.D., B.Sc. With 100 Illustrations. Crown 8vo., 7s. 6d. net.

HYGIENE. By J. LANE NOTTER, M.A., M.D., Professor of Hygiene in the Army Medical School, Netley, Colonel, Royal Army Medical Corps; and R. H. FIRTH, F.R.C.S., late Assistant Professor of Hygiene in the Army Medical School, Netley, Major, Royal Army Medical Corps. With 95 Illustrations. Crown 8vo., 3s. 6d.

ELEMENTARY SCIENCE MANUALS.

PRACTICAL, PLANE, AND SOLID GEOMETRY. By I. H. MORRIS and JOSEPH HUSBAND. Fully Illustrated with Drawings. Crown 8vo., 2s. 6d.

GEOMETRICAL DRAWING FOR ART STUDENTS. Embracing Plane Geometry and its Applications, the Use of Scales, and the Plans and Elevations of Solids. By I. H. MORRIS. Crown 8vo., 2s.

TEXT-BOOK ON PRACTICAL, SOLID, OR DESCRIPTIVE GEOMETRY. By DAVID ALLAN LOW (Whitworth Scholar). Part I. Crown 8vo., 2s. Part II. Crown 8vo., 3s.

AN INTRODUCTION TO MACHINE DRAWING AND DESIGN. By DAVID ALLAN LOW. With 153 illustrations. Crown 8vo., 2s. 6d.

BUILDING CONSTRUCTION AND DRAWING. By EDWARD J. BURRELL. With 308 Illustrations and Working Drawings. Crown 8vo., 2s. 6d.

AN ELEMENTARY COURSE OF MATHEMATICS. Containing Arithmetic; Euclid (Book I., with Deductions and Exercises); and Algebra. Crown 8vo., 2s. 6d.

ELEMENTARY SCIENCE MANUALS—*Continued.*

THEORETICAL MECHANICS. Including Hydrostatics and Pneumatics. By J. E. TAYLOR, M.A., B.Sc. With numerous Examples and Answers, and 175 Diagrams and Illustrations. Crown 8vo., 2*s*. 6*d*.

THEORETICAL MECHANICS—SOLIDS. By J. E. TAYLOR, M.A., B.Sc. (Lond.). With 163 Illustrations, 120 Worked Examples, and over 500 Examples from Examination Papers, etc. Crown 8vo., 2*s*. 6*d*.

THEORETICAL MECHANICS—FLUIDS. By J. E. TAYLOR, M.A., B.Sc. (Lond.). With 122 Illustrations, numerous Worked Examples, and about 500 Examples from Examination Papers, etc. Crown 8vo., 2*s*. 6*d*.

A MANUAL OF MECHANICS. With 138 Illustrations and Diagrams, and 188 Examples taken from Examination Papers, with Answers. By T. M. GOODEVE, M.A. Crown 8vo., 2*s*. 6*d*.

SOUND, LIGHT, AND HEAT. By MARK R. WRIGHT, M.A. With 160 Diagrams and Illustrations. Crown 8vo., 2*s*. 6*d*.

METALLURGY: an Elementary Text-Book. By E. L. RHEAD. With 94 Illustrations. Crown 8vo., 3*s*. 6*d*.

PHYSICS. Alternative Course. By MARK R. WRIGHT, M.A. With 242 Illustrations. Crown 8vo., 2*s*. 6*d*.

MAGNETISM AND ELECTRICITY. By A. W. POYSER, M.A. With 235 Illustrations. Crown 8vo., 2*s*. 6*d*.

PROBLEMS AND SOLUTIONS IN ELEMENTARY ELECTRICITY AND MAGNETISM. By W. SLINGO and A. BROOKER. Embracing a Complete Set of Answers to the South Kensington Papers for the years 1885-1899, and a Series of Original Questions. With 67 Original Illustrations. Crown 8vo., 2*s*.

ELEMENTARY PHYSIOGRAPHY. By J. THORNTON, M.A. With 13 Maps and 295 Illustrations. With Appendix on Astronomical Instruments and Measurements. Crown 8vo., 2*s*. 6*d*.

ORGANIC CHEMISTRY: the Fatty Compounds. By R. LLOYD WHITELEY, F.I.C., F.C.S. With 45 Illustrations. Crown 8vo., 3*s*. 6*d*.

INORGANIC CHEMISTRY, THEORETICAL AND PRACTICAL. By WILLIAM JAGO, F.C.S., F.I.C. With 63 Illustrations and numerous Questions and Exercises. Fcp. 8vo., 2*s*. 6*d*.

AN INTRODUCTION TO PRACTICAL INORGANIC CHEMISTRY. By WILLIAM JAGO, F.C.S., F.I.C. Crown 8vo., 1*s*. 6*d*.

PRACTICAL CHEMISTRY: the Principles of Qualitative Analysis. By WILLIAM A. TILDEN, D.Sc. Fcp. 8vo., 1*s*. 6*d*.

ELEMENTARY INORGANIC CHEMISTRY. By WILLIAM FURNEAUX, F.R.G.S. Crown 8vo., 2*s*. 6*d*.

ELEMENTARY GEOLOGY. By CHARLES BIRD, B.A., F.G.S. With Coloured Geological Map of the British Islands, and 247 Illustrations. Crown 8vo., 2*s*. 6*d*.

HUMAN PHYSIOLOGY. By WILLIAM FURNEAUX, F.R.G.S. With 218 Illustrations. Crown 8vo., 2*s*. 6*d*.

A COURSE OF PRACTICAL ELEMENTARY BIOLOGY. By J. BIDGOOD, B.Sc. With 226 Illustrations. Crown 8vo., 4*s*. 6*d*.

ELEMENTARY BOTANY, THEORETICAL AND PRACTICAL. By HENRY EDMONDS, B.Sc. With 342 Illustrations. Crown 8vo., 2*s*. 6*d*.

STEAM. By WILLIAM RIPPER, Member of the Institution of Civil Engineers. With 185 Illustrations. Crown 8vo., 2*s*. 6*d*.

AGRICULTURE. By HENRY J. WEBB, Ph.D. With 34 Illustrations. Crown 8vo., 2*s*. 6*d*.

40 *Scientific Works published by Longmans, Green, & Co.*

THE LONDON SCIENCE CLASS-BOOKS.

Edited by G. CAREY FOSTER, F.R.S., and by Sir PHILIP MAGNUS, B.Sc., B.A., of the City and Guilds of London Institute.

ASTRONOMY. By Sir ROBERT STAWELL BALL, LL.D., F.R.S With 41 Diagrams. Fcp. 8vo., 1s. 6d.

MECHANICS. By SIR ROBERT STAWELL BALL, LL.D., F.R.S. With 89 Diagrams. Fcp. 8vo., 1s. 6d.

THE LAWS OF HEALTH. By W. H. CORFIELD, M A., M.D., F.R.C.P. With 22 Illustrations. Fcp.8vo.,1s.6d.

MOLECULAR PHYSICS AND SOUND. By FREDERICK GUTHRIE, F.R.S. With 91 Diagrams. Fcp. 8vo., 1s. 6d.

GEOMETRY, CONGRUENT FIGURES. By O. HENRICI, Ph.D., F.R.S. With 141 Diagrams. Fcp. 8vo., 1s. 6d.

ZOOLOGY OF THE INVERTEBRATE ANIMALS. By ALEXANDER MACALISTER, M.D. With 77 Diagrams. Fcp. 8vo., 1s. 6d.

ZOOLOGY OF THE VERTEBRATE ANIMALS. By ALEXANDER MACALISTER, M.D. With 59 Diagrams. Fcp. 8vo., 1s. 6d.

HYDROSTATICS AND PNEUMATICS. By Sir PHILIP MAGNUS, B.Sc., B.A. With 79 Diagrams. Fcp. 8vo., 1s. 6d. (To be had also with Answers, 2s.) The Worked Solutions of the Problems. 2s.

BOTANY. Outlines of the Classification of Plants. By W. R. MCNAB, M.D. With 118 Diagrams. Fcp. 8vo., 1s. 6d.

BOTANY. Outlines of Morphology and Physiology. By W. R. MCNAB, M.D. With 42 Diagrams. Fcp. 8vo., 1s. 6d.

THERMODYNAMICS. By RICHARD WORMELL, M.A., D.Sc. With 41 Diagrams. Fcp. 8vo., 1s. 6d.

PRACTICAL ELEMENTARY SCIENCE SERIES.

ELEMENTARY PRACTICAL PHYSIOGRAPHY. (Section I.) By JOHN THORNTON, M.A. With 215 Illustrations and a Coloured Spectrum. Crown 8vo., 2s. 6d.

ELEMENTARY PRACTICAL PHYSIOGRAPHY. (Section II.). A Course of Lessons and Experiments in Elementary Science for the King's Scholarship Examination. By JOHN THORNTON, M.A. With 98 Illustrations and a Series of Questions. Crown 8vo., 2s. 6d.

PRACTICAL DOMESTIC HYGIENE. Stage I. By J. LANE NOTTER, M.A., M.D., and R. H. FIRTH, F.R.C.S. With 83 Illustrations. Cr. 8vo., 2s. 6d.

A PRACTICAL INTRODUCTION TO THE STUDY OF BOTANY: Flowering Plants. By J. BRETLAND FARMER, F.R.S., M.A. With 121 Illustrations. Crown 8vo., 2s. 6d.

ELEMENTARY PRACTICAL HYGIENE. Section I. By WILLIAM S. FURNEAUX. With Appendix to meet the requirements of the 1902 Syllabus of the Board of Education. With 146 Illustrations. Cr. 8vo., 2s. 6d.

ELEMENTARY PRACTICAL BUILDING CONSTRUCTION. By F. W. BOOKER. With Illustrations. Crown 8vo., 2s. 6d.

ELEMENTARY PRACTICAL SOUND, LIGHT, AND HEAT. Stage I. By JOSEPH S. DEXTER. With 152 Illustrations. Crown 8vo. 2s. 6d.

PRACTICAL MATHEMATICS. Stage I. By A. G. CRACKNELL, M.A., B.Sc. Crown 8vo., 3s. 6d.

ELEMENTARY PRACTICAL CHEMISTRY. Stage I. By G. S. NEWTH, F.I.C., F.C.S. With 108 Illustrations and 254 Experiments. Crown 8vo., 2s. 6d.

ELEMENTARY PRACTICAL PHYSICS. Stage I. By W. WATSON, F.R.S., D.Sc. With 120 Illustrations and 193 Exercises. Cr. 8vo., 2s. 6d.

ELEMENTARY BIOLOGY. By JOHN THORNTON, M.A. With 108 Illustrations. Crown 8vo., 3s. 6d.

THE ELEMENTS OF GEOMETRICAL DRAWING: an Elementary Text-book on Practical Plane Geometry, including an Introduction to Solid Geometry. By HENRY J. SPOONER, C.E., M.Inst.M.E. Crown 8vo., 3s. 6d.

ELEMENTARY PRACTICAL PHYSIOLOGY. By JOHN THORNTON, M.A. With 178 Illustrations (6 of which are Coloured). Cr. 8vo., 3s. 6d.

5,000/10/04.

Ingram Content Group UK Ltd.
Milton Keynes UK
UKHW040750240423
420680UK00004B/287